M000220061

Catechesis for the
New Evangelization

Catechesis for the New Evangelization

Vatican II, John Paul II, and the Unity of Revelation and Experience

Brian Pedraza

LIBRARY OF CONGRESS SURPLUS DUPLICATE

 The Catholic University of America Press | Washington, D.C.

Copyright © 2020
The Catholic University of America Press
All rights reserved
The paper used in this publication meets the minimum
requirements of American National Standards for Information
Science—Permanence of Paper for Printed Library Materials,
ANSI Z39.48–1984.
∞

Library of Congress Cataloging-in-Publication Data
Names: Pedraza, Brian, author.
Title: Catechesis for the new evangelization : Vatican II,
John Paul II, and the unity of revelation and experience /
Brian Pedraza.
Description: Washington, D.C. : The Catholic University of
America Press, 2020. | Includes bibliographical references
and index.
Identifiers: LCCN 2020010904 | ISBN 9780813232737 (paperback)
| ISBN 9780813232744 (ebook)
Subjects: LCSH: Evangelistic work—Catholic Church. |
Experience (Religion) | Revelation. | Vatican Council
(2nd : 1962–1965 : Basilica di San Pietro in Vaticano) |
John Paul II, Pope, 1920–2005.
Classification: LCC BX2347.4 .P43 2020 | DDC 268/.82—dc23
LC record available at https://lccn.loc.gov/2020010904

To Adrienne, mi segundo amor

Contents

Preface

Before one engages in the ministry of catechesis, one must first immerse oneself in contemplation of the mystery of Jesus Christ. One must sit at the feet of the Lord, who is the one true teacher of the faith, he who is the source, the goal, and the entire way through for all catechetical endeavors.

Papal preacher Fr. Raniero Cantalamessa once remarked about the universal catechism that, to teach it well, a person must first "eat the book." He drew this shocking yet powerful imagery from the call of the prophet Ezekiel. Showing him a written scroll and calling him to speak to the house of Israel, the Lord told the prophet to "eat what I give you" (Ez 2:8). Thus, a catechist must so immerse him- or herself in the word of God—must consume it—that it becomes a part of the catechist's very being. The word must become enfleshed in the life of the teacher. By this, not only will the catechist know the faith from the inside out, so to speak, but those taught will then witness a *living* faith in the person of their teacher.

Even so, the persistence necessary for contemplation comes in the present moment only with struggle. For us moderns, doing is prized over understanding—and why not, when the world is simply dubbed material to be manipulated, people and things are equated as objects for consumption, and our educational institutions are breeding grounds for pragmatism? The cultural forces at play coerce us into a posture of action and not contemplation, and to resist is necessarily to feel the constraint. And yet, the Gospel beckons us to remember "the one thing necessary" and that Mary chose "the good portion" (Lk 10:42). Standing within the stream flowing from this source, St. Thomas defends contemplation as the ultimate happiness of human life. But, as he states in article 6 of question 188 in the *Secunda Secundae*, one who hands on the faith must also teach from "the fullness of contemplation." Indeed, "as it is better to enlighten than merely to shine, so is it better to give to others the fruits of one's contemplation than merely to contemplate."

This book, then, is an exercise in contemplation, in hopes that it might overflow into action within the church's pastoral ministry. All of the postconciliar popes have identified the church's current mission in the Western world as one that can be characterized by what John Paul II called the "New Evangelization." Catechesis—the handing on or "echoing" of the faith—needs to take into account this new context, but doing so cannot solely be a practical matter. New methods, new media, and new ardor will surely play a role in this mission, but these practical matters must be guided by the church's attention to truth. The handing on of the faith is primarily theological before it is sociological, educational, or practical, because the faith is dependent upon God's self-revelation. This study thus examines the theoretical foundations of the New Evangelization precisely with the hope that it can help foster practical responses to what God has revealed about himself and humanity. It is, therefore, primarily a work of *catechetics* (catechetical theory) and not *catechesis* (catechetical practice). It is an attempt to be Mary before undertaking the important work of Martha.

The New Evangelization, of course, is another way of describing the vision of Vatican II. While the direct link between the two has been little studied, this book seeks to remedy this lack. The Council's teachings on revelation and the human person provide much of the material for what follows. The other primary source is the teaching of John Paul II since, as one of the most significant interpreters of the Council and as the ardent promoter of the New Evangelization, he stands as an important contributor to reflection on the church's current mission. His recent canonization is, for me, another reason to delve more deeply into his thought. There is more to be gained from one of the papacy's most prolific writers in history, I believe, especially when the church puts him forth as a model of holiness to be embraced by all the faithful.

Before proceeding, I am compelled to thank several people who helped me bring this book to completion. Among these are John

Grabowski, Chris Ruddy, and Bill Mattison, whose comments and suggestions have contributed to it greatly. I also thank my colleagues and students at the Catholic University of America and Franciscan Missionaries of Our Lady University, whose thoughts have sharpened my own. Likewise, my gratitude goes to John Martino and the staff at the CUA Press for helping bring this book to print. In a deeply important way, a word of thanks also belongs to those people, lay and ordained, who have taught me the faith as well as those whom I have had the honor of teaching.

Parts of chapters 1, 2, and 5 were previously published in two separate articles.[1] I thank Bill Murphy and the *Josephinum Journal of Theology* for allowing them to be republished here.

Last, I thank my family, both my family of origin and the one I have joyfully begun with my wife, Adrienne. My parents and brother are the community in which I was raised, and I continue to draw upon their love and support. My wife, Adrienne, is truly "bone of my bones, and flesh of my flesh." Because of her love and sacrifice, this book is, in many ways, as much hers as it is mine. The *communio personarum* I have found in her, along with our sons, has brought me the greatest peace and joy, while showing me that such communion takes steady and persistent receptivity and self-gift. To me, this shared life is an icon that offers a glimpse into the end that my theological and catechetical work hopefully serves—union with the communion of persons that is the Father, Son, and Holy Spirit.

May this work bear fruit for God's kingdom and in the lives of men and women in the church and in the world.

Brian Pedraza
Lent 2019

1. See Brian Pedraza, "Reform and Renewal in Catechesis: The Council, the Catechism, and the New Evangelization," *Josephinum Journal of Theology* 19, no. 1 (2012): 141–71, and *"Gaudium et Spes* and the Pedagogy of God: Conciliar Roots of the New Evangelization," *Josephinum Journal of Theology* 22, no. 1–2 (2015): 249–71.

Catechesis for the
New Evangelization

Introduction

Truth and Love: Christianity as Knowledge and a Way

> You shall love the Lord your God with all your heart, with all your soul, with all your mind, and with all your strength.
>
> **Mark 12:30**

> The whole concern of doctrine and its teaching must be directed to the love that never ends. Whether something is proposed for belief, for hope, or for action, the love of our Lord must always be made accessible, so that anyone can see that all the works of perfect Christian virtue spring from love and have no other objective than to arrive at love.
>
> *Catechism of the Catholic Church, no. 2*

It is the perennial concern—if not the central aim—of catechists that those who are being catechized receive the truth, yet not only receive it but accept it in such a way that it transforms the whole of their lives. In this way, the church's mission of handing on the faith embraces the first and greatest commandment: to love God not only in mind but with heart, soul, and strength. One could say in this light that Christian faith requires the turning over of the entire person to God. The "I believe" of the Christian—*Credo*—is not merely an exercise in intellectual assent. It is also an act of love.

Yet this unity of knowing and loving, one that embraces both the *quae* and the *qua* of the classic description of faith, comes in the present age only with struggle. Both recent magisterial teaching and the work of scholars have noted that, in the Western world, the church can no longer rest upon a Christianity that imbues society with identifying markers and hereditary traditions in order to sustain the faith.[1] Indeed, the fragmentation of faith and life is in some respects the hallmark of the modern Western world. As a consequence, the church must once again discover the ways in which the truths of the Gospel can speak to society and culture—the ways in which the experience of men and women can be addressed by the riches and wisdom of her long and fruitful tradition. In light of this context, Pope John Paul II called for a New Evangelization. In his words:

There is [a situation], particularly in countries with ancient Christian roots, and occasionally in the younger Churches as well, where entire groups of the baptized have lost a living sense of the faith, or even no longer consider themselves members of the Church, and live a life far removed from Christ and his Gospel. In this case what is needed is a "new evangelization" or a "re-evangelization."[2]

The late pope devoted the efforts of much of his pontificate to this purpose. Benedict XVI then took up the call of his predecessor in creating a pontifical council dedicated to this New Evangelization. And, more recently, Pope Francis has reiterated the importance of the church's "missionary option," especially by way of his apostolic exhortation *Evangelii Gaudium*.[3]

Undoubtedly, this papal call to renew the church's mission in the present age has great import for the ministry of catechesis. In its technical sense, catechesis is that ministry of the Word that takes the evangelized and baptized Christian and continuously forms him or her in

1. For examples of scholarly studies, see Robert T. O'Gorman, *The Church That Was a School: Catholic Identity and Catholic Education in the United States since 1790* (Washington, D.C.: United States Catholic Conference, 1987), and Joseph A. Komonchak, "Modernity and the Construction of Roman Catholicism," *Cristianesimo nella Storia* 18, no. 2 (1997): 353–85. Magisterial teaching will be addressed later.

2. John Paul II, *Redemptoris Missio*, no. 33, Vatican trans. (Boston: Pauline Books and Media, 1990), 46; also in AAS 83 (1991): 249–340. Henceforth, RM. Subsequent references to this document will be to this edition, noting the section number, followed by the page number in brackets. References to other church documents as well as other primary sources (such as patristic and medieval texts) will follow the same format.

3. Francis, *The Joy of the Gospel: Evangelii Gaudium*, no. 27, Vatican trans. (New York: Image, 2013), 24; also in AAS 105 (2013): 1019–1137. Henceforth, EG.

the faith to the point of maturity, especially by way of systematic teaching. Still, if catechesis could at one time be distinguished from the initial encounter with the Gospel, then today it cannot be so. For in the context of the New Evangelization, even the baptized are often found claiming a Catholic faith in name only, without having encountered the person of Jesus Christ and his Good News. The imparting of Christian doctrine in this context must be reconnected to what the Catechism calls "the love that never ends"—to the love *of* God in Christ that is its source and to the love *for* God in Christ that is its end. Thus, as past prefect of the Congregation for the Doctrine of the Faith, William Levada, has said, the New Evangelization requires a new catechesis.[4]

What should this new catechesis look like? What are its foundational principles? How would such a catechesis stand in continuity with the past and, at the same time, represent a development of the ministry of the Word? This book is aimed precisely at answering these questions, as I hope to offer a modest contribution to tracing the contours of the nature of catechesis in this time of the New Evangelization. Undoubtedly, in the theological and historical analyses that are to follow, that which is "new" will emerge into clearer view. Yet, it is also the case that, as often happens in periods of renewal, those elements that are foundational and enduring must be rediscovered or, at the very least, they must once again take their place at the center of the church's endeavors. Thus, this new catechesis will prove to be both ancient and new, embracing the past while being open to the present. In this way, the ministry of catechesis continues, as it hands on the faith as both knowledge and a way of life. The unity of truth and love is the path that the church must continuously tread.

Truth and Love: Moments from the Church's History

If Christianity is both knowledge and a way, then surely a few examples from the church's history can serve to show this dual nature of the Christian faith. While the choices are many, I simply wish to call to mind two moments from this history that can serve this purpose.

4. See William Joseph Levada, "New Evangelization Requires a New Catechesis," *L'Osservatore Romano*, English ed., January 7, 1998, 11.

The first moment recalls New Testament times where, at the shore of Galilee, we find the ordinary fishermen who encountered the apostolic call of Jesus. In this Rabbi—the title given to the Jewish teacher who expounded upon the Law—these fishermen discovered teachings that transcended those of other rabbis by the authority in which they were given.[5] Moreover, this authority was not simply a matter of rhetorical force. Other rabbis sought to explain the Law to their students from the position of an interpreter, as one standing beneath the Law; but Jesus placed himself in the very position of the Lawgiver. That is to say, in his teachings, he did not endeavor to bring his students to a deposit of knowledge that lay beyond himself, something that other rabbis did and, indeed, that all teachers aim to do. Rather, he claimed *himself* as the content of his teaching: "Rolling up the scroll, he handed it back to the attendant and sat down, and the eyes of all in the synagogue looked intently upon him. He said to them, 'Today this scripture passage is fulfilled in your hearing'" (Lk 4:20–21).[6] As one author puts it:

In the case of Socrates, once the disciple is in possession of doctrine, he can forget about the teacher. But what Christ does as teacher—as John's gospel shows clearly—is to reveal himself and his Father. When he asks the twelve, "Will you also go away?" Peter does not reply "We shall stay because we have understood your testimony, realize its truth, and can verify it." Rather his answer is deeply personal: "To *whom* shall we go? *You* have the words of eternal life."[7]

Face to face with such a teacher, the response of the disciple could not be the mere acceptance of teachings, but the acceptance of the Teacher as well. Likewise, though Jesus' teaching would necessarily be preserved in a form that could be apprehended by the intellect—later,

5. See Mt 7:28, Mk 1:22, and Lk 4:32.

6. On this point, see the interesting remarks offered by Pope Benedict XVI in *Jesus of Nazareth: From the Baptism in the Jordan to the Transfiguration*, trans. Adrian J. Walker (New York: Doubleday, 2007), 103–22. Benedict recalls the work of Jewish scholar and rabbi Jacob Neusner, who considers Jesus' teaching from the standpoint of placing himself within the gospel texts. After listening to the Sermon on the Mount and accompanying Jesus to Jerusalem, he retires to a town and speaks with the local rabbi there. This rabbi cites the Babylonian Talmud and offers an understanding of the law. In this imaginative scene, Neusner explains that Jesus' teaching is similar and that he subtracts nothing from the Law. The rabbi then asks, "Then what did he add?" to which Neusner replies, "Himself." See also Neusner, *A Rabbi Talks with Jesus* (Montreal: McGill-Queen's University Press, 2000), 108.

7. Gerald O'Collins, *Foundations of Theology* (Chicago: Loyola University Press, 1971), 30. Emphasis in the original. See also Jn 6:67.

the apostles would encourage new believers to "hold fast to the traditions" that were taught and to reject any other "gospel," even if, as Paul says, an angel were to proclaim it—it also demanded that disciples live it with the entirety of their lives.[8] To be a disciple of this Teacher was to live just as he lived, even to die as he died. From this it is more apparent why the apostolic church would come to identify itself as "The Way."[9] Thus, we can say that, for the burgeoning church, the acceptance of Christ's teachings was inescapably intertwined with the way in which hearers both enfleshed it and gave themselves over to it with their very lives. For the earliest Christians, to follow Jesus was a path of both truth and love.

Pressing a bit further in history, we find the same dynamic operative in the fifth century, this time in the life of Augustine of Hippo. In (then) Joseph Ratzinger's book *Introduction to Christianity*, he recalls an episode from Augustine's life in which the future bishop visited the wise and revered Simplicianus.[10] By this time, Augustine had already begun to accept the Catholic faith as true but could not harness the willpower to approach the waters of baptism. Mired by a past filled with sin, Augustine listened to Simplicianus tell the story of Marius Victorinus, an educated man so well-respected that he claimed a statue in the Roman forum.[11] As a philosopher who had encountered the Gospel, Victorinus believed that he had no need of entering the church, since his philosophical erudition had already led him to accept the basic tenets of Christianity. In his mind, the Christian faith could be reduced to ideas, a form of Platonism that need not be externalized by participation in ecclesial life:

Privately as between friends, though never in public, he used to say to Simplicianus, "I want you to know that I am now a Christian." Simplicianus used to reply, "I shall not believe it or count you as a Christian until I see you in the Church of Christ." At this Victorinus would laugh and say, "Is it then the walls of the Church that make the Christian?"[12]

8. See 2 Thes 2:15 and Gal 1:6–9.

9. See Acts 9:2, 18:26, 19:9, 19:23, 22:4, 24:14, 24:22.

10. Joseph Ratzinger, *Introduction to Christianity*, trans. J. R. Foster (San Francisco: Ignatius Press, 1990), 63–64.

11. *Confessions* 8.2–5. I have used St. Augustine, *Confessions*, trans. R. S. Pine-Coffin (New York: Penguin, 1961), 159–65.

12. Ibid., 160.

But of course such a reduction could not remain Victorinus's conviction so long as he pressed further and further into the Gospel. As has already been seen, to be a Christian is to accept the teachings of Christ, yet this is none other than accepting Christ himself. And in Victorinus's time, though Jesus had ascended centuries earlier, to give oneself over to him necessarily took the form of entering his Body on earth. Thus Victorinus, if he was to truly embrace the teaching of Christ, could not stay anchored to his Platonist position. Augustine's heart was pierced with longing in hearing the conclusion to Simplicianus's story: the philosopher eventually received baptism and entered into the life of the church, for, as Ratzinger explains, "Truth as mere perception, as mere idea, remains bereft of force; it only becomes man's truth as a way that makes a claim upon him, which he can and must tread."[13]

Ultimately, the "I believe" or *Credo* of the professing Christian is indeed the acceptance of true teaching, but in this very acceptance it must move the learner (*discipulus* in Latin), like Victorinus, to tread a new way of life. It is quite possible that our modern ears may be tempted to mistake the Christian faith, symbolized by the Creed, for a mere collection of well-worn statements. But from these two examples it is clear that it cannot be so. To be true disciples is to be like those ordinary men who first encountered Jesus Christ near the shore of the Sea of Galilee. There, at the birth of Christian learning, we find that belief takes on flesh in an entirely new manner of existence. For a Christian, *Credo* is an act of the intellect by which one acknowledges the teaching of Christ to be true, yet it is also an act of the will (empowered by grace) by which one offers him- or herself to this very Teacher—it is an act of self-offering to God in Jesus Christ.[14] Christianity necessitates both truth and love.

Truth and Love: From Vatican II to the New Evangelization

Even if both are essential to Christianity, recent history has offered occasions in which the unity of truth and love has been found want-

13. Ratzinger, *Introduction to Christianity*, 64.

14. Indeed, the word *credo* itself is the joining of two Latin words, *cor/cordis* (heart) and *do/dare* (to place). To believe, *credere*, while not neglecting the modern idea of intellectual assent, ultimately means to place one's heart in something. See *New Catholic Encyclopedia*, 2nd ed., s.v. "Creed."

ing. Catechists of the past several decades, and indeed Catholics of all stripes, often recall the era preceding the Second Vatican Council as one that witnessed certain aspects of separation. On the one hand it is said that Catholics often knew their faith, having memorized doctrines meticulously. In the United States, for instance, the Baltimore catechism is typically remembered—fondly by some and with disdain by others—in this regard. While the answer to the question "Why did God make you?" might have been known as if by reflex,[15] many catechists of the time began to question whether such memorized answers were reaching through the mind to the heart of American Catholics.[16] On the other hand, it could also be observed that many preconciliar Catholics seemed to embody the faith through cultural and social practices but, beyond the level of appearances, had not internalized its truth. In describing this phenomenon, pioneering Austrian scholar of the liturgy and catechesis Josef Jungmann wrote in 1936:

In many areas Catholicism has become *a traditional confession*—a pattern of local customs and practices, largely sustained by community pressures. Again we find a Catholicism whose religious capital consists for the most part in a sum of obligations—an uninspiring series of "musts" and "don'ts"—weighing heavily on the conscience but which must be borne, at least with minimal effort, if one is to save his soul. This *conventional Christianity* of traditional external practices and burdensome duties ... owing to its lack of inner dynamism ... often fails to survive or withers away to a bare sustenance level.[17]

At a perfunctory glance, we might be tempted to claim a paradox in the preconciliar situation that is illustrated by these examples: in the case of the memorization of the Baltimore Catechism, an overemphasis on truth at the expense of love; in the conventional Christianity of Jung-

---

15. The answer is given by the catechism "God made me to know Him, to love Him, and to serve Him in this world, and to be happy with Him forever in the next." See Part 1, q. 6, in J. L. Spalding, *A Catechism of Christian Doctrine Prepared and Enjoined by Order of the Third Plenary Council of Baltimore* (New York: Catholic Publication Company, 1885).

16. Reflecting upon her experience of such catechesis, Mary Perkins Ryan (at the time the editor of the only major catechetical journal in the United States) wrote, "This minimalistic and legalistic view of Catholic faith does not, of course, represent in any way the wealth of Catholic tradition and the living practice of the faith. But I think that is not an unfair summary of the main thrust of the *Baltimore Catechism* and its derivatives." See Ryan, "The Identity Crisis of Religious Educators," *Living Light* 5 (1969): 8.

17. Josef A. Jungmann, *The Good News Yesterday and Today*, ed. and trans. William A. Huesman (New York: W. H. Sadlier, 1962), 3–4. Emphasis in the original. This work is an abridged and translated edition of Jungmann's influential *Die Frohbotschaft und unsere Glaubensverkündigung* (Regensburg: Friedrich Pustet, 1936).

mann's description, the external markers of the way of love, yet void of truth. But such an appraisal would be superficial at best. In reality, truth is never fully accepted without becoming a way, and the way is never fully embarked upon without truth as a guide. Thus, Jungmann ultimately concluded that "to the degree that we grasp things with true understanding, will they influence us, particularly when we see them in their totality, that is, in their bearing on all our activity and striving."[18] In sum:

Religious teaching today cannot content itself with the mere handing on of hereditary formulas, nor can it assume, as once it did, that the traditional sum of customs, devotions, pious thoughts and practices, even intensively used, will avail to hold the faithful firmly in the Church and assure security and nourishment for their religious life. Today religious teaching must lead the faithful to a vital understanding of the content of faith itself, that they may interiorly grasp it, and thus grow to spiritual maturity and proper independence in religious life. It must lead in other words to the step of Christian formation.[19]

It is precisely on this basis that Jungmann sought to construct a new catechetical approach to handing on the faith, one with a renewed emphasis on the encounter with Jesus Christ as its unifying point. The Austrian scholar believed that only in this Christic center could the reunification of understanding and Christian living be achieved.[20]

Discerning ears will detect in these remarks on the preconciliar era the same struggles that trouble the church today. Indeed, the similarities between descriptions of the church in her preconciliar days and those of the present are striking. As noted earlier, Jungmann had recognized that catechesis during his time lacked an "inner dynamism" and a view of the "totality" of the faith. He had also recognized the ineffectiveness of a "traditional confession" or what today could be termed a "cultural Catholicism" for forming people in the faith. Such analyses were a strong indication of the aims of Vatican II, the Council in which Jungmann took part as a *peritus*, and the Council that, in response to the growing divide between faith and life, sought to engage the world with the church's teaching.

18. Ibid., 8.
19. Ibid., 7.
20. More will be said about Jungmann and his kerygmatic approach to catechesis in chapter 2.

More recently, Pope Benedict XVI, in addressing the dicastery of the New Evangelization in its first plenary meeting, offered a description of the present that echoes the concerns of Jungmann before the Council:

In the past decades, it was still possible to find a general Christian sensibility which unified the common experience of entire generations raised in the shadow of the faith which had shaped culture. Today, unfortunately, we are witnessing a drama of fragmentation which no longer acknowledges a unifying reference point; moreover, it often occurs that people wish to belong to the Church, but they are strongly shaped by a vision of life which is in contrast with the faith.[21]

From such a description it is apparent that the concerns that confronted the church in the period before the Second Vatican Council remain the concerns for the New Evangelization. Benedict, like Jungmann before him, acknowledges that the "Christian sensibility" passed on through markers of cultural Catholicism can no longer be a sustaining influence in the Western world. Faith and life, once synonymous, must now be reunited in a different fashion. Of utmost importance for the accomplishment of this goal is that a "unifying reference point" be found.

For both men this source of inner dynamism, this unifying point, is none other than Christ himself, the one who effectively unites God with humanity. Benedict XVI, in the same address to the Pontifical Council, explained that the answer to the present context lies in the proclamation of "the salvific mystery of the death and Resurrection of Jesus Christ"; thus, "the new evangelization must try to find ways of making [this proclamation] more effective—a proclamation without which personal existence remains contradictory and deprived of what is essential."[22] Separated by decades though speaking as if in tandem, Jungmann had likewise acknowledged:

However much Christianity may transcend this earth in its origin and its appointed goal, it must nonetheless develop and establish itself in this world. . . . *The living Christ should shine forth as the luminous central core* of all our preaching, our catechesis, and divine worship. From this center a new light should go

21. Benedict XVI, "Address of His Holiness Benedict XVI to Participants in the Plenary Assembly of the Pontifical Council for Promoting the New Evangelization, 30 May, 2011." Unless otherwise noted, quotations from papal texts, addresses, and homilies are from the Vatican translations found at http://www.vatican.va.

22. Ibid.

forth, as it were, *over the concerns of life, religious and ecclesiastical, moral and secular.* From this center must come the forces by which we shall once again conquer the world.[23]

The Christocentrism of all reality, then, is precisely what is at stake in a catechesis that can unify faith with life, the truth of the Gospel with the experience of modern men and women. For Jungmann and for Benedict XVI, for Catholic life before the Council and after it, Jesus Christ is the unifying point that can bring together the church's message and the longings of the human person.

It is in light of this context that John Paul II, as the originator of the New Evangelization, had devoted much of his scholarship and Petrine ministry to the question of the human person and the answer that is Jesus Christ. As his first encyclical states in its opening line, "The Redeemer of Man, Jesus Christ, is the center of the universe and of history."[24] He is this unifying center because he is both the "way 'to the Father's house' and ... the way to each man."[25] This unification of Christology and anthropology is the hallmark of his thought: it is the guiding factor in the way he interpreted the Second Vatican Council, and it remains the path he set forth in calling for the New Evangelization.

And if, as it has been seen, the descriptions of Jungmann and Benedict (while separated by seventy-four years) are markedly similar, then attention is necessarily drawn to that Council that lies between them. Vatican II was the great ecclesial event that was called to address the concerns of those like Jungmann who saw the divide between faith and life as the critical point needing the church's attention. It was, as one scholar notes, the Council that took the classic problem of reconciling nature and grace and raised it "to the level of social institutions"; it sought "to reconcile the Church with human culture in all its positive dimensions."[26] It is certainly curious and striking, then, that such a description fits squarely with the aims of the new period of evangeliza-

23. Jungmann, *The Good News Yesterday and Today*, 151 and 153. Emphasis mine.

24. John Paul II, *Redemptor Hominis*, no. 1, Vatican trans. (London: Catholic Truth Society, 1979), 3; also in AAS 71 (1979): 257–324. Henceforth, *RH*.

25. John Paul II, *Redemptor Hominis*, no. 13, 26–27. See also Jn 14:1.

26. John W. O'Malley, "Developments, Reforms, and Two Great Reformations: Towards a Historical Assessment of Vatican II," *Theological Studies* 44, no. 3 (1983): 406.

tion proclaimed by John Paul II, Benedict XVI, and now Francis. The Council's mission (to use Pope John XXIII's words) of reformulating the faith "in contemporary terms," of having the "the message of salvation more readily welcomed by men" so that it is "more widely known, more deeply understood, and more penetrating in its effects on men's moral lives," remains the mission of the New Evangelization.[27]

But if the intended aim of the Council persists in the present, then one of two conclusions must be made regarding Vatican II's efficacy and its relation to the current time. One may be tempted to claim that the teachings of the Council and their implementation have failed—Vatican II did not succeed in reconciling faith and life, and new efforts are now needed. As such, some have imagined the possibilities of another council in the near future.[28] Still, I believe it is fair to say that, even fifty years removed from the Council's close, such a conclusion would be premature. The effects of an ecumenical council cannot be fully measured within such a period.[29] The more likely conclusion is that the work of Vatican II is yet to be accomplished in its totality and that its teachings are still being received today. For his part, Ratzinger, as a cardinal in 1985, had already voiced the position that "the true time of Vatican II has not yet come," that its full reception is yet to be carried out.[30] Other commentators have likewise acknowledged that the full effects of the Council are yet to be seen.[31]

I believe that it is precisely for this reason that John Paul II, in initiating the present era of the New Evangelization, claimed that this apostolic mandate had its source in the very teachings of Vatican II. In fact, when describing his vision of implementing the Council in the new mil-

27. John XXIII, "Opening Address to the Council," trans. H. E. Winstone, in *The Encyclicals and Other Messages of Pope John XXIII*, ed. the staff of *The Pope Speaks* Magazine (Washington, D.C.: TPS, 1964), 430 and 433; AAS 54 (1962): 786–96.

28. See, for example, David Tracy, Hans Küng, and Johann B. Metz, *Toward Vatican III: The Work That Needs to Be Done* (New York: Seabury, 1978).

29. See Giuseppe Alberigo, "Vatican II et son héritage," in *Vatican II and Its Legacy*, ed. M. Lamberigts and L. Kenis (Leuven: Leuven University Press, 2002), 10. Alberigo describes the reception of a council as "long and tormented."

30. Joseph Ratzinger with Vittorio Messori, *The Ratzinger Report*, trans. Salvator Attanasio and Graham Harrison (San Francisco: Ignatius Press, 1985), 40.

31. O'Malley, for instance, in his article states that "we will still not be able perfectly to assess Vatican II, but we shall have moved 'towards an assessment,' which is all that I—or any historian at this stage—can hope to achieve." See O'Malley, "Developments, Reforms, and Great Reformations," 374.

lennium to the bishops of the United States, the pope explained that God was preparing the church "for a new springtime of the Gospel— for the beginning of the next Christian millennium—*through the extraordinary grace of the Council.*"[32] In John Paul's vision, this new springtime of evangelization is fundamentally tied to the ecumenical council that took place decades earlier. For the late pope, the New Evangelization "originated precisely at the Second Vatican Council."[33] Thus, the New Evangelization is the implementation of the Council in the present age.

John Paul II and Catechesis for the New Evangelization

How might modern catechesis contribute to the conciliar aim of re-unifying faith and life? A glance at the history of modern catechesis shows that the form of both the content and method of handing on the faith underwent significant changes in the decades leading up to and stemming from Vatican II, with varying degrees of success. If, in the United States, the Baltimore Catechism was the symbol of catechesis before the Council, then attention to life experience surely became predominant afterward. The works of scholars such as Gabriel Moran and Thomas Groome became the standard-bearers for catechesis in the second half of the twentieth century, and their emphases on experience and communal praxis emulated the trends of much of postconciliar theology. Toward the end of the century, however, dissatisfaction with the implementation of the Council's teachings and, in particular, with efforts to hand on the faith led to the 1992 promulgation of the *Catechism of the Catholic Church*, in some sense bringing the history of modern catechesis full circle.

Was this simply a case of pouring the ever-new wine of the Gospel into old wineskins? Did John Paul II, the pope who ordered the creation of and promulgated the new catechism, see the document as a pana-

---

32. John Paul II, "The Mystery of the Church," in *Springtime of Evangelization: The Complete Texts of the Holy Father's 1998 ad Limina Addresses to the Bishops of the United States*, ed. Thomas D. Williams (San Diego: Basilica Press; San Francisco: Ignatius Press, 1999), 46. Emphasis in the original. See also Paul VI, *Evangelii Nuntiandi*, no. 2, trans. the Vatican, in *The Catechetical Documents*, ed. Martin Connell (Chicago: Liturgy Training Publications, 1996); also in AAS 68 (1976): 5–76.

33. John Paul II, *Crossing the Threshold of Hope*, trans. Jenny McPhee and Martha McPhee (New York: Alfred A. Knopf, 2001), 160.

cea for the church's ills? Such an assertion would be ill-fitted to a man whose life's work had been squarely focused on the human person, including extensive attention to the role of experience in the praxis of men and women. Indeed, John Paul's own vision of catechesis within the church's mission of evangelization cannot be so easily pegged into old categories. The pope who gave us the catechism is also the pope who called our attention to human experience and, above all, the pope who directed the church's vision to Jesus Christ as the one in whom the faith of the church and the experience of the human person finds its fullest revelation. Thus, the main thesis of this book emerges: I believe John Paul II's Christocentric understanding of the human person can provide a framework for taking what is best from the various developments in modern catechesis while correcting deficiencies in each stage of those developments.

If the New Evangelization requires a new catechesis, then such a catechesis must effectively hand on the teachings of the church, yet do so in such a way that the catechized are able to encounter the Living Word—the person of Jesus of Christ—as the answer to the deepest concerns of life in the modern world. Such an approach must take into account the aims of the New Evangelization: to re-present the Gospel to places where Christianity has grown ancient roots but in which the flowering of the lived experience of the faith is no longer evident. Guided by the "compass" offered by John Paul II and reaffirmed by Benedict XVI and Francis, this catechesis must also find its source in the teachings of the Second Vatican Council.[34]

It is my aim, then, with John Paul II as a guide, to place into clearer focus the nature and purpose of this evangelizing catechesis. This endeavor proceeds in four steps: first, I examine the present theological foundations of catechesis in divine revelation and its reception by

34. Pope Benedict, in his first message after election, affirmed, "Pope John Paul II rightly pointed out the Council as a 'compass' by which to take our bearings in the vast ocean of the third millennium.... Thus, as I prepare myself for the service that is proper to the Successor of Peter, I also wish to confirm my determination to continue to put the Second Vatican Council into practice, following in the footsteps of my predecessors and in faithful continuity with the 2,000-year tradition of the Church." See Benedict XVI, "First Message of His Holiness Benedict XVI at the End of the Eucharistic Concelebration with the Members of the College of Cardinals in the Sistine Chapel, 20 April, 2005," Vatican, http://www.vatican.va/holy_father/benedict_xvi/messages/pont-messages/2005/documents/hf_ben-xvi_mes_20050420_missa-pro-ecclesia_en.html. Likewise, Pope Francis claims that his thoughts on evangelization are inspired by the Council, particularly *Lumen Gentium*. See EG, no. 17 [17].

the human person by way of the conciliar constitutions, *Dei Verbum* and *Gaudium et Spes*. Second, I take stock of the strengths and weaknesses of catechetics in the modern era, with an attention to its development in the twentieth century and the relationship of this development to the Council's teachings. Third, I turn to the scholarship and teaching of Karol Wojtyła/Pope John Paul II for the unique way in which it unites revelation and human experience. I make this turn for two reasons: because John Paul II was the main instigator of the New Evangelization, I believe he has important insights that are foundational for it to be carried out effectively. Likewise, because the core of his scholarship and teaching is a Christocentric understanding of the human person, he offers a way to unite revelation with human experience that is firmly rooted in the teachings of Vatican II. Fourth and finally, I return to the catechetical goal of this book: because John Paul II's anthropology effectively unites revelation with the human person, I believe it is also able to unify the best insights from the modern catechetical movement (and shore up its weaknesses) with the needs of the New Evangelization. More simply put, his understanding of the person is one that bears great importance for reuniting faith with life and, indeed, truth with love.

If my task is achieved, then it will remain for pastors and catechists to work out the necessary practical applications of these principles as they apply to their local communities.[35] Thus, this study encourages catechists—both ordained and lay—to work out further the implications of the conclusions reached here. It is my hope that, through this study, guidelines will emerge that can serve theologians in probing the foundations of the ministry of the Word and catechists in practicing their ministry in the field that is the world.

As a final note, some words are in order concerning the various documents and texts that are under study in this book. My review of Council documents will draw upon several commentaries of theologians, each providing a diversity of insights, some who even participated in the Council's proceedings. In doing so, I have attempted to avoid any tendentious notions of conservative or progressive/liberal interpretations of the Council, acknowledging that the fullest view is decided by

35. Though from time to time, especially in footnotes, I may address certain practical matters as proves fruitful for advancing the analysis.

the lived faith of the Body of Christ in history rather than by political categories.

As for Wojtyła/John Paul II's writings, the various qualifications offered by other commentators on his work are due here as well.[36] For instance, concerning matters of church authority, it should be noted that there are differences of authority in the writings of one who is a scholar (the younger Karol Wojtyła), one who is a bishop (Karol Wojtyła as bishop of Krakow), and one who is the pope (Pope John Paul II). The younger Wojtyła's works, such as *The Acting Person* and *Faith according to St. John of the Cross*, are those of a philosopher and a theologian, and as such their ideas are meant to be wrestled with and discussed by the scholarly community.[37] Works such as *Sources of Renewal*, the teachings of a bishop for the good of his diocese, bear the authority of a pastor and chief catechist in his particular diocesan community, though they can have broader influence when in communion with the universal ordinary Magisterium of bishops.[38] The apostolic letters and encyclicals of John Paul II claim special authority as part of the ordinary Magisterium of the pope; weekly catecheses such as those commonly called *Theology of the Body*, while still a part of the papal Magisterium, carry less weight, though it should be kept in mind that they can serve to elaborate on teachings already established that carry greater authority or serve as a backdrop against which these teachings can be read and interpreted.[39]

So, too, should it be considered that papal writings are often works of collaboration. The office of the papacy undoubtedly often utilizes the help of other pastors and theologians, especially in the construction of ecclesial documents. Nevertheless, John Paul II's papal writings bear

36. See, for instance, John S. Grabowski, "The Luminous Excess of the Acting Person: Assessing the Impact of Pope John Paul II on American Catholic Moral Theology," *Journal of Moral Theology* 1, no. 1 (2012): 116–47, especially his comments on scope and method in 121–24.

37. Karol Wojtyła, *The Acting Person*, trans. Andrzej Potocki (Boston: D. Reidel, 1979). Originally published as *Osoba I czyn* [The Person and the Act] (Krakow: Polskie Towarzystwo Teologiczne, 1969); Wojtyła, *Faith according to St. John of the Cross*, trans. Jordan Aumann (San Francisco: Ignatius Press, 1981).

38. Wojtyła, *Sources of Renewal: The Implementation of the Second Vatican Council*, trans. P.S. Falla (San Francisco: Harper and Row, 1980).

39. John Paul II, *Man and Woman He Created Them: A Theology of the Body*, trans. Michael Waldstein (Boston: Pauline Books and Media, 2006). References to the catecheses in this text will be cited as TOB and will follow Waldstein's system in which the number of the catechesis will be given first, followed by the paragraph number after the colon. The actual page number of the text will then be given in brackets.

the stamp of his approval and show the marks of his earlier thought. One can trace a common trajectory—as I hope this study shows—in terms of a consistent though developing anthropology that runs from the works of the younger Wojtyła to the teaching of John Paul II. As such, while bearing in mind these certain qualifications, I will consider his papal writings as his own. Still, while I am less concerned with the authority of the documents under review here—the content is what is truly at stake—I will refer to the writer as "Wojtyła" or "John Paul II" based upon the time when each piece was authored.

Concerning matters of translation, it is unfortunate that not all of Wojtyła/John Paul II's writings have been translated into English. Fortunately, John Grondelski has provided an invaluable bibliography in Kenneth Schmitz's study of the late pope's thought. It provides a list of available translations of nearly all of Wojtyła/John Paul II's written works as well as a list of helpful secondary literature. At times, these translations and the relevant secondary literature proved to be useful in navigating some of the difficulties present in the English translations of his work.[40]

Last, I have tried to augment much of my own analysis of Wojtyła/John Paul II's writings with his published personal bibliographical reflections, as well as his published interviews. Such sources are able to provide a more personal understanding of the scholarly ideas studied here.

---

40. Most notably, several authors have pointed out the insufficiency of *The Acting Person* as a translation of *Osoba I czyn*, particularly because the editor's preference for phenomenological terms has obscured the text's continuity with Thomistic philosophy. See Kenneth L. Schmitz's remarks in *At the Center of the Human Drama: The Philosophical Anthropology of Karol Wojtyła/Pope John Paul II* (Washington, D.C.: The Catholic University of America Press, 1993), 58–60. Grondelski's bibliography can be found at the end of the same work. For a different perspective, see Jameson Taylor, "The Acting Person in Purgatory: A Note for Readers of the English Text," *Logos* 13, no. 3 (2010): 77–104, who argues that the English revision is purposely intended to appeal to a wider and more phenomenologically oriented audience and therefore should be read on its own terms. I would contend that the attentive reader who is fairly versed in Thomism can recognize, even in the English translation, affinities with the thought of St. Thomas.

Chapter 1

Revelation and the Human Person according to Vatican II

In times past, God spoke in partial and various ways to our ancestors through the prophets; in these last days, he spoke to us through a Son.

Hebrews 1:1–2

In the Dogmatic Constitution on Divine Revelation, the [Council] looked at revelation as the act by which God communicates himself in a personal way.... God appears there as one who wishes to communicate himself, carrying out a plan which proceeds from love. Catechesis, then, ought to take its beginning from this gift of divine love.

General Catechetical Directory, no. 10

As masterful a catechist as he was a theologian, Augustine, around the turn of the fifth century, explained to the deacon Deogratias that his catechetical methods changed according to the hearer: "I am differently stirred according as he whom I see before me waiting for instruction is cultivated or a dullard, a fellow citizen or a stranger, a rich man or a poor man, a private citizen or a man honored by a public office, a man having some official authority, a person of this or that family, of this or that age or sex, coming to us from this or that school of philosophy, or from this or that popular error."[1]

Indeed, a catechist, as a good educator, recognizes that his or her methodology must change according to the times, the audience, and the various other contextual factors that come into play, be they social, cultural, or historical. Today, it is not uncommon for catechists to take their cues from the field of secular pedagogy and the advances in education and developmental psychology in order to gain new methodological insights. In fact, the first advances of the modern catechetical movement came from adherents of the so-called Munich Method, a secular educational advance in which content was made more applicable to students through the use of explanations and stories adapted to their common experience. Such advances in pedagogy have proven fruitful for the church since its encounter with Greco-Roman culture at its very beginnings. The fathers of the church were no strangers to harnessing what was useful from the surrounding culture, developing a Christian *paideia*, while rejecting those elements they deemed incompatible with the faith.[2]

Nevertheless, if catechesis is an enduring ministry in the church, it must rest upon a certain foundation that is unchanging, one that unifies catechesis in every age and that provides the measure for those elements that can and must be adapted.[3] Thus, while not disregarding the fruitfulness of the faith's encounter with secular pedagogies, it should be noted that the church ultimately does not take as its catechetical foundation these theories, nor any particular work of human achievement. As a ministry of the Word, catechesis rests upon an altogether different and unique foundation.

In his 1979 apostolic exhortation *Catechesi Tradendae*, Pope John Paul II offers the identity of this foundation when he explains that the

1. *De Catechizandis Rudibus* 15.23, in St. Augustine, *The First Catechetical Instruction*, trans. Joseph P. Christopher (New York: Newman, 1946), 50.

2. On the concept of the Christian appropriation of *paideia*, see Werner Jaeger, *Early Christianity and Greek Paideia* (Cambridge, Mass.: Belknap Press of Harvard University Press, 1961). Augustine's *De Doctrina Christiana*, while insightful for the field of biblical studies, can also be considered the bishop's treatise on Christian *paideia*. See Eugene Kevane, "Augustine's *De doctrina christiana*: A Treatise on Christian Education," *Recherches augustiniennes* 4 (1966): 97–129.

3. For Augustine, the heart of Christian instruction was what he called the *narratio*, a narration of the events of salvation history beginning with creation and continuing to the work of Christ in the church in the present. See *De Catechizandis Rudibus* 3.5 and 6.10.

church claims for itself an "original pedagogy of faith."[4] For John Paul, catechesis stems from God's own pedagogy of divine revelation and, therefore, is necessarily distinct from human pedagogies—that is to say that the "pedagogy of faith is not a question of transmitting human knowledge, even of the highest kind; [rather] it is a question of *communicating God's revelation in its entirety*."[5] Thus, while the work of educational theorists and the social sciences is indeed profitable to the church's catechetical mission, its usefulness is valued by the catechist only to the extent that it serves the irreducible originality of the church's faith.

Catechesis, then, as a ministry of the Word, rests upon the foundation of divine revelation. As Francis Kelly explains, "Catechesis is based on and directed by divine revelation," and as such it "serves revelation by being a means by which its message and mystery are made accessible and relevant to the women and men of each age."[6]

Indeed, this intrinsic relationship is manifested in the catechetical directory that was created by mandate from the Second Vatican Council and in its revision twenty-six years later. Issued by the Congregation of the Clergy, the *General Catechetical Directory* (1971) and the *General Directory for Catechesis* (1997) both ground their discussion of the nature and purpose of catechesis in Vatican II's Constitution on Divine Revelation, *Dei Verbum*. For the former, revelation is the way in which God communicates himself, accomplishing a plan that proceeds from love: "Catechesis, then, ought to take its beginning from this gift of love."[7] For the latter, God's revelation is itself a type of pedagogy consisting of words and deeds. Catechetical pedagogy is then modeled after this divine pedagogy, for it:

4. John Paul II, *Catechesi Tradendae*, no. 58, trans. *L'Osservatore Romano*, English ed. (Boston: St. Paul Editions, 1979), 48; AAS 71 (1979): 1277–1340. Henceforth, CT.

5. Ibid. Emphasis mine. Because John Paul II is ultimately an important subject for this study, I believe it is important to address the possible objection that, by beginning with his remarks on the nature of catechesis, I have therefore initiated a circular argument. I simply point out that it is his *anthropology* that later forms the material for the main lines of my argument; these statements regarding revelation and catechesis, besides carrying a certain magisterial authority, are echoed both by the work of scholars (as will be shown) and by other ecclesial documents such as the *General Catechetical Directory* of 1971 (thus written before *Catechesi Tradendae*) and the *General Directory for Catechesis* of 1997.

6. Francis D. Kelly, *The Mystery We Proclaim: Catechesis for the Third Millennium*, 2nd ed. (Huntington, Ind.: Our Sunday Visitor, 1999), 106.

7. Congregation of the Clergy, *General Catechetical Directory*, no. 10, Vatican trans., in *The Catechetical Documents*, ed. Martin Connell (Chicago: Liturgy Training Publications, 1996), 19. Henceforth, GCD.

transmits the words and deeds of revelation; it is obliged to proclaim and narrate them and, at the same time, to make clear the profound mysteries they proclaim. Moreover, since revelation is a source of light for the human person, catechesis not only recalls the marvels worked by God in the past, but also, in the light of the same revelation, it interprets the signs of the times and the present life of man, since it is in these that the plan of God for the salvation of the world is realized.[8]

In both documents the Council's teaching on revelation has a profound impact upon how catechesis is envisioned. As such, in order to better grasp the church's catechetical ministry it is necessary to first explore the teachings of Vatican II that, in the postconciliar period, give catechesis its foundation. As the *General Directory for Catechesis* suggests, the nature of revelation itself will be primary in this consideration, but so too will be the proper understanding of human experience in light of this revelation, for it is in "the signs of the times and the present life of man ... that the plan of God for the salvation of the world is realized." Both elements suggest that the truth itself and the way in which it is received by the human person remain the constant concern for catechesis.

The two main Council documents that garner the attention of this chapter are the Dogmatic Constitution on Divine Revelation, *Dei Verbum*, and the Pastoral Constitution on the Church in the Modern World, *Gaudium et Spes*.[9] These documents are significant for many reasons, not the least of which is the new theological ground they break:[10] the former is the church's first official document to focus exclusively on the nature of revelation itself, and the latter offers the "first time that a council has consciously endeavored to set forth a systematic account of Christian anthropology in an independent thematic concept," seeking to address the relationship between human experience and the faith

8. Congregation for the Clergy, *General Directory for Catechesis*, no. 39, also referencing *Dei Verbum*, no. 2 (Washington, D.C.: United States Catholic Conference, 1997), 37. Henceforth, GDC.

9. For Vatican II documents I have used the translation found in Austin Flannery, ed., *Vatican Council II*, vol. 1, *The Conciliar and Postconciliar Documents* (Northport, N.Y.: Costello, 1998).

10. Though the Council's aim was ultimately pastoral, it would be incorrect to oppose this pastoral orientation to the Council's doctrinal content. See John Paul II, *Fidei Depositum*, preface, Vatican trans., in *Catechism of the Catholic Church*, 1–6: "With the help of God, the Council Fathers in four years of work were able to produce a considerable number of doctrinal statements and pastoral norms which were presented to the whole Church" (as found in the beginning of the CCC [2]). See also Avery Dulles, "Vatican II: The Myth and the Reality," *America*, February 24, 2003, 7–11, esp. 9.

of the church.[11] This study proceeds, then, by examining the Council's teaching on revelation in *Dei Verbum* and its understanding of the human person present in *Gaudium et Spes*.[12] In analyzing these two documents this chapter seeks to gain helpful norms by which to evaluate the catechetical ministry of the Word. Chapter 2 will then provide an opportunity to examine the recent history of catechetics and to evaluate this history in light of the norms uncovered here. Ultimately, by returning to the teaching of Vatican II one can appropriately evaluate catechesis in the modern era and determine the contribution of this ministry in the New Evangelization.

Interpreting the Council

In initially approaching the teaching of Vatican II, a key to analyzing the conciliar documents undoubtedly lies in the hermeneutic of the Council itself. As the last fifty years have shown, the Council is considered by many as an event of great hope, and yet it garners tendentious interpretations as well. Often, the point of contention lies in the stance one takes toward *aggiornamento*, the updating of the church that coincides with the changing conditions of the modern world.

Having first emerged in the midst of Greco-Roman culture two millennia ago, the church has faced the ever-present challenge of confronting the world and the unique historical situations brought to the fore by men and women in every age. In the years leading up to the Council, this challenge took the form of a growing sense of human self-awareness and the discovery of the historical character of knowledge, along with progress in scientific, technological, and social realms. *Ad intra*, the church had uneasily navigated the Modernist heresy,[13] though not without

---

11. Walter Kasper, "The Theological Anthropology of *Gaudium et spes*," *Communio* 23, no. 1 (1996): 129.

12. This is not to say that the Council's other two constitutions, *Sacrosanctum Concilium* and *Lumen Gentium*, are insignificant for the New Evangelization. An adequate examination of the relevance of both for the church's ministry of the Word would require its own study.

13. Joseph Ratzinger, in *Theological Highlights of Vatican II*, trans. Henry Traub, Gerard C. Thormann, and Werner Barzel (New York: Paulist Press, 1966), 148, characterizes the "Modernist crisis" by the challenge brought to the church's faith by claims that the teachings of scripture and tradition were actually subject to the developments of human history. See also Brian Daley, "The Nouvelle Théologie and the Patristic Revival: Sources, Symbols, and the Science of Theology," *International Journal of Systematic Theology* 7, no. 4 (2005): 362–82, esp. 363.

staunchly reaffirming a theological system indebted to scholasticism.[14] *Ad extra*, many theologians of this period began to voice a certain unrest, finding such a neo-scholastic theology to be wedded to a fortress mentality, thus making it ill-equipped to handle the challenges of the modern world. Monumental figures such as Henri de Lubac, Jean Daniélou, Marie-Dominique Chenu, Karl Rahner, Hans Urs von Balthasar, and Yves Congar began to develop new lines of theological thought that could address the rising concerns of human experience and historicity. This so-called *nouvelle théologie* varied in scope and method, some (like Rahner) turning to the categories of modern philosophy and others (like de Lubac) believing a *ressourcement*—a return to the church's earliest sources—could help address the current situation.

Whatever their differences, the theologians of this era often shared two unifying perspectives: the inadequacy of neo-scholasticism, and the need to show the faith's relevance for the men and women of the present age. As Balthasar wrote in 1952, the church had "continued all too long after the Reformation to hand on the old intellectual framework of the middle-ages in her Counter-Reformation," and despite the widening horizon of modern concerns, "most of the church's representatives remained immersed in their own tradition, vigorously restoring it . . . unconcerned with the expanded field of view."[15]

This shared perspective undoubtedly carried over into the call for the Second Vatican Council. Nevertheless, the attempt to engage the modern world brought with it varying reactions—reactions that, in

---

14. The dominant theology in the years leading up to the Council, neo-scholasticism was the late nineteenth/early twentieth-century revival of the scholasticism of the Middle Ages. Often linked with Pope Leo XIII's approbation of Thomism in the 1879 encyclical *Aeterni Patris*, neo-scholastics retrieved the thought of such theologians as St. Bonaventure, John Duns Scotus, and especially St. Thomas Aquinas in order to address the needs of the church. Critics of this theology, as will be discussed more later, found it to be overly rationalistic and deductive, accusing it of attempting to confront the concerns of modernity by simply taking a defensive stance toward it. While such a claim may have some validity in regard to particular expressions of neo-scholasticism, it would be incorrect to broadly paint every neo-scholastic thinker with such a brush, even more so to claim that the writings of those such as St. Thomas no longer have bearing on the present. See John Paul II, *Fides et Ratio*, no. 43: "The Church has been justified in consistently proposing St. Thomas as a master of thought and a model of the right way to do theology." I have used the translation found in John Paul II, *Fides et Ratio*, Vatican trans. (Boston: Pauline Books and Media, 1998), 58; AAS 91 (1999): 5–88. Henceforth, FR. See also Aidan Nichols, "Thomism and the Nouvelle Théologie," *Thomist* 64 (2000): 1–19.

15. Hans Urs von Balthasar, *Razing the Bastions*, trans. Brian McNeil (San Francisco: Ignatius Press, 1993), 18.

many respects, persist in present attempts to interpret the Council. It is certainly true that a correct hermeneutic for Vatican II must include the idea of updating;[16] yet it is possible to overemphasize this idea to the point of creating a rift between the church before the Council and that which existed afterward.[17] Those who espouse such a position often see Vatican II's documents as products of compromise between traditionalist and progressive factions, claiming that the modernizing spirit of the Council must guide interpretation over and above the letter of its teachings.[18] Still there are others, decidedly fewer in number, who look upon *aggiornamento* with disdain. For these, the opening of the doors to modernity is a capitulation that forsakes the past.[19]

Rather than argue one-sidedly for a capitulation to modernity or, for that matter, for the repristination of an age long past, I would like to suggest that the proper hermeneutic for the Council is found in the words of the pope who first called it to order. For John XXIII, "it is absolutely vital that the church shall never for an instant lose sight of that sacred patrimony of truth inherited from the Fathers. But it is equally necessary for her to keep up to date with the changing conditions of this modern world."[20] His vision, in other words, reaches back to the past while simultaneously embracing the challenge of the present. That is to say that the pope who called the Second Vatican Council looked at

16. See Giuseppe Alberigo, "The Announcement of the Council: From the Security of the Fortress to the Lure of the Quest," in *History of Vatican II*, ed. Giuseppe Alberigo and Joseph A. Komonchak (Maryknoll, N.Y.: Orbis, 1995), 1:42: "Pope John wanted a Council that would mark a transition between two eras, that is, that would bring the Church out of the post-tridentine period and, to a degree, out of the centuries-long Constantinian era, into a new phase of witness and proclamation, and would also recover substantial and abiding elements of the tradition considered able to nourish and ensure fidelity to the gospel during so difficult a transition."

17. See Alberigo's chapter "The Christian Situation after Vatican II," in *The Reception of Vatican II*, ed. Giuseppe Alberigo, Jean-Pierre Jossua, and Joseph A. Komonchak (Washington, D.C.: The Catholic University of America Press, 1987), 23, where, according to the author, "reductionism is precisely the risk run by any assertion that the history of the Church has no before and after. A picture of church history as an even, unbroken line can indeed bring out the aspect of continuity, but it is also a picture of death, not life, of inertia, not of a journey toward the heavenly homeland."

18. Ibid., 21–24.

19. Archbishop Lefebvre was perhaps the most well known of this group. See Dulles, "Vatican II: The Myth and the Reality," 7, where he states, "While reformers caricature the preconciliar church as tyrannical and obscurantist, traditionalists idealize the preconciliar church as though it were a lost paradise."

20. John XXIII, "Opening Address to the Council," trans. H. E. Winstone, in *The Encyclicals and Other Messages of Pope John XXIII*, ed. staff of *The Pope Speaks* Magazine, 429.

the church diachronically, as standing in the stream of tradition that finds its source in Jesus Christ and runs through to the present.[21]

In his speech given to the Roman Curia in 2005, Pope Benedict XVI reaffirmed this hermeneutic of tradition, warning against what he called a "hermeneutic of discontinuity and rupture," one that saw the Council as an event manifesting a break with the tradition, resulting in a split between the preconciliar and postconciliar church.[22] Instead, he called for a "hermeneutic of reform," one of "renewal in the continuity of the one-subject church that the Lord has given us. She is a subject that increases in time and develops; yet always remaining the same, the one subject of the journeying People of God."[23] From such a position within tradition it is possible to embrace not only *aggiornamento*, but *ressourcement* as well. In fact, for Benedict and for many of the influential figures of the Second Vatican Council, the rediscovery of the treasures of the past is precisely what allows the church to confront the challenges of the present.[24]

My approach to the documents of Vatican II, therefore, will be one taken precisely from this stance within tradition. This hermeneutic will

21. John XXIII adds in his opening remarks, "What is needed is that this certain and immutable doctrine, to which the faithful owe obedience, be studied afresh and reformulated in contemporary terms. For this deposit of faith, or truths which are contained in our time-honored teaching is one thing; the manner in which these truths are set forth (with their meaning preserved intact) is something else." Ibid., 430.

22. See Benedict XVI, "A Proper Hermeneutic for the Second Vatican Council," in *Vatican II: Renewal within Tradition*, ed. Matthew L. Lamb and Matthew Levering (Oxford: Oxford University Press, 2008), x. Interestingly, such a hermeneutic can be applied to those who wish to remain in the past and to those who believe the church should capitulate to the present. In the first case, the perceived "rupture" is unwelcome; in the second, it is an enlivening change of antiquated positions.

23. Ibid. It would be facile to characterize the pope's remarks as the mere opposition of discontinuity and continuity in interpreting the Council. Rather, Benedict argues that true reform manifests continuity in foundational principles and possible discontinuity in contingent matters; false reform emphasizes discontinuity on both levels. Thus he goes on to explain, "It is precisely in this combination of continuity and discontinuity at different levels that the very nature of true reform consists. In this process of innovation in continuity we must learn to understand more practically than before that the church's decisions on contingent matters ... should necessarily be contingent themselves, precisely because they refer to a specific reality that is changeable in itself. It was necessary to learn to recognize that in these decisions it is only the principles that express the permanent aspect, since they remain as an undercurrent, motivating decisions from within. On the other hand, not so permanent are the practical forms that depend on the historical situation and are therefore subject to change."

24. See Marcellino D'Ambrosio, "Ressourcement, Aggiornamento, and the Hermeneutics of Tradition," *Communio* 18, no. 4 (1991): 530–54.

prove to be of decisive importance for our understanding of *Dei Verbum* and *Gaudium et Spes*.

Dei Verbum

My study of *Dei Verbum* will focus mainly on its first chapter, which concerns revelation itself, though it will include portions of the second chapter as well. I will analyze each article in turn; summarizing conclusions drawn from the analysis will be offered at the end of the chapter.

Article 1

The first article of the Constitution, the prologue, reaffirms the hermeneutic of tradition by stating its intention to follow "in the steps of the Councils of Trent and Vatican I."[25] As mentioned previously, Trent and Vatican I did not promulgate documents solely concerning the nature of revelation itself—Vatican II was breaking new ground in this regard—nevertheless, certain conclusions can be drawn from their teachings. For Trent, the "gospel" (the term we could, for our purposes, most closely identify with revelation) is the "source of the whole truth of salvation and rule of conduct" and is contained not only in the scriptures, but in unwritten traditions as well.[26] Even with the acknowledgment of a revelatory tradition (over and above sacred scripture), the issue of whether or not this tradition materially adds anything to revelation was one that caused great debate for the fathers of Vatican II. The teaching of Trent thus offered them the question "What can properly be termed the 'source' of revelation?" Is it scripture, tradition, both, or something else entirely?

As for Vatican I, the Council's main contribution to a theology of revelation coincides with the predominance of neo-scholasticism at the time: according to the second chapter of its Constitution, *Dei Filius*, God

25. *Dei Verbum*, no. 1 [750]. Henceforth, *DV*.

26. See Trent's Session 4, First Decree, where the Council declares that the Gospel is contained "in the written books and in the unwritten traditions which have been received by the apostles from the mouth of Christ Himself, or from the apostles themselves, at the dictation of the Holy Spirit"; from "Trent: 1545–1563," trans. Peter McIlhenny, in *Decrees of the Ecumenical Councils*, ed. Norman P. Tanner (Washington, D.C.: Sheed and Ward and Georgetown University Press, 1990), 2:663. See also Dulles, *Revelation Theology: A History* (New York: Herder and Herder, 1969), 49–50. This teaching is perhaps best understood as a response to the Protestant Reformation.

reveals "himself and the eternal laws [*decreta*] of his will."[27] Though it is important to point out that God's self-revelation is here acknowledged, the remaining teaching of the Council placed emphasis decidedly on the decrees. In this vein *Dei Filius*'s fourth chapter concludes that revelation is "a divine deposit committed to the spouse of Christ, to be faithfully protected and infallibly promulgated."[28] As such, revelation was mainly conceived as a deposit of propositional truths, some written in scripture, some handed on by church teaching, all of which were to be accepted with the obedience of faith.[29] Once again, a question was bequeathed to the fathers of Vatican II: is revelation fundamentally propositional in nature?

Considering Vatican II's desire to follow in the steps of these preceding councils, these two issues of revelation's sources and a propositional conception of revelation are themes that play an important role in the Council's teaching in *Dei Verbum*. In fact, the Constitution's answer to both questions ultimately becomes the heart of its teaching on revelation.

While more will be explained later, the prologue gives us a clue as to what will ultimately be the resolution to squaring these themes with more modern concerns. As de Lubac says in his commentary on the document, the clue is found in the first two words, those that give the Constitution its title. For the Council, revelation is *Dei Verbum*—the Word of God itself. Or perhaps, as article 2 shows, it is better to say here, the Word of God *himself*.[30]

27. *Dei Filius*, chapter 2, from "Vatican I: 1869–1870," trans. Ian Brayley, in Tanner, *Decrees of the Ecumenical Councils*, 2:806. The Latin text is found on the same page.

28. Ibid., chapter 4, 2:809.

29. See O'Collins, *Foundations of Theology*, 24: "Vatican I did speak expressly of God 'revealing himself.' But the trend to depersonalization was unmistakably there, so that revelation was presented as the disclosure of new truths about God, the communication of a body of doctrine, a privileged enriching of our knowledge about God.... From here it was only half a step to allowing 'correctness' of verbal expression and the sterile recitation of creeds to predominate over the lived experience of self-commitment to God."

30. Henri de Lubac, *La Révélation Divine*, 3rd ed. (Paris: Les Éditions du Cerf, 1983), 23: "These two first words, by which this doctrinal Constitution 'On Divine Revelation' will be designated, summarize very exactly its object. It consists of the Word of God. In the official text, they are written entirely in capital letters: therefore one cannot specify if they designate the word of God in general, taking it in a sense more or less abstract, or if they already directly indicate this White Knight of the Apocalypse who was named 'Word of God' and who carries a double-edged sword in his mouth, that personal Word, 'Word of life,' only Word of the Father, 'living wisdom and Son of God,' 'refulgence of his glory and image of his being,'—in short,

In Paul's letter to the Ephesians he expounds upon the "mystery of [God's] will"—in Christ every blessing of the heavens has been given and the mystery is revealed; in Christ all of humanity is chosen and returns to God, yet not only humanity, but all things "in heaven and on earth" (1:3–10).[31] As the scriptural foundation for the second article, Paul's words provide the heart of Vatican II's theology of revelation: God has given himself most perfectly in Christ, and in Christ humanity is brought into union with God. As Ratzinger notes, this conception of revelation is a *relecture* of the teaching of Vatican I. Whereas the first council had emphasized *aeterna voluntatis suae decreta* (the eternal decrees of his will), *Dei Verbum* chose *sacramentum voluntatis suae* (the mystery of his will), seeing in the Pauline word "mystery" (*sacramentum*) a stronger connection between God who is revealed and any possible decrees that may be associated with this revelation.[32] Thus, rather than revealing a mere deposit of truths, revelation reveals he who is truth itself.

Of course, it would be incorrect to take this personalistic affirmation as a relativization of propositions and the ability of words to convey truth—the scriptures and the doctrines of the church are not called into question here. But in choosing to emphasize God's *self*-revelation, the Council was able to recover the nature of revelation as attested to by the scriptures and the earlier Christian tradition. Just as Jesus the Teacher's doctrine was novel because, in it, he taught himself, the Council's affirmation importantly acknowledges that all Christian teaching must be able to ground itself in the source that is Christ.[33] Doctrine, in this case,

---

Jesus Christ. Without a doubt, it is suitable to leave them in their indetermination, that the result, then, will not take long at all to become clear" (translations from this text are my own). It is easy to see from the lavish scriptural imagery of de Lubac's prose his ultimate conclusion in the matter.

31. Paul's authorship of Ephesians is contested by some biblical scholars, though I have retained the Pauline reference in accord with the beginning of the letter. See Eph 1:1.

32. Ratzinger, "Chapter I: Revelation Itself," in *Commentary on the Documents of Vatican II*, ed. Herbert Vorgrimler, trans. W. J. O'Hara (New York: Herder and Herder, 1969), 3:171. The Latin texts in question are provided here as well. It is important to recall that Vatican I did acknowledge that revelation reveals God himself and not only the decrees of his will. It would be incorrect to accuse the First Vatican Council of intellectualism in this regard.

33. See St. Irenaeus, *Adversus Haereses* 4.34.1: "He brought all novelty by bringing himself, who had been announced"; from *The Ante-Nicene Fathers*, vol. 1, *The Apostolic Fathers with Justin Martyr and Irenaeus*, American ed., ed. and trans. Alexander Roberts and James Donaldson (New York: Charles Scribner's Sons, 1903), 511.

is revelation precisely because it participates in Christ's very person. To detach doctrine from such participation would be—as many claimed was witnessed in the theology of the manuals—to relegate Christ to the realm of the accidental:

The role of Jesus Christ in revelation [is] doubly effaced: he [is] neither the messenger par excellence nor the object par excellence of divine revelation. The object of faith [is] crumbled, almost pulverized: It [is] no longer God who [is] revealed, himself and his mysterious plan of salvation; man [has] to subscribe to a list of truths, which nothing [assures] him in advance that they [can] have between them and himself a substantial link. In the end, dogma [finds] itself as totally exteriorized, cut off from its finality, and faith [tends] to be no more than the blind submission to a *locutio Dei auctoritative docentis*.[34]

Rather than accept such a narrowly propositionalist understanding of revelation, the Council reaffirms in this article that "the most intimate truth which this revelation gives us about God and the salvation of man shines forth in Christ, who is himself both the mediator and the sum total of revelation."[35]

This personal conception of revelation calls attention to three other points of significance. First, such an understanding of revelation provides a way out of the contentious issue of scripture and tradition's material sufficiency. If the Council fathers had originally questioned whether one or both could be termed sources of revelation, in the end they concluded that there is actually only one Source, and from this Source scripture and tradition flow. Thus *Dei Verbum* in a later article states that "both of them, flowing out from the same divine well-spring, come together in some fashion to form one thing and move towards the same goal."[36] The one divine wellspring, as the Source of revelation, is none other than God himself.

Second, by affirming revelation's personal nature, the Council is likewise able to show revelation's corresponding dialogical character. Revelation manifests the *persona* of God and, as such, can only be received by persons. Thus, in what one commentator describes as "a passage that has few counterparts in ecclesiastical documents," *Dei Verbum* declares that "by this revelation, then, the invisible God, from the fullness of his love, addresses men as his friends and moves among them,

34. De Lubac, *La Révélation Divine*, 153–54.
35. DV, no. 2 [751].
36. DV, no. 9 [755].

in order to invite them and receive them into his own company."[37] This personal God, so evident in the events recorded in scripture, speaks and acts so that men and women can hear and perceive him—the very purpose of this self-revelation is that they are enabled to enter into communion with him. The dialogical nature of revelation, as it is found in salvation history, is highlighted in article 3.

Third, and here one can recall the reference to St. Paul's use of "mystery" (*sacramentum* in the Latin text of *Dei Verbum*), revelation is acknowledged to have a sacramental character. While sacramentality mainly concerns visible or material reality's ability to manifest the invisible, it can also denote the significance of both words and deeds in a given reality. As has already been noted, when God manifests himself in revelation, he does so in a personal way—that is, by way of word and action.[38] Sacraments likewise involve the same factors: the elevation of the host and the chalice are efficacious only in combination with the words of institution; the descent into and ascent out of the waters of baptism is united with the trinitarian formula to effect new birth. In a similar way, the acts of God in Israel's history often required the interpreting word of the prophets in order to bear salvific fruit, and the

37. See Francis Martin, "Revelation and Its Transmission," in Lamb and Levering, *Vatican II: Renewal within Tradition*, 57, and DV, no. 2 [751]. It is interesting to note with this point Joseph Ratzinger's *Habilitationsschrift* on St. Bonaventure's theology of history, which included the Franciscan doctor's understanding of revelation, particularly as it pertained to the scriptures. If, at the time of Ratzinger's theological formation, revelation was primarily conceived as the scriptures themselves, for Bonaventure the same cannot be said. For Bonaventure "it would have been impossible to refer to Scripture simply as 'revelation,' as is the normal linguistic use today. Scripture is the essential witness of revelation, but revelation is something alive, something greater and more: proper to it is the fact that it arrives and is perceived—otherwise it could not have become revelation. Revelation is not a meteor fallen to earth that now lies somewhere as a rock mass from which rock samples can be taken and submitted to the laboratory analysis. Revelation has instruments; but it is not separable from the living God, and it always requires a living person to whom it is communicated." From Ratzinger's *Milestones: Memoirs 1927–1977*, trans. Erasmo Leiva-Merikakis (San Francisco: Ignatius Press, 1998), 127; see also his Habilitation thesis, *The Theology of History in St. Bonaventure*, trans. Zachary Hayes (Chicago: Franciscan Herald Press, 1989). Not only does such a conception of revelation provide ample food for thought for the theology of revelation and for catechesis, but it also implies much about biblical studies and, as Ratzinger/Benedict XVI has consistently emphasized, the need to transcend merely historical approaches.

38. To speak of God in a "personal" way is necessarily to speak by analogy; nevertheless, the word "person," as it is used today, in many respects is Christian in origin. On this concept of person in theology, see Ratzinger, "Concerning the Notion of Person in Theology," *Communio* 17, no. 3 (1990): 439–54; and Grabowski, "Person: Substance and Relation," *Communio* 22, no. 1 (1995): 139–63.

actions of Jesus Christ were fully manifested in the words he spoke.[39] Furthermore, and by extension from these acts of God in history, the written words of scripture and the well-articulated words of church teaching continue to provide an aid to understanding the mysteries to which they refer.[40] Thus, one can say that the deeds of God in history require an interpreting word, and the words necessitate the deeds as their substantial content. As this second article states, the two "are intrinsically bound up with each other. . . . The works performed by God in the history of salvation show forth and bear out the doctrine and realities signified by the words; the words, for their part, proclaim the works, and bring to light the mystery they contain."[41]

This sacramental character is vital, first, in that it can help in giving further definition to the role of scripture and church teaching (that is, words) in the transmission of revelation today, a topic to be taken up later; and second, in that it broaches the theme of history, one of the primary challenges of modernity. This second theme is considered further in article 3.

Article 3

If revelation in its primary sense is more than a deposit of truths but is God manifesting himself to us by word and deed, then this manifestation must necessarily happen within history. By acknowledging this fact, the Council fathers were able to take on some of the most significant problems posed by modernity. For the church, the historical character of knowledge had posed a particularly difficult challenge in her confrontation with the Modernist heresy.[42]

39. See Avery Dulles, *Models of Revelation* (Maryknoll, N.Y.: Orbis, 1992), 67: "All revelation, inasmuch as it has the two dimensions of intelligibility and embodiment, is both manifestation and accomplishment. The Hebrew term *dabar*, meaning both word and event, suggests this duality. Thanks to the intrinsic correlation between the two dimensions, revelation has a sacramental structure."

40. René Latourelle, *Theology of Revelation*, trans. unknown (Staten Island, N.Y.: Alba House, 1966), 356: "Revelation is accomplished *through history*, but not without the interpretation of the word. It is presented as a complex of meaningful events proceeding from God and his plan for salvation. It follows that revelation is at once history and doctrine. It is doctrine about God, but a doctrine made up on the basis of God's activity in history." Emphasis in the original.

41. DV, no. 2 [751].

42. While the heresy of Modernism can be characterized by an emphasis on subjective experience and an evolutionary view of doctrine, the various figures connected with the heresy (e.g., Alfred Loisy and George Tyrrell) did not consider themselves part of a united front. In

The beginnings of the modern era (as opposed to the earlier Middle Ages or the more recent advent of postmodernity) are often traced to René Descartes, the seventeenth-century philosopher and mathematician who, having been trained by the Jesuits, had found their scholasticism wanting. Wishing to find a different foundation upon which all knowledge could be built, he postulated the now (in)famous *cogito ergo sum*, simultaneously incorporating systematic doubt about all perceived knowledge with the placement of human rationality at the center of reality.[43] This had a dual effect that rippled throughout modern history: should not the power of an individual's reason be acknowledged as the ground of all truth, rather than traditionally held formulations? And in doing so, should not such authoritative statements now be held subject to scientific examination, both of nature and of history? In the ripple that eventually reached the church in the late nineteenth and early twentieth centuries, the Modernist heresy indeed posed a difficult challenge, but with two sides. On its more objective side, the neo-scholastic and atemporal concept of propositional revelation was now suspect before the challenge of history: how could the church maintain the veracity of its teachings or the classic interpretation of its scriptures in the face of historical charges of development? And from its more subjective angle, this traditional deposit seemed unable to make any claim upon the interiority of human experience: should not men and women, along with their desires and concerns, be the determiners of revelation's claims? How could God speak—or at least be heard—if he does not speak precisely to *me*?[44]

From such a perspective it is easier to appreciate the vision posited by the Council fathers in *Dei Verbum*. As God's self-manifestation, revelation answers the historical charge by occurring as word and deed within

fact, it was Pius X, in 1907's *Pascendi Dominici Gregis*, who first referred to the work of such theologians as the Modernist heresy.

43. See René Descartes, Meditation Two, in *Meditations on First Philosophy*, 3rd ed., trans. Donald A. Cress (Indianapolis: Hackett, 1993), 19: "Here I make my discovery: thought exists; it cannot be separated from me. I am; I exist—this is certain. But for how long? For as long as I am thinking; for perhaps it could also come to pass that if I were to cease all thinking I would then utterly cease to exist."

44. It is not possible to outline all of the figures and themes that make up the Modernist heresy, but it is enough to recall here (and it will be necessary later as well) this dual challenge of history and experience. The condemnation of particular solutions to these challenges should not lead one to ignore the challenges themselves. Indeed, history/experience has become one of the pivotal points upon which theology and catechesis turn since Vatican II. For more on the heresy and the church's condemnation of it, see Latourelle, *Theology of Revelation*, 269–92.

history itself; it answers the existential concern by being the manifestation of the personal God to human persons who are its recipients. And it is in this third article where this line of thought is developed further.

In its first two sentences, the third article of the Constitution makes an intriguing distinction. The entire article could be summarized as a brief synopsis of the Old Testament, and, as such, one would expect to find in it references to events by way of the past tense; still, in the first sentence it begins with the doctrine of creation, and does so with verbs that speak of the present: "God, who *creates* and *conserves* all things by his Word, *provides* men with *constant evidence* of himself in created realities."[45] Immediately following this statement, the Council transitions to the past tense, stating that "furthermore, wishing to open the way to heavenly salvation, he *manifested himself* to our first parents from the very beginning."[46] Ratzinger notes the significance of the distinction made between God's creation and the revelation given to the various personages of history. In this "furthermore"—*insuper* in Latin—it is acknowledged that "creation was already oriented towards salvation," but beyond this, "the revelation to the patriarchs is separated from the creation and treated as a new action."[47] In the former, "evidence" of God is constantly provided—there is a testimony of him in created reality; yet, in the latter, God's salvific self-manifestation is offered to men and women in dialogical fashion. Francis Martin summarizes the framework of this article by remarking that "in modern Western theological thought the distinction is made rather between nature and grace. The document, while not denying this perspective, distinguished between nature and history."[48]

The theological import of this framework comes to the fore precisely by asking how the two components—creation and history—separately figure into the Council's conception of revelation. Thus, a first question can be asked: is creation revelatory? Initially, by speaking of God providing "constant evidence of himself in created realities," it might be assumed that the Council's answer is "yes." Because it takes place "by

45. DV, no. 3 [751]. Emphasis mine.
46. Ibid. Emphasis mine.
47. Ratzinger, "Chapter I: Revelation Itself," 173.
48. Martin, "Revelation and Its Transmission," 58. The distinction is no doubt a conceptual one. Creation involves both space and time, and, therefore, history is a part of it (creation is not an event of the past but requires God's willing of it in every "moment" in order to exist).

his Word," creation can be said to objectively manifest the presence of God. Bonaventure, exemplifying the Franciscan tradition, remarks that "every creature is a word of God, since it proclaims God."[49]

Nevertheless, it is the *insuper* of salvation history that leads one to give pause. The reason for history being a "further" development or, as Ratzinger says, a "new action" seems to lie precisely in that it involves the direct interaction of God with human persons. Thus, because revelation is—as the preceding article has indicated—principally personal and dialogical, it is only in God's communication to human persons that one can speak of revelation in its primary sense. Indeed, the unveiling of revelation (*re*/away–*velum*/veil) can refer to the perception of the receiver as much as the act of the Revealer. Revelation, it can then be inferred, only occurs when a person receives it.[50] This is not to deny the objective presence of God manifested through creation, but only to make a distinction in terms: in *Dei Verbum*, revelation in its proper sense is communicated by a personal God and received by human persons. Thus, the *insuper* of this article serves to reinforce the idea that revelation is a freely willed act of a personal God directed at human persons for the sake of their salvation. As such, any created reality is an occasion for revelation, but is not revelation itself.[51]

Already, in this first conclusion, the second concern of the article is broached, that of history's role in revelation. It is the distinct moments of salvation history acknowledged by the Council that offer clues to determining history's revelatory significance. Undoubtedly, these moments of self-manifestation—whether to Abraham or to Moses and the prophets—reveal that revelation requires history as a locus: "Revelation does not take place outside time, nor in a mythical time, the extra-temporal instant of beginning: it is an event which can be located in time. Through revelation God takes a role in human history, and his entry can be dated. Revelation makes history."[52]

49. St. Bonaventure, *Itinerium mentis in Deum*, chapter 2, no. 12, as quoted in *Verbum Domini*, no. 8. See Benedict XVI, *Verbum Domini*, Vatican trans. (Boston: Pauline Books and Media, 2010), 15; AAS 102 (2010): 681–787. Some theologians speak here of a "natural revelation," as distinguished from God's special revelation to persons in history. See, for instance, Dulles, "Faith and Revelation," in *Systematic Theology: Roman Catholic Perspectives*, ed. Francis Schüssler Fiorenza and John P. Galvin (Minneapolis: Augsburg Fortress, 1991), 1:94.

50. Recall Ratzinger's comments in footnote 37.

51. See Dulles, "Faith and Revelation," 94.

52. Latourelle, *Theology of Revelation*, 356. See also Gregory Baum, "Vatican II's Constitution

Nevertheless, while certain distinct moments are clearly given as stages in revelation, the question remains as to whether all of history is itself revelatory.[53] Undoubtedly, *Dei Verbum* gives weight to particular historical moments. The third article gives revelatory efficacy to specific events in which God is manifested to the patriarchs, a "succession of discontinuous interventions" in which "the events follow each other, but also prepare for each other."[54] The Council speaks of these discontinuous interventions as a sort of pedagogy in which God "taught [Israel] ... to recognize him as the only living and true God," as well as "to look for the promised Savior."[55] In such a vision, the specific and revelatory interactions of God, given in distinctly willed moments, are directed toward their fulfillment, that of the advent of Jesus Christ. As such, I believe it is fair to say that the unique history traced by the Old and New Testaments and now continued in the life of the church has special revelatory significance.

Nevertheless, especially considering how the Council had directed its concerns not only at Catholics but to the world, it must be asked how such a specific history of salvation can bear *universal* significance. At first glance, the scriptures seem to speak with no difficulty of the scandal of particularity: Israel is the chosen people, but as the elected firstborn of God it is to be a light to other nations, leading them to worship the one, true God.[56] In the New Testament, Jesus, as the firstborn consubstantial with the Father, manifests the extreme particularity of one person bringing salvation to all, Jew and Gentile alike. Still, such universal significance seems to rely on the efforts of messengers, that of prophets and apostles. The question remains as to whether those who

---

on Revelation: History and Interpretation," *Theological Studies* 28, no. 1 (1967): 61: "Revelation is thus primarily the self-disclosure of God in history in view of man's salvation"; and Jared Wicks, "Vatican II on Revelation: From Behind the Scenes," *Theological Studies* 71, no. 3 (2010): 640: "In its unfolding across history, God's revelation combines deeds and words, for it is history narrated and proclaimed, with events of 'mystery' anchoring the linguistic communication and doctrinal meaning."

53. For an explanation of such a theological stance, see Dulles's commentary on Wolfhart Pannenberg's equation of history with revelation in *Models of Revelation*, 58–60.

54. Latourelle, *Theology of Revelation*, 356.

55. DV, no. 3 [751].

56. See Is 49:6. See also Latourelle, *Theology of Revelation*, 353: "Actually, the scandal of particularism of revelation is inseparable from its historical character. If revelation is given to us in history and through history, as an event, it necessarily follows that this event is subject to the conditions of history: it must happen here rather than there, now rather than later, in one group rather than another."

do not encounter the faith of Israel or the Gospel of Christ are able to be saved. Here it is helpful to remember that the scriptures speak of God's universal salvific will (e.g., 1 Tm 2:4) and do not fail to mention righteous figures such as Melchizedek and Job who stand outside the walls of Israel and the church.[57] In this light it is fair to ask: can revelation occur in events outside of the history of Israel and the church?

In the face of such a difficult issue, it must be admitted that the Council's treatment of revelation's potential universality in this third article is limited in scope. *Dei Verbum* states that God "had never ceased to take care of the human race, for he wishes to give eternal life to all those who seek salvation by patience in well-doing."[58] Here, the document also references Romans 2:6–7, in which Paul speaks of all persons being judged by their works. Yet how God expresses such care for humanity in general is not discussed. As such, it may be helpful to note that some scholars speak of a distinction between the potential revelation given to all peoples and the unique revelation given in salvation history.[59]

Nevertheless, even if all of history is potentially deemed to be revelatory in some way, *Dei Verbum* gives no justification for separating this revelation from the person and work of Jesus Christ. As the previous article states, he is the "mediator and sum total of revelation" and not a mere point in history's continuous succession. That is to say that he is revelation's fullness and its peak, not simply one stop along the way. As de Lubac insightfully notes:

The Council does not therefore replace an idea of abstract and atemporal truths with the mere idea of the unfolding of a history of salvation.... For it replaces this idea of abstract truths with the idea of a truth in the highest concrete degree: the idea of the personal Truth, who appeared in history, works in history and, from the bosom of history, rules over all of history; this Truth in person who is Jesus of Nazareth, the "fullness of revelation."[60]

Thus, without aid of other Council documents, one can say that *Dei Verbum* highlights the significance of the unique salvation history given

57. Perhaps one of the most interesting passages related to this issue of particularity and universality is found in Exodus 3 when Moses encounters the burning bush and asks God's name. The name of God revealed to Moses, "I Am," simultaneously affirms God's transcendence and immanence. He is revealed as the ground of all being, and yet at the same time allegiance to him negates any allegiances to idols and gods who are not the one, true God.

58. DV, no. 3 [751].

59. See Dulles, *Models of Revelation*, 176.

60. De Lubac, *La Révélation Divine*, 58.

in the Judeo-Christian tradition while leaving open the possibility of revelation occurring in history at large. If God's ceaseless care for humanity, cited in this article, suggests the affirmation of this possibility, then it must be acknowledged that this revelation is always and everywhere connected to the person and work of Christ.[61] Without question the Council proclaims him to be (as de Lubac rightfully notes) the Lord of history, working from within its very bosom. The analysis of *Gaudium et Spes* in the second half of this chapter will be necessary to gain further insights into revelation's universal significance.[62]

Article 4

It is in this article that the Council expresses the fulfillment of God's pedagogy in the Old Testament. As the scriptural reference to Hebrews explains, "In times past, God spoke in partial and various ways to our ancestors through the prophets; in these last days he has spoken to us by a Son."[63] In Jesus Christ, revelation is "completed and perfected."[64] The use of the word "completed" (*complendo*) rather than "closed" is significant in that it represents a development of the then current interpretation of what was said in Pius X's *Lamentabili Sane Exitu*. The document of 1907 condemns the Modernist proposition that "revelation, constituting the object of the Catholic faith, was not completed

61. See the helpful chapter "Saving Revelation for All Peoples," in Gerald O'Collins, *Retrieving Fundamental Theology* (New York: Paulist Press, 1993), 79–86, where he traces other Council documents, finding such revelation to be always united to the work of Christ and his Spirit.

62. As Baum states, "This teaching is not worked out in detail here." Both Baum and Wicks refer to a schema written by Ratzinger and Karl Rahner in which the Council *periti* offer an account of revelation's universal significance. The unofficial draft, circulated in the Council's first few weeks, ultimately was not incorporated into the Constitution; nevertheless, some of their concerns were addressed. See Baum, "Vatican II's Constitution on Revelation," 63, and Wicks, "Vatican II on Revelation," 646–47. Also of note here are the recommendations Ratzinger made to Cardinal Josef Frings concerning early drafts of Council documents. See Wicks, "Six Texts of Prof. Joseph Ratzinger as *Peritus* before and during Vatican Council II," *Gregorianum* 89, no. 2 (2008): 233–311, especially 283: "We know today that the history of Israel and the Church occupies only a tiny part of the whole history of humankind, so that from a purely quantitative viewpoint salvation history almost disappears as a very minor part of world history.... A Council of today, which the whole world, including non-Christians, will be watching, should make it clear that it knows well the breadth, height, length, and depth, that is, the truly cosmic dimensions, of salvation in Christ, and that it is not imprisoned in the cage of a medieval worldview of history, within which it cultivates a kind of ecclesiastical provincialism."

63. DV, no. 4 [751], quoting Heb 1:1–2.

64. DV, no. 4 [752]. See AAS 58 (1966): 819: "Quapropter Ipse, quem qui videt, videt et Patrem ... revelationem complendo perficit ac testimonio divino confirmat."

with the apostles."[65] Within the scholastic framework of the time, such a teaching served to declare the substantial content of the deposit of faith as closed with the death of the last apostle. While maintaining the force of this teaching—for there can be no new public revelation in the church—Vatican II's description of revelation requires a *relecture* of Pius X's statement. If revelation is conceived primarily as a fixed deposit, then it indeed can be completed in the sense of being closed. But if revelation is the manifestation of the living God in Jesus Christ, then it is said to be complete, not in the sense that God arbitrarily stopped speaking when "the Apostle John breathed his final sigh," but in that, by speaking the Word who is Jesus Christ, God has said all that can be said.[66] Jesus is the fullness of revelation because, in him, God has spoken himself.[67]

This revealed Word is, in some sense, continually communicated to the church by "the Spirit of truth."[68] The Holy Spirit continues "to bear witness," as 1 John 5:6 declares.[69] In this regard, Francis Martin makes reference to the teaching of Leo the Great: "All those things which the Son of God both did and taught for the reconciliation of the world, we not only know in the account of things now past, but we also experience in the power of works which are present."[70] This continual communication of the once-and-for-all spoken Word is addressed further in the treatment of article 8 shown later.

Article 5

As revelation is directed toward human persons, it calls for the response of faith. This dialogical character of the Word of God recalls the words

---

65. Pius X, *Lamentabili Sane Exitu*, proposition 21, *Acta Sancta Sedis* 40 (1907): 473. Translation mine.

66. Dulles, "The Meaning of Revelation," in *Dynamics in Christian Thought*, ed. Joseph Papin (Villanova, Pa.: Villanova University Press, 1970), 76–77. Dulles notes that several Council fathers had requested an additional statement that revelation closed with the apostles. The drafting commission rejected the request but not without admitting that the wording as it stands "does not lack difficulties, and indeed from several points of view."

67. Ratzinger, "Chapter I: Revelation Itself," 175: "God does not arbitrarily stop speaking at some point of history and at some point of his discourse, although there would be much more to say, but Christ is the end of God's speaking, because after him and beyond him there is nothing more to say, for in him God has, as it were, said himself."

68. DV, no. 4 [752].

69. See Martin, "Revelation and Its Transmission," 60.

70. Ibid.

of the prophet Isaiah: "So shall my word be that goes forth from my mouth; it shall not return to me empty, but shall do what pleases me, achieving the end for which I sent it" (55:11). *Dei Verbum* introduces this end by using the Pauline phrase "the obedience of faith" (see Rom 1:5, 16:26). Echoing the self-manifestation of God that is revelation, this obedience of faith is one in which "man freely commits his entire self to God."[71] It is a returning self-gift to the God who first gives himself, and it is one that utilizes both the "intellect and will."[72] From this synthesis it is clear that the Council has been able to effectively integrate the intellectual and dogmatic faith called for by its conciliar predecessors with its own understanding of revelation's personal nature. This development is accomplished:

> by an understanding of revelation that is wholly Christological and that sees the dualism of word and reality reconciled in him who, as the true *Logos*, is at the same time the true ground of all that is real, and that consequently sees the antithesis between intellectual dogmatic faith and the yielding-up of one's whole existence in trust overcome through total acceptance coming from the person, which recognizes Jesus Christ as, indissolubly, both the truth and the way.[73]

In describing this act of faith, the Council stresses the work of the Holy Spirit. It is only by "the grace of God" that men and women can offer their entire selves in faith; it is the Spirit "who moves the heart and converts it to God" and "who opens the eyes of the mind."[74] And in this pneumatological emphasis, with the first chapter of the Constitution nearly coming to a close, the Council begins to open the way for its teaching on the Spirit's role in tradition—the way in which revelation, while completed in Christ, continues to be given to the church today. This foundation for tradition is laid in the article's last sentence, where "the same Holy Spirit constantly perfects faith by his gifts, so that revelation may be more and more profoundly understood."[75]

Article 6

The final article of the first chapter begins with the briefest summary of what has been said in the previous articles: "By divine revelation God

71. DV, no. 5 [752].
72. Ibid.
73. Ratzinger, "Chapter I: Revelation Itself," 177.
74. DV, no. 5 [752].
75. Ibid.

wished to manifest and communicate both himself and the eternal decrees of his will."[76] As every article of the chapter has shown, the *relecture* of previous teaching—the integration of the tradition with modern concerns—is accomplished effectively by removing revelation from a strictly intellectual and positivist domain and by emphasizing its deepest nature as the manifestation of God himself. If there is a temptation to discard previous tradition completely, to reject dogma and doctrine as unable to communicate the truth of God, then surely the Council does not embrace such a vision here.[77] By a hermeneutic of tradition, the dogmatic emphases of neo-scholasticism are replanted into their true ground.

In light of this affirmation of tradition it becomes easier to see why the first chapter concludes with a reiteration of Vatican I's teaching regarding the relationship of reason to revelation. Human reason is that which allows God to be known "from the created world" as the "first principle and last end of all things"; revelation, on the other hand, surpasses reason, though it allows things that reason could have known by its own power to be known "with ease, with firm certainty, and without contamination of error."[78]

If there is anything to add here it is that the teaching of Vatican I has indeed been reaffirmed, but in a new framework. The previous council had spoken of reason's powers, then of "supernatural revelation" given by God. Vatican II follows the reverse procedure: "It develops revelation from its Christological center, in order then to present the inescapable responsibility of human reason as one dimension of the whole."[79] In other words, the Council avoids an artificial separation between the human discovery of God by reason as a merely human work and the divine act of God's self-revelation. Even creation itself, as the third article has shown, is a work of God. It is better, in this sense, to speak of two unified but distinct aspects of knowing God. From the testimony of God

76. DV, no. 6 [752].
77. See Peter De Mey, "The Relation between Revelation and Experience in *Dei Verbum*: An Evaluation in the Light of Postconciliar Theology," in Lamberigts and Kenis, *Vatican II and Its Legacy*, 95–105. De Mey mistakenly faults the Council's teaching as being unable to renounce a "doctrinal model of revelation." He draws upon the work of those such as Rahner, who "deplored the 'objectivist structure'" of the first chapter, and Edward Schillebeeckx, who saw it largely as "a compromise between two conflicting conceptions."
78. DV, no. 6 [752–53].
79. Ratzinger, "Chapter I: Revelation Itself," 180.

("evidence," as the third article says) given in creation, "we can perceive God by the natural light of reason"; still, "this perception brings us only to the 'outer door,' as it were, of the mystery of God. It can grasp the fact of this mystery. But the nature of the mystery is closed to it."[80] It is, thus, in the historical interventions of God—a communication purely "from above"—that the mystery is fully revealed. Such a revelation must come from above, for there is no amount of human effort that can open the way of salvation and reveal God's innermost self. Reason can only perceive what testimony God offers in creation. Faith, then, is at its heart *a response* to the one who goes further (*insuper*) still—the one who, "from the fullness of his love, addresses men as his friends and moves among them in order to invite them into his own company."[81]

Chapter 2

If *Dei Verbum*'s first chapter concerns the nature of revelation itself, its second chapter explains how this revelation—summed up in Jesus Christ—is transmitted to future generations. Article 7 highlights that the revelation given in Christ was entrusted to the apostles and those associated with them, that they might hand it on to others "by the spoken word of their preaching, by the example they gave, by the institutions they established," along with what they had committed to writing.[82] Thus, revelation is handed on by sacred tradition and sacred scripture, both acting as "a mirror in which the church, during its pilgrim journey here on earth, contemplates God."[83]

In one sense, it could be said that scripture is given a place of preeminence in that its role occupies the remaining four chapters of the Constitution. Furthermore, as article 9 points out, "Sacred scripture *is* the speech of God as it is put down in writing," whereas "tradition *transmits* in its entirety the Word of God which has been entrusted to the apostles."[84] But to see the document advocating the priority of scripture would be to ignore the further statement that "both scripture and tradition must be accepted and honored with equal feelings of devo-

---

80. Walter Kasper, *Theology and Church*, trans. Margaret Kohl (New York: Crossroad, 1989), 24. See also Latourelle, *Theology of Revelation*, 338.
81. DV, no. 2 [751].
82. DV, no. 7 [753].
83. DV, no. 7 [754].
84. DV, no. 9 [755]. Emphasis mine.

tion and reverence."[85] This saying is justified by statements that show sacred tradition's role in actualizing scripture in the life of the church. As quoted earlier, tradition is said to transmit the Word of God *in its entirety*. In fact, article 8 claims that the recognition of the canon of the Bible is itself due to tradition. Furthermore, the understanding of the scriptures and therefore their actualization in the life of the church only occur by means of tradition. Such weighty statements imply a mutual dependence of the two streams of revelation on one another. Yet, to fully grasp the import of this relationship between scripture and tradition, I believe it is helpful to take a closer look at what the Council means when it uses the term *traditio* in speaking of how revelation is transmitted to future generations.

The previous analysis has noted the inadequacy of a (primarily) propositional conception of revelation. Admittedly, the distinction between revelation and its transmission is more easily navigated if revelation is a compilation of decrees, some written in the scriptures and some passed on by the means of an unwritten tradition. The words, both written and spoken, need only be passed on to future generations. But because revelation is truly the communication of the living God and calls for believers to respond with their very lives, its transmission must encompass something much greater. This transmission—lying at the heart of the meaning of *traditio* for the Council—takes on new meaning in the face of God's gift of himself: "For if the origin of tradition—that which stands at the beginning and must be passed on—is not a promulgated law, but communication in the gift of God's plenitude, then the idea of 'passing on' must mean something different than before."[86]

The Council's remarks on the Holy Spirit within the process of tradition help in understanding the nature of this "passing on." Toward the end of the first chapter, the Council had already begun to lay the groundwork for its teaching on tradition in mentioning the role of the Spirit in the faith of Christians. In the words of article 5, it is the Spirit who perfects faith that "revelation may be more and more profoundly understood."[87] It is here in the second chapter, specifically in article 8, that the Spirit's role is further clarified. Here the Council fathers ex-

85. Ibid.
86. Ratzinger, "Chapter II: The Transmission of Divine Revelation," in *Commentary on the Documents of Vatican II*, 3:181.
87. DV, no. 5 [752].

plain that tradition encompasses the whole of the church's "doctrine, life, and worship"—that through these three elements tradition "makes progress" (proficit)—and the Holy Spirit aids the church in growing "in insight into the realities and words that are being passed on."[88]

For the Council, then, it is the church's entire life that participates in the transmission of revelation today. Of course, it is rightfully said, as article 4 has shown, that revelation does have a certain once-and-for-all character—revelation is perfected, summed up, and completed in Jesus Christ. The Christ event is the fullness of revelation. Nevertheless, it is also correct to say that God still communicates himself—that is, he continues to speak the Word who is Christ—through the church's doctrine, life, and worship. There is no new content in this speaking, but it is indeed the same Christ who is spoken to the present. As article 8 explains, "God, who spoke in the past, continues to converse with the spouse of his beloved Son."[89] This is the sense in which revelation is transmitted by tradition.[90]

Thus, rather than being the growth in understanding of something recorded in the past, tradition is a growth in understanding of something that was completed in the past and yet is continually communicated to the present through the action of the Holy Spirit.[91]

The Holy Spirit's role is vital in this process of tradition, for it is the Spirit who is ultimately able to make present what occurred at history's apex—the revelation of Jesus Christ. Much in the same way the anamnesis of the liturgy both recalls and makes present the Paschal Mystery through the invocation of the Holy Spirit, so too does the church's

88. DV, no. 8 [754]. See AAS 58 (1966): 821: "Haec quae est ab Apostolis Traditio sub assistentia Spiritus Sancti in Ecclesia proficit."

89. DV, no. 8 [755].

90. See Frederick E. Crowe, "The Development of Doctrine and the Ecumenical Problem," *Theological Studies* 23, no. 1 (1962): 40: "One might say, therefore, that the material element of this phase of revelation will not be completed till the last day, but the formal element was completed nineteen centuries ago in the center of time in the Holy Land."

91. As Ratzinger explains, "This kind of new orientation simply expresses our deeper knowledge of the problem of historical understanding, which is no longer adequately expressed by the simple ideas of a given fact and its explanation, because the explanation, as the process of understanding, cannot be clearly separated from what is being understood. This interdependence of the two, which does not remove the ultimate basic difference between assimilation and what is assimilated, even if they can no longer be strictly isolated, is well expressed by the dialectic juxtaposition of the two clauses *Traditio proficit* and *crescit perceptio*." See "Chapter II: Transmission of Divine Revelation," 187–88.

tradition, by the same Spirit, make present what was completed in Christ. Ultimately, that tradition can transmit revelation in the present is "based on the fact that the Christ event cannot be limited to the age of the historical Jesus, but continues in the presence of the Spirit, through which the Lord who departed on the cross has come again, and through which he reminds his Church of what had happened"; thus the church "is led, as it remembers, into its inner significance and is able to assimilate and experience it as a present event."[92]

A final question remains, however. Indeed, it is one that is prompted by this formulation of tradition that is put forth in Dei Verbum. If in fact the church's doctrine, life, and worship are revelatory in their ability to make the manifestation of Christ a present reality, does this not place great importance on the experience of the faithful as a locus of revelation? Article 8 explains, as has already been noted, that tradition "makes progress" in the church and that there is a genuine "growth in insight" into divine revelation.[93] However, it adds that this progress and growth come about by "the contemplation and study of believers who ponder these things in their hearts," by "the intimate sense [intelligentia] of spiritual realities which they experience," and by the "preaching of those who have received . . . the sure charism of truth."[94]

I would like to draw specific attention to the second of this triad in which the word "experience" is used in relation to tradition's progress and growth. The Council fathers' choice of this word, itself a category that has "boomed in post-conciliar theology," is especially striking when one considers that there was a relative dearth in its theological use after the Modernist controversy.[95] Nevertheless, the fathers were

92. Ibid., 189–90. See also 175, where Ratzinger states that "subsequent history cannot surpass what has taken place in Christ, but it must attempt to catch up with it gradually, to catch up all humanity in the man who, as a man coming from God, is the man for all others, the area of all human existence and the one and only Adam." This concept of tradition, in which Ratzinger says "it is not difficult to recognize the pen of Y. Congar," was put forth by the French Dominican in several of his written works. See especially Congar's two-volume work La Tradition et les Traditions, published in English as Yves Congar, Tradition and Traditions, trans. Michael Naseby and Thomas Rainborough (New York: Macmillan, 1967).

93. DV, no. 8 [754].

94. Ibid. I have noted the Latin intelligentia after the Flannery translation of the word as "sense," because it bears great significance for how the passage is interpreted. See AAS 58 (1966): 821: "Apostolis Traditio sub assistentia Spiritus Sancti in Ecclesia proficit . . . ex intima spiritualium rerum quam experiuntur intelligentia."

95. See Alessandro Maggiolini, "Magisterial Teaching on Experience in the Twentieth Century: From the Modernist Crisis to the Second Vatican Council," Communio 23, no. 2 (1996): 225.

not afraid to appropriate the category of experience as a necessary part of their teaching on revelation, especially considering the need to give the faith existential relevance before the modern world.

Still, the problem that confronts any use of experience as a theological category is how one can avoid subjectivism in doing so. The Modernists had claimed that revelation was determined by experience, that human need had given rise to the various forms of religion throughout history, thus reducing divine revelation to human experience itself. Karl Rahner, in a lecture at the University of Münster, explained that though they may have given an answer that was "overhastily decided," the Modernists had nevertheless raised a question of "fundamental importance."[96] In the face of a perceived neo-scholastic extrinsicism, should not revelation be considered to speak to the present experience of men and women?

The Council's use of experience in *Dei Verbum* can be considered a validation of Rahner's point. The experience of believers has a rightful place in the church's concept of tradition and in the reception of revelation. Still, Vatican II avoided subjectivism in this appropriation of the word on two counts. First, rather than simply state that growth in insight into revelation comes "from the intimate experience of spiritual things" (*ex intima spiritualium rerum experientia*)—as in fact an earlier draft had stated—article 8 specifies that progress comes "from the intimate understanding of spiritual things which [believers] experience" (*ex intima spiritualium rerum experientia quam experientur intelligentia*).[97] The use of the word "understanding" as the object of the phrase (rather than "experience") highlights the use of the intellect in interpreting experience and gives weight to the cognitive dimension of knowing.[98]

Maggiolini's article as a whole is helpful in its tracing of the concept of experience in the church during the modern period.

96. See Rahner's "Observations on the Concept of Revelation," in Karl Rahner and Joseph Ratzinger, *Revelation and Tradition*, trans. W. J. O'Hara (New York: Herder and Herder, 1966), 10. Rahner believed that the church rightly condemned modernism for its immanentism but also thought it was evenly matched by what he took to be scholastic theology's extrinsicism. Rahner's own answer to the dilemma was widely influential in theology after the Council and had similar effect in postconciliar catechesis as well, as can be seen in the work of Gabriel Moran. Moran's thought will be briefly discussed in chapter 2.

97. The quote from the provisionary text is found in Maggiolini, "Magisterial Teaching on Experience," 240; the final text is in AAS 58 (1966): 821. Here, I have exchanged the Flannery translation of *intelligentia* as "sense" for what I believe to be a more accurate word, "understanding."

98. See Maggiolini, "Magisterial Teaching on Experience," 239–43.

Second, and perhaps even more substantial, is *Dei Verbum*'s explanation of the Magisterium's role in guarding divine revelation. The lived experience of the faith in the church is validated by those who, as article 8 points out, have "the sure charism of truth."[99] This idea is more fully fleshed out in article 10 when an explanation is given of the role of the Magisterium in relation to revelation. The beginning of the article reaffirms that both sacred scripture and sacred tradition make up a "single deposit of the Word of God," one that is meant to be adhered to by the entire church, lay and ordained alike.[100] "But," it continues, "the task of authentic interpretation of the Word of God, whether in its written form or in the form of tradition, has been entrusted to the living teaching office of the Church alone."[101] Thus, while the experience of the faithful has a significant role to play in the transmission of revelation, it is only the Magisterium—those given the "sure charism of truth"—that can guarantee the right interpretation and understanding of that experience, discerning authentic tradition from its inauthentic counterparts.[102]

Ultimately, then, the Council fathers validated the role of human experience in *Dei Verbum*'s understanding of divine revelation while taking steps to preserve it from subjectivism. One can fully agree with Alessandro Maggiolini when he states, "While the Modernist affair had led to an attitude of caution and a more careful consideration of the issue, it did not cause the Fathers simply to set aside the vocabulary of experience. True, they qualified this language of experience and secured it against possible misunderstandings, but they adopted and emphasized it all the same."[103]

99. DV, no. 8 [754].

100. DV, no. 10 [755]. Thus, while the Council placed the role of propositional revelation firmly on the foundation of God's self-revelation, it did not shy away from alluding to the classic phrase "deposit of faith."

101. Ibid.

102. *Dei Verbum* further explains that this is not an authority wielded arbitrarily, but since it takes the form of a gift (*charism*), it renders the teaching office as a servant. A note should also be made here of the more recent theological question concerning the role of the *sensus fidelium*. While the issue is worthy of its own theological study, I refer the reader to the articles by John J. Burkard that survey recent literature on the subject. See his "Sensus Fidei: Theological Reflection Since Vatican II (1965–89)," *Heythrop Journal* 34, no. 1 (1993): 41–59 and 123–36; "Sensus Fidei: Recent Theological Reflection (1990–2001) Part I," *Heythrop Journal* 46, no. 4 (2005): 450–75; and "Sensus Fidei: Recent Theological Reflection (1990–2001) Part II," *Heythrop Journal* 47, no. 1 (2006): 38–54.

103. Maggiolini, "Magisterial Teaching on Experience," 242.

In total, then, revelation is transmitted in the life of the church by scripture and tradition, served by the Magisterium. *Dei Verbum*, in chapter 2, makes clear the interrelatedness of all three elements. It is thus fitting that the chapter ends by stating, "In the supremely wise arrangement of God, sacred tradition, sacred scripture, and the Magisterium of the Church are so connected and associated that one of them cannot stand without the others. Working together, each in its own way under the action of the one Holy Spirit, they all contribute effectively to the salvation of souls."[104]

Gaudium et Spes

The beginning of this chapter noted that catechesis is founded upon divine revelation. As such, catechesis has a dual purpose: to communicate this revelation and to interpret present human experience in light of it. Or, in the words of the *General Directory for Catechesis*, not only does catechesis seek to communicate the mysteries of the faith, it must also examine the "signs of the times and present life of man."[105] What this suggests for the catechetical enterprise is that, not only must one understand the nature of revelation in itself, but present history and human experience must be understood in relation to this revelation. For, if revelation, as *Dei Verbum* explains, is dialogical and thus aimed at men and women in order to bring them into communion with God, then its reception becomes an essential aspect of its nature. As Gerald O'Collins puts it, "Central to any adequate exposition of revelation is the analysis of man's status and role in receiving revelation."[106]

For such an analysis it is important to examine the Pastoral Constitution on the Church in the Modern World, *Gaudium et Spes*. If at first it is not readily apparent why a document focusing on the church in the present era would provide such an anthropological focus, then perhaps a few comments on its development can offer more clarity.

When John XXIII first opened the Council, he offered an interesting metaphor to explain its purpose: as members of the church and yet as those who share an earthly existence with all of humanity, Catholic men

104. DV, no. 10 [756].
105. GDC, no. 39.
106. O'Collins, *Foundations of Theology*, 51.

and women have a two-fold obligation: "as citizens of earth and as citizens of heaven"; indeed, the Christian approach to life is to "strive with all zeal for evangelical perfection, and at the same time to contribute toward the material good of humanity."[107] As such, in the late pope's view, the Council's success should be measured not only by its ability to revivify the faith of believers, but also in its ability to speak to the modern world. The faith was, he claimed, not only a treasure for Catholics but "the common heritage of mankind."[108]

Certainly, most of the Council's documents served to contribute to the goal of revivifying the faith of Catholics—three of the four constitutions had generally been focused in such a direction: *Dei Verbum* had emphasized the Word of God in the church, *Sacrosanctum Concilium* had instigated renewal of the liturgy, and *Lumen Gentium* had defined the nature of the church in and of itself—that is to say, with a largely *ad intra* focus.[109]

But as for Vatican II's goal *ad extra*, it was not until the Council's fourth and final session that a document had been promulgated that exclusively sought to address the modern world; this document was *Gaudium et Spes*.[110] Part of the delay in issuing the Constitution lay precisely in the difficulty of crafting its argument. If the church was to speak to the modern world, should it use the language of faith or a vernacular common to all men and women? If it chose the former, would such a

107. John XXIII, "Opening Address to the Council," 428–29.

108. Ibid., 430.

109. This is not to say that the three constitutions showed no attempts to address the goal of speaking to the modern world. For instance, *Sacrosanctum Concilium*, in its introduction, explains that "the liturgy daily builds up those who are in the Church," and yet it "increases their power to preach Christ and thus show forth the Church, a sign lifted up among the nations, to those who are outside." Likewise, *Lumen Gentium's* title itself describes Christ's manifestation through the church as a "light to the nations," with the document describing the church as a sign and instrument "of communion with God and of unity among all men." See *Sacrosanctum Concilium*, no. 2, and *Lumen Gentium*, no. 1, respectively. As for *Dei Verbum*, I have already noted how the question of revelation to those outside of Judeo-Christian history was raised, if only briefly.

110. Charles Moeller explains that the Council's preparatory schemata barely addressed the issue: "Out of seventy schemata, only one was devoted to the social order." Likewise, Walter Kasper explains that only at the end of the Council's first session had it become evident that the nature of the church should be examined "in two parts devoted, respectively, ... to the Church in its self-understanding and to the Church looked at in its relation to the present situation of the world." See Moeller, "Pastoral Constitution on the Church in the Modern World: History of the Constitution," in *Commentary on the Documents of Vatican II*, ed. Herbert Vorgrimler, trans. W. J. O'Hara (New York: Herder and Herder, 1969), 5:2; and Kasper, "Theological Anthropology," 132.

Revelation and the Human Person according to Vatican II   47 theological description be inaccessible to non-Christians? Yet if it chose the latter, would it be sacrificing Christian identity in order to assert its relevance to the modern world? Walter Kasper describes the conundrum that faced the Council fathers as the search for "the Archimedean point" that could unify these concerns of identity and relevance.[111]

After multiple drafts, the fathers finally found such a unifying point. Recognizing that modern men and women long for meaning and for fulfillment, the fathers decided to place at the center of the document *the human person*—not the person as one who stands alone, but as one who is called, through the church, to union with God. The heading of part I of *Gaudium et Spes* is telling in this regard: "The Church and Man's Vocation." Man is the one who, in his joys and hopes (*gaudium et spes*), is in search of his calling.[112] Such an emphasis reconciles relevance with identity by speaking to the common experience of all men and women, while simultaneously identifying the Christian faith as the bearer of the fullness of life's meaning and *telos*. Thus, as Kasper explains, "Anthropology is the Archimedean point of the Pastoral Constitution, the basis for a dialogue with the world of today."[113]

After such a necessarily brief overview of the Constitution's history, it is easier to see why *Gaudium et Spes* garners attention here. It is the document that, while unprecedented in its *ad extra* orientation, is also unique in providing the first substantial conciliar outline of a theological anthropology. In other words, precisely because it seeks to address the modern world, it must necessarily show how the Word of God is to be correlated to the experience of all men and women. In its anthropological focus, it becomes a prime candidate for exploring how divine revelation is received by the human person.

It will be useful to approach this relationship between the Word of God and human experience that is offered by the Pastoral Constitution by means of the distinction put forth in the *General Directory for Catechesis*, that of "the signs of the times" and the "present life of man." This distinction has already been touched upon in the analysis of the concept of revelation in *Dei Verbum*, particularly in how the Council fathers faced

111. Kasper, "Theological Anthropology," 133.

112. Though "joy and hope" form the first words of the Constitution, they are followed by "grief and anguish." These, too, compel men and women to search for their vocation.

113. Kasper, "Theological Anthropology," 135.

the problems posed by modernity in history and existential meaning. Revelation, as noted earlier, when propositionally conceived, was considered suspect before both historical development and the human desire for meaning. Nevertheless, by defining revelation as primarily personal in nature, the Council was able to answer that revelation is word firmly united to deed in history; likewise, it is a word spoken by a personal God to human persons. Thus, it is both historical and *pro nobis*.

This dual-sided coin of modernity—reflecting both historical and existential concerns—is taken up in a particularly distinct way in *Gaudium et Spes*. In seeking to address the modern world, the document examines the relationship of the church's faith to *present* history (the here and now) and to the internal desires of modern men and women. Thus, it addresses human experience in both exterior and interior dimensions. Corresponding to these two dimensions, I believe that (A) an examination of the use of the phrase "signs of the times" and (B) a closer look at *Gaudium et Spes*'s anthropological framework will shed the further light needed to more fully grasp the Council's teaching on revelation in relation to present history and the human person.

Signs of the Times

One of the most striking characteristics of *Gaudium et Spes* is its reading of the "signs of the times." Its introductory survey of the situation of human beings in the modern world is a remarkable "snapshot" of the conciliar era.[114] The Council fathers speak of the rapid changes brought about by modernity, including political and social struggles for freedom, the rise of science and the technology that springs from it, gains in the rights of women and workers, globalization, and even the decline in religious practice of modern men and women. The image evoked by this survey is both optimistic and scrutinizing; modernity presents both reasons for hope and causes for concern. In total, the fathers describe the modern world as full of *inaequilibria* (imbalances) that are a symptom "of that deeper [*inaequilibrio*] that is in man himself."[115] It is this reading of an internal struggle in the human heart that allows the Constitution to proclaim Christ as the one who can "show man the

---

114. George Weigel, "Rescuing *Gaudium et Spes*: The New Humanism of John Paul II," *Nova et Vetera* 8, no. 2 (2010): 254.

115. *Gaudium et Spes*, no. 10. [910], Henceforth, *GS*.

way and strengthen him through the Spirit in order to be worthy of his destiny."[116]

While this proclamation of Christ is aimed at the Council's reading of the (then) modern world, one can still take from the Constitution a certain pedagogy of the signs of the times that endures. Thus, fifty years removed from the promulgation of *Gaudium et Spes* in 1965, our image of the world may include significant differences from the one described by the Council, and yet the Council's method of reading human experience and proclaiming Christ as its purification and fulfillment offers the church a way in which to undertake the New Evangelization. To better understand this pedagogy, we are helped by returning to the source of the phrase *signa temporum*.

In *Humanae Salutis*, the document by which he summoned the Second Vatican Council, Pope John XXIII first used the phrase "signs of the times," referencing Matthew 16:3 in doing so. For Pope John, the church needed to oppose the voice of those who only saw the world with eyes of condemnation. Rather, Christ "has not deserted the human beings he has redeemed"; as such, the church should know how to "recognize the signs of the times" that it might, "in the midst of all the hideous clouds and darkness, perceive a number of things that seem to be omens portending a better day for the Church and for mankind."[117] Later, in the 1963 encyclical *Pacem in Terris*, the phrase was used as a heading for what the pope perceived to be positive developments in (then) recent history.[118] From these two uses it can be gathered that, for John XXIII, "signs of the times" referred to the characterizations and events of current history that manifest the present condition of humanity. Though he especially wished to highlight those signs that could be perceived as positive, John XXIII indicated both the negative and positive character of such signs, thereby calling upon the church to distinguish between the two.

116. Ibid.

117. John XXIII, *Humanae Salutis*, no. 4, trans. Austin Vaughn, in *The Encyclicals and Other Messages of Pope John XXIII*, 387; AAS 54 (1962): 6.

118. See Richard Schenk, "Officium Signa Temporum Perscrutandi: New Encounters of Gospel and Culture in the Context of the New Evangelization" in *Scrutinizing the Signs of the Times in the Light of the Gospel*, ed. Johan Verstraeten (Leuven: Leuven University Press, 2007), 173. Schenk points out that the official Latin version of the text includes no headings, thus excluding the term; however, the Italian version uses the phrase four times, the English version once. Cf. John XXIII, *Pacem in Terris*, AAS 20 (1963): 257–304.

It was with this history in mind that the Council fathers utilized the phrase *signa temporum* in *Gaudium et Spes*, seeing such signs as particular insights into humanity that could provide the material needed for the church's dialogue with the modern world. Still, the use of the phrase in the Constitution only came with much debate. An earlier draft had linked the signs of the times with the Roman proverb *vox temporis vox dei*, thereby regarding "the voice of the age . . . as the voice of God."[119]

Such an equation of history with God's speaking itself came under scrutiny when it was compared to Matthew 16, the passage Pope John XXIII had originally referenced in his use of "signs of the times." In the gospel, Jesus' interlocutors ask him for a sign from heaven. Jesus replies somewhat antagonistically,

In the evening you say, "Tomorrow will be fair, for the sky is red"; and in the morning, "Today will be stormy, for the sky is red and threatening." You know how to judge the appearance of the sky, but you cannot judge the signs of the times. An evil and unfaithful generation seeks a sign, but no sign will be given it except the sign of Jonah.[120]

In this passage, "signs of times" bears a distinct Christological and eschatological meaning, one that is placed against the ability of his questioners to interpret present history. The ultimate sign of the time is Christ himself, along with his saving work, yet the Sadducees and Pharisees in question are unable to recognize him as such. The Gospel, then, seems to present a meaning of *signa temporum* that is directly antithetical to the Roman proverb.[121]

Because of this, the use of the phrase in subsequent drafts was altered, and it is notable that the official Constitution does not make

---

119. Ratzinger, "Part I: The Church and Man's Calling, Introductory Article and Chapter I," in *Commentary on the Documents of Vatican II*, ed. Herbert Vorgrimler, trans. W. J. O'Hara (New York: Herder and Herder, 1969), 5:115.

120. Mt 16:2–4.

121. Ratzinger, "Part I: The Church and Man's Calling," 115. See also the comments of the Reformed scholar Lukas Vischer, an invitee to the Council, as recorded in Schenk, "Officium Signa Temporum Perscrutandi," 178: "The text does not state in what fashion God speaks to us. It never names a criterion that would allow us to distinguish God's voice from any deceptive voices. It doesn't even mention that the phenomena of the times have a polyvalent character and thus are not easy to interpret. It settles for the simple statement of fact that God's voice is to be heard in our times. . . . The draft shows few traces of this epistemological problem. It speaks of God's voice as if it were easy to recognize. It opens the way for interpretations of history that are not grounded in the word of God. And the history of the Church is full of such interpretations" (emphasis in the original).

reference to the Matthean passage. In article 4, *Gaudium et Spes* states that:

At all times the Church carries the responsibility of reading [*perscrutandi*] the signs of the times and of interpreting them in the light of the Gospel if it is to carry out its task. . . . We must be aware of and understand the aspirations, the yearnings, and the often dramatic features of the world in which we live.[122]

The Council's use of the phrase, while bearing no referential notes to the biblical context, nevertheless should not be completely disassociated with the gospel passage. Rejecting the earlier draft's equation of history with the voice of God, the final document does recognize the need to scrutinize (*perscrutandi*) present history and human experience in order to ascertain what is genuinely a sign of the presence of God. Thus, the passage from Matthew and the use of the expression *signa temporum* in *Gaudium et Spes* share a common bond in that both refer to the reading of God's presence and activity in human history.[123] Nevertheless, they are distinct in that the gospel passage uses "signs of the times" to refer to the definitive presence of Christ (especially as a sign of history's final time), while the Council document refers to elements of human history that may or may not be genuine signs of his presence.[124]

Ultimately, then, the Council used the phrase in the sense in which John XXIII first did, as a reference to present history. The signs of the times are meant to be scrutinized by the church so that, inductively, she can present the Gospel message as the fulfillment of human yearnings. Considering the overarching goal of the document, along with the Council's overall intention regarding the relationship between faith and the world, *signa temporum* can be taken as "shorthand for the church's openness to and dialogue with the world that was the major goal of Vatican II."[125]

122. *GS*, no. 4 [905]. *Perscrutandi*, translated in the Flannery edition of the Council documents as "reading," has a more distinct meaning of "scrutinizing." See *AAS* 58 (1966): 1027: "Ad tale munus exsequendum, per omne tempus Ecclesiae officium incumbit signa temporum perscrutandi et sub Evangelii luce interpretandi."

123. See Mary Elsbernd and Reimund Bieringer, "Interpreting the Signs of the Times in the Light of the Gospel: Vision and Normativity of the Future," in *Scrutinizing the Signs of the Times in the Light of the Gospel*, 62–63.

124. More of Vischer's comments are telling in this regard: "To recognize the signs of the times one ought to distinguish the voice of God from any other voice no matter how persuasive it might be. Furthermore, the world is ambiguous, and evil is mixed up with good." As quoted in the *New Catholic Encyclopedia*, 2nd ed., s.v. "Signs of the Times."

125. Elsbernd and Bieringer, "Interpreting the Signs of the Times," 63.

With the rejection of *vox temporis vox dei* in favor of the church's need to scrutinize history, the Council gives further insight into the universality of divine revelation. Earlier, *Dei Verbum*'s limited statements on the subject were noted. The question was raised as to whether God speaks and acts in moments of history that stand outside the provenance of the Judeo-Christian tradition. The answer is clearly given in the affirmative by the use of "signs of the times" in *Gaudium et Spes*. Such signs can potentially reveal the presence of God working in current earthly realities and present history.

Nevertheless, the Council expressed caution in recognizing this fact. Article 11 of the Pastoral Constitution elaborates further on the church's need to scrutinize history:

The people of God believes that it is led by the Spirit of the Lord who fills the whole world. Moved by that faith it tries to discern in the events, the needs, and the longings which it shares with other men of our time, what may be genuine signs of the presence or of the purpose of God. For faith throws a new light on all things and makes known the full ideal which God has set for man, thus guiding the mind towards solutions that are fully human.[126]

The language here is evenhanded. The Holy Spirit is said to indeed fill the whole world, giving present history the ability to bear within it the presence of God. Nevertheless, in what Ratzinger terms a "felicitous touch," the Constitution describes the church as called to discern (*discernere*) which signs of the times are genuine bearers of this presence.[127] The spiritual practice of the discernment of spirits, most prominently seen in the Ignatian tradition, is thus reflected in these words.

It is only by the light of faith that the church can see in present human experience what is truly "of the Spirit." From this, what was stated in article 4 now stands out in greater relief: "The Church carries the responsibility of scrutinizing the signs of the times and of interpreting them *in the light of the Gospel*."[128] Thus, only from the vantage point of its faith—that is to say, only from the gift of revelation it has already received from God in Jesus Christ—can it see the ways in which the Spirit

126. *GS*, no. 11 [912].

127. Ratzinger, "Part I: The Church and Man's Calling," 116. See *AAS* 58 (1966): 1033: "Populus Dei, fide motus, qua credit se a Spiritu Domini duci qui replet orbem terrarum, in eventibus, exigentiis atque optatis, quorum una cum ceteris nostrae aetatis hominibus partem habet, quaenam in illis sint vera signa praesentiae vel consilii Dei, discernere satagit."

128. *GS*, no. 4 [905]. Emphasis mine.

moves and speaks in the entirety of human history. And being united to this history by its own humanity, it seeks to call those outside its visible walls to itself, presenting the truths of the faith as capable of fulfilling what is human, yet raising it up to full communion in Jesus Christ.[129] Thus, the "solutions that are fully human" are those that are, by their nature, open to union with God.[130]

Ultimately, then, the relationship between the church's mission of proclaiming the faith and the signs of the times is dialectical in nature. The church seeks to offer the world what can fulfill its "humanity"; yet, the world offers its humanity as a necessary avenue for the truth to be proclaimed. In the words of *Gaudium et Spes* 44, "The Church is not unaware how much it has profited from the history and development of mankind. It profits from the experience of past ages, from the progress

---

129. That the church is united to the world by its humanity presupposes an understanding of ecclesial identity that it is essentially sacramental. Thus, *Gaudium et Spes* builds on the foundation set by *Lumen Gentium*, by which the church is said to be "in the nature of a sacrament—a sign and instrument, that is, of communion with God and of unity among all men." Thus, before it is the People of God (chapter 2) or a hierarchically structured society (chapter 3), it is first mystery [*sacramentum*]. See *Lumen Gentium*, no. 1. See also de Lubac, *The Splendor of the Church*, trans. Michael Mason (San Francisco: Ignatius Press, 1999), 161: "Again, paradox; the mystical Bride, the Church with the hidden heart, is also a being very much visible among the beings of the world. . . . Like all human institutions, the Church has her exterior façade, her temporal aspect, often ponderous enough—chancelleries, code of law, courts. There is certainly nothing 'nebulous and disembodied' about her—far from it. She is no 'misty entity'; the fact that she is a mystery lived by faith does not make her any the less a reality of this world; she walks it in broad daylight, making her presence known to all and claiming her rights."

130. GS, no. 11 [912]. See also Ratzinger, "Part I: The Church and Man's Calling," 116–17: "Certainly the Church is tied to what was once and for all, the origin in Jesus of Nazareth, and in this sense it is obliged 'chronologically' to continuity with him and the testimony of the beginning. But because 'the Lord is the Spirit' (2 Cor 3:17) and remains present through the Spirit, the Church has not only the chronological line with its obligation of continuity and identity, it has also the moment, the kairos, in which it must interpret and accomplish the work of the Lord as present. The Church is not the petrification of what once was, but its living presence in every age. The Church's dimension is therefore the present and the future no less than the past. Its obedience to the Lord precisely as such must be obedience to him as pneuma, as summons today; it must be accomplished with discernment of spirits and must accept the risk of submitting at all times to such discernment. That is of course necessary in order that the moment of the Holy Spirit may not imperceptibly change into the momentary spirit of the age, and what is done under the appearance of obedience to the pneuma may not be in fact submission to the dictates of fashion and apostasy from the Lord. This shows the intrinsic connection between holiness and aggiornamento." Thus, what is accomplished here in *Gaudium et Spes* is a window into the Council's goal of *aggiornamento* as a whole, and the discernment of the signs of the times is likewise connected to the dynamic concept of tradition presented in *Dei Verbum*. In fact, what *Gaudium et Spes* implies here, which Ratzinger does not mention, is the inner connection between *ressourcement* and *aggiornamento*. The past becomes a norm for discerning the present.

of the sciences, and from the riches hidden in various cultures, through which greater light is thrown on the nature of man and new avenues to truth are opened up."[131] The church, therefore, as the Body of Christ, has both divine and human elements—in the words of *Lumen Gentium*, it is mystery. From this mystery, it offers to the world what it has received from God, and receives from the world a clarification and insight into its own humanity.[132]

This insight provides some further refinement in understanding the nature of divine revelation, especially in terms of the question regarding revelation in secular history. Is there revelation in history beyond that of the biblical and ecclesial tradition? The answer can only be reached in recognizing, as seen in the previous analysis of *Dei Verbum*, that revelation (by its own nature as dialogical) requires the perception of the one to whom God is being revealed. While this is true of the individual person, in a greater way, it is true of the church as a whole. As the one who is called to discern the signs of the times, the church is ultimately the subject who receives God's self-gift, and in perceiving it, responds in the returning self-gift of faith: "Thus God, who spoke in the past, continues to converse with the spouse of his beloved Son. And the Holy Spirit, through whom the living voice of the Gospel rings out in the Church—*and through her in the world*—leads believers to the full truth, and makes the Word of Christ dwell in them in all its richness."[133]

In this sense one can say that revelation is only received *in the church*. Any revelation "outside" the church (in the signs of the times) is then ordered to union with God in the church. Thus, the revelation to Israel recorded in the Old Testament is, as *Dei Verbum* 3 explains, ordered to the coming of Jesus Christ—which is ultimately to say, ipso facto, that it is ordered to his Body, the church. Likewise, the presence of God in the signs of the times is ordered to communion in the church. Indeed, this presence is recognized as revelatory by the very perception made pos-

131. GS, no. 44 [946].

132. See GS, no. 44 [946–47]: It is enriched by the world "not as if something were missing in the constitution which Christ gave the Church, but in order to understand this constitution more deeply, express it better, and adapt it more successfully to our times. . . . Whoever contributes to the development of the community of mankind on the level of family, culture, economic and social life, and national and international politics, according to the plan of God, is also contributing in no small way to the community of the Church insofar as it depends on things outside itself."

133. DV, no. 8 [755]. Emphasis mine.

sible by the church's faith. It should be noted that the faith that allows it to perceive this presence encompasses the revelation it has already received from the scriptures and by its doctrine, life, and worship—that is, from sacred tradition. Then, in discerning God's speaking and acting in present history, it thus incorporates the sign into its own tradition. The sign of the times, in one sense "outside" its walls, is now fulfilled by being brought "within," becoming an avenue for the proclamation of the Kingdom. Thus, in the greater context of *Gaudium et Spes* 44, the church:

profits from the experience of past ages, from the progress of the sciences, and from the riches hidden in various cultures, through which greater light is thrown on the nature of man and new avenues to truth are opened up. The Church learned early in its history to express the Christian message in the concepts and language of different peoples and tried to clarify it in the light of the wisdom of their philosophers: it was an attempt to adapt the Gospel to the understanding of all men and the requirements of the learned, insofar as this could be done. Indeed, this kind of adaptation and preaching of the revealed Word must ever be the law of all evangelization.[134]

In a way, this understanding of revelation in the signs of the times is analogous to what has already been said regarding creation and revelation. Just as creation itself is not revelation but is an occasion for it, so too is present history and human experience an occasion for the church to perceive God's acting and speaking.

But another explanation may be of further help in understanding this dynamic concept of revelation in the church and the world. At the Council, in discussing a draft of what would eventually become *Dei Verbum*, the Melkite archbishop Néophytos Edelby offered the Eastern churches' understanding of tradition in relation to history.[135] In markedly liturgical language, Edelby described the proclamation of the scriptures that occurs in the liturgy as a "consecration of salvation history"— that is, an offering of God's actions in history back to God himself—a recapitulation reminiscent of the offering of bread and wine. Yet, Edelby continued, "this consecration requires some kind of epiclesis—that is to say, the invocation and the action of the Holy Spirit." Strikingly, he explained that this "epiclesis is precisely sacred tradition," and with-

134. GS, no. 44 [946].
135. An English translation of this remarkable speech, from which my quotations are taken, can be found in the appendix of O'Collins, *Retrieving Fundamental Theology*, 174–77.

out this tradition, "the world's history is incomprehensible and sacred scripture remains a dead letter." History, then, can be an offering of the presence of Jesus Christ to the Father, when it is subsumed by the Holy Spirit into the church's living tradition.

I believe it is important to reemphasize, in this dynamic concept of tradition, that the revelation received by the church in its scriptures and already put forth in its doctrine, life, and worship becomes the norm for discerning the ways in which God continues to speak today. Here it may be helpful to make a distinction—latent in the dynamic understanding of tradition put forth in *Dei Verbum*—between the Body of Christ understood diachronically (*dia*/through–*chronos*/time) and synchronically (*syn*/with–*chronos*/time). While both viewpoints are legitimate and necessary, the first recognizes those who make up the church throughout time and therefore includes Christians of the past, united to the present in the communion of saints; and the second recognizes the rightful place of the people of God in the present era, a people who are found in virtually every corner of the world. The synchronic understanding lends legitimate voice to the present concerns of the people of God in the modern world. Yet the diachronic understanding shows that the scriptures and church teaching are not external impositions upon the freedom of the present experience of the Body of Christ. Rather, they are objective manifestations of the revelation already received by the people of God in the past and, since the church by nature is united to this experience, it must continue to be informed by it. Scripture and doctrine are, thus, not external to the present church but make up a central part of its very identity.

Ultimately, then, the revelation received in the past is the means for discerning the revelation of God today. The signs of the times are discerned *by the light of the Gospel*. It is necessary to stress this point in the face of incorrect interpretations of the Council's teaching that would claim experience as the determiner of revelation's claims,[136] or further,

136. It is important to remember here the amendment to *Dei Verbum*, mentioned earlier, concerning the role of experience in tradition. In article 8, it is the understanding [*intelligentia*] of spiritual realties experienced that helps tradition make progress in the church, rather than experience itself. That revelation is a norm for present experience is a teaching in *Gaudium et Spes* that is sometimes left aside in the wake of the positive value of dialogue with the world. For an example of the impact on moral theology when this teaching is left aside, see Michael G. Lawler and Todd A. Salzman, "Human Experience and Catholic Moral Theology," *Irish Theological Quarterly* 76, no. 1 (2011): 35–56. The authors rightfully consider the role of experience in moral theology, but give it preeminence over scripture, tradition, and reason.

that the world in and of itself is already in some sense "Christian."[137] For the Council, present human experience is only properly seen in the light of the church's faith, responding to God's self-revelation.

The Human Person

Having examined the relationship of revelation to what I have called the exterior dimension of human experience—present history—it now remains to turn to experience's interior dimension—that is, to the *subject* of experience—namely, the human person. This is a central concern for catechesis, following divine revelation, because it "springs from the very end of catechesis, which seeks to put the human person in communion with Jesus Christ."[138]

The human person is, one should recall, the "Archimedean point" in which the Council fathers believed the faith of the church could be brought to bear upon the modern world. Men and women, by their *gaudium et spes* and *luctus et angor*, are in search of their true calling—in search of fulfillment. And here the Council proposes that this vocation is none other than union with God in Jesus Christ.

Such a bold claim is better understood against the backdrop of theological history, particularly the pre–Vatican II neo-scholastic context already mentioned toward the beginning of this chapter. The critics of neo-scholasticism had found its theology unable to speak to the needs of the modern world. Of special note is the work of Henri de Lubac, who challenged certain Thomistic interpretations of the relationship between nature and grace. According to de Lubac, the scholastic view of this relationship had, to ill effect, established the conception of a natural order with its own ends, independent of the supernatural order and its call to divine life in God.[139] The effect of such a conceptually two-tiered world was the divorce of faith from life. In opposition to

137. Jared Wicks points to a letter in de Lubac's memoirs in which the theologian staunchly opposed an interpretation of *Gaudium et Spes*, and indeed the Council as a whole, in which "there would no longer be any true evangelization in view for the future," since the "so-called 'profane' world [was] already Christian in reality, independent of any evangelical revelation." See Wicks, "Further Light on Vatican Council II," *Catholic Historical Review* 95, no. 3 (2009): 546–69, especially 559–62; and de Lubac, *At the Service of the Church*, trans. Anne Elizabeth Englund (San Francisco: Ignatius Press, 1993), 341.

138. GDC, no. 116.

139. See de Lubac, *Surnaturel: Études historiques* (Paris: Desclée de Brouwer, 1991) and his later work *Le mystère du surnaturel*, now published in English as *The Mystery of the Supernatural*, trans. Rosemary Sheed (New York: Crossroad, 1998).

such a vision, de Lubac drew upon passages from St. Thomas in which the angelic doctor expressed a *desiderium natural visionis dei*.[140] Recent objections to de Lubac's thesis, however, claim that an innate desire in human nature would place a demand on God, thereby removing the gratuitousness of grace.[141] Regarding this dilemma, David L. Schindler notes:

It is essential to keep this problematic in mind when we consider the technical issues involved in de Lubac's explicit argument on the subject of the supernatural. On the one hand, if grace did not somehow—always already—touch the soul of every human being, the Christian fact would remain a "private" matter of urgent concern only to those who were already believers. On the other hand, if the order of grace were not essentially gratuitous—that is, did not really add something to nature that could not be anticipated or claimed by nature itself—then the Christian fact would lose its newness and its proper character as divine gift. In either case, Christianity would lose its essentially missionary and indeed apologetic impetus: in the former case, men and women would have no good—that is, profound—reason for *becoming* Christian; and, in the latter case, they would—effectively—*already be* Christian.[142]

While it is not my intention to rehearse a debate in which no small amount of ink has already been spilled,[143] I do believe that the tension

---

140. See, for example, *Summa Theologiae* I-II, q. 3., a. 8: "If therefore the human intellect, knowing the essence of some created effect, knows no more of God than 'that He is'; the perfection of that intellect does not yet reach simply the First Cause, but there remains in it the natural desire to seek the cause. Wherefore it is not yet perfectly happy. Consequently, for perfect happiness the intellect needs to reach the very Essence of the First Cause. And thus it will have its perfection through union with God as with that object, in which alone man's happiness consists." From St. Thomas Aquinas, *Summa Theologiae* (henceforth ST), trans. Fathers of the English Dominican Province (Allen, Tex.: Christian Classics, 1948), 602.

141. See ST I, q. 75, a. 6 [368]: "A natural desire cannot be in vain."

142. From Schindler's preface in de Lubac's *Mystery of the Supernatural*, xvi. Emphasis in the original.

143. See, for instance, the support of de Lubac's position in Nicholas J. Healy, "Henri de Lubac on Nature and Grace: A Note on Some Recent Contributions to the Debate," *Communio* 35, no. 4 (2008): 535–64; John Milbank, *The Suspended Middle: Henri de Lubac and the Debate Concerning the Supernatural* (Grand Rapids, Mich.: Eerdmans, 2005); and the critique of it in Stephen A. Long, "On the Possibility of a Purely Natural End for Man," *Thomist* 64, no. 2 (2000): 211–37; Thomas Joseph White, "The 'Pure Nature' of Christology: Human Nature and *Gaudium et Spes* 22," *Nova et Vetera* 8, no. 2 (2010): 283–322; Guy Mansini, "The Abiding Theological Significance of Henri de Lubac's *Surnaturel*," *Thomist* 73, no. 4 (2009): 593–619; and Lawrence Feingold, *The Natural Desire to See God according to St. Thomas Aquinas and His Interpreters*, 2nd ed. (Naples, Fla.: Sapientia Press of Ave Maria University, 2010). For another position, different from either of the two sides, see Servais Pinckaers, "The Natural Desire to See God," *Nova et Vetera* 8, no. 3 (2010): 627–46.

latent in the theological issue is important for our reading of *Gaudium et Spes*. An evangelizing catechesis must reckon in some way with the question of how men and women come to desire communion with God.

And considering that it is the logic of the document to present the human person as one who is ultimately fulfilled by union with God in Christ, the question remains of how the Council fathers perceived the relationship between nature and grace, especially as it informs the *telos* of the human person. Admittedly, the tension between the two positions is present, at least implicitly, in the document. On the one hand, it seems that the fathers were comfortable with recognizing a legitimate autonomy for humanity—that is, one conceived apart from supernatural grace.

Thus, as has already been seen in the previous examination of *signa temporum*, the claim is made that the Christian faith can help find solutions to the world's problems that are "fully human."[144] Such a position is strengthened when article 36 states that there is a rightful autonomy of the natural order: "By the very nature of creation, material being is endowed with its own stability, truth, and excellence, its own order and laws."[145] By deduction, the activities of men and women would, by their nature, have specific natural ends.

A certain anthropological weight is added to this position in article 12, in which the question is asked, "What is man?," to which the answer is given, "the image of God."[146] Such a conception of the human person, while drawing from biblical tradition, makes no explicit reference to the advent of Christ or the faith of the church.[147] Rather, what seems to be expressed in this definition is the fact that the human person stands over everything else, bearing a certain dignity and freedom. Five articles later, this rendering of humanity seems to be confirmed when it is stated that "freedom is an exceptional sign of the image of

144. GS, no. 11 [912].

145. GS, no. 36 [935]. The section is titled "Rightful Autonomy of Human Affairs."

146. GS, no. 12 [913]. The *imago dei* could easily be called the hinge of the Council's anthropology in *Gaudium et Spes*. See the study by Anthony O. Erhueh, *Vatican II: The Image of God in Man* (Rome: Urbaniana University Press, 1987), especially chapters 2 and 3.

147. See Luis Ladaria, "Humanity in the Light of Christ at the Second Vatican Council," in *Vatican II: Assessment and Perspectives*, ed. René Latourelle (New York: Paulist Press, 1989), 2:396: "Humanity's definite vocation is its divine vocation: therefore, we must refer to Christ so as to understand not only the Christian but also humanity in general. Yet, we cannot help noticing that in the majority of passages dealing with human beings as created in the image of God no reference is made to Christ."

God in man" and that "God willed that man should 'be left in the hand of his own counsel.'"[148] Indeed, regarding this use of the *imago dei* one author can state that "the fundamental content of the image is liberty. Man is like God because he is free."[149]

Without allusions to the Christian revelation, such a definition of the image of God is, for Walter Kasper, "rather static and flat."[150] Likewise, Ratzinger explains the problem posed by beginning with such a rendering of humanity by referring to the conciliar debate regarding article 12:

It seemed to many people . . . that there was not a radical enough rejection of a doctrine of man divided into philosophy and theology. They were convinced that fundamentally the text was still based on a schematic representation of nature and the supernatural viewed far too much as merely juxtaposed. To their mind it took as its starting-point the fiction that it is possible to construct a rational philosophical picture of man intelligible to all and on which men of goodwill can agree, the actual Christian doctrines being added to this as a sort of crowning conclusion. The latter then tends to appear as a sort of special possession of Christians, [about] which others ought not to make a bone of contention but which at bottom can be ignored.[151]

Certainly, the Council intended to build an anthropology that begins with man as he is known by all (article 12); that addresses both his fall into sin (article 13) and his remaining dignity and freedom (articles 14–17); and yet that culminates in Jesus Christ, the new man who reveals the human vocation of union with God (article 22). But as conceived here, it is possible to read the Constitution as advocating a natural end for humanity, leaving its connection to the supernatural end of union with God unclear.

On the other hand *Gaudium et Spes*, in attempting to show the fulfillment of humanity in Christ as the new man, makes several statements

148. GS, no. 17 [917], referencing Sir 15:14.

149. Antonio B. Lambino, *Freedom in Vatican II: The Theology of Liberty in Gaudium et Spes* (Manila: Loyola School of Theology, 1974), 24. Lambino's study is insightful, especially in highlighting the difference between the freedom to choose and the Pauline idea of the "liberty of the sons of God" (Rom 8:21). Regarding article 17, he notes (on page 15) that an earlier draft had included the Pauline notion of filial freedom, yet it was removed from the text. The *relatio* explained, "The liberty of the sons of God is no longer treated in this article because it is a different form of liberty from that treated here."

150. Kasper, "Theological Anthropology," 138. See also David L. Schindler, "Christology and the Imago Dei: Interpreting *Gaudium et Spes*," *Communio* 23, no. 1 (1996): 156–84.

151. Ratzinger, "Part I: The Church and Man's Calling," 119.

that seem to justify a *desiderium natural visionis dei*. Recognizing the dilemma as posed by Ratzinger regarding article 12, one could respond that, earlier, the document had already claimed Jesus Christ as "the key, the center, and the purpose of the whole of man's history" by virtue of his position as "the image of the invisible God [and] the firstborn of all creation."[152] Likewise, in what has become "the standard and the short formula" of the entire Constitution, article 22 states that "it is only in the mystery of the Word made flesh that the mystery of man truly becomes clear."[153] For "Christ the new Adam, in the very revelation of the mystery of the Father and of his love, fully reveals man to himself and brings to light his most high calling."[154] Such a profound statement serves to explain the deepest truth of the Council's teaching in its dialogue with the world, that God is "the last end of man," that he "opens up to [man] the meaning of his own existence, the innermost truth about himself," and that God alone "can satisfy the deepest cravings of the human heart."[155]

Faced with such seemingly paradoxical statements, what can we make of the Council's teaching on the human person? Is de Lubac vindicated in the teaching of *Gaudium et Spes*, or are his recent neo-Thomist interlocutors shown to be correct?[156] More to the point, how can the church evangelize modern men and women—by calling upon a longing for the divine in the deepest part of who they are or by claiming that their human desires are both fulfilled *and elevated to new heights* by the revelation of God in Jesus Christ?

In truth, I believe that the poignant teaching of *Gaudium et Spes* 22 can be interpreted from both de Lubacian and neo-Thomist positions.[157]

---

152. GS, no. 10 [911], referencing Col 1:15.
153. Kasper, "Theological Anthropology," 137, and GS, no. 22 [922], respectively.
154. GS, no. 22 [922].
155. GS, no. 41 [940].
156. "Neo-Thomist" is a broad term and, at the time of the Council, could encompass those such as Chenu and Rahner, who in many ways would be odd company for the more recent Thomists arguing against de Lubac's position.
157. As Mansini points out, "*Gaudium et spes* does not commit itself to any technical, ontological theses on the natural desire nor on the relation of nature to grace. The text asserts no more than does Sacred Scripture, which is to say, it asserts a narrative unity between the First and Last Adam, and so by implication no more than a narrative unity between nature and grace, and so, also by implication, no more than a narrative unity between the philosophical knowledge of man and nature and the theological knowledge of Christ and grace." See "Abiding Theological Significance," 618.

The Constitution does not spell out the ontological underpinnings of its statement. But from the standpoint of practical considerations for the church's ministry, two conclusions can be made.

First, there is an actual agreement between the two positions regarding the role of revelation in illuminating the human desire for God. Interestingly enough, de Lubac claimed that the natural desire for the vision of God was itself structural, but not necessarily conscious.[158] He recognized that there were clearly many men and women who felt no essential lacuna in their lives. Thus, for de Lubac, it is only by revelation that one can recognize this structural calling.[159] While rejecting any such structural desire, the strongest advocates of the neo-Thomist position similarly recognize the importance of revelation for eliciting in human beings a desire for their ultimate end. Thus, Stephen Long can say that the "graced appetite for beatific vision proceeds, not from mere natural evidence, but from the active agency of God upon the soul through supernatural grace"—that is, we desire union with God only "*after the fact of revelation* and under the light of grace."[160]

On the practical level, then, and from both sides of the issue, the conscious desire for union with God—whether natural or supernatural, so to speak—can only come about after one has perceived God's revelation. Thus, the important article 22 of the Pastoral Constitution offers its insight by claiming that Christ, "*in the very revelation* of the Father and of his love," reveals man to himself.[161] Evangelization, therefore, cannot rest in the comfort of human aspirations and goals in hopes of affirming some form of implicit faith, but must always present the explicit revelation of Christ in order to call men and women to union with God.

Second, and in conjunction with what has just been said: if revelation is necessary to awaken the desire for God in others—as de Lubac

158. See chapter 11, aptly titled "The Unknown Desire," of de Lubac's *Mystery of the Supernatural*, especially 208: "But is the desire for the beatific vision really, in its full nature and force, also to be known by reason alone? This I do not believe."

159. Ibid., 209: "I say that the knowledge that is revealed to us of that calling, which makes certain of that end, leads us to recognize within ourselves the existence and nature of that desire."

160. Long, "On the Possibility of a Purely Natural End for Man," 223. See also Feingold, *Natural Desire to See God*, 193–94: "The natural desire to see God spoken of by St. Thomas cannot be understood to indicate the underlying finality of rational nature itself, because for St. Thomas, we are not ordered to the vision of God by virtue of our nature, *but by virtue of grace*." Emphasis added both here and earlier.

161. Emphasis mine.

himself claimed—there remains little practical reason to posit an ontological natural desire for the beatific vision.[162] De Lubac's thesis, of course, was born out of concern for the living reality of the church in its ministry; he had therefore judged the perceived neo-scholastic split between nature and grace to be detrimental precisely because he had seen its effects on the church and its relation to the world.[163] But his rendering of the *desiderium natural* as structural, yet not necessarily conscious, seems to belie his rightful pastoral concerns. Faith, as the graced, free commitment of the entire self to God (recalling *Dei Verbum* 5), is a reality that requires human consciousness and freedom. As such, an unknown desire cannot be called upon by the church to present the Gospel. This concern seems especially acute today in the face of secularized—even atheistic—Western cultures in which many men and women claim no great dissatisfaction in their earthly lives. In this sense, the neo-Thomist account seems most useful for dialogue with people who do not readily accept that there is "something missing."

Yet, in accepting this ontological foundation, one does not have to settle for a sharp wedge between nature and grace, thereby leaving men and women to their earthly happiness. It is helpful here to recall *Dei Verbum*'s epistemological vision of the knowledge of God in which reason and revelation are distinct yet unified aspects of a Christological whole. In such a sacramental vision, the integrity of reason is legitimized while simultaneously being seen as open to the correction and transcendence of revelation. Thus, by reason, Christians can attempt to show others the existence of the Creator who gives human life and indeed all reality its meaning.[164] Then, at the right time and with the aid of grace, the

162. See Mansini, "Abiding Theological Significance," 606–7 and 615. Mansini makes a pivotal distinction between who and what a human person is: "When de Lubac says he could not be himself without the desire for God, he is telling the truth; but it is a truth about his person, not his nature."

163. See de Lubac, *Mystery of the Supernatural*, xxxv: "Though the dualist—or, perhaps better, separatist—thesis has finished its course, it may be only just beginning to bear its bitterest fruit. As fast as professional theology moves away from it, it becomes so much more widespread in the sphere of practical action. While wishing to protect the supernatural from any contamination, people had in fact exiled it altogether—both from intellectual and from social life—leaving the field to be taken over by secularism. Today that secularism, following its course, is beginning to enter the minds even of Christians."

164. "Meaning" is something that can only be given and perceived by rational beings. Here one of the greatest differences between the theist and the nontheist becomes evident: If God exists, then everything in the universe has meaning and purpose. If God does not exist, then the universe is meaningless; it is, to put it bluntly, just "stuff." The only other alternative for the

revelation of Jesus Christ can be proclaimed in such a way that it cuts at the joints and marrow of life—its boldness, though unforeseen, purifies reason and brings its findings into clearer view.[165] It takes the One through whom creation finds meaning and gives him flesh and bone.

In a similar way, if reason and revelation are distinct yet unified aspects of a Christological whole, then surely the same can be said of creation and redemption.[166] In the presence of those who are seemingly satisfied with their earthly lives, Christian revelation can recognize the integrity (perhaps a better formulation than *Gaudium et Spes* 36's "rightful autonomy") of that happiness, but then lead such men and women to the very source of that happiness, God himself. This Source, no doubt, transcends the earthly counterpart *ad infinitum*; nevertheless, God is able to draw men and women to himself precisely because his truth and goodness have already been perceived, albeit imperfectly, in the goodness of his creation. The Gospel is thus proclaimed as the fulfillment and surpassing of the happiness already experienced (however limited) on the level of nature. Ultimately then, not only is the church sacramental by nature, but the world itself is sacramental. What is human or "purely natural" claims its own integrity, yet this integrity is open to the transcendence of God.[167]

---

latter position is for meaning to be imposed on reality by the rationality of human beings, there being nothing to stand in the way, in any given moment of history, of the will of the majority or that of the most vocal or powerful.

165. See Heb 4:12. C. S. Lewis's impressive prose in *Miracles: A Preliminary Study* (New York: Macmillan, 1947), 132–33, is a testimony to this vision: "Let us suppose we possess parts of a novel or a symphony. Someone now brings us a newly discovered piece of manuscript and says, 'This is the missing part of the work. This is the chapter on which the whole plot of the novel really turned. This is the main theme of the symphony.' Our business would be to see whether the new passage, if admitted to the central place which the discoverer claimed for it, did actually illuminate all the parts we had already seen and 'pull them together.' . . . If it were genuine, then at every fresh hearing of the music or every fresh reading of the book, we should find it settling down, making itself more at home, and eliciting significance from all sorts of details in the whole work which we had hitherto neglected."

166. See Jn 1:1–18. See also St. Athanasius, *De Incarnatione Dei Verbi* 1.1: "There is thus no inconsistency between creation and salvation for the One Father has employed the same Agent for both works, effecting the salvation of the world through the same Word Who made it in the beginning." This translation comes from St. Athanasius, *On the Incarnation*, trans. and ed. a Religious of CSMV (Crestwood, N.Y.: St. Vladimir's Seminary Press, 1993), 26.

167. Stephen Long gives a helpful analogy in describing this dynamic, one that draws upon St. Thomas's concept of "obediential potency," in which human nature is "passively susceptible of a definite and distinct range of actuation under the active agency of God." For Long, "the similitude of the stained-glass window illumined by the sun's rays well bespeaks the character of the doctrine of obediential potency as applied to the relation of nature and grace. The

In more anthropological terms, what has just been stated can be related to the human person as the "image of God," first mentioned in *Gaudium et Spes* 12 yet brought to light most fully in article 22. As made in his image, man by nature has the potential to be united with God, though he is (without revelation) unaware of it, and could not actively accomplish it by his own powers. Marred by sin yet spurred to progress, he is, in his earthly nature, one who experiences both *luctus et angor* and *gaudium et spes*. Yet, in the revelation of Jesus Christ—fully God and fully man—man's nature is healed from sin, but, further, called to and given the ability to be united to God. By the Incarnation, human nature is thus both "restored" and "raised to a dignity beyond compare."[168] That is to say, just as Jesus's two natures were distinct but united, so too do men and women maintain the integrity of their human natures while finding both reparation and surpassing fulfillment in divine union.[169] Revelation, then, rejects what is sinful in man (*via negationis*), affirms what is good in him (*via positionis*), and elevates him to communion in the life of the Trinity (*via eminentiae*).[170] Thus, we can rightly recognize that "it is only in the mystery of the Word made flesh that the mystery of man truly becomes clear."[171]

---

stained-glass window, were it cognizant, could not 'know what it was missing' were it never to irradiate its bright colors under the influence of the sun. It would be a window, still, and function as part of the structure—though it would, in a given respect, not be fulfilled. It would be what it is, not fail to be part of the whole structure of which it would form an integral part, nor lack its own participation in the good of the whole as a specific perfection. Yet its nature stands properly revealed only under the extrinsic causality of the sun's illumination: seeing it so illumined, we know what stained-glass truly is for." See Long, "On the Possibility of a Purely Natural End for Man," 236. See also ST III, q. 9, a. 2, ad. 3: "The beatific vision and knowledge are to some extent above the nature of the rational soul, inasmuch as it cannot reach it of its own strength; but in another way it is in accordance with its nature, inasmuch as it is capable of it by nature, having been made to the likeness of God. . . . But the uncreated knowledge is in every way above the nature of the human soul."

168. GS, no. 22 [922–23].

169. See Mansini, "Abiding Theological Significance," 607: "What we are can be the same, indeed, is the same, whether we are called to grace and glory or not. Sharing in the divine nature does not give us another nature. Deification does not make us no longer men." See also White, "'Pure Nature' of Christology," 320–21.

170. Walter Kasper insightfully recognizes this triple dynamic in Paul's account of Christ as the New Adam, from which *Gaudium et Spes* 22 finds its scriptural foundation. See his *Theology and Church*, 82–93, especially 82–87.

171. GS, no. 22 [922].

Norms on Revelation and the Human Person

With the analysis of *Dei Verbum* and *Gaudium et Spes* complete, it is now possible to formulate some summarizing norms regarding divine revelation and the human person. Such norms serve the purpose of allowing us to evaluate the church's catechetical ministry, that which is founded upon the pedagogy of God as given in revelation and received by the human person. Five particular norms can be established:

(1) *Revelation is Christocentric.* Revelation is the personal self-gift of God to human persons, and this self-gift is most fully manifested in the person of Jesus Christ. He is the one who, in his person, unites humanity (and indeed all of creation) to the Father, through the Holy Spirit. Jesus is thus "the fullness of revelation," and this encompasses both revelation that preceded his historical appearance on earth and revelation that occurs afterward: the Old Testament serves as a pedagogy by which the people of God were prepared for his coming, and the church now perpetuates his presence in history, transmitting revelation by scripture and tradition and likewise perceiving all revelatory activity in the world by the light of the Gospel. Still, revelation is Christocentric not only in terms of content but also in terms of its aim: God reveals himself that humans may know and love him. The goal of revelation—illuminated by the Incarnation—is the communion of God and man.

(2) *Revelation is dialogical, and its goal is faith.* The self-gift of God in divine revelation involves both the objective manifestation of God in his word and the perception of a receiving personal subject. As a whole, this receptive subject is the church, but individually, it is its members. In the face of revelation, man is able to make a returning self-gift of faith. This faith encompasses not only the intellect but the will—indeed, the entire person.

In this sense, revelation not only reveals God but also humanity in its ultimate vocation. The human person can find some sense of earthly happiness but is ultimately and surpassingly fulfilled by union with God in Jesus Christ. This vocation lies in Jesus Christ, for Christ is not merely a revelatory exemplar, but is "the way, the truth, and the life" (Jn 14:6). Only by participation in him is the human person ultimately fulfilled.

(3) *Scripture and tradition faithfully transmit revelation to every age.* Jesus, as the fullness of revelation, made himself known through words and deeds. He continuously manifests himself in history through his body,

the church, by way of words and deeds—each requiring the other in the unity of revelation. Thus scripture, as the inspired Word of God, bears special importance in recalling and making present the specific salvation history that culminated in the coming of Jesus Christ. Likewise, the teaching of the Magisterium, as the preaching of the word offered through the charism of serving and safeguarding the truth, perpetuates revelation in the life of the church. Furthermore, the self-gift of God in Jesus Christ is communicated to future generations by the power of the Holy Spirit, and this occurs not only through the church's teaching, but by its life and worship.

One of the greatest implications of this principle is that the words of scripture and doctrine, which is to say propositional communication, cannot be pitted against the personal conception of revelation. Indeed, divine revelation is primarily God's self-revelation, yet words interpret the deeds of God in history. Likewise, the formulation of the church's faith into propositional statements (scripture, doctrines, creeds) allows future generations to stand in continuity with the past while providing these generations with norms by which to interpret present revelatory action.[172] Thus, handed on (*traditio*) by the church to its newest members, these revelatory propositions are then returned to her (*redditio*), united to the "flesh" of new human experience, with scripture and tradition forming a dynamic unity encompassing the church's life, doctrine, and worship throughout time.

(4) *The Magisterium and the faithful play integral roles in the progress of tradition.* The dynamic of *traditio* and *redditio* in the life of the church shows that tradition only makes progress in time by means of the life of the entire Body of Christ in history. The faithful have an important role to play in the process, particularly in the way they understand their experience of revelation in their daily lives. Coinciding with this fact, it is ultimately the role of the Magisterium—as servant of the Word of God and in utilizing the charism of faithfully safeguarding the truth—to faithfully in-

---

172. Here one could note with Chesterton what he shrewdly termed the "democracy of the dead." See G. K. Chesterton, *Orthodoxy* (London: Image, 1959), 45: "If we attach great importance to the opinion of ordinary men in great unanimity when we are dealing with daily matters, there is no reason why we should disregard it when dealing with history or fable. Tradition may be defined as an extension of the franchise. Tradition means giving votes to the most obscure of all classes, our ancestors. It is the democracy of the dead." Then he poignantly adds, "Tradition refuses to submit to the small and arrogant oligarchy of those who merely happen to be walking about."

terpret revelation in this living tradition and in the scriptures. The Magisterium must be, therefore, astutely attentive to the experience of those they serve, just as the faithful must take up a posture of trust toward those who serve them. A true *sense of the faith*, to recall a phrase of one of the Council's other constitutions, is only possible within this unity.[173]

The recognition of this unity of the Body of Christ in history is particularly important in the face of views of the church that would see the lay faithful in opposition to the Magisterium or, more precisely, place their present experience in opposition to the church's past teaching. The Council's teaching affirms no such dichotomy. The Magisterium and the faithful together make up the Body of Christ, each bearing necessary roles: "The eye cannot say to the hand, 'I do not need you,' nor again the head to the feet, 'I do not need you.'"[174] Likewise, scripture and doctrine are not external impositions on the present church but make up a central part of its very identity.

(5) *Human experience is a locus of revelation, and it must be interpreted in the light of the Gospel.* Since revelation is dialogical and must be received by human persons, human experience becomes a necessary locus of revelation. The revelation that stands as already perceived by the church becomes the norm by which present experience is interpreted. Revelation thus has a triple effect on experience in both its exterior (present history) and interior dimensions (existential meaning): the *via negationis*, *via positionis*, and *via eminentiae*. First, revelation exposes what is sinful in human experience, rejecting what is unconformable to the reality of creation and humanity's ultimate vocation. Second, revelation acknowledges what is legitimately true and good in human experience, affirming this truth and goodness in terms of its rightfully human purpose. Third, not only does revelation affirm this truth and goodness in experience, but it opens up a new horizon transcending experience's previous boundaries, opening the way for present history to reveal the surpassing presence of God and elevating the nature of man to supernatural union in the life of the Trinity.

With these norms in hand this study now turns to the recent history of catechesis in the church, bearing in mind that it is the pedagogy of God—witnessed in revelation—that serves as the model for all of the church's catechetical activity.

173. See *Lumen Gentium*, no. 12. The article teaches that the *sensus fidei* belongs to all the faithful, a universal agreement extending from the bishops to the laity.
174. 1 Cor 12:21.

Chapter 2

The History of Modern Catechetics

And for this reason we, too, give thanks to God unceasingly, that, in receiving the word of God from hearing us, you received not a human word but, as it truly is, the word of God, which is now at work in you who believe.

1 Thessalonians 2:15

Pedagogy of faith is not a question of transmitting human knowledge, even of the highest kind; it is a question of communicating God's revelation in its entirety. Throughout sacred history, especially in the Gospel, God himself used a pedagogy that must continue to be a model for the pedagogy of faith. A technique is of value in catechesis only to the extent that it serves the faith that is to be transmitted and learned; otherwise it is of no value.

Catechesi Tradendae, no. 58

The church's practice of the catechetical ministry is undergirded by the way in which it perceives and understands God's speaking and acting in the world. At its innermost core, catechesis is based upon divine revelation.[1] As if to remind the church of all time of this foundational prin-

---

1. See John T. Ford, "Revelation and Catechesis as Communication," *Living Light* 9 (1972): 21: "Every catechesis, as a ministry of the word, is based on a theology of the word—on a theology of revelation."

ciple, St. Paul explains that the word that is echoed in the church from person to person and generation to generation is "not a human word but, as it truly is, the word of God."

God's revelation of himself, in its own way a divine pedagogy, is therefore the model of catechetical pedagogy. Commissioned to preach the Word of God to all peoples in all times, the church must hand on what it receives. That is to say, it must imitate this divine pedagogy, and, further, it must participate in it. The late French Dominican Pierre-André Liégé put it succinctly: "This ministry must reproduce, as far as possible, the very forms in which God revealed himself."[2]

Still, if catechesis is founded upon divine revelation, it follows that any *relecture* or progression in the church's understanding of revelation will necessarily compel changes in the way it hands on the faith.[3] As chapter 1's analysis of *Dei Verbum* and *Gaudium et Spes* has shown, the church's understanding of revelation did indeed progress from the neo-scholastic emphases of Vatican I. Aided by the thought of an emerging new theology, Vatican II sought to engage the experience of the modern world, grounding the concept of a doctrinal *depositum fidei* in a more personalistic conception of revelation, one that included the locus of human experience in its historical and existential dimensions.

Coinciding with this development, catechists likewise began to shift from time-worn models of catechesis that emphasized the memorization of doctrine to anthropological approaches based upon human experience. The modern catechetical movement, the name given to this renewal of the church's ministry, thus inaugurated a monumental shift in the way in which the church practiced the pedagogy of faith.

The goal of this chapter, then, is to trace this development of the modern catechetical movement and to take stock of its contributions to present catechetical models. In doing so, my intent is to focus on what the movement has bequeathed to post–Vatican II catechesis. I do so without necessarily accepting generalizations that would term the period of postconciliar catechesis as one of "destruction";[4] likewise, I do

2. Pierre-André Liégé, "The Ministry of the Word: From Kerygma to Catechesis," in *Sourcebook for Modern Catechetics*, ed. Michael Warren (Winona, Minn.: St. Mary's Press, 1983), 1:313–14; and D. S. Amalorpavadass, "Catechesis as a Pastoral Task of the Church," in *Sourcebook*, 1:343.

3. See Anne Marie Mongoven, *The Prophetic Spirit of Catechesis: How We Share the Fire in Our Hearts* (New York: Paulist Press, 2000), 87–88.

4. See Michael J. Wrenn, *Catechisms and Controversies: Religious Education in the Postconciliar Years*

not perceive postconciliar catechesis as a sort of superior achievement that liberates catechesis from the evils of older models.[5] Knowing that I myself am an inheritor of this catechesis—both as one who was taught by it and as one who seeks to practice it—I recognize it both for its outstanding achievements and for the aspects in which further development is needed. Much like the interpretation of the Council itself, a hermeneutic of tradition is needed to properly receive and assess the movement—a hermeneutic that stands in continuity with foundational principles and yet that is open to reform in matters of contingency.

The norms on revelation and human experience from chapter 1, therefore, will serve as the measure for the contributions of the modern catechetical movement. This serves a dual purpose: first, and recalling the overall aim of this study, if the New Evangelization requires a new catechesis, such a catechesis must recognize that the new springtime of the Gospel heralded by popes John Paul II, Benedict XVI, and Francis finds its source in the Second Vatican Council. Second, comparing the results of the movement with the established norms recalls the foundational premise that catechesis is always undergirded by divine revelation. The ministry of the Word transmits, to recall Paul's phrase, "not a human word, but as it truly is, the word of God."[6] Put differently, "God himself used a pedagogy," and this pedagogy "must continue to be a model for the pedagogy of faith."[7]

(San Francisco: Ignatius Press, 1991), 115–16. While Wrenn's insights are sometimes keen and are able to provide a different look at the history of the catechetical renewal than one normally finds, his prose nevertheless often carries a polemical tone—one that makes his own message harder to hear by those who would most likely disagree with him.

5. See Kenneth R. Barker, *Religious Education, Catechesis, and Freedom* (Birmingham, Ala.: Religious Education Press, 1981), 45: "The movement from catechism to kerygma was ultimately another form of slavery, since it still involved an imposition upon the individual from outside the realm of personal experience. The attempts to find a truly anthropological catechetics in the most recent era of the movement are attempts to make room in catechetics for human freedom."

6. 1 Thes 2:13.

7. CT, no. 58 [48]. Recently, Petroc Willey has convincingly argued for the renewal of catechesis based upon the pedagogy of God. See the excerpt from his doctoral dissertation published as David James P. Willey, *Philosophical Foundation for a Catechesis in the Light of the Pedagogy of God: Excerptum theseos ad Doctoratum in Philosophia* (Rome: Pontificia Università Lateranense, 2010); and the chapters published as Petroc Willey, "An Original Pedagogy for Catechesis," "The Pedagogue and the Teacher," and "The Pedagogy of God: Aim and Process," in *The Pedagogy of God*, ed. Caroline Farey, Waltraud Linnig, and M. Johanna Paruch (Steubenville, Ohio: Emmaus Road, 2011), 15–79.

The Modern Catechetical Movement: A Movement in Three Phases

Though far less recognized than its biblical and liturgical counterparts, the modern catechetical movement was the renewal of catechesis, underway since the turn of the twentieth century, which coincided with the renewal in theology that was taking place at the time. Much like the adherents of *la nouvelle théologie*, catechists of the movement shared a common distaste for neo-scholasticism—represented by an emphasis on catechism instruction—and sought a better way of reconciling the faith with the lives of the catechized. Also similar to their theological counterparts, these catechists differed in their approach to catechetical *aggiornamento*: some turned to modern advancements in philosophy, sociology, psychology, and education; others believed the proper integration of faith and life could only occur within the context of a *ressourcement*—that is, they believed the earlier tradition supplied key resources for catechetical renewal.

These varying approaches to catechetical *aggiornamento* can be witnessed in the theoretical shifts that took place in the movement, shifts that, generally speaking, cut the twentieth century into thirds. Berard Marthaler provides an approach to this history that serves as a helpful organizational scheme for what follows:

Up to the present the modern catechetical movement has evolved through three more or less distinct phases. The first began with a quest to find a more effective method than the one then in use and gradually evolved into a second phase, which was more concerned with content than method. And most recently, the third phase sees catechetics broadening its ken to include a variety of educational ministries and instructional strategies.[8]

Following this outline, the remainder of this chapter surveys the modern catechetical movement in its three phases, noting its effects on ecclesial teaching and pastoral practice. The survey is followed by a brief discussion of two ecclesial documents that manifest the effects of the renewal, along with an examination of the work of the American educator Gabriel Moran in order to highlight a concrete example of an inheritor of the movement, one who paid particular attention to the role of divine revelation in catechesis. The norms from chapter 1 are then

8. Marthaler, "The Modern Catechetical Movement," in Warren, *Sourcebook*, 276.

compared to the movement in order to see those gains that must be affirmed, the developments that should be corrected, as well as those that stand in need of further growth. The chapter ends with an appraisal of catechesis as it stands today, noting the needs that must be addressed by catechesis for the New Evangelization—needs that stem from comparing the modern catechetical movement with Vatican II's teaching on divine revelation and the human person.

The First Phase: The Search for a Better Method

Historical Survey of the First Phase: The Munich Method

The modern catechetical movement takes its start in German-speaking countries in the early twentieth century. Up to that point, catechesis had mainly taken the form of the instruction of children from catechisms, a pedagogical method that marked the inheritance of the proliferation of catechisms since the Council of Trent[9] and the predominance of neo-scholasticism at the time.[10]

In the United States, the Baltimore Catechism became the symbol of this type of instruction. Its method of well-organized questions and answers, coupled with the setting of the religious classroom, became the hallmark of American catechesis in the preconciliar period. William Loewe's reflections are representative of an entire generation of American Catholics: "The catechesis which regards faith as chiefly a matter of assent to propositions is a familiar childhood memory to many of us."[11]

While an emphasis on the memorization of doctrine may have been a valuable asset for the church in previous eras, by the turn of the twen-

---

9. The history of catechisms can be traced further back to the Middle Ages, where the precursors of catechisms were found in manuals of preparation for confession. See Josef A. Jungmann, "Religious Education in the Late Medieval Times," in *Shaping the Christian Message: Essays in Religious Education*, ed. Gerard Sloyan, 38–62. (New York: Macmillan, 1959), 41. The first catechism, Berard L. Marthaler explains, was *The Lay Folks' Catechism* of 1357, a book of instructions by which archbishop of York and lord chancellor of England, John Thoresby, endeavored to educate the clergy in hopes they would catechize the faithful in their care. But it was not until Martin Luther published his catechisms, and the Council of Trent, in turn, published the *Roman Catechism*, that such books of instruction became largely influential in the Catholic Church. See Marthaler's *The Catechism Yesterday and Today: The Evolution of a Genre* (Collegeville, Minn.: Liturgical Press, 1995), especially 12–14 and 21–41.

10. See Marthaler, *Catechism Yesterday and Today*, 108.

11. William P. Loewe, "Revelation: Dimensions and Issues," *Living Light* 16 (1979): 155.

tieth century, many commentators were starting to claim that such a methodology was significantly less effective in its ability to pass on the faith in all its vitality. Negative appraisals were nearly ubiquitous, so much so that today one can scarcely read a history of the period without being reminded of the fact. In the words of Johannes Hofinger:

Let us recall the lengthy, difficult, and pictureless catechisms of those days, splendid models no doubt of precise formulation of the Church's doctrine, but equally splendid models of a completely unpsychological presentation of that doctrine. To make matters worse, children were generally required to learn these unchildlike catechisms by heart, word for word. We do not need to say that the result in many cases was mere mechanical memorizing of abstract texts, the meaning of which was often grasped in part or perhaps not at all; and that these memorized texts offered the well-meaning, but helpless, child next to no nourishment for his religious life.[12]

Other appraisals did not shy away from harsher terms. For some the doctrinal model of catechesis, with its "exclusive use of the question and answer method," was "a pedagogical strait jacket."[13] Indeed, for others, the method represented a "minimalistic and legalistic view of the Catholic faith"; that is to say, it was ultimately "authoritarian and fear-centered."[14]

In hindsight, perhaps one need not speak so harshly of the catechetical method employed by teachers of the time and their predecessors. Doctrinal catechesis had, after all, been a stabilizing force for the church in the Counter-Reformation[15] and had borne fruit in places in which parents had faithfully raised their children in a Christian environment.[16] Still, by the early 1900s—a period centuries removed from the

---

12. Johannes Hofinger and Francis J. Buckley, *The Good News and Its Proclamation: Post–Vatican II Edition of The Art of Teaching Christian Doctrine* (Notre Dame, Ind.: University of Notre Dame Press, 1968), 3–4.

13. Gerard S. Sloyan, *Speaking of Religious Education* (New York: Herder and Herder, 1968), 16. See also Jacques Audinet, "Catechetical Renewal in the Present Situation," in *The Medellin Papers: A Selection from the Proceedings of the Sixth International Study Week on Catechetics Held at Medellin, Columbia, August 11–17, 1968*, ed. Johannes Hofinger and Terence J. Sheridan (Manila: East Asian Pastoral Institute, 1969), 59.

14. Ryan, "Identity Crisis of Religious Educators," 8.

15. Marthaler gives a generally positive account of the *Roman Catechism* in *Catechism Yesterday and Today*, 40.

16. Hofinger and Buckley, *Good News and Its Proclamation*, 4: "In earlier times the children of good Christian parents had grown up naturally, as it were, into good Christian living. Religious instruction in the schools had only a supplementary role; it organized and deepened the religious knowledge already acquired by the children in their homes and in their parish community."

Counter-Reformation—it was clear in the eyes of many catechists that such a method had overstayed its welcome.

Such discontent formed the milieu from which the modern catechetical movement would emerge. The first phase of renewal arose from Austria and Germany, in part because the Marxist presence there had all but assured the change from a religious culture to a secular one.[17] Hofinger, a figure destined to play a substantial role in catechetical renewal, recalled:

Late nineteenth-century socialism was imbued with Marxist aversion for church and religion; the liberalism of the time was vehemently anticlerical and in favor of religious indifferentism. Already then it was evident that the conventional way of teaching religion was disastrous for children of families that were irreligious, if not antireligious. It caused resentment, which compounded the contempt for religion which they experienced at home.[18]

Though this was the case in Hofinger's native land of Austria, the growing secularism of the West in general did not leave other countries, including the United States, immune from religious indifference.[19]

Faced with such a situation, catechists such as the priests Heinrich Stieglitz and Wilhelm Pichler turned to modern psychology in order to make the teaching of religion more effective.[20] They believed that conforming the contents of the catechism to the developmental capacity of their students could help produce a firmer grasp of the faith in the catechized. Thus, they helped establish what is now termed the "Munich Method" of catechesis. Based on the educational psychology of Johann Friedrich Herbart, this method of presentation, explanation, and application was a text-developing approach as opposed to the text-explanatory approach then in use.[21] Now, instead of mere memoriza-

---

17. Austria and Germany are often recalled for their role in the beginning of catechetical renewal; Pierre Ranwez points to similar developments in France after the First World War. See his "General Tendencies in Contemporary Catechetics," in Shaping the Christian Message, 113: "A pastoral letter written in 1922 by Monseigneur Landrieux, Bishop of Dijon, became a kind of manifesto of the catechetical revival. 'Instead of going in directly by the open doors of the child's imagination and sense perception, we waste our time knocking on the still bolted doors of his understanding and his judgment,' wrote the Bishop."

18. Hofinger, "Looking Backward and Forward: Journey of Catechesis," Living Light 20, no. 4 (1984): 350.

19. See Hofinger and Buckley, Good News and Its Proclamation, 4–5.

20. See Hofinger, "Looking Backward and Forward," 350.

21. See Thomas F. Gleeson, "History and Present Scene in Religious Education," Teaching All Nations 2 (1974): 74.

tion, catechesis consisted of the presentation of a story (often biblical), the highlighting of particular doctrinal points that could be gleaned from the story, and the offering of ways in which the teaching could be applied practically to students' lives.[22] The content of catechesis, found in the catechism, was thus supplemented by a method drawn from creative psychological insights.

The Munich Method found validation at a series of catechetical congresses (most notably Vienna in 1912 and Munich in 1928) in which catechists gathered to discuss the ministry of the Word.[23] There, "scientific and practical lectures were given; the best literature, both Catholic and Protestant, was on display; and formal and informal discussions were held."[24]

Ultimately, the Munich Method held sway in Europe for three decades. It also gained some popularity in the United States through the work of Joseph J. Baierl, Anthony Fuerst, and Rudolph G. Bandas, though without garnering universal acceptance.[25] Nevertheless, the search for a new method, born from the emerging secular milieu and from discontent with question-and-answer methodology, had indeed initiated the first phase of the modern catechetical movement.

General Observations on the First Phase

Interestingly, histories of the catechetical renewal remember the first phase more for what it left behind than what it brought about in terms of renewal. While the advent of the Munich Method is surely recognized as a major achievement, the flight from neo-scholasticism is by far the first phase's most recognizable characteristic. The so-called "manual

22. See Marthaler, "The Modern Catechetical Movement in Roman Catholicism: Issues and Personalities," in Warren, *Sourcebook*, 276. See also Luis Erdozain, "The Evolution of Catechetics: A Survey of Six International Study Weeks on Catechetics," in Warren, *Sourcebook*, 88: "This method was still further amplified by the 'École active' popularized in Italy by Maria Montessori, in France by Quinet, and in Spain by Manjón. Following the principle that a child learns not simply by listening but even more by doing, this school stressed the value of action. And so the above schema was rounded off by a fourth function, that of the child's activities."

23. Hofinger notes that the first catechetical congress in Vienna actually occurred as part of the International Eucharistic Congress that was held at the time. See Johannes Hofinger, "J. A. Jungmann (1889–1975): In Memoriam," *Living Light* 13 (1976): 352.

24. Mary Charles Bryce, "Evolution of Catechesis from the Catholic Reformation to the Present," in *A Faithful Church: Issues in the History of Catechesis*, ed. John H. Westerhoff III and O. C. Edwards Jr. (Wilton, Conn.: Morehouse-Barlow, 1981), 227.

25. See Marthaler, "Modern Catechetical Movement," 276–77.

theology" and the catechisms that mimicked it in simplified form were regarded by catechists as holdovers of an outdated pedagogy.[26]

According to D. S. Amalorpavadass, the theology of revelation implicit in such catechism-based pedagogy can be characterized as "mostly notional and abstract, overessentialist and objectivist, exclusively of the past and static, impersonal and individualistic."[27] As such, revelation was largely seen "as the manifestation of doctrines beyond humanity's understanding"; these doctrines were, according to the theologian, "articles of faith about God, the world, and humanity's salvation, done in an impersonal way, in a distant past, dropped, so to say, from heaven outside the context of history with no reference to the community of men and women."[28]

Inheriting from neo-scholasticism an emphasis on revelation as a divine deposit of truths, catechetical theory relegated the teaching of the faith strictly to the use of the catechism.[29] If divine revelation is seen mainly in terms of a collection of propositions, then catechesis need only pass on these propositions with the hope of students committing them to memory. Accordingly, catechesis was seen as "handing on the revealed doctrines, the emphasis being on *what* we have to communicate or on *teaching* the truths."[30]

It would, of course, be unfair to characterize all neo-scholastic theology of the time—and the resulting catechesis—in such impersonal terms. Likewise, such critical analyses have the advantage of hindsight—the reformers of the first phase foreshadowed the systematic reflection upon divine revelation that was to emerge in the next few decades, and the characterizations of catechism-based approaches often found today manifest that development. Even so, the concerns of the first phase were much more pedagogically based than theological in nature.

26. Ibid., 277. For more on neo-scholastic manuals and why they were lamented by many of the influential theologians of Vatican II, see Wicks, "A Note on 'Neo-Scholastic' Manuals of Theological Instruction, 1900–1960," *Josephinum Journal of Theology* 18, no. 1 (2011): 240–46.

27. Amalorpavadass, "Catechesis as a Pastoral Task," 1:344.

28. Ibid. See also José M. Calle, "Catechesis for the Seventies," *Teaching All Nations* 7 (1970): 93: "The classical Aristotelian categories of the official standard theology were utterly inadequate to explain the existential personalism which is of the very essence of Christianity."

29. The scholastic emphasis itself was not an innovation, but harkened back to the words of scripture. See 1 Tm 6:20 [Vulg.]: "O Timothee, depositum custodi."

30. Amalorpavadass, "Catechesis as a Pastoral Task," 1:344. Emphasis in the original.

Pedagogically, they were reacting against what they perceived as a conflation of content and method in catechesis. In other words, the method of instruction was absorbed by the content, because the content—the catechism—itself had become the method.[31] The question asked by the Jesuits Gatterer and Krus thus became emblematic of the period: "Shall we keep the catechism as it is, or shall we teach it by means of Bible History?"[32]

Nevertheless, from the theological perspective, one can sense in this question hints of the developing theology of revelation that would eventually emerge in the decades leading up to the Council. Finding the older method of memorization to be inadequate, some began to discover in the catechetical practice of the early church a different emphasis upon salvation history.[33] The use of Bible stories in the first phase's methodology, therefore, was not solely the product of the desire to make doctrine more psychologically appealing. Rather, it was claimed:

Bible History and the Catechism comprise the same subjects, namely, divine revelations; but whereas the former contains them in concrete and historical narratives, the latter expresses them in the form of abstract, doctrinal statements. Hence, Bible History is the root out of which the Catechism should grow; it should, consequently, prepare the way for the latter.[34]

Thus, though the first phase of the modern catechetical movement developed out of what were primarily pastoral and pedagogical concerns, it nevertheless evidenced important theological underpinnings that would become more prominent in the later phases. So, too, it should be noted, did the first phase's pastoral concerns focus squarely on the need to reconcile faith and life—the search for better methodology was compelled precisely because the mere memorization of doctrine had failed to take practical effect in students' lives. Such remarks serve to show that the need to reconcile faith and life, so prevalent in the theological milieu leading up to the Second Vatican Council, also manifested itself in pastoral practice—indeed it was the pastoral realm

31. See Marthaler, *Catechism Yesterday and Today*, 108; and Joseph J. Baierl, Rudolph G. Bandas, and Joseph Collins, *Religious Instruction and Education* (New York: Joseph F. Wagner, 1938), 138–39.

32. M. Gatterer and F. Krus, *The Theory and Practice of the Catechism*, trans. J. B. Culemans (New York: Frederick Pustet, 1914), 103.

33. Ibid., 121–22.

34. Baierl, Bandas, and Collins, *Religious Instruction and Education*, 36.

that gave proponents of a new theology their most forceful argument.

Ultimately, then, the catechetical renewal was born from the context of neo-scholastic theology and the resultant emphasis on catechism instruction. The Munich Method was the initial attempt of the renewal to establish the distinction between what was to be taught and the method used to accomplish the task. In this particular model of catechesis the content remained the doctrines of the catechism, but the method utilized sought to relay these doctrines through presentation, explanation, and application. As pioneers in the field, the catechists of the first phase of the modern catechetical movement had recognized a need and appropriately developed catechesis in order to address it.

Even so, this development itself eventually came to be seen as inadequate. With 1928 marking the climax of the first phase,[35] a second phase was on the horizon, ushered in by the Austrian Jesuit Josef Jungmann and his student Johannes Hofinger.

The Second Phase: Kerygmatic Catechesis

Historical Survey of the Second Phase: Josef Jungmann

When it was published in 1936, Josef Andreas Jungmann's *Die Frohbotschaft und unsere Glaubensverkündigung* garnered "immediate, vigorous and, as was to be expected, partisan" reaction.[36] Jungmann, a Jesuit and member of the faculty of the University of Innsbruck, is most commonly remembered as a scholar of the liturgy—today his book on the history of the liturgy, *The Mass of the Roman Rite*, is widely recognized as a classic.[37] Nevertheless, it was this book on catechesis, abridged and published in English as *The Good News Yesterday and Today*, that caused remarkable debate and instigated a monumental shift in the ongoing catechetical renewal.[38]

---

35. Erdozain, "Evolution of Catechetics," 88.

36. Bibliographical information for Jungmann's influential work is found in the introductory chapter of this volume. The quote is from William A. Huesman's preface to Jungmann, *Good News Yesterday and Today*, vi.

37. See Jungmann, *The Mass of the Roman Rite: Its Origins and Development*, trans. F. A. Brunner (London: Burns and Oates, 1959). This study, undertaken during the years Hitler had closed down the theology department at Innsbruck, contributed greatly to Jungmann's selection as a *peritus* at the Second Vatican Council, where his influence is largely seen in the drafting of *Sacrosanctum Concilium*.

38. While catechists were favorable to the work, many in the theological establishment

Such immediate, vigorous, and partisan reactions to Jungmann's work can be seen as part of the larger debate on la nouvelle théologie that took place before the Council. Because it challenged the reigning neo-scholastic framework, this new theology was embraced by those who advocated renewal and rejected by others who saw it as a challenge to theological orthodoxy.[39] Yet, while some of the proponents of reform turned to modern advancements in fields such as psychology and philosophy in order to bring renewal, Jungmann placed himself in the company of those who advocated renewal through a return to the sources of Christian tradition—that is, through ressourcement.[40] His book The Good News Yesterday and Today, along with the rest of his catechetical writings, therefore took what was happening on the theological plane and translated it into the realm of catechetics.[41]

Given that Jungmann's work coincides with this preconciliar push for the reunification of faith and life, it is not surprising to find that his analysis of the then current situation in Europe is marked by what he

were less so. The book seemed destined to an initial condemnation from ecclesiastical authorities but was pulled from publication by Jungmann's Jesuit superiors to avoid this from happening. See Hofinger, "Looking Backward and Forward," 352.

39. The Dominican Réginald Garrigou-Lagrange is often credited with having popularized the term la nouvelle théologie. He used "new" in a pejorative sense, believing the proponents of this theology to have broken from the tradition of the church while embracing the tenets of Modernism. See his "La nouvelle théologie où va-t-elle?," Angelicum 23, no. 3–4 (1946): 126–45.

40. See Jungmann, The Good News Yesterday and Today, 17: "Today we are experiencing something of a renaissance of early Christianity. Nor should one wonder that an age like ours, which feels its very foundations shaking, should look back to the beginnings of Christian history where principles were distinct and tangible, contrasts sharp and clear, forms fresh and vigorous. The main value in this turning back to early Christianity ought not to be seen in the fact that we here meet with examples of great holiness and courageous witness (these can be found in all ages), nor in the relatively high level of religious-moral life in these Christian communities; but rather in the pristine spirit and single-mindedness of its Christian life and in the clarity of its ideals—ideals not broken up and watered down, but dynamically alive in the consciousness of the faithful, providing the assurance and impetus needed for the conquest of a pagan world."

41. In a review of the English edition, James Carmody writes that "almost the whole of the philosophy behind the reform movement in the Church, what Pope John XXIII called an aggiornamento, is contained within the brief compass of this book." See Carmody, review of The Good News Yesterday and Today, by Josef Andreas Jungmann, Theological Studies 24, no. 3 (1963): 502. See also Daniel M. Ruff, "From Kerygma to Catechesis: Josef A. Jungmann's Good News Yesterday and Today," Living Light 39, no. 1 (2002): 72: "In the end, The Good News . . . must be said to have anticipated and to have helped clear the way for many of the theological emphases that would be vindicated and highlighted at the Second Vatican Council. These included an insistence on Christ in the role of mediator and savior, a general re-emphasis on the importance of God's word and its kerygmatic proclamation, and a ringing affirmation of the legitimate demand that academic theology be reformulated in a way that takes contemporary life experience better into account."

termed a "conventional Christianity" or a "traditional confession."[42] By this he meant that the ritualized customs and memorized doctrinal formulae of the church, having emerged from the faith of previous ages, had become detached from present life. He explained:

Christian customs have become a protective armor shielding religious life. In fact, one might say that there is religious life stored up in them. For the custom itself evolved out of an intensely lived religion, just as the protective bark of a tree develops from the life of a tree. Nor could religious life maintain itself without a sound armor of custom, no more than a tree could flourish without its bark or a plant without its stalk.[43]

Yet, for Jungmann, the bark of conventional Christianity had become but a shell:

Of course, it can also happen that, underneath the protective bark of custom, life itself dies out or is restricted to a few pitiful strands of living tissue, while the tree continues to appear outwardly great and mighty.[44]

The external markers of Christianity, or even more, the rudimentary memorization of the faith's doctrinal tenets, thus were no longer attached to their living center. Christianity had, according to the liturgical and pastoral theologian, become a faith residing on the surface level of believers' lives, with belief and practice being fragmented into dogmatic and moral stipulations without their rightful unifying core.[45] Any catechetical solution to this fragmentation, therefore, would have to move beyond the mere development of methodology; rather, it would need to reattach the words and deeds of Christianity to their source of life.

Jungmann's solution was to return to the heart of the church's message, both for her members and for the world—the proclamation of Jesus Christ and the salvation that is found in him. "We must," he

42. Jungmann, *Good News, Yesterday and Today*, 3.
43. Jungmann, "An Adult Christian," *Worship* 27, no. 1 (1952): 6.
44. Ibid.
45. See Jungmann, "Theology and Kerygmatic Teaching," in Warren, *Sourcebook*, 213: "It is not really ignorance of the basic points of Christian doctrine that we regret. Most people know all the sacraments; they know about the person of Christ, as well as about Our Lady, Peter and Paul, Adam and Eve, and a good many others. They know enough about the commandments of God and the Church. But what is lacking among the faithful is a sense of the unity, seeing it all as a whole, an understanding of the wonderful message of divine grace. All they retain of Christian doctrine is a string of dogmas and moral precepts, threats and promises, customs and rites, tasks and duties imposed on unfortunate Catholics, whilst the non-Catholic gets off free. They are averse to believing in and acting up to their beliefs, a reluctance which, in an atmosphere of unbelief and materialism, soon leads to disaster for the individual Catholic."

wrote, echoing St. Clement Hofbauer, "really preach the Gospel all over again."[46] As such, his approach to catechesis became identified with the *kerygma*, the Greek word used by New Testament writers to denote the Gospel message that was preached by Christ and the apostles.[47]

Undoubtedly, at the center of Jungmann's kerygmatic proposal is the person of Jesus Christ, the one who unites God with humanity.[48] Thus kerygmatic catechesis presented a Christocentric antidote to the problem of unifying faith and life: in the face of a fragmented Christianity, "Christ shines forth as the luminous core who illumines every question, every doctrine, every commandment."[49] Furthermore, "from this center a new light should go forth, as it were, over all the concerns of life, religious and ecclesiastical, moral and secular. From this center must come the forces by which we shall once again conquer the world."[50]

This kerygmatic center is, for Jungmann, made accessible in two ways. First, to properly grasp Christ, one must turn to the testimony of the scriptures. That is to say, one must come to see Christ not so much from "the scientific refinement of concepts" offered by scholasticism, but from the economy of salvation.[51] Thus, "in a word," kerygmatic catechesis "will prefer the original, simple modes of expression of Sacred Scripture to the sharply defined language of the School."[52] Mani-

---

46. Jungmann, *Good News, Yesterday and Today*, 11.

47. See Mk 1:14 and Acts 2:14, among many other examples. The word *kerygma* is "used in its verbal form some 61 times to describe the proclamation of the kingdom of God and of the 'gospel of God' (Rom 1:2)," and "it was employed in an almost technical sense by the New Testament authors to signify the manner in which an authorized preacher announced the truth that 'the kingdom of God has come upon you (Mt 12:28, Lk 11:20).... The content of the kerygma is the gospel of Christ (cf. Mk 1:14), what is to be believed (Rom 10:18), or simply the logos, or word (Acts 17:11, 2 Tm 4:2)." See *New Catholic Encyclopedia*, 2nd ed., s.v. "Kerygma."

Related to this kerygmatic catechetical model, Jungmann's work also came to be seen in conjunction with the push for a kerygmatic form of theology, over and above the neo-scholastic form. This perhaps caused the greatest unrest for opponents of his thought. Nevertheless, their perception was not entirely true. While some of Jungmann's associates advocated for a new form of theology in the seminaries, Jungmann himself did not "intend to set up a new theology against dogmatic theology. The discussion . . . on the need for a kerygmatic theology has been sidetracked far away from the real question. The main point is not that of an independent theology but that of the special rules for preaching in the light of theology." See Jungmann, "Theology and Kerygmatic Teaching," 217.

48. See Jungmann, "Christ's Place in Catechesis and Preaching," *Lumen Vitae* 7 (1952): 533–42.

49. Jungmann, *Good News, Yesterday and Today*, 11.

50. Ibid., 153.

51. Ibid., 35

52. Ibid.

festing the patristic interest of the *ressourcement* movement, Jungmann's approach to the scriptures was modeled after that of the church fathers. He inherited from them the belief that Christ was the hermeneutical key to both the Old and New Testaments and that both portions could be considered as one "*narratio* of God's saving design for humanity."[53] Salvation history was therefore integral to encountering Christ and to reunifying the fragmented elements of the faith.[54]

Furthermore, for Jungmann, not only is the presence of Christ encountered in the economy of salvation as told in the scriptures, but his economy is made present in the liturgy.[55] Jungmann believed that the liturgy held a unique formative power: "One should not expect an easy familiarity with the central doctrines of faith to grow out of skillful teaching alone. Lived, *but above all prayed*, dogma will prove to be the best school."[56] The sacredness of the liturgy and its evocation of the holy were particularly formative, for "liturgical prayer is pre-eminently filled with a sense of the majesty of the infinite God, ever mounting to Him and impressing on men's souls that He is the final goal of all human striving.... Our young people will never grasp the seriousness and sublimity of the thought of God in a more vital way than through the power of the liturgy."[57]

In sum, Jungmann's proposal was to return catechesis to the dynamic impulses of the church's beginnings, to recenter the message

53. Michael Warren, "Jungmann and the Kerygmatic Theology Controversy," in Warren, *Sourcebook*, 194.

54. See Mary C. Boys, *Biblical Interpretation in Religious Education: A Study of the Kerygmatic Era* (Birmingham, Ala.: Religious Education Press, 1980), 77. Boys's study is especially useful for the way in which it connects biblical studies with catechesis, as she quite skillfully displays familiarity with both fields.

55. See Jungmann, "Liturgy and the History of Salvation," *Lumen Vitae* 10 (1955): 261–68. Here Jungmann mentions the work of scholars who appropriated Platonic thought in order to explain how Christ is made present in the liturgy, as well as that of Odo Casel, who is widely recognized for reintroducing the idea that the liturgy makes present the "mystery" of the event of salvation.

56. Jungmann, *Good News, Yesterday and Today*, 114. Emphasis mine.

57. Ibid., 114–15. Jungmann's research into the history of the liturgy clearly played a role in this aspect of kerygmatic catechesis. Recalling the liturgy of the early church, he admired that "there was a living liturgy. The liturgy was both Christian school and Christian instruction; the liturgy enriched the parents interiorly to such an extent that they were enabled to instruct their children; the liturgy made the Christians coalesce into one community. Through the liturgy, i.e., through the word of God which it contains and through the strength of its sacraments, pagan society became a Christian society." See Jungmann, "The Pastoral Effect of the Liturgy," *Orate Fratres* 23, no. 11 (1949): 491.

upon Jesus Christ and his saving work, made accessible by the breadth of the narration of salvation history and the formative effect of the liturgy. In its kerygmatic form, catechesis could then reunify the faith with the understanding of believers and tie to their center the various elements of doctrine and custom that made up "conventional Christianity."

Historical Survey of the Second Phase: Johannes Hofinger and the Study Weeks

While such groundbreaking ideas had caused an immediate stir in Europe, the popularizing of Jungmann's thought is owed in large part to the work of his student Johannes Hofinger.[58] Having studied under Jungmann at Innsbruck, Hofinger took his teacher's ideas and gave them an expanded international voice.[59] He is perhaps best known for his leadership and organization of the catechetical Study Weeks, international gatherings in which bishops, missionaries, and catechetical experts came together to discuss the ministry of the Word, particularly as it applied to missionary contexts.

These Study Weeks, in one sense, provide a unique view into the modern catechetical movement, for they act as a prism in which to view the movement as a whole.[60] Over the period of a mere decade, one can witness the transformation of catechetical models from an emphasis on the kerygma to the theoretical and practical embrace of human experience that dominated postconciliar thought in the late twentieth century. As such, Hofinger's international gatherings form the bulk of the remainder of this chapter's historical survey of the modern catechetical movement. The study week at Eichstätt belongs to the second phase of the movement and thus is covered here. The study weeks at Bangkok, Manila, and Medellín will be analyzed as part of the third phase.[61]

---

58. See Barker, *Religious Education, Catechesis, and Freedom*, 49.

59. This includes the lectures he gave at the University of Notre Dame in 1955, the first time kerygmatic catechesis had been brought to the United States. See footnote 10 of Hofinger, "J. A. Jungmann: In Memoriam," 359.

60. See Warren, "Introductory Overview," in Warren, *Sourcebook*, 23.

61. While other study weeks took place during the period between 1959 and 1968, I will concentrate on these specific study weeks because they highlight particular shifts that were taking place in the catechetical movement. A complete list of the study weeks is as follows: Nijmegen 1959, Eichstätt 1960, Bangkok 1962, Katigondo 1964, Manila 1967, and Medellín 1968.

Eichstätt   The study week at Eichstätt that took place in 1960 is called by Berard Marthaler a "landmark in the history of modern catechetics."[62] Though taking place some twenty-four years since Jungmann had reintroduced the kerygma to catechesis, the study week's proceedings, published in English as *Teaching All Nations*, manifest the broad acceptance of the kerygmatic proposal.[63] In the introduction to the proceedings, Hofinger confidently explains that the "kerygmatic ideal" can be found in every paper, in the study week's conclusions, and in the program designed by the participants for the future of catechesis. Indeed, "anyone who seriously studies the papers read and the conclusions reached at Eichstätt will not be able to entertain the slightest doubt that the kerygmatic viewpoint is, for modern catechetics, both characteristic and basic."[64]

This predominance of kerygmatic catechesis proclaimed by Hofinger—while not necessarily disclosing the whole of the proceedings—is perhaps best evidenced by a paper presented by the German professor Josef Goldbrunner of the University of West Berlin. In it, he recalls the initial turn to psychological methodology as found in the catechetical movement's first phase. While offering the Munich Method and "learning by doing" methodology modest praise, he interestingly likens such methods to the gospel depiction of Martha: "Martha, Martha, you are busy with many things."[65] For Goldbrunner, the busyness of such methodology takes a secondary place to Mary's part, for "only one thing is necessary," the message of the Kingdom of God—that is, the kerygma.[66] Ultimately, the German professor emphasizes the need of

62. Marthaler, "Modern Catechetical Movement," 280.

63. Hofinger, ed., *Teaching All Nations: A Symposium on Modern Catechetic*, trans. Clifford Howell (New York: Herder and Herder, 1961 (note that the book *Teaching All Nations* is distinguished from the journal that bears the same name). Portions of the study week's conclusions are also published in Warren, *Sourcebook*, 30–39.

64. Hofinger, introduction to *Teaching All Nations*, xv.

65. Josef Goldbrunner, "Catechetical Method as Handmaid of Kerygma," in *Teaching All Nations*, 110. The gospel paraphrase is Goldbrunner's.

66. Ibid. On the following page, Goldbrunner, with an example that seems to recall his Mary-Martha analogy, explains the transformative power of the kerygma in a way that, I believe, captures the spirit of the renewal proposed by Jungmann: "Let us explain the role of the kerygma in religious education through a comparison. A young girl is doing her housework reluctantly, slowly, and wearily. Her mother who lies sick in bed sadly watches the joyless activities of her daughter. Suddenly, the doorbell rings and the postman delivers a letter for the young girl, which she opens and reads. The mother witnesses in amazement a sudden transformation which now comes over her daughter. She returns to her work singing and refreshed

both "sisters," so to speak, while nevertheless recognizing the priority of catechesis' Marian aspect over its "Marthian" one.[67]

This kerygmatic priority mentioned in Goldbrunner's paper is also well-evidenced by the final conclusions put forth by the study week. These conclusions, published in a summary report, affirm the psychological advances of the catechetical movement's first phase while embracing the "conclusions reached by the recent kerygmatic renewal."[68] Likewise, they explain that "the chief aim of this kerygmatic renewal is to present the truth of our faith as an organic whole. Its core is the Good News of our redemption in Christ. Its fruit should be the grateful response of our love."[69]

While much can be said for Hofinger's proclamation of the kerygmatic movement's acceptance—indeed, one author refers to Eichstätt as an "echo" of Jungmann's thought[70]—it would be incorrect to claim the proponents of kerygmatic catechesis as the only significant voice at the study week. According to Alfonso Nebrada, a Jesuit who was heavily involved in the proceedings, there was a certain tension present between the Germans who advocated the kerygmatic approach and the French-speaking participants, especially those from Paris and the Belgian *Lumen Vitae* institute, who advocated a pedagogy of signs.[71] The four signs underscored by the French theologians and catechists—Bible, Liturgy, Doctrine, and Witness—were incorporated into the general conclusions as a sort of compromise.[72] In the words of the program for future catechesis put forth by the participants, the kerygma should be considered "our message," while the four signs are "our method."[73]

---

with keen interest and joy, and swiftly accomplishes all her duties. She is like a different person, like one reborn. What news did the letter bring? Her fiancé will be here in a week! This news, this message of a future event, makes its effect felt in the present. The message has the power to change the existence of the young girl."

67. Ibid., 121.

68. "General Conclusions," in *Teaching All Nations*, 387.

69. Ibid.

70. Bryce, *Pride of Place: The Role of the Bishops in the Development of Catechesis in the United States* (Washington, D.C.: The Catholic University of America Press, 1984), 134. See also, Gleeson, "History and Present Scene," 79.

71. See Alfonso Nebrada, "Some Reflections on Father Gleeson's Paper on History and Present Scene in Religious Education," *Teaching All Nations* 11 (1974): 85.

72. Ibid. Nebrada notes that "it is thus a little misleading to simply state that [the tetrad of signs] form [an] essential part of the kerygmatic renewal."

73. "Programme of the Catechetical Apostolate," in *Teaching All Nations*, 394 and 398. Anne Marie Mongoven traces the pedagogy of signs back to Joseph Colomb, a Sulpician priest who

Tensions notwithstanding, I believe one can rightly call the study week at Eichstätt the climax of the kerygmatic movement. Jungmann's proposals, first issued in 1936, had found general approval and international voice over twenty years later, especially through the work of his disciple Hofinger. Through Hofinger's consistent championing of his master's thought, especially seen in his organization of the gathering at Eichstätt, kerygmatic catechesis came to be seen as a watershed in catechetical renewal.[74] In this light, the Bavarian study week of 1960 stands as the high point of the second phase of the modern catechetical movement.

General Observations on the Second Phase

While the first phase of catechetical renewal can be recalled for the introduction of a new catechetical method, the second is recognized for the stress it placed on content. In the former, the content of the catechism was retained while being supported by methodological advances in psychology and education. But, in the latter, the adequacy of this content itself was challenged. While recognizing the importance of the propositional formulae of doctrine, Jungmann believed the content of catechesis was to be found ultimately in the Gospel message— that is, the kerygma.[75]

The shift from method to content coincided with the shifts in theology that were occurring at the time, as noted earlier.[76] Most important-

---

was concerned with awakening "the spiritual sense of the child by drawing out the Christian meaning of their human experiences." Colomb firmly believed that intellectual knowledge presupposed personal experience. See Mongoven, *Prophetic Spirit of Catechesis*, 48–49; and Joseph Colomb, *Aux Sources du Catéchisme: Histoire Sainte et Liturgie*, 2nd ed. (Paris: Société de Saint Jean L'Évangéliste, 1949), 1:9: "Doctrine will appear more real if it is known from a personal experience by the child, if it is presented as this same experience put into formulas, in words" (translation mine). Marthaler, "Modern Catechetical Movement," 280, refers to the work of George Delcuve, Marcel van Caster, and Andre Godin in popularizing the pedagogy of signs.

74. Cardinal Valerian Gracias, archbishop of Bombay, delivered the closing remarks of the study week in which he gave special attention to the efforts of Hofinger: "Obviously the lion's share of our gratitude goes to Father Hofinger, S.J., who, to fulfill his mission, has been seven times round the world, and is threatening to undertake an eighth world tour! God has blessed him with a slender frame—a sign of health and energy, without any encumbrances, with an infinite capacity for study and work, a consuming zeal, a gift for driving hard his secretaries; and with inestimable, priceless ability to sleep to order!" See Valerian Cardinal Gracias, "Concluding Address," in *Teaching All Nations*, 377–78.

75. See Hofinger, "J. A. Jungmann: In Memoriam," 356; and Erdozain, "Evolution of Catechetics," 89.

76. Erdozain traces the theological influence on Jungmann even further back to the scholars

ly, a different understanding of divine revelation was beginning to take hold, one that challenged the earlier emphasis on a deposit of faith. As one paper presented at Eichstätt put it, "As the form of revelation God did not, therefore, choose universally valid dogmas, but a clear, gripping event, one which he allowed to take place and then caused to be proclaimed."[77]

Thus one can say that, while the first phase of renewal had shown hints of a budding new conception of revelation, it was the second phase that reaped the results of its growth. No longer was revelation seen in the static conception that was attributed to the theological resurgence of scholasticism. Rather, it was claimed, God manifested himself through the events of salvation history, culminating in the coming of his Son, Jesus Christ. God's plan of redemption "did not take the form of a philosophical system but that of a series of historical events making gloriously manifest God's incredible love of man. It is revealed to us in the form of joyful tidings, the Good News brought by Christ, which we should receive with alacrity through faith and which we should respond to with love."[78]

Certainly, this new theological foundation and the emphasis on the kerygma were developments that were well-received by catechists who had grown weary of catechism instruction. Nevertheless, in recognizing the kerygmatic movement's advances, one should also note that Jungmann, Hofinger, and many of those they influenced never viewed themselves as a rupture with the church's theological or catechetical tradition. Rather, they were at pains to show that their work was a progression that developed the tradition without ever rejecting it outright. Theologically, Jungmann faced many detractors who believed he had strayed from theological orthodoxy; still, from the vantage point of the present, it is clear that he wished to return to the sources of theological tradition, sources that pushed further back than neo-scholasticism's embrace of the Middle Ages. So too did Jungmann recognize that doc-

---

of Tübingen—calling the Austrian Jesuit a "champion of this tradition." See "Evolution of Catechetics," 87–89.

77. Klemens Tillman, "Origin and Development of Modern Catechetical Methods," in *Teaching All Nations*, 92. Today one can recognize that, while Tillman's remarks bear some truth, the totality of revelation is nevertheless manifested by deeds *and words*. Part of the scandal of the Incarnation is that God not only takes on human flesh, but he also uses human words.

78. Léopold Denis, "Advantages and Difficulties of Modern Methods in Mission Catechesis," in *Teaching All Nations*, 95.

trine—the objective form of revelation embraced by neo-scholasticism—was not to be discarded, but was to be regrounded in the person and work of Jesus Christ:

Unity of doctrine becomes evident only if the Person of Jesus Christ is the center. Do not separate Christ from His work, salvation through the Church. Do not represent Christ with empty hands. His coming into this world, His passion, His resurrection, are not "autonomous" events, from which, at most, certain moral lessons derive; they should demonstrate their redemptive meaning.... When speaking of grace, the Church, the sacraments, we cannot content ourselves with clear definitions and comprehensive enumerations patiently elaborated by theological experts; we must connect them with the Sanctifier, the Head of the Church, the first Dispenser of the sacraments.[79]

This desire to remain within the tradition while developing it manifested itself in how the kerygmatic scholars viewed the catechetical movement as well. Jungmann and Hofinger recognized the value of the advancements in methodology that had occurred in the movement's first phase.[80] Jungmann himself advocated a version of the Munich Method, though with his own modifications and emphases.[81] The turn to content advocated by both men, therefore, was not a break with the first phase but a development of it. Hofinger, even as he began to sense the emergence of a third phase on the catechetical horizon, wrote, "It is of great importance that we should never let the promising progress of our days make us minimize the great work accomplished by the pioneering leaders of earlier stages of the catechetical renewal"; indeed, a new stage "can in no way mean any break with the past, but only a further homogeneous development of our catechetical heritage."[82]

79. Jungmann, "Christ's Place in Catechesis and Preaching," 535–36. See also Jungmann, *Announcing the Word of God*, trans. Ronald Walls (New York: Herder and Herder, 1967), 66: "In every separate point of doctrine the objectively existing reference to the person of Christ should always shine through the exposition, thus drawing it together to form a unity, a living cosmos"; and Hofinger and Buckley, *Good News and Its Proclamation*, 6: "The realization became evermore widespread that a true catechetical renewal must also concern itself with the content of religious instruction. This does not mean, of course, that traditional Catholic doctrine be changed in order to conform with modern fashions of thought, nor that it be watered down to suit the secularized outlook of modern society. Far from it."

80. See Hofinger and Buckley, *Good News and Its Proclamation*, 5–6.

81. See the chapter "General Method," in Jungmann, *Handing on the Faith: A Manual of Catechetics*, trans. A. N. Fuerst (New York: Herder and Herder, 1962), 174–221.

82. Hofinger, "Contemporary Catechetics: A Third Phase?," *Chicago Studies* 2, no. 3 (1963): 268.

The Third Phase: The Anthropological Turn

Historical Survey of the Third Phase: Emerging Missionary Concerns of the Study Weeks

While Eichstätt is rightly considered the climax of the kerygmatic renewal, there, at the Bavarian study week, the signs of further development were already beginning to make themselves known. As mentioned previously, French-speaking catechists and theologians had advocated the pedagogy of signs as a catechetical method to augment the kerygma.

Indeed, prior to Eichstätt, the catechetical atmosphere in France had already begun to witness a shift in approach toward anthropological—or, one could say, experiential—concerns.[83] The influences upon this shift were varied, but certainly numbered among them is the research of the Swiss developmental psychologist Jean Piaget.[84] With particular attention to how children learn, Piaget posited four stages of cognitive development, each manifesting a progressive difference in kind in the mental capacities of a child.[85] The implication for cat-

---

83. The word "anthropology" is referred to in catechetics much like the way it is referenced in relation to *Gaudium et Spes*. It refers simultaneously to human experience in exterior (present history) and interior (the person's longings, joys, struggles, etc.) dimensions. See D. S. Amalorvapadass, "Workshop on Recent Developments in Catechetics," in *Teaching All Nations* 4 (1967): 377: "It must be noted that anthropology as understood in the continental sense and as used in the catechetical movement is concerned with man whole and entire, with human experience and human values. It implies attentiveness to man, reflection on him and on his varied situations in life"; and Joseph Bournique, "The Word of God and Anthropology," *Teaching All Nations* 4 (1967): 371: "The catechetical movement uses this term with a very specific meaning. It is not to be limited to ethnography nor to cultural anthropology. It means attentiveness to man, reflection on man, and consists in discovering, describing, and analyzing the major situations in which man finds himself, such as: man's struggle against his environment; man at work; man transforming his environment; man's relationship with other men (family relationship, love, hate, solitude). It will consider how man treats himself, tries to understand himself, his fight for integrity and freedom, and how he faces death, etc. Anthropological research in catechetics tries to discover what these situations mean for man. It is an investigation also into the way Jesus Christ in revelation has taken all that is human unto Himself. It is finally an attempt to show how the deepest human problems and Christ's assumption of our nature render God's mystery visible and fulfill His plan."
84. See Marthaler, "Modern Catechetical Movement," 279.
85. See Boys, *Biblical Interpretation in Religious Education*, 213–14. Boys includes Piaget as one of the many influences that led to the fall of the salvation history hermeneutic in both catechesis and biblical studies. A helpful summary of Jean Piaget's work is given in his *Science of Education and the Psychology of the Child*, trans. D. Coltman (New York: Viking Press, 1971), 30–33. See also Piaget and Bärbel Inhelder, *The Psychology of the Child*, trans. H. Weaver (New York: Basic Books, 1969), a work that Piaget describes as a "synthesis, or summing up, of our work in child psychology" (xv).

echesis, and indeed for all educational activity, was that the developmental structure of a person's mind determined what was to be learned in any given situation.[86]

Another influence upon the anthropological shift in catechesis was the work of Joseph Colomb, a Sulpician priest and professor of catechetics in Paris, who highlighted the role of experience in religious learning.[87] For Colomb, human experience held the place of primacy in relation to content:

I cannot understand a book about mountains and valleys, if I have not seen and travelled through both in my country, if I have no experience of what a mountain (or at least a hill) and a valley is. All knowledge from books or words presupposes some personal experience. If this is lacking, or the books and words do not correspond with it, they mean nothing. They can be learnt by heart, they can nourish oral comprehension, [but] they do not become part of the living man. All living comprehension is built on experience; then it ranges this experience, becomes conscious of it, and prepares further experience, avoiding useless wanderings and profiting still more by it.[88]

Such an emphasis on experience, along with the pedagogy of signs, gave the Eichstätt study week a secondary voice that grew louder in the international gatherings that were to follow.[89]

---

86. Such a conclusion was heavily influenced by at least two sources. First, Piaget's theory manifested a Darwinian influence in that he believed the knower to be conditioned by his or her environment, the resulting process of accommodation and assimilation becoming the driving force behind developmental evolution. See Piaget and Inhelder, *Psychology of the Child*, 6. Likewise, Piaget embraced a Kantian epistemology in claiming the mind's structures to be the determiner of meaning. Thus he claimed that "one can feel very close to the spirit of Kantianism (and I believe I am close to it)," but maintained that his scientific approach enabled a "much richer constructivity, although ending with the same characteristics of rational necessity and the structuring of experience as those which Kant called for to guarantee his concept of the *a priori*." See Piaget, *Insights and Illusions in Philosophy*, trans. W. Mays (London: Routledge and Kegan Paul, 1972), 58.

Piaget's developmental theory is still widely used, both in secular and religious education. For the latter, see Thomas Groome's *Christian Religious Education: Sharing Our Story and Vision* (San Francisco: Harper and Row, 1980), 239–57. While Groome's theory has much to recommend it, I do not believe that such a constructivist, or Kantian, epistemology can ultimately be reconciled with catechesis based upon divine revelation.

87. See Mongoven, *Prophetic Spirit of Catechesis*, 45 and 48–51.

88. Colomb, "Teaching Catechism as a Message of Life," in *Readings in European Catechetics*, ed. G. Delcuve and A. Godin, trans. unknown (Brussels: Lumen Vitae Press, 1962), 128.

89. It is apparent from the published texts of Eichstätt that the anthropological concern was already being weighed, even by Hofinger. In the latter's introduction to *Teaching All Nations*, he notes that "another point which had become increasingly clear in recent years was the failure of catechesis to adapt the Christian message to the people whom we have to instruct. We are,

Bangkok   The anthropological concerns of the catechists at Eichstätt planted seeds that began to blossom at the 1962 study week at Bangkok. In the move from Europe to Asia, the role of human experience took on greater importance for the catechetical enterprise, especially because Christians made up only a minority of the Asian population. As Hofinger explained, Western catechesis had initially developed as the teaching of those who had already professed faith, and thus, in the past, no special preparation was needed for hearers to embrace the Gospel. But "this is surely not the case with the unbeliever we approach in mission countries," nor, for that matter, "with the would-be convert and the fallen-away Catholic whom we try to bring home to the sheepfold of the Lord."[90]

Recognizing the needs of an evangelizing catechesis for mission lands, the scholars who gathered at Bangkok began to reassess the emphasis on content that had begun with the kerygmatic renewal and had reached its peak in the German study week. The question arose: before one can even begin to speak of content—the Good News—must not the hearer be prepared to receive it? Must not his or her experiences be mined for those places that can make the message more accessible, more palatable? In the words of Alfonso Nebrada, "The problem is not whether to be theocentric or Christocentric, but to be decidedly anthropocentric in approach. . . . The basic principle is 'to take man as he is and where he is.'"[91]

Most important to this discussion was the advent of a new stage in the evangelization process, that of the "pre-evangelization" of unbelievers.[92] First advanced by the writings of Pierre-André Liégé, this stage preceded the preaching of the kerygma, indeed, made a way for it by

---

indeed, only just beginning to cope with this problem." See Hofinger, introduction to *Teaching All Nations*, xii. See also Léopold Denis's essay "Advantages and Difficulties of Modern Methods," 95–107, in the same volume.

90. Hofinger, "Contemporary Catechetics: A Third Phase?," 267. Here one begins to see the concerns of the New Evangelization in germ.

91. Nebrada, "Some Reflections," 89.

92. See the helpful chart in Nebrada, "East Asian Study Week on Mission Catechetics: 1962," in Warren, *Sourcebook*, 46, which outlines the stages of pre-evangelization, evangelization, and catechesis proper. Nebrada's report is the official summary report of the Bangkok study week. See also Jean-Paul Labelle, "An Appraisal of the Catechetical Situation in Southeast Asia," *Teaching All Nations* 4 (1967): 284–85, where the author states that the three stages from Bangkok were "canonized by Vatican II in the *Decree on the Missionary Activity of the Church* [nos. 10–14]."

giving attention to the religious, cultural, and societal milieu of those to be evangelized.[93] One author describes it as a preparation that, "taking man as he is and where he is, makes a human dialogue possible and awakens in him the sense of God, an indispensable element for opening his heart to the message."[94] More specifically, pre-evangelization probes the experience of the hearer, seeking the places in this experience that help effect a sense of God and rooting out those obstacles that would keep him or her from accepting the Gospel.[95] Ultimately, then, before catechesis proper, and even before the kerygma can be initially proclaimed, one must consider the experience of the human person.

With this, the participants at Bangkok had caused a shift in the catechetical landscape, though there were other contributions as well. Of note is the fact that a concern for missionary evangelization had necessarily broadened catechesis' purview. Until then, most had limited catechesis to the teaching of children, but now it was clear that an evangelizing catechesis should be aimed at adults, at least as the normative form, for adult conversion—that is, the response of a free, consciously chosen gift of self on the part of the person evangelized—is the main concern of the missionary.[96] Likewise, even after pre-evangelization has taken place, the content of catechesis must be adapted "according to analogies, images, or forms of expression familiar to people of a given region or culture."[97]

Also of note, Bangkok's emphasis on evangelization led to a renewed emphasis on the baptismal catechumenate as the fundamental

93. See Erdozain, "Evolution of Catechetics," 93.

94. Gleeson, "History and Present Scene," 79.

95. See Theodore G. Stone, "The Bangkok Study Week," *Worship* (1963): 186–87: "The guiding principle of pre-evangelization is anthropocentric, because we must start from the non-believer and carefully respect his spiritual situation. This means taking the other seriously, his person, his conscience, his truths—even though these be fragmentary. It requires being alert to the non-believer's current interests and cares. The study week used the phrase 'positive apologetics' to describe this: 'Positive apologetics proceeds from a true understanding and appreciation of whatever is good and acceptable in a man's culture. It consists in taking due consideration of the man with whom we speak, and in removing the personal obstacles which prevent his ready acceptance of the kerygma.'"

96. See Mongoven, *Prophetic Spirit of Catechesis*, 54. The ripple effects of this shift are seen in the GCD when it states that "catechesis for adults, since it deals with persons who are capable of an adherence that is fully responsible, must be considered the chief form of catechesis. All other forms, which are indeed always necessary, are in some way oriented to it." See GCD, no. 20 [23].

97. Nebrada, "East Asian Study Week," 45.

process by which one converts and becomes a Christian.[98] Thus, the ancient liturgical practice gained new life as a modern school of catechesis.[99]

In sum, one can say that the East Asian study week provided two new overarching themes to the modern catechetical movement. First, if the kerygmatic movement had provided the initial impetus for joining evangelization and catechesis, then here at Bangkok both elements permanently joined hands.[100] The missionary context of the proceedings, by its very nature, placed catechesis under the umbrella of evangelization. Second, as noted earlier, the participants brought focused attention to the role of human experience. As one author put it, the participants "shifted from concern about the content of catechesis to the *subjects* of catechesis."[101] While it would be incorrect to say that Bangkok relegated content to the background entirely, it is nevertheless true that the beginnings of a new phase of renewal emerged from the study week's proceedings. The groundwork had been laid for an anthropological turn in modern catechesis.

Manila With the Second Vatican Council closing only two years prior, the participants of the 1967 study week in the Philippines saw in the conciliar documents an affirmation of the anthropological concerns of the renewal. A summary report of some of the discussion groups explains their overall approach to the Council:

[The Church] is called to become incarnate in local cultures, to dialogue sincerely with all Christians, all believers, and also with those who do not profess

---

98. Ibid., 47–48.

99. An outstanding introduction to the fourth-century baptismal catechumenate can be found in Edward Yarnold, *The Awe-Inspiring Rites of Initiation: The Origins of the RCIA*, 2nd ed. (Collegeville, Minn.: Liturgical Press, 1994). Here, once again, the ripple effects of the catechetical movement are felt, as the GDC states that "the model for all catechesis is the baptismal catechumenate." This should not be seen as limiting catechesis to the very practice of the liturgy, nor as a call to the strict imitation of the catechumenate in all catechetical settings. Rather, the catechumenate should "inspire the other forms of catechesis in both their objectives and in their dynamism." See GDC, no. 59 [53].

100. Nebrada notes that the first two phases of the modern catechetical movement paved the way for Bangkok's contribution, since they already envisioned catechesis apart from a Christian culture. See "East Asian Study Week," 45.

101. Mongoven, *Prophetic Spirit of Catechesis*, 54 (emphasis mine). Mongoven is not entirely correct with this assertion. It is true, as I have argued, that a noticeable shift took place; nevertheless, the summary report states that "the emphasis is on content more than on method. . . . Method is a servant but an indispensable one." See Nebrada, "East Asian Study Week," 43–44.

any religion. From being a ghetto the Church is called to give herself to the modern world, to share in its hopes and anxieties and to collaborate with all men of good will for the building of human communities of brotherhood, equality, justice, and peace. In so doing the Church would witness to the values of Christ in a manner intelligible and acceptable to men of our times.[102]

A key element in this perspective on the Council is the incarnational approach to local cultures, by which the discussion groups meant that the faith is to take the form, so to speak, of those to be catechized. In this incarnational approach, the emphasis is clearly on accessibility and intelligibility—on what the church shares with the experience of others—rather than condemnation or an ecclesial stance defined as a "ghetto" mentality.

Thus, as other papers suggested, more attention should be "devoted to finding out what 'is good in the minds and hearts of men,' what 'is true and holy in other religions,' and how to 'promote the spiritual and moral good found among those professing these religions, as well as the values in their society and culture.'"[103] Rather than imposing seemingly foreign dogmas, the church must harness "anthropological signs" and the ways in which "man expresses his fundamental aspirations in different societies."[104] In sum, in the past catechists had "stressed too much the aspects of rupture, judgment, and condemnation. Today we should stress Christianity as continuity and fulfillment."[105]

The freshness of this anthropological approach brought with it new challenges. First, if Christianity is described as "continuity and fulfillment," does this not imply that God is already at work in human experience apart from the church? And if so, would this not furthermore imply that salvation is already taking place before the kerygma is preached and accepted? Faced with reconciling their missionary impulses with Vatican II's teaching on the salvation of non-Christians, the participants at Manila wrestled with finding new motivation for the missionary apostolate.[106] As a corollary to this issue, the challenge of

---

102. "The Implications of Vatican II for the Mission in Asia," *Teaching All Nations* 4 (1967): 320–21. The author of the report is unnamed. The third issue of this volume of *Teaching All Nations* contains reports and papers from the Manila study week.

103. Labelle, "Appraisal of the Catechetical Situation," 286, referencing *Lumen Gentium*, no. 17, and *Nostra Aetate*, no. 2.

104. D. S. Amalorpavadass, "Workshop on Recent Developments," 379.

105. "The Implications of Vatican II," 322.

106. See John Bovenmars, "Vatican II and the Motivation of the Missionary Apostolate,"

pluralism began to emerge, especially in light of the encounter between Christianity and the Asian religions. If these religions indeed contain elements that are good and true, then perhaps conversion need not imply their outright rejection. Such elements could "be maintained even when someone is converted to Jesus Christ."[107]

It would be a mistake, nonetheless, to ascribe to all the participants at Manila an approach to human experience that exclusively emphasized its continuity with the faith. Some like George Delcuve posited a scheme in which the relationship between the faith and experience was characterized by Incarnation (continuity), Death (discontinuity), and Resurrection (transcendence).[108] For Delcuve, the continuity manifested in finding what is good and true in human experience must be balanced by the need for "people to become conscious of the limitations of those values, either profane or religious."[109] Any so-called "seeds of the Word," to use the patristic phrase, must be liberated, purified, and completed by the Gospel.[110]

Even with these considerations, the general tenor of Manila's proceedings gives weight to the anthropological aspects of catechesis over the theological ones. To use the phrasing of one of the study week's reports: in approaching non-Christians "we feel that Christianity would do well to meet them not vertically but horizontally. . . . In other words,

---

Teaching All Nations 4 (1967): 313–16. A helpful insight is given by Bovenmars when he states on pages 313–14, "The fundamental motivation of missionary activity is to be sought in the plan of God to communicate his life to men, not individually, but by constituting them into one holy people, which is the body of Christ and the temple of the Holy Spirit." See *Lumen Gentium*, no. 16. A more recent approach to this issue is found in Roch Kereszty, "Why a New Evangelization? A Study of Its Theological Rationale," *Communio* 21, no. 4 (1994): 594–611.

107. See "The Implications of Vatican II," 321: "It is particularly necessary to have a theology of the plurality of religions and the mission of the Church in this context. . . . Our attitude towards religions like Buddhism in many cases does not seem justifiable. In the past conversion to Christianity meant often a total denial of one's religious and cultural tradition and a rejection of all that was Buddhist. . . . Similarly it was said that missionaries generally took it for granted that a follower of Confucius had to give up his loyalty Confucius in order to be loyal to Jesus Christ. However the well-known convert Dom Lou points [out] that this is a totally mistaken idea and he professes to be a Confucianist and a Christian. Brahmabhanduev Upadhyaya, a famous Bengali convert, stated: 'I am Hindu by birth, I am Catholic by rebirth, I am a Catholic Hindu.' And the Buddhist monk Vajrapanna quite recently expressed his conviction that his loyalty to the Buddha did not prevent him from following the teaching of Jesus Christ."

108. See George Delcuve, "Some Reflections on Dialogue as Used in Pre-Evangelization," *Teaching All Nations* 4 (1967): 347.

109. Ibid.

110. Delcuve, "A Few Suggestions for Renewal in Catechetics after Vatican II," *Teaching All Nations* 4 (1967): 282.

it is through immanence that we lead them to transcendence."[111] The universal dimensions of the faith, brought to the fore by the Council, were received by the catechists at Manila as truths that "can make Christians aware of the spiritual riches of all mankind and at the same time make others see in Christianity the fulfillment of their own highest aspirations."[112]

Medellín In the year following the gathering in the Phillipines, emerging challenges in Latin America summoned pastors, catechists, and missionaries from around the world to gather once more, this time in Colombia. The atmosphere of unrest in Latin America caused the participants to reassess their understanding of catechesis with a particular urgency, for it provided the context of a "sub-continent boiling with indignation at the widening gap between rich and poor, the overfed and the starving. [The study week] was attended by priests, and not a few bishops, who were burdened with the thought that their people were deprived of the very necessities of life."[113] In stark terms, Jacques Audinet presents the tension that confronted the catechists of Medellín: "What is the value of what we are doing? Wouldn't it be better to commit oneself to another task—to give up catechizing and evangelizing in order to build the city of men?"[114]

The participants at Medellín did not eject the ecclesial dimensions of their work, but the surrounding unrest certainly played an important role in forming their catechetical vision. Coincident with the theology of liberation that was emerging from the same context, the catechesis promoted by the 1968 study week manifested an expansion of the priority of human experience to include social and communal dimensions, a strong emphasis placed upon human freedom and praxis, and an institutional embrace of pluralism.[115]

111. "The Implications of Vatican II," 322.

112. Ibid., 324.

113. Terrence J. Sheridan, "The Occasion," in *The Medellín Papers: A Selection from the Proceedings of the Sixth International Study Week on Catechetics Held at Medellín, Columbia, August 11–17, 1968*, ed. Johannes Hofinger and Terrence J. Sheridan (Manila: East Asian Pastoral Institute, 1969), 11. Sheridan continues, "It was the fact that the Sixth International Catechetical Study Week was held in a continent boiling with unrest and in an atmosphere of near revolution that called for the most outspoken declarations about the position of the Church and of catechetics."

114. Audinet, "Catechetical Renewal in the Present Situation," 58–59.

115. This study week was largely influential on the Second General Conference of Latin American Bishops (CELAM) of 1968, and indeed was its predecessor by a week. The conference

In one sense, Medellín takes up the role of experience precisely where Manila had left it: "Catechesis must be determined not only by the pastoral situation, but by what is most characteristic of today, namely, the problem of man himself, anthropology."[116] But in accepting the priority of anthropology, the participants at Medellín pushed beyond the conclusions of their predecessors, especially by viewing revelation within present experience. Their words are stronger in this regard: "Our contemporaries will not discover God—and if at all they discover him one day—except in man, at the very heart of interrogations on himself."[117]

Such an entering of the divine into what was previously considered the realm of the secular had immense consequences for the role of experience in catechesis. The theology of *Gaudium et Spes*, especially a particular reading of its use of the signs of the times, became the paradigm for Medellín's catechetical approach. Thus, one of the published general conclusions states:

Contemporary catechesis, in agreement with a more adequate theology of revelation, recognizes in the historical situations and in authentic human aspirations, the first sign to which we must be attentive in order to discover the plan of God for the men of today. Such situations therefore are an indispensable part of the *content* of catechesis.[118]

Human experience, therefore, is not a mere opening to revelation, nor a medium by which the content of catechesis is relayed. Rather, it is the content of catechesis itself.

The practical method that emerged from this new view took place in three stages. First, a catechist must help a group identify—in fact, be present to—its current situation. After cultivating this self-awareness, the catechist must then walk with the group, helping the people to see and live within the dynamic process by which their situation constantly changes. Finally, the catechist is to name Jesus and his teachings by

is often remembered for raising ecclesial awareness of liberation theology. See Komonchak, "Christ's Church in Today's World: Medellin, Puebla, and the United States," *Living Light* 17 (1980): 108–20. For more on liberation theology, see Gustavo Gutiérrez, *A Theology of Liberation: History, Politics, and Salvation*, rev. ed., trans. and ed. Caridad Inda and John Eagleston (New York: Orbis, 1988).

116. D. S. Amalorpavadass, "Guidelines for the Production of Catechetical Material," in Hofinger and Sheridan, *Medellín Papers*, 100.

117. Ibid., 101, quoting Jean Le Du.

118. Conclusion 11, from "General Conclusions of the International Study Week," in *The Medellín Papers*, 217. Emphasis mine.

way of a language that emerges from the life of the group itself. Such a catechesis is not imposed, but emerges from within the life of the community.[119]

One of the defining characteristics of this process is the emphasis it places on communal and social life. The participants at Medellín validated the experiential concerns of their predecessors, but found in the past a tendency to focus on experience in its individual dimension. But in the turmoil of Latin American society, the experience of injustice was the property belonging not only to one but many. If God reveals himself in the present, then he is at work not only in the aspirations and fears of an individual but in the history of society as well, past, present, and future.[120]

Furthermore, the participants argued that this revelation must—if it is to speak to the heart of Latin Americans—be made known in the community's struggle for liberation. Catechesis cannot rest contently with forming the catechized in the life of the church but must give priority to liberating praxis, critiquing unjust establishments and aiding the community in freeing itself from such institutions.[121] Thus, the catechists of Medellín felt they could not respond to injustice with "a more or less lucid, speculative perspective but on the basis of a will to act and become involved."[122]

In this light, one paper drew upon the work of the famous Brazilian educator Paulo Freire in recommending a liberating catechesis.[123] For

119. This is the method of Audinet, given in "Catechetical Renewal in the Present Situation," 63–67, and reiterated by Teresita E. Nitorreda, "The Search for New Meanings," in *The Medellín Papers*, 68–71. In sum, as Audinet puts it on page 67, "catechesis becomes the place where the Christian group creates its experience of Faith and invents a new language to express it."

120. See Conclusion 10, from "General Conclusions," 216: "Among the different forms of existence, community life has particular importance. Catechesis therefore cannot limit itself to the individual dimensions of life." See also Mongoven, *Prophetic Spirit of Catechesis*, 57. An interesting connection can be made—though to my knowledge it has not been done—between this shift in the Study Weeks and the influential theologies of Karl Rahner and his student Johann Baptist Metz. Rahner emphasized the role of human experience by paying particular attention to subjectivity and human transcendence. Metz critiqued his teacher, claiming that Rahner had ignored the political and social dimensions of Christianity. See Metz's *Faith in History and Society: Toward a Practical Fundamental Theology*, trans. David Smith (New York: Crossroad, 1980), 163–64.

121. See Erdozain, "Evolution of Catechetics," 99: "One should point to the option made in advance by the congress, one very characteristic of its attitude: the primacy of *action*" (emphasis in the original). See also Bryce, "Evolution of Catechesis," 228.

122. Erdozain, "Evolution of Catechetics," 99.

123. Antonio Cechin, "Evangelizing Men as They Are," in Hofinger and Sheridan, *Medellín Papers*, 131–36.

Freire, whose work continues to influence both secular and religious education today, "to educate is not to introduce someone into a ready-made world, but to help him transform the world."[124] Freire was adamantly opposed to any notion of content that could be deposited by the teacher into the mind of the learner—what he termed the "banking" model of education.[125] Rather, his method is one that seeks to make learners conscious of their surrounding situation, cultivating a critical attitude toward it, that they may free themselves from it by means of their own power and realizations. At Medellín, the method was "characterized by a certain spirit of rebellion, in the most human meaning of the expression."[126]

The critical eye fostered by this form of catechesis was to be aimed not only at so-called secular society but at the church as well, for it forms part of society.[127] Thus, as one author states, if the church had condemned aspects of the world in the past, it now must become "conscious of the fact that she is a part of the very structure she is condemning and that the whole social life of the Church emphasizes this identification. She cannot claim to be blameless when around her thousands are starving: she cannot say she is only concerned with spiritual matters."[128]

Along with the expanded role of experience and an emphasis on liberating praxis, Medellín also made a strong push for recognizing the value of pluralism in the catechetical enterprise.[129] In a sense, this

124. Ibid., 131.

125. See Paulo Freire, *Pedagogy of the Oppressed*, 30th Anniversary ed., trans. Myra Bergman Ramos (New York: Continuum, 2006), 72. Thomas Groome's understanding of religious education is largely influenced by Freire's work, including his opposition to a "banking" model of education. See Groome, *Christian Religious Education*, 175–77. From my own reading of Freire, it is unclear how his model of education can be appropriated by catechesis without correction on a fundamental level. Though he opposes outside content, liberating praxis can never be achieved, in a truly ecclesiological and theological sense, by remaining solely within the experience of the catechized. Revelation always maintains a transcendent character. Though not specifically addressing Freire, Lorenzo Albacete's thoughts are helpful in this regard. See Albacete's "The Praxis of Resistance," *Communio* 21, no. 4 (1994): 612–30.

126. Cechin, "Evangelizing Men as They Are," 131.

127. See François Houtart, "Reflections on the New Thinking in Latin America," in Hofinger and Sheridan, *Medellín Papers*, 72.

128. Ibid., 72–73. See also Berard Marthaler, *Catechetics in Context: Notes and Commentary on the General Catechetical Directory Issued by the Sacred Congregation for the Clergy* (Huntington, Ind.: Our Sunday Visitor, 1973), 13.

129. See ibid., 17.

valuing was the consequence of the other experiential and praxis-based emphases. Social experience undoubtedly varies from culture to culture, and liberation refuses any type of rigid conformity.[130] Thus, the participants were especially weary of attempts to establish a rigid catechetical system and the imposition of any notion of content that would originate from outside the local community. This is evidenced in the appeal they made to Cardinal Villot, president of the Congregation of the Clergy—the congregation charged, at the time, with creating a catechetical directory for the entire church (the *General Catechetical Directory* of 1971). The participants urged him to relay to Roman authorities that the directory *not* be presented to national hierarchies as a normative document, but that "it be promulgated in such a way that it leaves the national hierarchies free to exercise that flexibility of approach and expression so clearly indicated by the exigencies of this moment in history."[131]

In sum Medellín is, to use the words of Mary Charles Bryce, "a high-water mark" in the experiential phase of the modern catechetical movement.[132] It took the anthropological and experiential emphases of Bangkok and Manila and elevated them to new heights. Ultimately it defined catechesis as "the action by which a human group interprets its situation, lives it, and expresses it in the light of the gospel."[133] Thus, in this study week, one can see the completion of the transformation of catechesis in the modern era: from the imparting of the catechism, catechesis had indeed made an anthropological turn.

General Observations on the Third Phase

Looking back on the progression of the modern catechetical movement, Berard Marthaler notes that, "just as the proclamation of the word was the dominant characteristic of the second phase of the ... movement, the *interpretation of experience* is the distinguishing feature of the third phase."[134] Indeed, the earlier kerygmatic stage had placed Christ as the Word of God at the center of catechesis, but now, in this

---

130. Ibid., 19.

131. Nebrada, "Special Commission on International Cooperation," in Hofinger and Sheridan, *Medellín Papers*, 209. See also Conclusion 7, in "General Conclusions," 215.

132. Bryce, "Evolution of Catechesis," 228.

133. Audinet, "Catechetical Renewal in the Present Situation," 62.

134. Marthaler, "Modern Catechetical Movement," 282. Emphasis mine.

third phase, the need was felt to give greater attention to humanity. What had ultimately caused the shift?

The history of the movement indicates that the challenges emerging from missionary contexts and the ensuing focus on evangelization became the driving force of the anthropological turn.[135] Alfonso Nebrada, who is often cited as one of the main instigators of this turn, both summarized the issue and posed the question that would launch the third phase:

If you start by presuming that your audience believes, you are frequently just begging the question. This was the case in Japan. The Japanese missionaries felt a need to prepare the people before introducing them to the kerygma. The kerygma is a challenge from God urging man to make a decision. But before man can respond, he must realize he has been addressed. And that is the problem. If you start by presenting the Christian fact, you sense somehow that the audience feels as if you were talking to somebody else. They remain untouched. The words they hear mean little or nothing to them. They do not feel themselves challenged. Let us put the discussion in the form of a question. "Is a crisis developing in the kerygmatic movement?"[136]

135. The concern for evangelization was no doubt the main impetus for moving from the kerygmatic to the anthropological phase, but other factors played a role as well. For Mary Boys, the full account of the dénouement of the kerygmatic approach is incomplete without mentioning various theological, cultural, and educational factors. Theologically, new theologies of revelation (e.g., that of Gabriel Moran) were beginning to emphasize that revelation is less a matter of words or events but, rather, recognizing God in human experience. This will be analyzed in detail later. Likewise, biblical scholars began to abandon *Heilsgeschichte* as an approach to the scriptures, finding the notion of the New Testament fulfilling the Old to be a dogmatic imposition on the scriptural text and one that often fails to acknowledge the integrity of Judaism. Second, and with a distinctive focus on the United States, the 1960s provided an environment of social upheaval in which authority and more traditional religious categories were placed in doubt. Finally, education of both the secular and religious type began to manifest humanistic concerns and the influence of revisionist, praxis-based approaches. See chapter 3 of Boys, *Biblical Interpretation in Religious Education*, 140–273.

It is appropriate, I believe, to recognize that while Boys seems to approve of the jettisoning of salvation history by biblical studies and finds its use in catechesis exemplifying a "scriptural naiveté," it is nevertheless a notion that has its foundations in the tradition and can be rightly used in catechesis today, with appropriate distinctions. See, e.g., Pontifical Biblical Commission, *The Interpretation of the Bible in the Church*, trans. John Kilgallen and Brendan Byrne (Boston: Pauline Books and Media, 1993), 82–86 and 91–94; and Benedict XVI, *Verbum Domini*, nos. 37–40 [58–66, especially 64–65]. See also DV, nos. 12 and 16.

136. Nebrada, *Kerygma in Crisis?* (Chicago: Loyola University Press, 1965), 46. Nebrada's influence on the experiential phase is unquestionable; however, it would be incorrect to state that he advocated the rejection of the kerygma in favor of a method that focused solely on experience. Rather, he firmly believed in the necessity of both. Even at Medellín, at the height of the third phase, he acknowledged, "Let us repeat: the kerygma retains all its youthful freshness and appeal. The difficulty lies in how to *prepare* our youth to discover it and thus welcome

Nebrada's question was able to pierce through the perceived weaknesses of the kerygmatic establishment, being aided especially by what was seen as a lack in the kerygmatic theology of revelation.[137] For some, the catechesis of proclamation, while attempting to move past the catechetical scholasticism of the past, had erred by simply replacing the emphasis on doctrine with that of scripture. Exchanging "the old scholasticism with the new biblicism" had accomplished nothing, critics argued, in the way of reunifying the faith with life in the modern world.[138] It had merely replaced ineffective doctrinal propositions with facts of a history long past. Perhaps no one has been more vigorous in applying this critique of the kerygmatic model than Gabriel Moran, who explained his opposition in a work published in 1966:

The crucial question here is whether one is starting with real people and their real experience, elucidating that experience by an ever open and ever widening interpretation; or whether one begins with a set of truths that are self-interpretive and are imposed from the outside. And I would claim that a description of past events is—especially for a child—a set of propositional truths. A teacher with imagination can reconstruct a story from the past in a way that will catch the child's attention, but there is no way to make the events of some past life recorded in a story the facts of one's own life. The experience that Moses had of God may have been personal, concrete, and existential; but Moses is dead.[139]

While Moran's critique is both clear and forceful, what remains unclear is how much it can rightly be applied to the thought of Jungmann and Hofinger. Jungmann, for instance, did not seem to confine his vision of catechesis to the retelling of biblical stories; rather, salvation history was a means for encountering Jesus Christ and a way of manifesting Christ's lordship over all of history.[140] Likewise, the kerygmatic

---

it. This is the problem of catechesis" (emphasis in the original). See Nebrada, "Fundamental Catechesis," in Hofinger and Sheridan, Medellín Papers, 42.

137. See Calle, "Catechesis for the Seventies," 94.

138. Ibid. See also Gleeson, "History and Present Scene," 79–80; and Erdozain, "Evolution of Catechetics," 100–101. See Barker, Religious Education, Catechesis, and Freedom, 62, who goes so far as to claim that the kerygmatic worldview remained "supernaturalist."

139. Gabriel Moran, Catechesis of Revelation (New York: Herder and Herder, 1966), 46. This work is the second half of Moran's doctoral dissertation, published in two books. The first is Theology of Revelation (New York: Herder and Herder, 1966).

140. See Jungmann, Handing on the Faith, 106: "A presentation of a history of redemption, which reaches its culmination in Christ, makes it abundantly clear that he is the chief element of Christian doctrine. It also demonstrates in a very emphatic fashion that the Christian message is

emphasis on Christ's presence made manifest in the liturgy seems to belie the force of Moran's assessment. Ultimately, then, it is difficult to reconcile a view of kerygmatic catechesis as the mere recounting of past events with the total impulses, tenor, and content of Jungmann and Hofinger's work.

Still, it is quite possible that catechists influenced by this work were ill-equipped or unaware of its comprehensive outlook. Even the well-trained catechist, if uncritically accepting the rise of historical-critical approaches to the scriptures, could fall into the trap of approaching the Word of God as a distant artifact.[141] Thus, the reduction of the kerygmatic program to the telling of biblical events long past in actual catechetical practice may be where Moran's critique finds its real force.

Whatever the case, a new theology of revelation was being heralded by the catechesis of the third phase, one that looked for God less in past events than in the experience of the present. As such, this theology of revelation had the effect of shifting the focus of catechesis from the

---

rooted in the course of world history. At the same time the grandiose plan inherent in universal history is unfolded. Every event that takes place in the world is connected in some way or another with the kingdom of God, to which all men have been called."

141. A contributing factor to this misunderstanding of kerygmatic catechesis is undoubtedly found in the rise of historical-critical methods of interpreting scripture. Such methods are fruitful and necessary, especially for establishing the literal sense of scripture. Yet, when practiced apart from the church's tradition, the analogy of faith, and a view of the unity of the entire Bible, they become methods that remove the sacred text from the worshipping community in which it finds its rightful home (see DV, no. 12). As such, scripture becomes a dead letter, and Christ—the real focus of the kerygmatic emphasis on scripture—becomes extrinsic to the events of much of biblical history. With this point it is interesting to note the remarks of Gerard Sloyan, who in 1964 spoke at a gathering of catechists, theologians, and catechetical scholars: "Relevance, the Christ-life here and now, are matters that are being deferred because so much time is required to relate the Emmanuel prophecy to Jesus the Messiah or to reconstruct the post-exilic situation. Relating Assyria to the monolithic threats of bigness in the young lives of students, making Syria and Ephraim meaningful in terms of all the 'deals' they have witnessed by age fifteen in which canny men of little faith agree to sup with the devil—we are not finding time for that. Besides, it is mere accommodation. It departs from the primary literal sense. In other words, I find us retreating from the real work of catechetics because it is proving so satisfactory to teachers at the moment to give biblical lectures to young people. The reason? Well it is such a relief from the many years we spent giving them theological lectures. We have discovered the Bible lately, and we rush impetuously to share our treasure without taking time to do with it what the church has always done: teach Christ from it." Scripture will not find its rightful place as a source of catechesis until a new way of interpreting the texts, one that unifies the literal and spiritual senses, becomes the norm. See Gerard Sloyan, "Catechetical Crossroads," *Religious Education* 59, no. 2 (1964): 148–49. The entire article is worth noting both for the way it captures the initial embrace of the catechetical renewal in the United States and for the personal anecdotes of its author, a scholar who played a large role in bringing the insights of the renewal from Europe across the Atlantic.

realm of the sacred to that of the secular. Mary Perkins Ryan, as the editor of the only peer-reviewed catechetical journal in the Unites States, wrote in 1969:

Now, to many of us at least, the focus has radically changed. We realize that we are to look for God in daily life, in human experience, in human history.... We find Christ's presence not only in the assembled Christian community, in the scriptural word, and in liturgical celebrations, but also wherever love is present and active and where there is need of love—and his "sacral" modes of presence are to help us celebrate and discern and respond to his "secular" ones, not the other way around. Daily life can indeed be worship, both in the sense of a wondering, awestruck delight in God's presence, and in the sense of self-offering to his will. But liturgy, the formal worship of the Church, does not confer meaning or sacredness on daily life; it clarifies and celebrates the meaning already given human life by God in the risen Christ.[142]

The affirmation for this change was, Ryan noted, found in the Council's promulgation of *Gaudium et Spes*.[143] Catechists of the third phase believed that the Constitution, especially in the role it gave to reading the signs of the times, reversed the direction of catechetical interpretation. Rather than referring to the secular experience of the catechized to help them understand the sacred (i.e., scripture, liturgy, doctrine), catechesis would now refer to the sacred in order to interpret the secular.[144] In this light the general conclusions of Medellín, as already noted, state that catechesis must recognize "in the historical situations and in the authentic human aspirations [of the catechized], the first sign to which we must be attentive."[145]

This understanding of revelation, therefore, prompted a method in which the catechist sought to make hearers consciously aware of their present experience, that they might search for the meaning of it in light

142. Ryan, "Identity Crisis of Religious Educators," 11. Emphasis in the original.
143. Ibid., 12. See also Bournique, "Les Congrès de Manille," *Catéchèse* 29 (1967): 512.
144. See Calle, "Catechesis for the Seventies Part II," *Teaching All Nations* 7 (1970): 226: "It has been said that the revealed truths verbalized by the Magisterium and the biblical events found in the Holy Scripture are the source, the point of departure and the content of Catechesis. But are they? Properly speaking they are not. It is not the *written content* of Divine Revelation that must be considered as the source and point of departure of catechesis but the *living act* of God's self-communication to man, namely the on-going saving action of God as He actually reveals himself today within the mysterious ambiguity of human aspirations and of human history.... This is also the meaning of the Council's admonition: 'The Church has always the duty of scrutinizing the signs of the times and of interpreting them in the light of the Gospel.' Emphasis in the original.
145. Conclusion 11, in "General Conclusions," 217.

of the Gospel.[146] Such a method makes human experience part of the very "content of catechesis."[147]

It is in this affirmation that one finds one of the most remarkable aspects of the overall progression of the catechetical renewal. The modern catechetical movement, it can be recalled, emerged as a reaction to the conflation of content and method: the content of the faith—symbolized by the catechism—had overshadowed the method of teaching to the point where it became the method itself. The first phase of renewal, therefore, sought to correct this conflation in its embrace of the Munich Method, a pedagogical tool that could relate the content of the faith to the experience of the catechized. The pioneers of the second phase, while maintaining the methodological advancements of their predecessors, then took on the challenge of renewing the content of catechesis. In their heralding of the kerygma, this content was reattached to its Christological center, and the previous methods were refined to relate the proclamation of Christ to human experience. But here in the third phase, the movement comes full circle, and a complete transformation can be seen: in the words of Anne Marie Mongoven, now "the method of catechesis is a content."[148] Human experience is no longer a means to grasping the faith—it is the substance of the faith itself. In sum, "catechesis has become the interpretation of human experience."[149]

Assessing the Renewal

The modern catechetical movement emerged from a situation in which the content of the faith had become the method; yet, in its third phase, it heralded a pedagogy in which the method had become the content. This closing of the circle ultimately raises the question: did the renewal correct one conflation only to end up in another?

Answering such a pivotal question will ultimately require the use of the norms derived from the teaching of Vatican II in chapter 1. But, before making the comparison between the catechetical renewal and

---

146. See Calle, "Catechesis for the Seventies Part II," 227.

147. Conclusion 11, in "General Conclusions," 217.

148. Mongoven, *Prophetic Spirit of Catechesis*, 57. See also Piet Schoonenberg, "Revelation and Experience," in Warren, *Sourcebook*, 310; and Erdozain, "Evolution of Catechetics," 101.

149. Schoonenberg, "Revelation and Experience," 304.

the teaching of the Council, I believe some initial steps can be taken to aid in forming the beginning of an answer. The first step lies in an examination of the postconciliar ecclesial documents that manifest the influence of the catechetical movement, the second, in taking a closer look at the work of a scholar whose writings played an important role in implementing the catechetical renewal in the United States. The former offers a sense of the effect of the renewal on the church in its universal dimensions; the latter provides a more focused look at the difficulties of implementing the renewal in a particular region of the church.

The Renewal's Effect on Ecclesial Teaching

Two postconciliar documents in particular display the inheritance of the catechetical renewal. The *General Catechetical Directory* of 1971, published by decree from Vatican II, has been called a "symbol" of the ecclesial affirmation of the movement's best insights.[150] Likewise, Paul VI's apostolic exhortation *Evangelii Nuntiandi* stands as a landmark in the church's reflection on the ministry of the Word. It is a document that clearly evidences the effects of the renewal on the church worldwide in the aftermath of the Council.[151] I will consider both documents in turn.

The *General Catechetical Directory* is most certainly a consequence of the Second Vatican Council, but it is one that was unforeseen. Berard Marthaler notes that its creation was instigated by the recommendation of Bishop Pierre Marie Lacointe of France, who had "correctly anticipated that others would urge the resumption of a project left unfinished at the end of the First Vatican Council, namely, the redaction of a universal catechism for children."[152] Indeed at Vatican I, "next to the debates and discussions on the matter of papal infallibility," the call for such a catechism had "occupied more of the council's time than any other single issue."[153] Thus, it seemed likely that Vatican II would be "the logical time and place to act on that 'unfinished' business" of its predecessor.[154]

---

150. See Mongoven, "The Directories as Symbols of Catechetical Renewal," in *The Echo Within: Emerging Issues in Religious Education*, ed. Catherine Dooley and Mary Collins (Allen, Tex.: Thomas More, 1997), 131–32; and Mongoven, *Prophetic Spirit of Catechesis*, 64.

151. Here one could certainly include Pope John Paul II's *Catechesi Tradendae*, as well, but since John Paul II remains the focus of the next part of this study, I will examine his exhortation on catechesis in chapter 5.

152. Marthaler, *Catechetics in Context*, xvi.

153. Bryce, *Pride of Place*, 78.

154. Ibid., 139.

Lacointe's suggestion, while not anticipated, eventually gained traction. While some bishops, including those from the Eastern churches, argued for a catechism to ensure the uniformity of the faith in the face of growing diversity, it was eventually concluded that such a task was not feasible. Rather, other bishops argued, because "conditions differ greatly from country to country and individual to individual," it would be more useful to commission a catechetical directory.[155] Such a directory would contain rules and norms for catechesis, as well as the principal tenets of doctrine, leaving the application of these to Episcopal Conferences.[156] The directory would, therefore, be a reference text that could be applied to the varying experiences of the many cultures and peoples encompassed by the church.

The publication of the *General Catechetical Directory* thus became the official position of the Council.[157] It is not possible here to comprehensively cover the structure of the directory, along with the various insights it provides into the catechetical ministry, though this has been done elsewhere.[158] Still, I do think some mention can be made of those elements that evidence the effect of the modern catechetical movement. First and foremost among these is the fact that the directory itself, in a certain sense, embodies the flight from catechetical scholasticism that lay at the origin of the renewal. The Council fathers' recognition that publishing a universal catechism was not the proper course of action at

155. Marthaler, *Catechetics in Context*, xvii. Joseph Ratzinger, though greatly responsible for the eventual creation of the *Catechism of the Catholic Church*, likewise found the proposal to be untenable at the time. See Ratzinger and Cristoph Schönborn, *Introduction to the Catechism of the Catholic Church* (San Francisco: Ignatius Press, 1995), 12: "I expressed the opinion then that the time was not yet ripe for such a project, and I continue to believe that this evaluation of the situation was correct. Jean Guitton, it is true, is reported to have said that the present catechism comes twenty-five years too late, and in a certain respect one may agree with him in this assertion. On the other hand, it must also be said that in 1966 the full extent of the problem had simply not become visible; that a process of fermentation had just begun which could lead only gradually to the clarifications necessary for a new common word."

156. Marthaler, *Catechetics in Context*, xvii–xviii.

157. The directive for its creation is found in *Christus Dominus*, no. 44. See Maurice Simon, *Un Catéchisme Universel pour L'Église Catholique: Du Concile de Trente à Nos Jours* (Leuven: Leuven University Press, 1992), 284. For more on this history and the eventual creation of a new universal catechism, see Pedraza, "Catholic Disagreements and the Catechism's 25th Anniversary," *Church Life: A Journal for the New Evangelization* (October 24, 2017), http://churchlife.nd.edu/2017/10/24/catholic-disagreements-and-the-catechisms-25th-anniversary/.

158. Marthaler's *Catechetics in Context*, cited earlier, is the most comprehensive reference in English.

the time is, in a certain regard, a vindication of the rejection of the older way of doing catechesis.[159]

Second, and in conjunction with what has just been said, the directory situates catechesis in the Council's developed theology of revelation. Part Two, titled "The Ministry of the Word," begins by reiterating the teaching of *Dei Verbum* and ends by placing catechesis upon this foundation. It therefore explains how the Word reveals himself, then describes catechesis as a ministry of this Word, that which is "intended to make men's faith become living, conscious, and active, through the light of instruction."[160] In short, "God appears as one who wishes to communicate himself, carrying out a plan which proceeds from love. Catechesis, then, ought to take its beginning from this gift of divine love."[161] In such a conception of catechesis, the directory has clearly embraced the vision of catechesis that reinserts the doctrinal emphases of neo-scholasticism into the greater totality of the person of Jesus Christ while acknowledging the unity of revelatory words and deeds.[162] The modern catechetical movement's constant attention to the need for a more adequate theology of revelation is thus manifested here.

Last, because catechesis is aimed at a living, conscious, and active faith, the directory establishes that the chief form of the ministry is the catechesis of adults.[163] While seeming to be, on the surface, a simple expansion of the catechetical audience, this declaration is actually an affirmation of one of the greatest gains of the movement, for it moves

159. See Berard L. Marthaler, "Catechetical Directory or Catechism? *Une Question Mal Posée*," in *Religious Education and the Future*, ed. Dermot A. Lane (New York: Paulist Press, 1986), 55–70. Marthaler ultimately claims that directories should not be opposed to catechisms, expressing that both have to be adapted to the needs of nations and more local regions. Indeed, the GCD claims that "the greatest importance must be attached to catechisms published by ecclesial authority" in no. 119 [68]. Nevertheless, that Marthaler's article is even necessary reveals the nature of the tensions that have been and continue to be present in catechetical scholarship since the Council. The question can only be *mal posée* if it was posed in the first place.

For another perspective, see Eugene Kevane, Introduction to *Teaching the Catholic Faith Today: Twentieth Century Catechetical Documents of the Holy See* (Boston: Daughters of St. Paul, 1982), liii–lvi, where Kevane correctly situates the directory as a product of John XXIII's council, yet also gives numerous examples in which the pontiff also stressed the importance of catechisms.

160. GCD, no. 17 [22], quoting *Christus Dominus*, no. 14. Interestingly, the directory calls the ministry of the Word an "act of living tradition"; it gives "voice to this living tradition, within the totality of tradition." See no. 13 [20].

161. GCD, no. 10 [18–19].

162. See GCD, nos. 11–12, 39–41.

163. See GCD, no. 20. See also Mongoven, "Directories as Symbols," 135.

faith from pure notional assent—for example, the memorization of doctrines by children—to the commitment that can only be realized most fully in adults: a commitment of the entire person. Such an adult commitment requires that catechesis address human experience and freedom in order to show the faith's relevance for the whole of life.[164]

While acknowledging these important aspects, those that form the heart of the renewal's third phase, the directory nonetheless issues a word of caution. It does so by stating that the church is entering into a sort of catechetical "crisis," flanked on one side by those who claim that "the issue here [is] merely one of eliminating ignorance of doctrine," yet on the other by those "who are inclined to reduce the Gospel message to the consequences it has in men's temporal existence."[165] Here the directory, at the very same time, finds fault with those who reject the results of the catechetical renewal entirely, as well as those who push the third phase's conclusions to the point of being discontinuous with previous tradition. It likewise envisions a catechesis in which content is united to method while nevertheless remaining distinct from it. Thus, in accord with the teaching of Vatican II itself, the directory clearly embraces a catechetical hermeneutic of tradition.

Certainly, with the noted cautions, the *General Catechetical Directory* manifests clear indications of affirming the catechetical renewal. It is, however, not the only evidence of the movement's effect on ecclesial teaching. Pope Paul VI's *Evangelii Nuntiandi*, promulgated in 1975, is likewise a testament to the long-lasting effects of the renewal.[166] The product of the pope's reflection upon the 1974 Synod of Bishops on evangelization, the exhortation echoes the consistent refrain of the catechetical movement, especially in its third phase, that catechesis must be intimately tied to the mission of evangelization.[167] Thus, rath-

164. See GCD, nos. 26 and 74 on experience and 61 on human freedom. Regarding experience, no. 74 [49] is notable for the way it both affirms experience and cautions that it "must be illuminated by the light of revelation.... This task, even though it is not without its difficulties, must not be overlooked." This somewhat moderates Mongoven's claim in *Prophetic Spirit of Catechesis*, 67, that the directory "moved the church from an instructional model of catechesis into an anthropological model which focused on the experience of people and their faith."

165. GCD, no. 9 [17].

166. I have used the version found in Pope Paul VI, *Evangelii Nuntiandi*, Vatican translation, in *The Catechetical Documents*, 157–99; AAS 68 (1976): 5–76. Henceforth, EN.

167. Michael Warren, in his brief introduction to Piere-André Liégé's "Ministry of the Word: From Kerygma to Catechesis," 1:313, claims that "one finds clear echoes of Liégé's thought in Pope Paul VI's apostolic exhortation on evangelization, *Evangelii Nuntiandi*, echoes

er than seeing catechesis as a stage that follows an evangelizing initial stage, the document sees evangelization as the totality of the church's mission, with catechesis as an aspect of the whole. In the words of Paul VI, evangelization is "the grace and vocation proper to the Church, her deepest identity."[168]

According to the pope, evangelization consists of various factors, including personal witness, preaching, the Liturgy of the Word, the utilization of mass media, person-to-person contact, the celebration of the sacraments, and popular piety. Most important for this study is the statement in article 44 that "a means of evangelization that must not be neglected is that of catechetical instruction."[169] An evangelizing catechesis, the pope notes, must "form patterns of living" rather than remaining "only notional."[170] Likewise, echoing the *General Catechetical Directory*, it must be given not only to children but to "adults who, touched by grace, discover little by little the face of Christ and feel the need of giving themselves to him."[171]

One cannot help but also note the comparatively large amount of space Paul VI devotes to the liberating aspect of evangelization in articles 29–39. The direct concerns of the study week at Medellín and the affirmation of those concerns in the gathering of Latin American bishops that immediately followed are evidenced in his words.[172] The pope acknowledges the role of liberation in the church's mission, explaining that the duty of "assisting the birth of this liberation, of giving witness to it, [and] of ensuring it is complete . . . is not foreign to evangelization."[173] Indeed, there are "profound links" between evangelization and liberating praxis, including "links of an anthropological order, because

---

which suggest that Liégé himself may have written one of the earlier drafts of that important document." Liégé, it can be recalled, was one of the first to speak of pre-evangelization as a stage in the catechizing of people in missionary lands.

168. EN, no. 14 [161].

169. EN, no. 44 [173]. See Liégé, "Ministry of the Word," 1:321: "There are not two kinds of faith nor two successive stages of faith—stage of conversion, stage of doctrinal belief—but two dialectic elements of Christian faith, one living reality."

170. Liégé, "Ministry of the Word," 1:321.

171. Ibid.

172. See especially EN, no. 30 [168], which mentions the "Bishops from the Third World" who voiced the concerns of people engaged in the "struggle to overcome everything which condemns them to remain on the margin of life."

173. Ibid.

the man who is to be evangelized is not an abstract being but is subject to social and economic questions."[174]

While acknowledging these anthropological aspects of liberation, the pope nevertheless gives an appropriate caution, reminiscent of the concerns of the General Directory in warning against those who would limit the Gospel's effects to the temporal sphere. Thus, along with the anthropological links between evangelization and liberation there also stand "links in the theological order, since one cannot dissociate the plan of creation from the plan of redemption."[175] More specifically, and with a keen insight into the nature of the church, Paul VI explains:

We must not ignore the fact that many, even generous Christians who are sensitive to the dramatic questions involved in the problem of liberation, in their wish to commit the Church to the liberation effort are frequently tempted to reduce her mission to the dimensions of a simply temporal project. They would reduce her aims to a man-centered goal; the salvation of which she is the messenger would be reduced to material well-being. Her activity, forgetful of all spiritual and religious preoccupation, would become initiatives of the political or social order. But if this were so, the Church would lose her fundamental meaning.[176]

Thus, once again, the catechetical movement—especially in its concluding phase—is affirmed, yet it is also cautioned about becoming trapped in its rightful anthropological concerns. An anthropological catechesis must include a transcendent dimension, one open to that which is greater than human experience and that can ultimately redeem it.

With similar balance, *Evangelii Nuntiandi* also considers the affirmation of pluralism that Medellín had championed in its proceedings. Article 61 speaks of the church's universality, but it is immediately followed by article 62's mention of the local churches. Thus, the church is, as the first Christians believed, a "being spread throughout the universe ... which neither space nor time can limit"; yet the "universal Church is in practice incarnate in the individual churches made up of such or such an actual part of mankind, speaking such and such a language, heirs of a cultural patrimony, of a vision of the world, of a historical past, of a particular substratum."[177] The effect of this dual affirmation

174. EN, no. 31 [168].
175. Ibid.
176. EN, no. 32 [168–69].
177. EN, nos. 61 and 62, respectively [182–83].

is appropriately twofold: evangelization must "take into consideration the actual people to whom it is addressed," speaking to their experience; yet it also "risks losing its power and disappearing altogether if one empties or adulterates its content under the pretext of translating it; if, in other words, one sacrifices this reality and destroys the unity without which there is no universality, out of a wish to adapt a universal reality to a local situation."[178] Evangelization, therefore, must always integrate the local with the universal; catechesis, as an aspect of evangelization, must do the same. Indeed, the faith must become incarnate in the experience of the catechized, but it must also retain its universal dimension lest the faith of a local community become detached from the faith of the church at large.

Altogether, the ecclesial vision of catechesis in the postconciliar documents is balanced in its affirmation of the modern catechetical movement. Both the *General Catechetical Directory* and *Evangelii Nuntiandi* willingly appropriate the best insights of the renewal, though, in them, one gains a sense of the great difficulty faced in practically implementing these insights. It seems that *aggiornamento*, whether conciliar or catechetical, is destined to garner interpreters who find in it a substantive break with the tradition.[179] These ecclesial documents, however, envision a catechetical renewal in which the best elements of each era's pedagogy—even that of the days of catechism instruction—are embraced and integrated into the present practice of the ministry of the Word.

The Effect of the Renewal as Seen in the Writings of Gabriel Moran

A second step toward assessing the modern catechetical movement lies in examining its effects on catechesis in a particular region of the church. I especially have in mind the United States, both because it is my own country and because, as a Western nation, it is a point of focus for the New Evangelization. But even more, I believe it deserves particular attention for the way in which it manifests the effect of the third phase of the catechetical renewal.

The third phase of the movement, with its experiential focus, was undoubtedly the most influential contributor to catechetical practice in

---

178. EN, no. 63 [184].

179. Of course, some welcome the perceived break; others reject it as an unwelcome accommodation to the present.

the church after the Council. Though this focus emerged from missionary lands, it has since become a predominant paradigm for catechesis in the Western world. As Thomas Groome states, "A counting of heads among contemporary theorists indicates that there has been a significant shift toward a mode of knowing that is relational, experiential, and active"; Groome advocates a praxis-based approach to religious education.[180]

In the United States, experience has, in particular, come to dominate much of the catechetical landscape. Marthaler notes that "experience is a theme which runs through the educational literature of the United States like a haunting melody."[181] The melody is, for catechesis, heard at its loudest in the work of the religious educator Gabriel Moran.[182] Moran, "in the decade after the publication of his two works *Theology of Revelation* and *Catechesis of Revelation* . . . had unrivaled influence on catechesis in the United States," and the main lines of his thought persist in much of the catechetical scholarship of the present.[183]

As such, I believe it will be helpful to briefly discuss Moran's work, for he represents one of the most influential inheritors of the catechetical renewal in American catechesis. This brief look also provides the benefit of tying the theories of the third phase of the movement to a specific vision of catechesis that has been widely influential in actual educational practice. While it will not be possible to cover his work comprehensively, I wish to bring attention to the salient points of his thought—those that bear particular importance for this study.

Gabriel Moran's writings on catechesis and revelation are significant in that they, for many American educators and theologians, provided the theological foundation for the demise of the kerygmatic phase. Alfonso Nebrada, it can be recalled, had asked at the cusp of the third

---

180. Groome, *Christian Religious Education*, 146. See also his "Remembering and Imaging," *Religious Education* 98, no. 4 (2003): 511–20; and "Old Task: Urgent Challenge," *Religious Education* 78, no. 4 (1993): 492–96.

181. Marthaler, "Modern Catechetical Movement," 282. He continues, "Some contend it is simply another aspect of American pragmatism. Despite a certain abhorrence among Roman Catholics for John Dewey's philosophy of education earlier in the century, his influence in contemporary catechetics is as unmistakable as it is pervasive." For Dewey's role in the acceptance of experiential catechesis in the U.S. see John Dewey, "Religious Education as Conditioned by Modern Psychology and Pedagogy," *Religious Education* 69, no. 1 (1974): 6–11.

182. See Boys, *Biblical Interpretation in Religious Education*, 244–47.

183. Marthaler, "Modern Catechetical Movement," 281.

phase whether the kerygma was entering into a time of crisis. As one study notes, while Nebrada had "raised the catechetical question," it was Gabriel Moran who ultimately "formulated the theological response."[184]

Moran's response to the question is decidedly affirmative. His work seeks to correct what he deems to be an inadequate notion of divine revelation present in the kerygmatics' approach and in the earlier neo-scholastic method. He does so mainly by removing divine revelation from the notion of objective content—whether conceived as doctrinal statements or the proclamation of specific events of history—and placing it in the consciousness of the human person. The guiding thought of his work is captured in a line from an article published in 1964: "When the word 'revelation' is used as a noun in the objective sense and when one asks where this exists, the only answer would seem to be: in the consciousness of man."[185] Thus, for Moran, "man does not believe in statements or truths, nor does he believe in events; he believes in God revealed in human experience and consciousness."[186]

The writings that gave him prominence as a catechetical scholar, *Theology of Revelation* and *Catechesis of Revelation* (both published in 1966), can be considered an explication of this principle. While the former focuses primarily on revelation as the personal and existential experience of God's presence, the latter offers the implications of this notion for catechetical ministry.

In the first book, Moran defines revelation in terms of intersubjectivity. Thus, it is a "historical and continuing intersubjective communion in which man's answer is part of the revelation"; or once again, "revelation is a personal union in knowledge between God and a participating subject in the revelational history of a community."[187] This understanding of revelation is articulated by Moran by means of modern epistemological and ontological categories. For instance, he criticizes the tendency of the past to identify knowledge with "concepts and words"—thereby rejecting the earlier scholastic view—instead opting for the position that "human knowledge is the inner presence of being

---

184. Didier-Jacques Piveteau and J. T. Dillon, *Resurgence of Religious Instruction: Conception and Practice in a World of Change* (Notre Dame, Ind.: Religious Education Press, 1977), 53.

185. Gabriel Moran, "What Is Revelation?," *Theological Studies* 25, no. 2 (1964): 225.

186. Ibid.

187. Moran, *Theology of Revelation*, 50 and 93, respectively.

to itself mediated by its relation to the other."[188] The union of knower and known is therefore not merely cognitive, though it is "brought to full reflexive consciousness only by progressive conceptual expression and dialogue."[189] Applied to the realm of theology, the union between God and human persons is, for Moran, foundationally present before one even forms concepts or words about it.

Here one catches echoes of the philosophy of Joseph Maréchal or, more precisely, the theological appropriation of it by Karl Rahner.[190] Rahner's mix of Thomism with Kantian epistemology had led him to famously posit that human beings are, in the transcendence of their own subjectivity, always and already in contact with God as the ground of all being.[191]

The Rahnerian influence upon Moran is most readily apparent when he speaks of the way in which God reveals himself to the individual:

188. Ibid., 84. Contrast this with the position of Aquinas, in which all knowledge comes by way—indeed, only by way—of concepts and words. See ST I, q. 16, a. 2.

189. Moran, Theology of Revelation, 85. If such a description of revelatory knowledge seems a bit inaccessible, then surely one can take heart in the fact that even the estimable Avery Dulles claims that Moran's "thought on this subject is by no means easy to follow." See Dulles, Models of Revelation, 105.

190. See Moran, Theology of Revelation, 34: "Within the Catholic tradition and more immediately related to our subject, the ontology of knowledge in the work of Joseph Marcéhal and Karl Rahner would seem to be of incalculable importance for a theology of revelation." Indeed, the index of the book indicates Rahner's influence on Moran more than any other scholar. See Joseph Maréchal, Le point de départ de la métaphysique, vol. 5, 2nd ed. (Paris: Desclée de Brouwer, 1949); and the summa of Rahner's thought, Foundations of Christian Faith: An Introduction to the Idea of Christianity, trans. William V. Dych (New York: Crossroad, 1978).

191. Rahner's work is, in part, an attempt to address the Kantian critique of reason by claiming that, rather than God being a useful but unverifiable assumption of practical reason, he is in fact the ground from which all human knowing finds its foundation. Two great difficulties with Rahner's thesis, bearing some importance for this study, come to mind, the first being how one can adequately distinguish between the natural, so to speak, orientation of humans to being and the gratuitous supernatural existential that is present in every person. It is helpful to recall that Rahner's thesis was, in part, a response to the controversy surrounding de Lubac's claim concerning the natural desire to see God. Rahner posited that the unthematic communion with God was an "existential" precisely so as to say that it is not a matter of human nature but rather one of "existence." For his part, de Lubac considered Rahner's solution unsatisfying. See chapter 6, footnote 2 of Mystery of the Supernatural, 102: "Really, to the extent that this 'existential' is conceived as a kind of 'medium' or 'linking reality,' one may object that this is a useless supposition, whereby the problem of the relationship between nature and the supernatural is not resolved, but only set aside." The second difficulty is an extension of the first, for, if it is difficult to adequately distinguish the transcendence of human subjectivity from the gratuity of God's action, then it becomes unclear how any notion of God's revelation can escape from the confines of subjectivism. For more on this critique, see Paul D. Molnar, "Can We Know God Directly? Rahner's Solution from Experience," Theological Studies 46, no. 2 (1985): 228–61.

The foundation of the individual's revelatory experience, therefore, resides in the gracious presence of the Spirit who penetrates human existence at its highest point, thus affecting "the *a priori* 'mental horizon' which we are conscious of in being conscious of ourselves." . . . [Thus, God] does not intermittently offer "truths" for man's mind. Instead, he begins by knowing and loving man with a love that is transforming. When that divine activity in man's life emerges into conscious experience, man comes to know the one who is closer to him than he is to himself.[192]

If, as Moran holds, such an ontological and epistemological foundation undergirds the human encounter with divine revelation, it then follows that catechesis must abandon the notion of transmitting content:

There is a very important sense in which every Christian receives (or takes part in) revelation immediately; that is, he receives it not from men or books but from the indwelling Spirit. The definite part that holy Scripture, Church doctrine, official teachers, and other believing Christians play is a large one and we shall look to these shortly. What I wish to oppose here, nevertheless, is the supposition that revelation can be something outside man, something which can be passed down over the centuries, something which can be delivered to man by other men. God reveals and man believes; there is no revelation unless God is now acting and unless a human consciousness is now responding.[193]

Moran's vision of catechesis is thus much more focused on the present encounter with God than it is on particular words or formulations handed on from the past. Still, he does not, as is apparent in the previous quotation, entirely dismiss the role of propositions in the revelatory process. For Moran, "God completes the revelational process by speaking words of human love"; such words draw "forth from the pre-reflexive, entitative, and intentional union a wealth of meaning. . . . The revelatory experience for the individual is thus made complete by the word drawing grace into the conscious experience of faith."[194] In this light it is notable that Moran clearly does not neglect to recommend the teaching of scripture and doctrine in catechesis, even holding them to be necessary parts of the process.[195] They are, furthermore, not merely human attempts to express the unthematic knowledge of God

192. Moran, *Theology of Revelation*, 149–50, in part quoting Rahner.
193. Ibid., 92.
194. Ibid., 151.
195. See, for instance, Moran, *Catechesis of Revelation*, 76–89 and 103–15, in which he respectively addresses the place of both in catechesis.

but are inspired and divinely guided formulations against which a student must weigh his or her experience.[196] As such I believe that, while the Rahnerian foundation to his catechetical theory is not necessarily the most firm, Moran has nevertheless formulated an understanding of catechesis in *Theology of Revelation* and *Catechesis of Revelation* that can be adequately reconciled with ecclesial teaching concerning the ministry.

While the ecclesial context of catechesis is rightly recognized in Moran's earliest writings, the same cannot be said, by his own admission, in the works that were to follow. Within a few years after the publication of *Theology of Revelation* and *Catechesis of Revelation*, Moran's vision of revelation and catechetical ministry had changed considerably. Now, in a striking turn, he believed that catechesis was better off fading to nonexistence.[197]

The shocking boldness of such a claim can only be understood against the backdrop of two simultaneous developments: on the one hand, Moran's acceptance of the growing American vision of education and, on the other, his developing understanding of revelation, which was an outgrowth of his earlier conception. In terms of education, Moran's later works evidence a general acceptance of progressivism in educational practice. He rejected the pedagogy by which a teacher communicates a body of content to his or her students; rather, he insisted upon "helping a person to think in a manner that will enable him to find his own answers at a later time."[198] Such an educational philosophy regards teachers as "underminers," so to speak, for they help students chal-

---

196. See Moran, *Theology of Revelation*, 113: "The ordinary personal experience of the Christian must be constantly measured for its truth against the Church's objective norm"; and Moran, *Catechesis of Revelation*, 109: "It is theologically false to drive a wedge between the gospel and later doctrinal reflections as if the latter were mostly corruptive. What is needed is not less doctrinal reflection upon the gospel by students, but much more of it. Provided that the students are reflecting upon the reality testified to by the holy Scripture, then the more doctrinal the teaching is, the better."

197. See Moran, *Design for Religion: Toward Ecumenical Education* (New York: Herder and Herder, 1970), 9: "Two years ago I published a collection of essays on religious education entitled *Vision and Tactics*. At the time, a priest from the Midwest wrote me a letter highly critical of the book. He wanted to know why I did not treat real practical issues like the catechetical material from publishers. I wrote back to him and suggested . . . that the problem of catechetics is that it exists. After saying that a field should not exist it is difficult to get excited about some of the practical problems of the field." See also Moran's republished article, "The Intersection of Religion and Education," in *Who Are We? The Quest for a Religious Education*, ed. John H. Westerhoff (Birmingham, Ala.: Religious Education Press, 1978), 237.

198. Moran, *Vision and Tactics: Toward an Adult Church* (New York: Herder and Herder, 1968), 21.

lenge and critique the orthodoxy of tradition.[199] From this perspective, there can actually be no real field of "catechesis" that is distinct from education in general, for the educator is less concerned with any version of content—even religious content—but is much more concerned with raising the critical consciousness of his or her students. The unexpected but logical conclusion follows: the more successful a religious educator is, the more the field of catechesis disappears.[200]

In this educational philosophy, one can already begin to glimpse the second factor that contributed to Moran's proclamation of a catechetical death knell. For, just as he claimed there can ultimately be no specific Christian education, so too did he advance that there can be no specific claim to revelation by Christians. Divine revelation, occurring in human experience, is "ecumenical" by nature, which is to say that "a God who has involved himself in partnership with all men is revealed wherever there are men."[201] As such, the church should "give up the language of 'revealed truths' and 'Christian revelation,'" for "Christianity is set squarely within the context of a world history where Christians must search for the truth with everyone else."[202]

In a sense, Moran's new position was simply the outgrowth of what he had previously claimed when he wrote *Theology of Revelation* and *Catechesis of Revelation*. To claim that revelation is universal is easily deduced from the position that all human beings are always and already in contact with God in the very subjectivity of their experience. The difference in these later works, however, lies in his new understanding of what was particularly Christian. Previously, he had held that the scriptures and church teaching were objective norms by which to measure experience and that they claimed such a role precisely because they were products of divine, and not just human, action. But now he held that Christianity

---

199. Moran, *Design for Religion*, 14–15: "[Teachers] are usually dumbfounded when they are charged with undermining the faith of their students and destroying Catholic tradition. They ought to recognize that to a large extent the accusation is valid. They are underminers not mainly because they have failed as teachers but because the educational process itself has that effect upon faith and tradition. . . . One has only to engage in the educative process at all for this undermining to occur. This fact is obscured in many arguments over the orthodoxy of what is being taught. The more important question is whether the words orthodoxy and education are at all compatible." This critical pedagogy resonates with the method of Medellín, though obviously pushes further than the study week's own conclusions.

200. Ibid., 15.

201. Ibid., 40.

202. Ibid., 41.

was merely "one of the necessary embodiments of man's permanent religious quest."[203] As such, so-called objective norms are human in origin and thus changeable; they are, in a reversal of his previous position, subject to the true norm of experience:

People who demand that there be a higher norm of truth than human experience are asking for an idol. Man has no recourse in his life except to turn to what is finite. He can submit, as he is always tempted to submit, to a text or a ruler or an institution built by his own hands. There is no lack of things available and waiting for divinization. His only other alternative is to follow his own human experience and to pursue it wherever it takes him. If there be a God, must not his voice be heard within the experience of a man who listens with all other men for the voice of the divine?[204]

Working from this new perspective, Moran began to manifest a stronger aversion to objective norms. By 1972 he claimed that, because revelation is at its core an interpersonal relationship, all truth is therefore relative: "Being relative or related to others becomes the stabilizing and guiding factor for each statement of truth. The whole matrix of interrelationships becomes the starting point for understanding."[205] Furthermore, the imposition of absolutes was an affront to human autonomy. For Moran, freedom is "given with humanness and must be experienced and asserted as the primary category of life."[206] Indeed, the relativity of truth—contrary to the Christian criticism of modern notions of freedom—is demanded by freedom itself: "It is not relationship but one particular kind of relation that is incompatible with freedom, namely, that arrangement whereby someone else is in control and has the answers before the questions are asked."[207]

203. Ibid., 42. Moran continues, "The main problem is not that the church thought it had a message but that it forgot that the message was its own. The church's message is the church's and not God's. . . . There is quite a definite message of Christianity and it is neither more nor less than *an interpretation of the whole of experience*" (emphasis mine). Interestingly, Guy Mansini finds the same development in Rahner, from the initial publication of his *Hearer of the Word* to the revised edition, *Hearers of the Word* (edited by J. B. Metz) and his later works. See Mansini's "Experiential Expressivism and Two Twentieth-Century Catholic Theologians," *Nova et Vetera* 8 (2010): 125–41, especially 131–41. An insightful critique of Rahner's approach to universality and particularity, one that I believe is helpful when likewise applied to Moran's work, is offered by Joseph Ratzinger in *Principles of Catholic Theology: Building Stones for a Fundamental Theology*, trans. Mary Frances McCarthy (San Francisco: Ignatius Press, 1987), 162–71.

204. Moran, *Design for Religion*, 45–46.

205. Moran, *The Present Revelation: The Search for Religious Foundations* (New York: Herder and Herder, 1972), 9.

206. Ibid., 52.

207. Ibid.

Ultimately, then, the scholarship of Gabriel Moran came to give greater weight to present experience over the past, human freedom over absolute truth, and universality over particularity. He thus exploded the boundaries of ecclesial ministry by arguing for its very nonexistence. Such a bold claim may seem unpalatable to many catechists today, and some may find Moran's later positions opposed to the earlier works that made him influential in the first place. While this may be the case, I believe it is fair to say that the seeds of catechetical discontent were sown in his earlier writings. In them, though Moran had rightly recognized the place of scripture and doctrine in the revelatory process, he nevertheless showed a tendency to prefer the present to the exclusion of the past, embracing an understanding of revelation that, once taken to an extreme, failed to adequately reconcile the particularity of the church with the universality of God's speaking and acting. Catechetically, this likewise opened the door to an inadequate reconciliation of scripture and church teaching—as objective manifestations of revelation—with the subjectivity of human experience.[208]

Comparing the Modern Catechetical Movement to the Teaching of Vatican II

Moran's work is but one example of no doubt many in which an educator or catechist seeks to come to terms with the challenges of the modern world. The balance between the immanence of human experience and the transcendence of divine revelation, between the plurality of human life and the universality of the faith, is an issue that emerges from the heart of the modern catechetical movement to confront the church in the New Evangelization.[209] Catechesis for the New Evangelization must ultimately address and resolve this tension if it is to effectively speak to the experience of men and women today.

Here it is helpful to remember the Council's teaching on revelation and the human person, for the pedagogy of the church must always stem from and participate in the pedagogy of God—that is, it must

208. This trajectory persists in Moran's recent works. See, for instance, *Believing in a Revealing God: The Basis of the Christian Life* (Collegeville, Minn.: Liturgical Press, 2009).

209. This is evident not only in the church's ministry of catechesis but also in the practice of theology. The confluence of revelation and experience is, in a certain sense, at the heart of the teaching of Vatican II and thus affects the entirety of the church's reflection on revelation and its meaning for the modern world.

stem from the way in which God reveals himself and calls upon men and women to respond in faith. The norms from chapter 1, therefore, can serve as a summary of the relevant teaching of the Council and can likewise act as guidelines by which to measure the modern catechetical movement. Such a comparison can bring to light those aspects of the movement that are substantial gains while revealing elements that require further updating or correction.[210]

(1) *Revelation is Christocentric.* The history of the modern catechetical movement testifies to the fact that the greatest problem with preconciliar catechism instruction was its lack of connection to the person and work of Jesus Christ. In this sense, some within the neo-scholastic tradition had unwittingly strayed from the thought of the master they wished to imitate. St. Thomas had explained that "the believer's act [of faith] does not terminate in the propositions, but in the realities [that they express]."[211] But, detached from the person of Christ, such propositions are condemned to become the facts of trivia, like the names and dates of a history book that are often forgotten in a short while. Certainly, the first phase of renewal tried to remedy this type of pedagogy, striving to make doctrine meaningful by use of accessible stories; however, apart from the use of gospel accounts in this context, such methodological advances remained susceptible to the same problem— doctrine remained disconnected from Christ.

The second phase was better in this regard, and it stands as the most clearly Christocentric of the movement. Jungmann's assertion that Christ is the center of all reality, both secular and spiritual, was a definitive call to reconnect all aspects of the church's faith to their rightful unifying core. Thus, for the kerygmatics, all doctrine refers to life in Christ, all liturgical actions effect communion with Christ, and the whole of the scriptures speaks the one Word who is Christ.

210. In no way do I claim that the practice of every catechist in his or her respective time period will necessarily fit into the categories offered by this comparison, nor in the previously discussed history of the catechetical renewal, for that matter. It very well may be that certain catechists of the first phase were quite masterful in connecting church teaching to the person and work of Christ or that catechists of the third phase clearly and distinctly avoided the problems of subjectivism. Nevertheless, the progression of the phases of the catechetical movement themselves suggests the need for categorization and appraisal; likewise, comparing the phases of the renewal to the teaching of the Council must also be done in order to ascertain how to proceed in the time of the New Evangelization. One must necessarily try to understand the past in order to act in the present.

211. ST II-II, q. 1, a. 2, as quoted in *CCC*, no. 170 [146].

The catechists of the third phase, however, found the work of their predecessors to be too narrowly ecclesial in scope. They attempted to show the relevance of the faith for the world precisely by claiming that revelation is to be found in the world—that is, in present history and experience. Still, in the end, without strong ties to scripture and doctrine—pointing to the person of Jesus Christ—such catechesis risks becoming ambivalent to the claim that Christ is the fullness of revelation. As the *General Catechetical Directory* and *Evangelii Nuntiandi* caution, the pedagogy of the third phase—even with the best of intentions—can become trapped in the subjectivity of the human image rather than open the way for humanity to be transformed into the image and likeness of God.

(2) *Revelation is dialogical, and its goal is faith.* This teaching of the Council is increasingly manifested in the successive phases of the movement. Each, perceiving a growing indifference amongst the catechized to the faith of the church, evidenced in its own way the foundational truth that revelation is aimed at human persons and calls forth a living faith. In this light, the first phase, even though the personal conception of revelation had not yet become dominant, was nevertheless the initial attempt to make the church's faith more accessible to human experience. The Munich Method, while lacking the theological and anthropological depth of the later phases, certainly sought to make the Word of God recognizable, that students might better be able to respond with living faith. Catechesis of the second phase advanced this notion by emphasizing the revelatory self-gift of Christ and the ultimate vocation of the human person in him. Christ was, for Jungmann, the one who unites humanity with God in his very person. Catechesis of the third phase went further still, highlighting the dialogical nature of revelation by seeing it within present history and experience. Though not without its difficulties—especially in navigating the unity and distinction between revelation and experience—it nevertheless appropriately saw that God speaks to men and women, not only in the past but in the present.

(3) *Scripture and tradition faithfully transmit revelation to every age.* Just as the first phase of the renewal did not have the advantage of an articulated personalistic theology of revelation, neither did it have the benefit of the dynamic concept of tradition that was to be advanced in

the teaching of the Council. Nevertheless, catechists of this phase did believe that the scriptures and teachings of the church were objective means of handing on divine revelation. When using biblical stories to relay doctrine, they likewise manifested in a rudimentary way the revelatory unity of words and deeds that forms the progress of tradition throughout time.

Catechists of the second phase, backed by the emerging new theology, highlighted this revelatory unity especially by way of their integration of scripture, doctrine, and liturgy. The words of scripture manifested the deeds of God. In the dynamic action of Christian worship, these words then combined with the actions of the liturgy to make those very deeds present. The words of church teaching, furthermore, referred back to this liturgical union, forming a more dynamic whole in which Christ was continually proclaimed to the church.

Catechists of the third phase varied in their appropriation of scripture and tradition and the unity of revelatory words and deeds. In the latter study weeks, revelatory deeds became much more prevalent than words, for the words were found to be inaccessible to hearers in missionary lands. At Medellín, for instance, liberating deeds became the heart of catechesis, with the words of the church's past becoming secondary to those that emerged from the life of the local community. In the United States, the latter work of Gabriel Moran manifests a further decrease in the role of scripture and doctrine in the educational process, as words became subject to the norm of present experience. Tradition, which by necessity includes that which must be handed on from the past, was made susceptible, even on the fundamental level, to the demands of human freedom and critical consciousness.

(4) *The Magisterium and the faithful play integral roles in the progress of tradition.* This norm emphasizes the importance of the entire Body of Christ in the progress of tradition throughout history. Certainly, all three phases of the renewal evidence this role of the Body of Christ, though each does so in a different way. While blanket statements cannot be faithfully applied in every situation, tendencies to either a diachronic or synchronic view of the church manifest themselves in the catechetical renewal.

The first phase is perhaps weighted to the past to the neglect of the present. Undoubtedly, the catechists of this phase wished to make the teachings of the church more accessible to their students, but their use of the catechism and biblical stories only addressed present experience in a rudimentary way. The second phase was certainly more balanced in its consideration of the diachronic and the synchronic. The words and deeds of salvation history—manifested in scripture and doctrine and actualized in the liturgy—were rooted in the person of Jesus Christ so as to speak to the experience of the current era. Christ's rule over salvation history included not only the events of the Old and New Testaments, but the events of present history as well. In practice, however, the kerygmatic method—at times hampered by historical-critical methodology—often confined the stories of scripture to the past. If salvation history is portrayed as closed with the New Testament, it becomes removed from the experience of the church in the present. Finally, the third phase was able to overcome the weaknesses of its predecessors by emphasizing the synchronic experience of the Body of Christ; however, in opposing any content originating from outside the community, it unwittingly embraced the present at the expense of the past.

A second consideration is raised by this norm—namely, the respective places of the Magisterium and the lay faithful in the progress of tradition. A necessary caution is in order, for it would be overly generalized and, in fact, ultimately superficial to view the Magisterium as the preserver of the past while considering the experience of the lay faithful to be the sole vehicle for change in the present.[212] However, there is a sense, evidenced in the weighing of each phase's diachronic or synchronic tendencies, in which the catechetical movement gave greater weight either to Magisterial teaching or to the experience of the laity in its developing understanding of catechesis. In this light, it is perhaps fair to say that the first two phases underscored the role of the Magisterium more so than that of the lay faithful, for, in both phases, the teaching of the past was considered the interpretive norm for the present. The third phase, however, precisely by emphasizing present experience, at times gave more emphasis to the lay faithful than to Magisterial teaching; when done so, as evidenced in Moran's writings, the experience of the present becomes the vehicle for critiquing the past.

212. Moran has a tendency to embrace this dichotomy. See, for instance, *Design for Religion*, 13, where he perceives a "conflict between, on the one hand, many teachers of religion in Catholic school and CCD and, on the other hand, church authorities and conservative critics."

As such, the weakness of the first two phases lies in their inability to account for the experience of the faithful; the weakness of the third phase is its tendency to oppose this experience to the past teaching of the church—in its feeblest iterations it fails to acknowledge the Magisterium as the final interpreter of revelation.

(5) *Human experience is a locus of revelation, and it must be interpreted in the light of the Gospel.* Already, in the comparison with the previous norm, the movement's relationship to the fifth and final norm is glimpsed. Revelation—by its very nature—challenges aspects of human experience and affirms others, while ultimately transcending experience altogether. The first two phases, by holding to the interpretive authority of objective forms of revelation, clearly acknowledged revelation's negating function. The catechized were to conform their lives to the demands of church teaching and to the proclamation of the Kingdom.

The positive character of revelation, by most accounts, was seen in varying amounts, if at all, in the earlier phases. The affirmation of experience, therefore, is rudimentarily evidenced in the first phase while gaining some ground in the second. As a consequence of this, the eminent character of revelation is only scarcely recognizable in the first phase—for experience can only be transcended if it is affirmed in the first place. Likewise, the kerygmatic phase displayed the eminent character of revelation when speaking of humanity's vocation as communion in Jesus Christ, but it was less visible when catechists, in practice, limited catechesis to the mere recounting of scripture.

The third phase, on the other hand, most clearly evidences revelation's positive function. It does so by affirming experience as revelation itself. The redemptive and transcendent dimensions of revelation, however, are acknowledged with difficulty in the concluding stage—as the *General Catechetical Directory* and *Evangelii Nuntiandi* warn, the anthropological turn is susceptible to a reductionist tendency, shying away from the critique of present experience and failing to reach beyond rightful human concerns.

Reform and Renewal of Catechesis

The comparison between the modern catechetical movement and the teaching of Vatican II highlights both the strengths and weaknesses of the renewal. From the vantage point of the Council, the movement is marked by a certain unresolved tension between what must be handed on from the past and the experience of the present. One of the general conclusions of the study week at Medellín summarizes this tension well:

In each case catechesis has its fundamental message that consists in uniting two aspects of total reality. This unity is complex, differentiated, and dynamic. It exists: between human values and the relationship to God; between the projects of men and the salvific project of God, realized in Christ; between human history and the history of salvation; between the experience of man and the revealing action of God; between the progressive realization of Christianity within time and its eschatological fulfillment. This is why catechesis lives in permanent tension between continuity and rupture.[213]

The history of the renewal shows that the relationship between this "continuity and rupture" has not always been worked out with great success. An oscillation is apparent in modern catechetics—a swing of the pendulum—in which one could rightly say, to answer a previous question, that indeed catechesis emerged from one conflation to end up in another. At both ends of the pendulum's arc, content and method—and likewise the relationship between revelation and experience—are indistinguishable, with one taking over the role of the other.

The result of this pendulum swing is that the experiential focus that marks much of postconciliar catechesis is often viewed in opposition to doctrinal content. Indeed, recent catechetical scholarship will often emphasize one side over the other. For instance, John Cavadini, after participating in a conference at Boston College dedicated to "Handing on the Faith," confesses, "I found myself worrying throughout the conference about one fairly consistent omission. Virtually absent from the papers and the discussions, apart from a few comments made by a couple of the participants, was any consideration of 'Handing on Catholic Faith' as handing on the faith, that is the teachings of the faith, the doctrines which express and elaborate the mysteries of the faith as summarized in the Creed."[214] At the same conference, with a nod that would

---

213. Conclusion 12, from "General Conclusions," 217.

214. John C. Cavadini, "Continuing the Conversation," in Handing on the Faith: The Church's Mission and Challenge, ed. Robert P. Imbelli (New York: Herder and Herder, 2006), 214. Emphasis in the original. He continues, "If we were to judge from these papers, which represent a good range of liberal to conservative opinion, one might conclude that we have discovered an unexpected

seem to express the need for a return of content-based catechesis for today's adolescents, Mary Johnson referred to a large sociological study on Catholics and religious education. In this study "the content of religious education programs was a sore spot. Some respondents reported that there was no content in their programs at all. Those who spoke in that vein describe their experience: 'It was insufficient.' 'It was silly.' 'It was abysmal.' 'We got nothing in depth.' 'We got God loves you, but not much else.'"[215] Much of the blame for this lack of substantial religious knowledge in young adults is placed by Richard Rymarz on experiential methods: "One important reason behind the lack of religious content knowledge is the reluctance of teachers to move beyond the experiential world of students and to pass on knowledge that they should possess."[216]

Still others remain less enthusiastic about a return to doctrine in handing on the faith. There is perhaps no greater evidence of this than the various negative scholarly reactions to the universal catechism, first called for at the Extraordinary Synod of 1985 and now published as the *Catechism of the Catholic Church*.[217] Because of Vatican II's earlier decision

consensus among liberals and conservatives, namely, that doctrinal catechesis is of such little importance or significance in the life of the Church that it is not even worthy of mention in papers considering how Catholic faith is to be handed on in the twenty-first century."

215. Dean R. Hoge, William D. Dinges, Mary Johnson, and Juan L. Gonzalez Jr., *Young Adult Catholics: Religion in the Culture of Choice* (Notre Dame, Ind.: Notre Dame University Press, 2001), 136. Johnson and her colleagues continue, "One of the most cogent comments about the lack of content and its implications for her life was made by a college senior: 'It was too vague. I would hesitate to call it teaching or learning. I don't think much was taught, and I certainly don't think much was learned from my perspective. I think my lack of knowledge is what made me disinterested in the Catholic Church.'" Johnson's address at the Boston College conference can be found in "Religious Education in Its Societal and Ecclesial Context," in *Handing on the Faith: The Church's Mission and Challenge*, ed. Robert P. Imbelli (New York: Herder and Herder, 2006), 24–25.

216. Richard M. Rymarz, "Who Is This Person Grace? A Reflection on Content Knowledge in Religious Education," *Religious Education*102, no. 1 (2007): 63.

217. See David Tracy, "World Church or World Catechism: The Problem of Eurocentrism," *Concilium* 204, no. 4 (1989): 28: "The hope for an adequate 'world catechism' seems, at best, illusory"; and Emilio Alberich, "Is the Universal Catechism an Obstacle or a Catalyst in the Process of Inculturation?," *Concilium* 204, no. 4 (1989): 94: "At this point in time, there are many who have criticized the proposed compendium of doctrine, and it is also important to point out that experts and researchers in catechetics have not received the proposal of a universal catechism with much enthusiasm." In contrast to these positions, see Dulles, "The Challenge of the Catechism," *First Things* 49 (1995): 46–53; Joseph Ratzinger's 1983 lecture, "Handing on the Faith and the Sources of the Faith," in *Handing on the Faith in an Age of Disbelief*, by Ratzinger, Dermot J. Ryan, Godfried Danneels, and Franciszek Macharski, trans. Michael J. Miller (San Francisco: Ignatius Press, 2006), 15: "An initial and momentous error down this road [of catechetical

to opt for a directory over a universal catechism, many considered it—
and indeed still do—a reversal of the *aggiornamento* called for by the
Council and a rejection of the renewal brought about by the modern
catechetical movement.[218] Indeed, after hearing of the synod's request,
the internationally recognized journal *Concilium* devoted an entire issue
to critiquing the idea of a universal catechism. The critiques are summarized well by the editors, Johann-Baptist Metz and Edward Schillebeeckx, when they write that the synod's decision "betrays the opinion
that the crisis of religion is primarily doctrinal and not above all a crisis
of Christian individuals and of institutions and their praxis."[219]

In the United States the debate once again came to the forefront
of catechesis due to the publication of a doctrinal framework for high
school curricula by the United States Conference of Catholic Bishops.[220] In articles published in *America* in September of 2009, William
O'Malley and Alfred McBride disagreed over their assessments of the

---

crisis] was doing away with the catechism and declaring in general that the literary genre 'catechism' was outmoded"; and Ratzinger's remarks regarding the "Current Doctrinal Relevance
of the Catechism of the Catholic Church, 9 October, 2002," Vatican, http://www.vatican.va/
roman_curia/congregations/cfaith/documents/rc_con_cfaith_doc_20021009_ratzinger
-catechetical-congress_en.html: "The *Catechism of the Catholic Church*, which Pope John Paul II
gave to the Christian world ... responded to a universal expectation felt everywhere in the
Church; while in some segments of the Catholic intellectual world of the West it met skep-
ticism, indeed, rejection. After the epochal turning point of the Second Vatican Council, the
catechetical tools used until then seemed insufficient, no longer on par with the consciousness
of faith as it was expressed by the Council." Berard Marthaler finds Ratzinger's remarks "either
disingenuous or misunderstood because he knew that the idea of catechisms was neither sup-
pressed nor obsolete," citing the publication of the Dutch Catechism in 1966. However, considering the overwhelming academic backlash to the idea of a universal catechism, Marthaler's
remarks become hard to understand. See his "The Ecclesial Context of the Catechism," in *Introducing the Catechism of the Catholic Church: Traditional Themes and Contemporary Issues*, ed. Berard L.
Marthaler (New York: Paulist Press, 1994), 13.

218. See Marthaler, "Catechetical Directory or Catechism?," 56: "The compilation of
such a compendium seems to run counter to the spirit if not the letter of the Second Vatican
Council"; Mary Collins and Berard L. Marthaler, preface to *Introducing the Catechism of the Catholic
Church*, vi: "How do we reconcile the proposal of the Synod [of 1985] with Vatican II's refusal to
authorize a catechism for the universal Church?"; and Wilkie Au, "Holistic Catechesis: Keeping
Our Balance in the 90s," *Religious Education* 86, no. 3 (1991): 349: "Critics of the [Catechism]
suspect that, despite all reassurances to the contrary from episcopal authorities, it is a co-
vert attempt to reverse, rather than to reinforce, the directions of post–Vatican II catechetical
renewal."

219. Johann-Baptist Metz and Edward Schillebeeckx, "Editorial," *Concilium* 204, no. 4
(1989): 4.

220. Secretariat for Evangelization and Catechesis, *Doctrinal Elements of a Curriculum Framework for the Development of Catechetical Materials for Young People of High School Age* (Washington, D.C.:
United States Conference of Catholic Bishops, 2008).

document. For O'Malley, it "exemplifies how Jesus did not teach" and thus "remains as personally uninvolving as the Baltimore Catechism.... There is no attempt to make the material even vaguely relevant to [students'] lives and felt needs."[221] His judgment of the catechetical theory undergirding the framework even goes so far as to apply descriptions of "indoctrination" and "brainwashing." McBride, on the other hand, in defending the bishops' document, explains that it "takes the divine love story of revelation and expresses it in an orderly, systematic fashion, which the human mind demands."[222] He welcomes the doctrinal emphasis, emphasizing that students "have a right and a need to know the teachings of Christ and the Church."[223]

Ultimately, then, recent scholarship offers no lack of evidence that the tensions that emerged from the catechetical renewal are yet to be resolved. Undoubtedly, the church has gained much from the movement, but there remain clear indications of the further development needed for catechesis to play an effective role in the New Evangelization.

Yet how should the church proceed? I believe that a resolution to the challenges brought about by the catechetical renewal will not be found by advocating one swing of the pendulum over another—even less so by the advent of some new advance in educational theory. Rather, the solution can only be found by taking a stance within the dynamic current of the church's tradition. Put differently, it seems clear that the challenges brought about by the catechetical renewal are similar—if not intimately tied to—the challenge of implementing the renewal called for by the Second Vatican Council. Here, Catherine Dooley's observations on the connection between the implementation of the catechetical renewal and the greater ecclesial renewal are telling:

The creativity and enthusiasm that followed the Second Vatican Council quickly turned to discontent and dissatisfaction. The mass in the vernacular, the revision of the rubrics, the increased participation of the laity, mitigation of fasting and abstinence laws, ecumenical dialogue and openness to religious pluralism, questioning of traditional teaching and values were obvious signs of a Church in transition and of issues yet to be resolved. Religious ed-

221. William J. O'Malley, "Faulty Guidance: A New Framework for High School Catechesis Fails to Persuade," *America*, September 14, 2009, 14.

222. Alfred McBride, "A Sturdy Framework: A Defense of the Bishops' New High School Catechesis," *America*, September 28, 2009, 16.

223. Ibid., 17.

ucation/catechesis, which implemented many of the liturgical changes and reflected current thinking in biblical studies and Vatican II theology, became the focal point of the backlash. "Crisis" and "polarization" were words frequently used to describe the reaction to the "new catechetics."[224]

If such a connection exists between catechetical and conciliar renewal, then there is fault to be found—as is true with the Council—in approaching catechesis with a hermeneutic of discontinuity. In such a view, the handing on of the past and the experience of the present are necessarily in conflict. Yet, from a stance within tradition, the past and the present are united in the one subject that is the church; the church must grow and develop, but in this growth and development retains "her inmost nature and true identity."[225] This is not, of course, an external imposition of an interpretation on ecclesial history by Pope Benedict XVI. For, as chapter 1 has shown, this hermeneutic of tradition stems from the very purpose of the Council envisioned by John XXIII and, indeed, emerges from the Council's own reflection on revelation and the modern world. For John XXIII the "deposit of faith, or truths which are contained in our time-honored teaching, is one thing; the manner in which these truths are set forth (with their meaning preserved intact) is something else."[226] Likewise, in *Dei Verbum* and *Gaudium et Spes*, revelation is completed in the Word who is Jesus Christ, yet this Word is continually spoken to the church today; thus it is only in the light of the Gospel, received in the past, that one is able to truly see the present.

In order to appropriate this hermeneutic of tradition in catechesis, one is helped by returning to the thought of arguably the most influential scholar of the modern catechetical movement. Johannes Hofinger, as the mind behind the Study Weeks, is universally heralded for instigating the international gatherings that serve as a lens for viewing the renewal as a whole. Yet, to my knowledge, very little of catechetical scholarship has focused on his conclusions regarding the renewal, conclusions that grew more urgent in tone toward the end of his life. At the cusp of the third phase Hofinger had, it can be recalled, voiced the concern that "this third stage can in no way mean any break with the past, but only

224. Catherine Dooley, "The Religious Education Curriculum in Catholic Schools," in *The Catholic Character of Catholic Schools*, ed. James Youniss, John J. Convey, and Jeffrey A. McLellan (Notre Dame, Ind.: University of Notre Dame Press, 2000), 160.

225. Benedict XVI, "A Proper Hermeneutic for the Second Vatican Council," xiv.

226. John XXIII, "Opening Address to the Council," 430.

a further homogeneous development of our catechetical heritage."[227] Eleven years later, in an article published in the United States, Hofinger clearly embraced the third phase's concern for evangelization;[228] however, in citing certain obstacles to this evangelizing mission, he noted both "traditionalism" and "secularism." The former emphasizes "the valuable religious heritage which former generations have transmitted to us," though without "the necessary discernment and without the indispensable adaptation to our present situation."[229] The latter stands at "the opposite extreme," for it "contents itself with trying to build up a paradise in this transitory world"; yet while doing so, "it contradicts the very core of the Christian message, the Paschal Mystery of Christ, and its fulfillment in our life with Christ."[230] In each case, the catechetical scholar clearly had no intention of denying the content of the faith, nor the importance of human experience; rather, he lamented the catechetical swing of the pendulum that divided one from the other.[231]

Such a lament became most clearly distilled in a piece Hofinger wrote, published in the year of his death.[232] In it, he surveyed the entire renewal, including the first phase's search for a better method, the second phase's heralding of the kerygma, and the third phase's championing of human experience. However, in a surprising turn, he ended the article by describing his assessment of the third phase as a *eulogy*: "All I have stated in praise of the third phase of the catechetical renewal

227. Hofinger, "Contemporary Catechetics: A Third Phase?," 268.

228. Hofinger, "Evangelizing Catechesis: Basic Principles," *Living Light* (1974): 338: "In recent years not a few National Centers and Diocesan Departments of Religious Education, especially in Latin America, changed their official designation, preferring to be called Centers and Departments of 'Evangelization and Catechesis. . . .' The change in emphasis . . . is easily understood in the light of the present pastoral situation. There is an immense multitude of baptized Christians but only a rather limited number of Christians who really live their Christian commitment. This is becoming as true in the northern hemisphere—in the U.S., Canada, and Europe—as it is in the southern."

229. Ibid., 344.

230. Ibid., 347.

231. Ibid., 344: "[Traditionalism] does not, of course, consist in the acceptance and appreciation of the valuable religious heritage which the former generations have transmitted to us. Such acceptance and appreciation is obviously good and desirable"; and 347: "Understood as worldliness, secularism is something different than a sincere and deep appreciation of human values and of this visible world made by God for man. It is precisely the longest and most significant document of Vatican II, the pastoral Constitution on the Church in the Modern World, which insists upon these values and upon the commitment of man to fulfill his task in the world."

232. See Hofinger, "Looking Backward and Forward," 348–57.

I truly mean as a convincing eulogy. . . . The human approach to cat-echetics has in fact not come to an end. Its valuable achievements must be further developed and must be passed on to coming generations as a precious heritage. But at the same time the person-centered approach as a particular phase of catechesis should give way to a fourth phase still to come."[233]

A faithful catechist to the end, he used vivid imagery to explain the need for this new phase:

The specific contribution of the three phases of catechetical renewal can be compared with the different phases we find in the construction of a build-ing. The pioneers did the hard and dirty groundwork; the kerygmatic renewal built a noble construction on that basis, but it still needed a crowning roof. The promoters of the human approach provided us with a fine roof; but un-fortunately, instead of placing the roof upon the walls, they constructed the roof on the grounds beside the edifice; and now it needs a fourth phase for elevating this valuable roof to its proper place upon the walls.[234]

Catechesis for the New Evangelization, then, must place the roof upon the walls. It must address human experience, yet connect that experience to the heritage of the past, with both finding their unity in the person of

233. Ibid., 355.
234. Ibid., 356. See also Hofinger, "The Catechetical Sputnik," in *Modern Masters of Religious Education*, ed. Marlene Mayr (Birmingham, Ala.: Religious Education Press, 1983), 32: "By the time [the *General Catechetical Directory* and the *National Catechetical Directory for Catholics in the United States*] appeared, religious education had been unfavorably influenced by a formidable wave of secularism and an unreadiness to accept normative directions of the church. Due to this situa-tion in the last fifteen years, religious education in home and school suffered a serious setback."
Hofinger was not the only major figure to notice the challenges of the third phase. Al-fonso Nebrada, one of the phase's founders, so to speak, wrote of a "subtle assumption" of certain anthropological approaches that "nagged" him and left him "uneasy"—namely, the assumption "that Faith is something easily come by, which can only be pre-supposed or readily 'taught,' and then needs only to be focused on the revelation-laden human experience." By this he meant to defy the notion that—quite contrary to the third phase's methodology—one could find revelation in human experience apart from explicit faith. Thus, in his determination, catechesis of the third phase often confused implicit and explicit faith. Likewise, Nebrada also acknowledged the important place of content in catechesis: "It would be distressing if, by the all-too-natural *law of the pendulum*, we swung too wide to another extreme. It is one thing to move now from the unacceptable past tendency of insisting on indoctrination and teaching of 'Christian truths' as the main task of religious education. It is another matter to go to the opposite pole of watering things down to the point of declaring ourselves satisfied with stress-ing human experience and human values under the claim that objectively they are Christian anyhow and there is thus no need to spell out their Christian specificity or explore its full-blossomed Christian implications. . . . It is one thing not to separate; quite another thing alto-gether is to *identify to the point of confusion*" (emphasis mine). See Nebrada, "Some Reflections," 92–96, especially 95.

Jesus Christ. Catechesis for the New Evangelization must therefore become the fourth phase envisioned by Hofinger before he passed away.

I believe that, to conclude this assessment of the modern catechetical movement, three things are apparent when attempting to reformulate catechesis as Hofinger envisioned it, which is to say, from a stance within tradition. First, I cannot help but think that the flight from neo-scholasticism that marked the beginning of renewal was itself, though perhaps unwittingly, an occasion for discontinuity. Theologically speaking, scholarship both preceding and coming after the Council, even when seeking to be faithful to the church, sometimes evidences an aversion to scholasticism and its rightful contributions to the development of the church's faith.[235] Catechetically, this same dynamic is manifested in the aversion to content—especially when this content takes the form of the Catechism. The Council never intended to do away with the objective forms of revelation that were received by the previous experience of the church; it only regrounded this deposit in the person of Jesus Christ. The deposit of faith, including the rich treasure of the scriptures and the church's doctrinal formulations, was prized catechetically in the apostolic age[236] and in the early church;[237] it would be a mistake to see

235. An example of a scholastic development that has often been deemed an innovation can be found in the study of sacraments and the liturgy. Joseph Ratzinger notes that in liturgical theology, many scholars question the scholastic emphasis on the "Real Presence" of Jesus Christ in the Eucharist, finding in it a "hitherto unknown realism, indeed naturalism ... forcing its way into Eucharistic doctrine, [with] the large views of the Fathers ... giving way to a static and one-sided idea of the Real Presence." Yet, he goes on to explain, this emphasis on the Real Presence "is not a misunderstanding due to losing sight of what is central, but a new dimension of the reality of Christianity opening up through the experience of the saints, supported and illuminated by the reflection of the theologians. At the same time, this new development is in complete continuity with what had always been believed hitherto." See Ratzinger, *The Spirit of the Liturgy*, trans. John Saward (San Francisco: Ignatius Press, 2000), 85–91, especially 87–89. For an example of a scholar who finds fault with the scholastic emphases in liturgical theology, see Louis-Marie Chauvet, *Symbol and Sacrament: A Sacramental Reinterpretation of Christian Existence*, trans. Patrick Madigan and Madeleine Beaumont (Collegeville, Minn.: Liturgical Press, 1995). Cf. Christopher Ruddy, "*Ressourcement* and the Enduring Legacy of Post-Tridentine Theology," in *Ressourcement: A Movement for Renewal in Twentieth-Century Catholic Theology*, ed. Gabriel Flynn and Paul D. Murray (Oxford: Oxford University Press, 2012), 185–201, especially 187: "It would be a strange *ressourcement*, after all, that simply regarded centuries of thought as a new Dark Ages or that reduced complex eras and theologies to brief, sometimes dismissive summaries in textbooks."

236. See 2 Tm 1:13–14: "Take as your norm the sound words that you heard from me, in the faith and love that are in Christ Jesus. Guard this rich trust with the help of the Holy Spirit that dwells within us"; and 2 Thes 2:15: "Therefore, brothers, stand firm and hold fast to the traditions that you were taught, either by an oral statement or by a letter of ours."

237. St. Cyril of Jerusalem, a fourth-century mystagogue and one of the premier sources of

revelation in its propositional form as an innovation of the Middle Ages and their reprise in neo-scholasticism.[238]

Following from this, the *Catechism of the Catholic Church* cannot be viewed as a reversal of conciliar *aggiornamento*. Only a hermeneutic of discontinuity could make such a claim. Rather, in accord with John XXIII's desire to see the sacred patrimony of the faith communicated to the experience of today, and in light of Vatican II's own regrounding of the deposit of faith in the personal revelation of God in Jesus Christ, the Catechism is rightly said to be a direct fruit of the Council. It is not a book meant to be memorized by children; it is a faithful and systematic presentation of:

the teaching of Sacred Scripture, the living Tradition in the Church and the authentic Magisterium, as well as the spiritual heritage of the Fathers, Doctors, and saints of the Church, [allowing] for a better knowledge of the Christian mystery and for enlivening the faith of the People of God. It [takes] into

---

patristic catechesis, speaks in his fifth catechetical lecture of the nature of faith, expressing in his own way the classic distinction between *fides quae* and *fides qua*: "Hold fast to the teachings which are now delivered to you, and 'write them on the tablet of your heart.' Guard them with care else by chance the enemy may despoil those who have grown remiss, or some heretic may pervert the traditions entrusted to you. Faith is like opening a deposit account at the bank, as we have now done; but it is God who is the author. 'I charge thee,' as the Apostle says, 'in the sight of God, who gives life to all things, and in the sight of Jesus Christ, who bore witness to that great claim before Pontius Pilate,' that you keep this faith which is delivered unto you, without stain until the coming of our Lord Jesus Christ. A treasure of like has now been committed to you, and the Master will require the deposit at the time of His coming" (5.12 and 13). I have used the translation found in *The Fathers of the Church*, vol. 70, *The Works of Saint Cyril of Jerusalem*, trans. L. P. McCauley and A. A. Stephenson (Washington, D.C.: The Catholic University of America Press, 1969), 144–47. Cyril's understanding of a "banking model" of education, thus, can be considered a corrective to that which is opposed by Paolo Freire and, in turn, Thomas Groome.

238. See, for instance, Sloyan, "Catechetical Crossroads," 147: "The worst service we could do to the cause, I think, is to fall in with the erroneous assumption that a return to sources, a preaching of the gospel at full strength, is somewhat *new*. We may not tolerate this abuse in our hearing, least of all concur in it by declaring ourselves proponents of the 'new theology' or the 'new catechetics.' ... It is the novelties introduced in the twelfth century, or the fifteenth, or the nineteenth, that we cannot abide—the human traditions that our Lord Jesus identified as adulterating the pure Word of God, even while he upheld strongly a theory of the development of doctrine in Israel" (emphasis in the original). For a different perspective, more in line with what I am advocating here, see Jungmann, *Good News Yesterday and Today*, 27: "A comparison between the proclamation of the faith of the early Church, as just outlined, and a modern catechism or theological compendium presents a rather profound contrast. On the one hand we find a simple message, a graphic picture; and on the other, a complicated structure of concepts, divisions, distinctions. But the contrast is no greater, we are justly reminded, than that between the seed and the full-grown plant of the parable of God's Kingdom. Despite differences of appearance, both are of the same nature."

account the doctrinal statements which down the centuries the Holy Spirit has intimated to his Church. It [also helps] to illumine with the light of faith the new situations and problems which had not yet emerged in the past.[239]

As such, the Catechism has even been heralded as the "Catechism of the Second Vatican Council."[240]

Second, and in accord with the kerygmatic emphasis of Jungmann and Hofinger, even as it recovers doctrine as an objective form of revelation that has been prized since its very beginning, the church must connect these teachings to their source. Without the person of Christ as their unifying core, doctrinal teachings become, at the most, pieces of information that must compete with an endless and seemingly more compelling stream of information offered by a media-powered and technologically driven age. At the least, they are unintelligible fragments that fail to have their proper bearing on the life of the Christian or, for that matter, the rest of the world. Thus, just as *Dei Verbum* affirmed that Christ is the fullness of revelation, so too must catechesis for the New Evangelization offer this very same fullness, even as it hands on the faith in an integral, systematic, and life-giving way. Catechesis, in this sense, must always be evangelizing because it must always proclaim the person of Jesus Christ.[241]

239. *Fidei Depositum*, no. 2, as found in the beginning of *CCC*, 4.

240. John Paul II, "Address of John Paul II to the International Catechetical Congress Held to Observe the 10th Anniversary of the Publication of the Catechism of the Catholic Church, 11 October, 2002," Vatican, http://www.vatican.va/holy_father/john_paul_ii/speeches/2002/october/documents/hf_jp-ii_spe_20021011_congresso-catechistico_en.html. See also J. Augustine Di Noia, Gabriel O'Donnell, Romanus Cessario, and Peter John Cameron, *The Love That Never Ends: A Key to the Catechism of the Catholic Church* (Huntington, Ind.: Our Sunday Visitor, 1996), 20: "Thus, even though it was not explicitly mandated by the Council, the Catechism deserves to be called, at least unofficially, the 'Catechism of Vatican II.'" This renewed vision of seeing the Catechism in accord with conciliar renewal is one that deserves further study. Some preliminary work has been done, for instance Brian Daley's essay on the Catechism's recovery of a Trinitarian perspective, "A Mystery to Share In: The Trinitarian Perspective of the New Catechism," *Communio* 21 (1994): 408–36; the Catechism's renewal of moral theology, via the thought of Servais Pinckaers, in John Corbett, "Pinckaers et le nouveau catechisme," trans. Giovanna Brianti, in *Renouveler toutes choses en Christ*, ed. Michael S. Sherwin and Craig Steven Titus (Fribourg: Academic Press, 2009), 173–89, as well as Craig Steven Titus, "Servais Pinckaers and the Renewal of Catholic Moral Theology," *Journal of Moral Theology* 1, no. 1 (2012): 43–68; and Petroc Willey's chapter, "The Catechism of the Catholic Church and the New Evangelization," in *The New Evangelization: Faith, People, Context, and Practice*, ed. Paul Grogan (New York: Bloomsbury, 2015), 209–20.

241. See Pedraza, "Participation over Imitation: Communion in Christ and Catechesis for the New Evangelization," *Church Life: A Journal for the New Evangelization*, 2013, 27–34.

Finally, as a third conclusion stemming from the assessment of the renewal, not only must catechesis for the New Evangelization recover objective forms of revelation and ground it in the person of Christ, but it must unite this revelation to human experience. To recover the Catechism (or the use of sacred scripture, the Creed, etc.) without this attention to experience would be tantamount to pouring new wine into old wineskins. Likewise, to teach the faith, even in a kerygmatic fashion, without engaging human experience would be to throw the seed of the Gospel on untilled land. Both the initial work of pre-evangelization and that of engaging the signs of the times are important tasks offered by the third phase of the renewal that must be undertaken by catechists, yet done so without falling prey to subjectivism or the simple conflation of divine revelation with human experience.

One can recall here that for the Council the human person was, to use Kasper's phrase, the Archimedean point in which the faith could be reconciled with the modern world. As such, catechesis must brace itself against subjectivism by appropriating a better anthropology in order to reconcile revelation and experience in a more fruitful way, consonant with tradition. Indeed, this anthropology must include a theological dimension that allows for the affirmation of experience's revelatory character while, at the same time, allowing experience to be redeemed and ultimately transcended by revelation. In this sense, such an anthropology must be genuinely Christological as well.

With this final conclusion the path for the rest of this study is opened, for I believe that the thought of one philosopher and theologian, in particular, can provide the adequate anthropology needed for the ministry of the Word to flourish in the New Evangelization. As one who participated in the Second Vatican Council and who devoted great energies to articulating a philosophical and theological understanding of the human person consonant with the Council's teaching, Karol Wojtyła/Pope John Paul II stands as an important figure in both conciliar and catechetical renewal. As such, keeping in mind the ultimate goal of renewing catechesis in the present era, this study turns to his thoughts on the human person, as seen by the light of human reason and the light of Jesus Christ.

Chapter 3

The Human Person in the Light of Reason

The man gave names to all the cattle, all the birds of the air, and all the wild animals; but none proved to be the suitable partner for the man.

Genesis 2:20

Being in the image of God the human individual possesses the dignity of a person, who is not just something, but someone. He is capable of self-knowledge, of self-possession, and of freely giving himself and entering into communion with other persons. And he is called by grace to a covenant with his Creator, to offer him a response of faith and love that no other creature can give in his stead.

Catechism of the Catholic Church, no. 357

As vicar capitular and then archbishop of Kraków, Karol Wojtyła took part in the Second Vatican Council from its very beginning.[1] Among his various contributions to the Council's proceedings some have noted his insistence upon the personalistic conception of God's self-revelation

1. Wojtyła's participation in the Council is traced by George Weigel in *Witness to Hope: The Biography of Pope John Paul II* (New York: Cliff Street, 1999), 160–72; Rocco Buttiglione in *Karol Wojtyła: The Thought of the Man Who Became Pope John Paul II*, trans. Paolo Guietti and Francesca Murphy (Grand Rapids, Mich.: William B. Eerdmans, 1997), 187–99; and George Huntston Williams in *The Mind of John Paul II: Origins of His Thought and Action* (New York: Seabury, 1981), 164–85.

in the debates that led to the promulgation of *Dei Verbum*;[2] his ecclesiological vision of a unified People of God, bearing a transcendent dimension that extends beyond mere sociology, in the preparatory stages of *Lumen Gentium*;[3] and the impassioned plea for religious freedom, surely born from the experience of his native Poland,[4] in the discussions that eventually led to the promulgation of *Dignitatis Humanae*.[5] These contributions, in many ways, embodied the constant concerns of his academic and pastoral work, and they undoubtedly played their respective roles in forming the conciliar documents. But perhaps even more than these interventions during the Council, it is Wojtyła's interpretation of the Council *after* its conclusion that defines his greatest contribution to the legacy of Vatican II. Later, as John Paul II, he would be characterized as the "Conciliar Pope," for his papacy of twenty-seven years was, by his own admission, squarely focused on the Council's implementation.[6]

Still, even before his election to the papacy and the ensuing focus on conciliar-based renewal, Cardinal Wojtyła had penned a much lesser-

2. Weigel, *Witness to Hope*, 161.

3. See Wojtyła's first official intervention, as quoted by Williams, *Mind of John Paul II*, 169: "This transcendence of the People of God in the living forth by virtue of the sacraments ought to presuppose the transcendence of this Church itself in respect to whatever society in the natural order and in respect to the whole of the earthly city. For in this manner the People of God in the Church make a similitude of the mystery of the Incarnation itself, for at one and the same it remains linked to humanity in whatever the human society or community, and, it also transcends humanity." See also Buttiglione, *Karol Wojtyła*, 187–88.

4. See John Paul II, *Crossing the Threshold of Hope*, 157–58: "I had the particular fortune of being able to participate in the Council from the first day to the last. This was in no way to be taken for granted, since the Communist authorities in my country considered the trip to Rome a privilege and entirely under their control. If, then, under such circumstances I was given the opportunity to participate in the Council from beginning to end, it can rightly be judged a special gift from God."

5. Williams, *Mind of John Paul II*, 177, once more provides a translation of his intervention in this regard: "It is not enough to say in this matter 'I am free,' but rather 'I am accountable.' This is the doctrine grounded in the living tradition of the Church of the confessors and martyrs. Responsibility is the summit and necessary complement of liberty. This ought to be underlined so that our Declaration will be seen to be intimately personalistic in the Christian sense, but not as derived from liberalism or indifferentism. The civil powers ought to observe most strictly and with great sensitivity religious liberty as much in a collective as in a personal sense." Williams notes that this intervention was made with a "sonorous voice of compelling authority." See also Weigel, *Witness to Hope*, 163–66.

6. See Williams, *Mind of John Paul II*, 164, as well as John Paul's introduction to *Fidei Depositum*, as found in the beginning of *CCC*, 2: "For me, then—who had the special grace of participating in it and actively collaborating in its development—Vatican II has always been, and especially during these years of my Pontificate, the constant reference point of my every pastoral action, in the conscious commitment to implement its directives concretely and faithfully at the level of each Church and the whole Church."

known work in which he reflected specifically on the implementation of Vatican II. The work, *Sources of Renewal*, is aimed at helping the people of his own archdiocese appropriate the riches of the Council's teaching: its purpose, as Wojtyła states in the introductory chapter, is to introduce them "to the relevant documents of Vatican II, but always from the point of view of translating them into the life and faith of the Church."[7] As such, it contains valuable insights into the interpretation of the Council that lay at the foundation of his papacy and, by extension, his call for a New Evangelization.

Wojtyła's desire to translate the Council's teachings into the life of faith is, of course, consonant with the purpose of Vatican II as a whole. The reconciliation of faith and life, as chapter 1 of this study recalls, was the hope that stirred John XXIII to call the Council to order. This same concern is echoed in the words of Wojtyła when he writes:

Vatican II . . . while preserving its pastoral character and mindful of the purpose for which it was called, profoundly developed the doctrine of faith and thus provided a basis for its enrichment. . . . [Yet] the Pastors of the Church were not so much concerned to answer questions like "What should men believe?," "What is the real meaning of this or that truth of faith?" and so on, but rather to answer the more complex question: "What does it mean to be a believer, a Catholic, and a member of the Church?"[8]

Wojtyła's words suggest that the aim of the Council—and its conception of faith—are dual-sided. The *robust objectivity* of the church's faith—the theological virtue of faith given by God, as well as the divine revelation that such faith claims knowledge of—is one thing, while the *subjective appropriation* of that faith is still another. Undoubtedly, the latter existential sense only exists by virtue of the former; nevertheless, to see the faith of the church translated into the lives of believers was the ultimate goal of conciliar renewal.

As such, *Sources of Renewal* employs a peculiar phrase—the "enrichment of faith"—when speaking of the Council's overall intention. The phrase embodies the faith of the church in both its objective and subjective dimensions:

The enrichment of faith which we regard as the fundamental pre-requisite for the realization of Vatican II is to be understood in two ways: as an enrichment

7. Wojtyła, *Sources of Renewal*, 11.
8. Ibid., 17.

of the content of the faith in accordance with the Council's teaching, but also, originating from that content, an enrichment of the whole existence of the believing member of the Church. This enrichment of faith in the objective sense, constituting a new stage in the Church's advance towards the "fullness of divine truth," is at the same time an enrichment in the subjective, human, existential sense, and it is from the latter that realization of the Council is most to be hoped for.[9]

Here, in these words, one begins to sense a certain way of approaching the reunification of faith and life that was both the goal of the conciliar era and, in a particular way, the modern catechetical movement. In this vision, the "subjective, human, existential" character of faith is firmly wedded to faith in its objective sense—as in the faith of the church, the truth revealed by God. And yet, by distinguishing the importance of the subjective aspect, Wojtyła clearly recognizes the contribution subjectivity can and must make to the church in the modern era. If what the Polish cardinal says here is true, then one can draw two immediate implications for the goal of this study: first, the experiential concerns of the modern catechetical movement are justified and are of paramount importance for the church in the New Evangelization; and second, the tension between the objectivity of divine revelation and the subjectivity of human experience is ultimately a false dichotomy, for the living out of faith is fundamentally tied to the objectivity of the church's faith as its foundation.

Thus, in Wojtyła's reading of the conciliar goal, one finds important implications about how to advance catechesis in a way consonant with the direction indicated by Hofinger at the end of his life. Here one finds a way to reintegrate the anthropological phase of the catechetical renewal with the previous phases, to "place the roof upon the walls," so to speak.

Therefore, the next portion of this study is dedicated to explicating the understanding of ecclesial faith that was put forth by Wojtyła in *Sources of Renewal* and that was, as I believe can be argued, expanded in the pontificate of John Paul II. Still, as is clear in Wojtyła's unique descriptions of the conciliar goal, this understanding of faith is only grasped in its fullness by way of that which lies at the very core of his thought. Those most familiar with the writings of Wojtyła/John Paul II

9. Ibid., 18.

know that it is a Christocentric reading of the human person that serves as the foundation for the entirety of his academic and pastoral work.[10] Ultimately, to understand his reading of the Council, one must understand his thoughts on the human person.

This chapter, therefore, explores the philosophical anthropology put forth by Karol Wojtyła, while chapter 4 explores the way in which Wojtyła/John Paul II appropriated this anthropology theologically. The former considers the person in the light of reason, the latter in the light of revelation. If the human person is, to recall Walter Kasper's phrase, the Archimedean point by which the faith and the modern world can be reconciled, then the work of these two chapters is to provide just the sort of anthropological foundation necessary to accomplish the conciliar aim. These chapters are, therefore, an attempt to show how the human quest for fulfillment can be met by the answer that is the self-revelation of God. Only in this union of revelation and experience can catechesis accomplish the aim of the Council and succeed in the New Evangelization.[11]

Wojtyła's Anthropology: The Structure of Personal Fulfillment

Before setting out to explore Wojtyła's philosophical look at the human person, an initial word is in order. Readers of Wojtyła's philosophical

10. See, for instance, Grabowski, "The Luminous Excess of the Acting Person," 144–45, where the author keenly observes that both proponents and critics of the late pope's thought "have plucked the fruit of individual insights or ideas which support their own positions while ignoring the tree which supports and unifies them. That 'tree' is the human person, a dynamic acting subject, addressed by Christ in the existential drama of salvation, and called to fulfillment through the grace-powered action expressive of the gift of self. The individual insights or ideas gleaned from the late pope's thought are intelligible and fruitful because of the anthropology which nourishes them." See also Peter Simpson, *On Karol Wojtyła* (Belmont, Calif.: Wadsworth, 2001), 7, who states that there is "one idea or object that runs through the whole of Wojtyła's work like an ever-recurring theme, the theme of the human person."

11. It is not my intention, in this chapter, to cover Wojtyła's philosophical anthropology comprehensively. For such a task, there are many capable guides. Along with Schmitz's *At the Center of the Human Drama*, Buttiglione's *Karol Wojtyła*, and Simpson's *On Karol Wojtyła*, one could also add Jarosław Kupcak, *Destined for Liberty: The Human Person in the Philosophy of Karol Wojtyła/John Paul II* (Washington, D.C.: The Catholic University of America Press, 2000). Simpson's book is especially helpful for its clarity in contextualizing the thought of Wojtyła, whose work is often characterized as dense and, at times, lacking in helpful examples. Here, I seek to raise only those points that pertain directly to the unification of experience and objectivity, as well as those concerning human fulfillment.

texts often find them difficult because of his attempt to draw from the resources of both metaphysics and phenomenology simultaneously. The combination of the two is not without its difficulties. As one author puts it, "Thomists are skeptical of Wojtyła's phenomenological inclinations even as phenomenologists suspect that underneath it all Wojtyła's phenomenology is rooted in Scholasticism."[12] As an indication of this uncommon blend, the difficult prose of his main philosophical work, *The Acting Person*, has even led some in his native land of Poland to quip that the book was written "with full foreknowledge that he would one day be pope and that he would then require it as reading for priests in purgatory."[13]

All witticisms aside, the challenge of reading Wojtyła's texts inevitably requires a concerted effort at explaining the intricacies of his thought and the terminology he introduces, all of which can lead to one "losing the forest for the trees," so to speak. Thus, in the following analysis, I have attempted to explain the details of his philosophy where appropriate, all the while endeavoring to keep in mind the greater picture of his understanding of the human person. For Wojtyła, both metaphysics (especially the philosophy of St. Thomas) and phenomenology are necessary to provide an adequate picture of the human person, one that can illuminate humanity in all of its dimensions.

The metaphysical grounding, therefore, is essential because Wojtyła seeks to examine how the person reaches fulfillment, a question that necessitates the study of being and its causes and ends. This focus on the human being and his or her fulfillment likewise provides a bridge by which one can unite Wojtyła's thought with the theological and catechetical concerns of the present work. Here, both the conciliar aim of addressing the modern world and the catechetical renewal's anthropological thrust reveal the common concern of how to present the faith as the fulfillment of the human person.

Likewise, the phenomenological analysis is essential to Wojtyła's

12. Taylor, "Acting Person in Purgatory," 77. Cf. John J. Conley, "The Philosophical Foundations of the Thought of John Paul II: A Response," in *The Thought of Pope John Paul II: A Collection of Essays and Studies*, ed. John M. McDermott (Rome: Editrice Pontificia Università Gregoriana, 1993), 28: "I believe that the distinctive union between phenomenological method and neo-scholastic analysis of the moral act explains part of the difficulty many of us experience when reading the pope's documents. I often have the impression of banging into scholastic steel as I wander through the phenomenological fog."

13. Schmitz, *At the Center of the Human Drama*, 62.

project precisely because of the modern focus on subjectivity and human experience. Yes, personal fulfillment requires the categories of causality and ends, but the modern era has questioned the adequacy of such universal categories, opting instead for a focus on personal and communal experience. Often, for modern eyes, fulfillment cannot be offered by any outside authority, least of all the church, but must be the result of a free choice made in light of what is most pertinent to the chooser. Here, freedom is paramount, for the modern human being is a "master of nature" who can "freely decide what to do with nature. He is not bound by any preexisting purposes in nature, but sets his own purposes."[14] In giving preeminence to this personal freedom, so too does subjective experience gain the upper hand over any supposed objective reality. In other words, "the demands of the knower take precedence over the demands of being."[15] There is, perhaps, no stronger affirmation of this approach to experience than that offered by George Berkeley when he states that *esse est percipi* (to be is to be perceived).[16]

Even if one should reject these modern emphases in their extreme forms, the questions brought to the fore by the modern world cannot simply be brushed aside. Thus, Wojtyła's embrace of phenomenology is an attempt to address these very challenges. Here, Wojtyła's emphasis on experience can prove fruitful for this study, especially in light of the anthropological concerns of the Council (especially in *Gaudium et Spes*) and the catechetical renewal's later attention to human experience and liberating praxis.

Ultimately, then, Wojtyła is guided by the question of human fulfillment and the role experience plays in its attainment—both of these, Wojtyła claims, are united in the freely chosen act of a person. The following, therefore, is an attempt to trace the structure of the human person and his or her act, utilizing Wojtyła's metaphysical and phenomenological analyses. I begin with Wojtyła's understanding of the person and his or her dignity, a dignity that is revealed in a particular

14. Waldstein offers this comment on the modern, scientific vision of humanity in his introduction to John Paul II, *Man and Woman He Created Them*, 41.

15. Kenneth L. Schmitz, "Selves and Persons: A Difference in Loves?" *Communio* 18, no. 2 (1991): 193.

16. See Berkeley's *Principles of Human Knowledge* (1710), nos. 2 and 3, in George Berkeley, *"Principles of Human Knowledge" and "Three Dialogues,"* ed. Howard Robinson (Oxford: Oxford University Press, 1996), 24–25.

way by personal subjectivity. The chapter then moves to how Wojtyła is able to transcend this interiority to unite the person with objective and fulfilling reality, especially by way of the conscious and freely chosen act. Finally, I consider what Wojtyła takes to be the greatest form of this act—the act of love—and, stemming from this, the role other persons play in human fulfillment. With each step, I hope both the greater picture and the intricate details—the forest and the trees—prove to be mutually illuminating of Wojtyła's project.

The Dignity of the Human Person

It may seem strange to begin philosophical reflections on the human person by way of a passage from scripture, but in the case of Karol Wojtyła, it is not unwarranted. His reflections on the person are ultimately influenced by what God has revealed; this will be explored further in chapter 4. But, for now, it is enough to turn to the line from Genesis that begins the present chapter, to turn to the moment in which the man, Adam, encounters the rest of the world only to discover that he is unique among the created order. In the face of the other animals, he realizes there is no "suitable partner" for him. Historically, Christian philosophers have placed this difference between the human person and the rest of creation precisely at the level of the intellect and will—as St. Thomas says, echoing Boethius, "*Person* signifies what is most perfect in all nature—that is, a subsistent individual of a *rational nature*."[17] This rational nature instills humanity with a certain dignity. Whereas other animals "think" in rudimentary ways, humans not only think, but they understand—they grasp meaning;[18] indeed, humans can even think about thinking (as Descartes captures so well). Likewise, just as animals "choose" according to instinct and the necessities of life, humans choose according to the understanding acquired by their intellects.[19] As such, in freedom, they can forgo the instinctual and, furthermore, even choose the unnecessary. In sum, humans have the unique ability to think about truth precisely because it is true, and to choose what is good precisely because it is good.

17. ST I, q. 29, a. 3 [158]. The first emphasis is in the original; the second is mine. This rational nature encompasses both the intellect and the will.

18. On this difference between human thinking and that of other animals, see the dialogue of Evodius and Augustine in the latter's *On Free Will* 2.3.8–9.

19. See ST I, q. 59, a. 1.

Ultimately, then, this rational nature is the source of human transcendence over the rest of the world. Men and women share many things with their fellow creatures, among them existence and material bodies; perhaps, with plant and animal life, one could even argue an immaterial soul—but rationality seems the sole property of human life for earthly beings. As Wojtyła explains (drawing upon St. Thomas), this transcendence of rationality is the mark of a *person*; moreover, it constitutes the person as the most perfect of all beings:

St. Thomas continually has recourse to a definition of the person. This is the well-known and widely used definition formulated by Boethius: *persona est rationalis naturae individua substantia*. . . . The human being is an individual (*individua substantia*) of a rational nature. A rational nature does not possess its own subsistence as a nature, but subsists in a person. The person is a subsistent subject of existence and action—which can in no way be said of a rational nature. . . . St. Thomas says that this being is objectively the most perfect being. Its perfection is undeniably the result of its rational, and thus spiritual, nature, which finds its natural complement in freedom. Both of these spiritual properties of the nature—reason and freedom—are concretized in the person, where they become properties of a concrete being, which exists and acts on the level of a nature that has such properties. The person, therefore, is always a rational and free concrete being, capable of all those activities that reason and freedom alone make possible.[20]

Wojtyła correctly pinpoints Thomas's reliance on Boethius for the definition of "person," and it is noteworthy that he finds nothing in this definition to contradict. Nevertheless, the challenges of modernity and the atrocities he experienced in his native Poland had led him to believe that the unique dignity of the human person could not be captured *solely* by reference to the Boethian and Thomistic view of the person, one he characterized as "very objectivistic."[21] Rather, this objective view must

20. Karol Wojtyła, "Thomistic Personalism," in *Person and Community: Selected Essays*, trans. Theresa Sandok (New York: Peter Lang, 1993), 167. Wojtyła's emphasis on the person as a concrete, existing being can be traced to the influence of Existential Thomists such as Étienne Gilson and Joseph de Finance. Whereas one can speak of a rational nature while remaining within the realm of the abstract, the same cannot be said, for Wojtyła, in speaking of a person. A person is not a mere abstract termination (or ending point) of a rational nature; rather, a person is always a concrete, existing being. See Jarosław Kupcak, *Destined for Liberty*, 52, and Schmitz, *At the Center of the Human Drama*, 51, footnote 27.

21. Wojtyła, "Thomistic Personalism," 170. On this and the following page, Wojtyła notes that St. Thomas's anthropology is precisely what makes subjectivity possible. While it "gives us an excellent view of the objective existence and activity of the person . . . it would be difficult to speak in his view of the lived experience of the person."

be enriched by an examination of the subjective aspect of the person in order to meet modern preoccupations head on. According to Wojtyła, from Descartes forward, modern philosophy has given witness to a "gradual process of a kind of hypostatization of consciousness," one in which human subjectivity has become separated from its ontological foundations.[22] Likewise, after feeling the full force of the Communist occupation of his homeland, the Polish philosopher could plainly state that the dialectical materialism of Marxist thought had led not to the promotion of human dignity but rather to the subjugation of it.[23] While clearly not in agreement with these philosophical and political reductions of the human person, Wojtyła maintained that, in an attempt to dialogue with the modern world, any recovery of a realist understanding of humanity must include a concrete examination of the person in all of his or her objectivity *and* subjectivity.[24]

His project, therefore, is twofold: first, it is aimed at entering into the moment of lived experience in order to show that such experience

22. Ibid., 169. This tearing of human subjectivity from the body of the material world is traced from Bacon to Descartes to Kant by Michael Waldstein in his introduction to John Paul II, *Man and Woman He Created Them*, 36–63.

23. See John Paul II, *Memory and Identity: Conversations at the Dawn of a Millennium*, trans. unknown (New York: Rizzoli, 2005), 9–10: "What happened in Poland after the Marxists came to power had much the same effect as the philosophical developments that occurred in Western Europe in the wake of the Enlightenment. People spoke, among other things, of the 'decline of Thomistic realism' and this was understood to include the abandonment of Christianity as a source for philosophizing. Specifically, the very possibility of attaining to God was placed in question. According to the logic of *cogito ergo sum*, God was reduced to an element within human consciousness; no longer could he be considered the ultimate explanation of the human *sum*.... Man remained alone: alone as creator of his own history and his own civilization; alone as one who decides what is good and what is bad, as one who would exist and operate *etsi Deus non daretur*, even if there were no God. If man can decide by himself, without God, what is good and what is bad, he can also determine that a group of people is to be annihilated"; and Wojtyła, "The Person: Subject and Community," in *Person and Community*, 220: "The problem of the subjectivity of the person—particularly in relation to human community—imposes itself today as one of the central ideological issues that lie at the very basis of human praxis, morality (and thus also ethics), culture, civilization and politics.... This aptly describes the situation in Poland today with respect to the whole political reality that has arisen out of Marxism, out of dialectical materialism, and strives to win minds over to this ideology."

24. See Wojtyła, "Subjectivity and the Irreducible in the Human Being," in *Person and Community*, 212–13: "As the need increases to understand the human being as a unique and unrepeatable person ... the category of lived experience takes on greater significance, and, in fact, key significance. For then the issue is not just the metaphysical objectification of the human being as an acting subject, as the agent of acts, but the revelation of the person as a subject *experiencing* its acts and inner happenings, and with them its own subjectivity" (emphasis in the original).

is both necessarily grounded in and open to what transcends it.[25] Thus Wojtyła believes that, by phenomenologically examining the subjectivity of experience, he can show its inherent need for objectivity. If successful, he can then reestablish the connection between phenomenon and foundation and, from this, show modernity the true foundations of human dignity. Second, his project likewise acknowledges that, in the modern preoccupation with experience, there lies an important contribution that subjectivity can make in revealing the dignity of *each specific* human person. This is because, in the self-efficacy that is present in a consciously willed act, a person's subjective awareness and offering of him or herself become a unique locus of this dignity—only I, in my own freedom, can choose this specific act and thereby make a gift of myself.[26]

Thus, for Wojtyła, there is an aspect of human dignity that goes beyond having a rational nature. Yes, a rational nature, as evidenced by Adam in the garden or by every man and woman in the midst of the world, reveals the worth of humanity in comparison to other creatures. But it is one's subjectivity, in a particular way, that reveals (not *causes*) the singular worth of that person, not only in comparison to other creatures, but, even more, in relation *to other persons*. As the Catechism similarly explains, "The human individual possesses the dignity of a person, who

25. "Lived experience," for Wojtyła, is the experience of a particular person that, in a certain sense, cannot be reduced to anything else precisely because it is the experience of that person. See Wojtyła, "Subjectivity and the Irreducible in the Human Being," 214: "The experience of the human being cannot be derived by way of cosmological reduction; we must pause at the irreducible, at that which is unique and unrepeatable in each human being, by virtue of which he or she is not just *a particular human being*—an individual of a certain species—but *a personal subject*" (emphasis in the original). Wojtyła's method, then, is to "pause at the irreducible" and to explore what that lived experience reveals. On the same page he is mindful that, in this pausing, while "we cannot complete this picture [of the person] through reduction alone, we also cannot remain within the framework of the irreducible alone (for then we would be unable to get beyond the pure self)."

26. This unique dignity of each specific person is therefore manifested by one's consciousness, especially in what Wojtyła calls consciousness' reflexive function. He explains that consciousness has a twofold purpose: first, in its *reflective* function, it mirrors what is cognized by the intellect, including the knowledge of objects and the person himself. Still, "it is one thing to *be* the subject, another to *be cognized* (that is, objectivized) as the subject, and still a different thing to *experience* one's self as the subject of one's own acts and experiences" (emphasis in the original). Thus, consciousness also has a reflexive function that allows a person not merely to know himself in an act, but to experience himself as the one who is acting. The person then "owes to consciousness the subjectivation of the objective." See Wojtyła, *Acting Person*, 44 and 42, respectively.

is not just something, but someone. He is capable of self-knowledge, of self-possession, and of freely giving himself and entering into communion with other persons."[27] Such an analysis of the human person helps explain why the suppression of even one person's freedom—even for the supposed sake of the good of all—is an offense to human dignity. Because of Poland's past Wojtyła was no stranger to this truth.

Ultimately, then, it is because of the modern emphasis on subjectivity that Wojtyła's philosophical "evangelization" of modernity is aimed precisely there, at its deepest concern. It should be reemphasized that in his embrace of the subjective dimensions of personhood, in no way does Wojtyła accept the modern dichotomy between this subjectivity and the objective aspects of the person. Rather, for the Polish philosopher, personhood encompasses both the robust objectivity of human nature—body, soul, passions, intellect, will, etc.—and the unique subjectivity of the person revealed in consciousness.[28] The former acts as an ontological anchor, while the latter provides a unique look into the person, one that captures in a particular way the dimension of human freedom. Many commentators have pointed out that this distinctive combination of the philosophies of being and consciousness—what

27. *CCC*, no. 357 [91]. This aspect of human dignity is captured in a retreat Wojtyła gave to university students in 1962, where he distinguishes between the relative importance of human beings (manifested by their achievements) and their absolute importance (given by human nature). See John Paul II/Karol Wojtyła, *The Way to Christ: Spiritual Exercises*, trans. Leslie Wearne (San Francisco: HarperSanFrancisco, 1984), 4–5. Peter J. Colosi traces this emphasis on the unique dignity of *each* person to Wojtyła's study of Max Scheler, who claimed that each person has an "individual value essence." This uniqueness explains why objects such as chairs are replaceable but not humans, and why people love persons not only for certain traits that can be found in others but for the totality of their personhood. See Colosi's "The Uniqueness of Persons in the Life and Thought of Karol Wojtyła/Pope John Paul II, with Emphasis on His Indebtedness to Max Scheler," in *Karol Wojtyła's Philosophical Legacy*, ed. Nancy Mardas Billias, Agnes B. Curry, and George F. McLean (Washington, D.C.: Council for Research in Values and Philosophy, 2008), 61–99, especially 69–70. Wojtyła does not, of course, express this dimension of human dignity by way of the word "essence" as does Scheler, particularly because of Wojtyła's grounding in Thomistic metaphysics. Rather, he places this dimension of uniqueness in personal self-efficacy.

28. See Wojtyła, *Acting Person*, 19. This insistence on maintaining the unity of subjectivity with objectivity, even when practicing the phenomenological method, is an emphasis of the Lublin Thomism of which Wojtyła played a significant part. On this form of Thomism centered in Poland, see Stefan Swiezawski, "Karol Wojtyła at the Catholic University of Lublin," in Wojtyła, *Person and Community*, ix–xvi; Roger Duncan, "Lublin Thomism," *Thomist* 51 (1987): 307–324; and Josef Seifert, "Karol Cardinal Wojtyła (Pope John Paul II) as Philosopher and the Cracow/Lublin School of Philosophy," *Aletheia* 2 (1981): 130–99. As Seifert explains, Lublin Thomism was a school of phenomenological realism that sought to avoid the subjectivism of the later Husserl.

Wojtyła termed a "Thomistic Personalism"—is owed in large part to his studies of the thought of St. Thomas and the phenomenologist Max Scheler.[29] Ultimately, in this Thomistic Personalism, there can be no opposition between person and nature but only a proper integration of the two concepts.[30]

From the Inside Outward: Entering into Experience and Transcending It

The point of departure for overcoming the divide that stands between subjectivity and objectivity lies in the scholastic axiom *operari sequitur esse* (action follows being). For Wojtyła, not only must the statement be logically true, but, because it is so, it can provide a pathway by which to travel through experience to the reality of being itself: "If *operari* results from *esse*, then *operari* is also—proceeding in the opposite direction—

29. See, for instance, George F. McLean, "Karol Wojtyła's Mutual Enrichment of the Philosophies of Being and Consciousness," in Billias, Curry, and McLean, *Karol Wojtyła's Philosophical Legacy*, 15–29; Kupcak, *Destined for Liberty*, 80; and Schmitz, *At the Center of the Human Drama*, 36–37. As pope, John Paul II would write in *Fides et Ratio*, no. 83 [104–5], "Metaphysics should not be seen as an alternative to anthropology, since it is metaphysics which makes it possible to ground the concept of the person's dignity in virtue of the person's spiritual nature. In a special way, the person constitutes a privileged locus for the encounter with being, and hence with metaphysical enquiry. Wherever men and women discover a call to the absolute and transcendent, the metaphysical dimension of reality opens up before them: in truth, in beauty, in moral values, in other persons, in being itself, in God. We face a great challenge at the end of this millennium to move from *phenomenon to foundation*, a step as necessary as it is urgent. We cannot stop short at experience alone; even if experience does reveal the human being's interiority and spirituality, speculative thinking must penetrate to the spiritual core and the ground from which it arises" (emphasis in the original). Ultimately, then, I think it fair to call Wojtyła's philosophy a "mutual enrichment" of Thomistic metaphysics with phenomenological personalism in the sense that he enters into the "phenomenon" in order to penetrate to the "foundation."

30. See Wojtyła, *Acting Person*, 78–82, and "Thomistic Personalism," 170, where he condemns the modern opposition of subjectivity to objectivity. In *Memory and Identity*, 12, John Paul states that many of the modern moral evils are born from "the rejection of what ultimately constitutes us as human beings, that is, the notion of human nature as a 'given reality'; its place has been taken by a 'product of thought' freely formed and freely changeable according to circumstances. I believe that a more careful study of this question could lead us beyond the Cartesian watershed. If we wish to speak rationally about good and evil, we have to return to Saint Thomas Aquinas, that is, to the philosophy of being. With the phenomenological method, for example, we can study experiences of morality, religion, or simply what it is to be human, and draw from them significant enrichment of our knowledge. Yet we must not forget that all these analyses implicitly presuppose the reality of the Absolute Being and also the reality of being human, that is, being a creature. If we do not set out from such 'realist' presuppositions, we end up in a vacuum."

the most proper avenue to knowledge of that *esse*."[31] Thus, if the reality of the human person is expressed in human acts, then these acts, in turn, can provide access to the reality of the person.[32] Here lies a pivotal consideration for Wojtyła's project. He desires to enter into experience to show its reliance upon objectivity, but it is not simply any experience that will do. Rather, it is the experience of self-efficacy that provides the bridge needed to cross from consciousness to real being.[33] It is the experience of a consciously willed act.[34]

Why is this emphasis upon intentional acts so necessary for uniting the subjective and objective realms? First, it is because such an act is one that is always willed toward something. Its very structure relies upon the actuality of legitimate realities, both the actuality of the one willing and that of the good being willed. This is one of the blunt *givens* of human experience; Wojtyła feels no temptation to fall into subjectivism here because the experience of efficacy—when given an unbiased look—demands objectivity. Human choices affect and effect real lives.

31. Wojtyła, "Person: Subject and Community," 223.

32. As others have noted, this is the reason for the title of Wojtyła's main philosophical work, Acting Person. In fact, as George Weigel points out in a note in *Witness to Hope*, 175, the Polish title of the book, *Osoba y cczyn*, "is translated, literally, *Person and Act*: a title that retains the tension between subjective consciousness and objective reality in which Wojtyła is trying to work." See also Wojtyła, *Acting Person*, 10: "For our position is that *action serves as a particular moment of approaching—that is, of experiencing—the person.*" Emphasis in the original.

33. For Wojtyła, this experience of self-efficacy is the experience of personal choice in which "there is between a person and action a sensibly experiential, casual relation which brings the person ... to recognize his action to be the result of his efficacy; in this sense he must accept his actions as his own property and also, primarily because of their moral nature, as the domain of his responsibility." See Wojtyła, *Acting Person*, 67.

34. Wojtyła came to focus on the importance of the human act by way of his studies on Scheler and Immanuel Kant. Scheler had formulated his philosophy, in part, as a critique of Kant's understanding of moral obligation. Because of the sharp divide between theoretical and practical reason in Kant's philosophy, moral obligation was separated from the experience of the world. Thus, for Kant, morality was not a response to perceived values but was the compulsion of the will to follow the categorical imperative. In contrast, Scheler focused morality primarily on the phenomenological experience of values, passively received from one's encounter with the world. However, Wojtyła stipulated, Scheler's approach was an overreaction to the Kantian priority of the will, leaving the person too passive in the face of these perceived values. Ultimately, while Kant emphasized the importance of duty and Scheler the importance of experienced values, neither provided an integral account of human morality. For Wojtyła, the experience of values is an important component in reconnecting morality with the objective world, but the role of the will must be considered as well. Thus, it is the consciously willed act that provides the best approach to morality. For this influence of Scheler and Kant on Wojtyła's philosophy, see Schmitz, *At the Center of the Human Drama*, 42–50; and Tadeusz Slipko, "Le développement de la pensée éthique du Cardinal Karol Wojtyła," *Collectanea theologica* 50, special issue (1980): 61–87.

Against Descartes's *cogito*, Wojtyła exclaims, "In reality, does man reveal himself in *thinking* or, rather, in the actual *enacting* of his existence? In observing, interpreting, speculating, or reasoning ... or in the confrontation itself when he has to take an active stand upon issues requiring vital decisions and having vital consequences and repercussions?"[35] Thus, in the face of a modern temptation to subjectivism Wojtyła posits the immense weight of lived reality. Human life is indeed concerned with subjective values and impressions, but these are bound up in the greater question, "How should I live?," and the consequences that flow from answering it.[36]

It is notable that, in this recognition of the undeniably objective consequences of conscious acts, Wojtyła likewise acknowledges that it is only by such acts that a person *reveals* him- or herself. But this revelation is not simply the unveiling of what was always there before. It is, rather, the unveiling of what was always there in potential *and* what is, likewise, now coming to be. That is to say, the conscious act manifests one's latent abilities while, at the same time, actualizing them—by such an act the person truly fulfills him- or herself.[37] Indeed, in this light,

35. Wojtyła, *Acting Person*, vii. Emphasis in the original. See also Simpson, *On Karol Wojtyła*, 12.

36. See John Paul II, *Crossing the Threshold of Hope*, 200: "By this point the war had ended and the controversies with Marxism were in full swing. In those years, my greatest involvement was with young people who asked me questions, not so much about the existence of God, but rather *about how to live*, how to face and resolve problems of love and marriage, not to mention problems related to work. The memory of those young people from the period following the German occupation has always remained with me. In a certain sense, with their doubts and with their questions, they also showed me the way. From our meetings, from my sharing in the problems of their lives, a book was born, the content of which is summarized in the title *Love and Responsibility*. My book on the acting person came later, but it was also born of the same source" (emphasis in the original).

37. See Wojtyła, "Person: Subject and Community," 225: "The human self gradually both discloses itself and constitutes itself—and it discloses itself by constituting itself." In *Acting Person*, 25, Wojtyła points out that St. Thomas referred to this type of act as an *actus humanus* (e.g., ST I-II, q. 6, a. 1). The emphasis upon the *actus humanus* is consonant with Wojtyła's constant concern for the unique dignity of a human being. Joseph Rice explains that this emphasis is even found in Wojtyła's preference for one of the two Polish words used for "humanity." See Rice's "On the 'Proper Weight of a Man': Reexamining the Poetic Foundations of Wojtyła's Theory of Participation," in Billias, Curry, and McLean, *Karol Wojtyła's Philosophical Legacy*, 297: "Polish, moreover, has two terms for humanity, one abstract, and the other concrete; here, Wojtyła refers to 'humanity' not as *ludzkosc* (a universal reference to the abstract idea of man), but as *czlowieczenstwo* (a reference to the always unique and unrepeatable, personal 'I'), that which makes one human—and that, for example, which a cruel man might be accused of lacking. Thus 'humanity' has, in each man, what Wojtyła calls the 'concrete, specific weight of personal being.'"

one could rightly say that it is only by way of such acts that the human quest for meaning and fulfillment is traveled.[38]

The best way to explore this understanding of self-efficacy is to proceed by way of what Wojtyła recognizes to be the human experience of *transcendence*. "Etymologically," he explains, "transcendence means to go over and beyond a threshold or boundary (*trans-scendere*)."[39] In every consciously willed act, a person is necessarily transcending him- or herself, though this happens in two different ways—corresponding to a distinction Wojtyła makes between horizontal and vertical transcendence. With the former, experience reveals that human acts are always directed toward specific objects, beyond the self, that are encountered as goods. Such transcendence corresponds to what is normally taken to be the intentional nature of a human act, and it is exemplified in actions as simple as the selection of food or as complex as the choice of a future spouse.[40] Yet, with the latter, experience manifests the fact that such actions involve a moment of determination in which the person moves him- or herself toward the perceived good. In this moment, the vertical dimension of transcendence is manifested because the person, in a sense, stands over him- or herself in order to make a choice.

Perhaps another way of explaining this "standing over" is to say that, in vertical transcendence, as is the case with its horizontal counterpart, a person is directed toward an object, though, in this instance, the object is the self. In a moment of conscious choice, one is simultaneously the subject and the object of his or her action: one not only wills the external good, but also wills him- or herself toward that good. This is described

---

38. See Wojtyła, "Person: Subject and Community," 232: "The picture of personal subjectivity that unveils itself before us in experience would be incomplete if we failed to include the element of fulfillment. If action is the avenue to knowledge of the person (*operari sequitir esse*), then we must necessarily examine the expression 'to fulfill an action.' This expression seems in a most basic way to refer not just to the reality of the action, the *actus humanus*, but also to the reality of the human being, the subject who fulfills the action. This is not an accidental expression. An action as an *actus humanus* is this actual fullness in the order of *operari*. The person, however, is always included within the compass of the action's fulfillment." The translator's footnote on page 260 notes that the phrase "to fulfill an action," in the original Polish, encompasses the dual meaning of which Wojtyła is speaking: "In Polish ... the same verb (*spelniac*) is used in the phrases 'to perform an action' (*spelniac czyn*) and 'to fulfill oneself' (*spelniac siebie*). Spelniac literally means to bring to completion or fullness. Wojtyła here is playing on the similarity of the phrases to bring home his point that when we fulfill (perform) an action we simultaneously fulfill ourselves as well."

39. Wojtyła, *Acting Person*, 119.

40. Ibid. See also Simpson, *On Karol Wojtyła*, 27.

by Wojtyła as self-determination,[41] and this self-determination is a fact uniquely manifested in consciousness: "The person, the acting ego, also experiences the awareness that he is the one who is determined by himself and that his decisions make him somebody, who may be good or bad."[42] Simply put, in a deliberate act, one's consciousness experiences that I, the *subject*, direct myself, the *object*. This is none other than the conscious experience of human freedom.

Transcendence: Freedom Directed toward Fulfillment

Thus far, Wojtyła's patient attention to lived experience has revealed a dynamic structure of human transcendence in which the person chooses different objects encountered as goods and, in this choosing, proves to be a self-determining being.[43] The human person is endowed with freedom, and consciousness itself bears witness to this fact. Nevertheless, Wojtyła perceives in this analysis of freedom a certain dynamism—a propulsion toward personal fulfillment. For, why would one choose a particular good if it did not represent the realization of a desire latent in that person? "The tendency toward the fulfillment of oneself," Wojtyła claims, "shows that this self is somehow incomplete."[44] Thus, the experience of freedom is proof that a person is simultaneously confronted with a desire for fulfillment and a sense of contingency. A person makes choices not simply out of sheer willfulness, but because the goods encountered represent some sort of satisfaction to the one who chooses.[45] Thus, for Wojtyła, freedom is intimately tied to the quest for human fulfillment.

41. Wojtyła, Acting Person, 112: "Self-determination puts the ego, that is to say, the subject, in the place of the object."

42. Ibid., 113.

43. Wojtyła recognizes that self-determination can be limited by the constraints of one's nature, as well as things such as habits, vices, and acts that "happen" to a person. The goal of becoming a fulfilled person thus includes what he calls "integration," whereby transcendence incorporates or overcomes these elements of human existence. See Acting Person, 189–219.

44. Wojtyła, "Person: Subject and Community," 232–33.

45. Thomas Ryba notes, "Though transcendence is experienced in fulfillment, the quest for fulfillment also makes the person aware that fulfillment is contingent on the external world." See his "Action at the Moral Core of Personhood: Transcendence, Self-Determination, and Integration in the Anthropology of John Paul II," in Billias, Curry, and McLean, Karol Wojtyła's Philosophical Legacy, 253. Emphasis in the original.

The metaphysical grounding of Wojtyła's understanding of this fulfillment can be traced back to his embrace of Thomistic metaphysics. In particular, St. Thomas's notion of potency and act and his theory of participation play prominent roles in Wojtyła's analysis of the person and his or her acts. Regarding the first of these Thomistic principles, certainly one of the most celebrated appropriations of Aristotelian thought lies in Thomas's blending of the Greek philosopher's metaphysical categories of potentiality and actuality with a Christian understanding of God as Being itself:

Aristotle's primary metaphysical distinction was between potentiality and actuality, and, for him, being is ultimately actuality. Such a doctrine could not be the last word for a theologian reflecting on creation and on the statement in Exodus 3:14, "I am, that I am," which seems to say that God is Being. Aquinas took up the distinction between essence and existence already employed by the Muslims and used it to deepen Aristotle's conception. Existence he did not construe as an accident accruing to essence, as Avicenna had it, but rather, as the very act of existing of the essence.[46]

The existential Thomist Étienne Gilson expresses this identity of being and act even further:

Not: to be, then to act, but: to be is to act. And the very first thing which "to be" does, is to make its own essence to be, that is, "to be a being." This is done at once, completely and definitively.... But the next thing which "to be" does, is to begin bringing its own individual essence somewhat nearer [to] its own completion.[47]

46. Arthur Hyman and James J. Walsh, "Thomas Aquinas," in *Philosophy in the Middle Ages: The Christian, Islamic, and Jewish Traditions*, 2nd ed., ed. Arthur Hyman and James J. Walsh (Indianapolis: Hackett, 1973), 504–5. See also Thomas Aquinas, *Summa Contra Gentiles* I, ch. 43.

47. Étienne Gilson, *Being and Some Philosophers*, 2nd ed., trans. unknown (Toronto: Pontifical Institute of Medieval Studies, 1952), 184, as quoted in W. Norris Clarke, *Person and Being* (Milwaukee: Marquette University Press, 2004), 8. See also ST I, q. 42, a. 1, ad. 1 [214]: "The first effect of form is being, for everything has being by reason of its form. The second effect is operation, for every agent acts through its form." Wojtyła, in an article published in the Catholic weekly *Tygodnik Powszechny*, offered his own explanation: "Each being is its own essence, that which we understand quite simply as signifying that which is a given being (*quidditas*).... Contrary to [its] accidents, the substantial being in itself is the subject of existence and action: it exists, therefore, and acts in an autonomous way.... Acting actualizes the essence of a given being: that which it is in potentiality becomes, thereby, a reality. And it is, therefore, the realization of all that a given being is in potentiality that constitutes its finality; for it corresponds to its nature, and, consequently, contributes to the awakening of the aspirations and the activity of a given being." See Wojtyła, "Nature et perfection," in *En esprit et en vérité: Recueil de textes 1949–1978*, trans. Gwendoline Jarczyk (Paris: Le Centurion, 1980), 117. My translation from French to English.

All beings, therefore, are "in act," so to speak, for to exist is to act. Now, aside from God (who, as Being itself, alone is Pure Act), all beings can be expressed by the dynamic relationship between potency and act.[48] As Gilson points out, for these there is a sort of first act that is the movement from nonexistence to existence.[49] The second act, then, is to move "nearer to completion."

This is precisely the metaphysical vision that Wojtyła willingly inherits.[50] For the Polish disciple of St. Thomas, there are not "yet any other conceptions and any other language which would adequately render the dynamic essence of change—of all change whatever occurring in any being—apart from those that we have been endowed with by the philosophy of potency and act."[51] Indeed, his own emphasis on the conscious act of the human person is, in its own way, a gloss on this dynamic concept.[52] For Wojtyła, it is the conscious act that allows a person to transcend him- or herself—to leave one's current state in order to move "nearer to completion": it is the conscious act that most fully

48. Potency is the limiting factor for created beings. See Clarke, "The Limitation of Act by Potency," in *Explorations in Metaphysics: Being—God—Person* (Notre Dame, Ind.: University of Notre Dame Press, 1994), 65–88, especially 67: "No act or perfection can be found in a limited degree in any being unless it is conjoined with a really distinct limiting principle whose nature is to be a potency for act." Clarke's article is an excellent introduction to the both the Aristotelian and Platonic roots of the act-potency relationship.

49. For St. Thomas, because God is Being itself, he is Pure Act and thus is his own existence. For created beings, one can make a distinction between their essence and existence—I can think of a tree, but that tree need not actually exist. But with God, his essence is his existence, for it is impossible to make such a distinction in a being who is Being itself. Ultimately, then, in a (created) person, essence and existence can be correlated with potency and act. The first "act" of a person is that of existing itself. The second act is to move nearer to completion. Wojtyła's primary concern is with such second acts. See John F. Wippel, *The Metaphysical Thought of Thomas Aquinas: From Finite Being to Uncreated Being* (Washington, D.C.: The Catholic University of America Press, 2000), 107–8.

50. See Wojtyła, "In Search of the Basis of Perfectionism in Ethics," in *Person and Community*, 48: "[St. Thomas's] philosophy of being takes full into account the whole dynamism of reality. Reality is dynamic, for we observe that beings undergo change. A change is always the actualization of some potency. The actualization of potency consists in the real coming-into-existence of something that previously existed only in potency—in other words, really did not exist. Once a being has already begun to exist and continues to exist, actualization is the perfection of that being." See also Wojtyła, *Acting Person*, 63.

51. Wojtyła, *Acting Person*, 64.

52. Still, Wojtyła is clear that even unconscious acts, that is, unwilled acts that happen in a person (e.g., the beating of the heart) are also metaphysically representative of the movement from potency to act. See *Acting Person*, 64. Nevertheless, it is the *actus humanus* that can fulfill a human being in a uniquely personal way.

leads to the fulfillment of a person's potency.[53] Thus, transcendence is not only an experiential datum; it is a metaphysical reality as well.

This embrace of potency and act leads to a further concept in St. Thomas's thought—his theory of participation.[54] In a sense this theory has been latent in the discussion of potency and act just discussed, for how could a person move nearer to completion or fulfillment if he or she did not somehow come to participate more fully in Being? Drawing upon the influence of Augustine on St. Thomas, Wojtyła explains that every being can be "measured," so to speak, in accord with the degree to which it participates in Being: "The perfection of created beings is essentially related to God: God is the fullness of existence, and creatures participate in this fullness because they owe their existence to God. [Furthermore,] the more perfect they are, the more they participate in the unconditional fullness of existence that is God."[55] Such a metaphysical vision conceives of a hierarchy of beings, with higher beings participating more fully in Being than lower ones. Yet, in returning

53. Ibid., 112: "The performing of an action is at once the fulfillment of the person. Here 'fulfillment' may be regarded as having a correlative meaning with 'actualization' and thus with the metaphysical meaning of the term 'act.'"

54. Thomas's theory of participation is a blending of Aristotelian and neo-Platonic (including Augustine's) thought, and it largely came to prominence in Thomistic scholarship in the twentieth century by way of those such as Cornelio Fabro, Louis Geiger, and, in the United States, W. Norris Clarke. See Clarke's "The Meaning of Participation in St. Thomas," in his *Explorations in Metaphysics*, 89–101. The importance of this theory of participation in Wojtyła's project has received little attention, though there are some who point out its significance. See, for instance, McLean, "Karol Wojtyła's Mutual Enrichment of the Philosophies of Being and Consciousness," 16–18; and Rice, "On the 'Proper Weight of a Man,'" 297–324. The latter is unique in that it unites what is normally taken to be an altogether different understanding of participation (Wojtyła's analysis of acting together with others) with this Thomistic/Augustinian notion.

55. Wojtyła, "On the Metaphysical and Phenomenological Basis of the Moral Norm," in *Person and Community*, 77. See also page 76: "In beings we find different degrees of perfection, which are connected with the different degrees in which the three cofactors of the good— mode, species, and order—occur with respect to different beings.... The perfection of every created being is in this sense 'measurable.' Only Divine Being is beyond the scope of mode, species, and order. As a good in every respect, God excludes all measures of good, while at the same time constituting their basis: every mode, species, and order has its cause in God."
Though secondary to the topic at hand, it should be pointed out that Wojtyła believes that moral norms are able to be conceived precisely because of this participatory relationship with God as the fullness of Being and Goodness. Reason apprehends the good and measures it according to the hierarchy of goods, allowing it to conceive of moral norms for human action. Norms are, therefore, not external impositions on one's freedom, but flow from the person's own cognition of the truth about the good. For more on the role of moral norms in the thought of Wojtyła/John Paul II, see Adrian J. Reimers, *Truth about the Good: Moral Norms in the Thought of John Paul II* (Ave Maria, Fla.: Sapientia Press, 2011).

to a focus on the person and the conscious act, such a vision also implies that human acts have the ability to bring the person into a greater share of this participation. By moving "nearer to completion," to use Gilson's terminology, a person partakes more fully of Being.

A distinctly moral element is added to this theory of participation when one considers that, in the Thomistic synthesis, goodness and being are convertible.[56] Goodness has its objective measure in God, who is Goodness itself. As such, it is not simply any conscious act that can effect a greater participation in Being. Only a good act—not an evil one—can be efficacious in this sense.[57] For Wojtyła, "fulfillment is reached only through the good, while moral evil leads or amounts to, so to speak, nonfulfillment."[58] One could even say, therefore, that good acts actualize a person's existence, while evil ones lead, in some sense, to his or her own nonexistence.[59]

Here in this context, then, lies the important moment of delibera-

---

56. See ST I, q. 5, a. 1.

57. See Wojtyła, "In Search of the Basis of Perfectionism," 48–49; and Wojtyła, *Acting Person*, 98–99: "It is man's actions, his conscious acting, that make of him *what* and *who* he actually is. This form of the human becoming thus presupposes the efficacy of causation proper to man.... It is man's actions, the way he consciously acts, that make of him a good or a bad man—good or bad in the moral sense. To be 'morally good' means to be good as a man. To be 'morally bad' means to be bad as a man. Whether a man, because of his actions, becomes morally better or morally worse depends on the nature and modalities of his actions. The qualitative moments and virtualities of actions, inasmuch as they refer to the moral norm and ultimately to the dictates of conscience, are imprinted upon man by his performing the action" (emphasis in the original). It is clear for Wojtyła, following St. Thomas's understanding of participation and the formation of moral norms, that moral goodness is not merely socially defined but is measured objectively.

58. Ibid., 153. Thus, as Wojtyła notes on page 155, the person's transcendence is linked to the classic understanding of the Transcendentals (i.e., truth, goodness, and beauty): "The transcendence of the person understood metaphysically is no abstract notion; the evidence of experience tells us that the spiritual life of man essentially refers to, and in its strivings vibrates with the ... innermost attempts to reach truth, goodness, and beauty. We may thus safely speak of the role of these absolute modes of values that accompany the experience of personal transcendence."

59. Ibid.: "This approach appears somewhat convergent with the view that all evil, including moral evil, is a defect [or, more commonly, a privation]. The defect occurs in the moral order and thus in the axiological order from which it is instilled into the existential-ontological order; for the significance of moral values for the person is such that the true fulfillment of the person is accomplished by the positive moral virtuality of the action and not by the mere performance of the action itself. Morally evil virtualities of action, on the other hand, lead to nonfulfillment even though the person is acting. When performing an action the person fulfills himself also from the ontological point of view. Thus we come to the conclusion that the deepest significance with respect to the real existence of morality can be grasped as man's fulfillment, whereas his allegiance to evil means in fact nonfulfillment."

tion in any given conscious act. This is the moment in which a person, in freedom, determines his or her own self by choosing the path that leads either to fulfillment or nonfulfillment. Wojtyła even recognizes in this potential fulfillment the more classical conception of what the Greeks called *eudaimonia*, or happiness.[60] Human happiness is precisely what is at stake in a moral act. By such an act, one either participates more fully in Being, becomes more fully good, and reaches further fulfillment; or one heads further into nonexistence, becomes more evil, and grows frustrated by nonfulfillment.

Of course, such deliberation is not the proper realm of the will alone. Logically speaking, one can only choose a good or evil act *after* weighing and considering the goodness of the available options. So to what does this deliberation belong? It belongs to one's conscience and to the intellect that forms this conscience by recognizing the truth about the good. Here, Wojtyła once again expresses his fidelity to both subjectivity and objectivity—the modern preoccupation with conscience as the moral authority of decision making is acknowledged, yet it is firmly wedded to the cognition of truth by the intellect.

One's conscience is, undeniably, an experiential datum. The weight of a person's conscience is so prevalent in Western culture that it has become popularized, though perhaps incorrectly, by the familiar image of the angel on one shoulder, whispering what is the right thing to do, with the devil on the other, offering his temptations by way of the other ear.[61] Today one is more apt to hear the term used, at least in the public

60. Ibid., 174–75. It is possible to see the convergence of a virtue ethics approach to morality with this emphasis on happiness/fulfillment and its achievement by good acts. See Wojtyła, "Person: Subject and Community," 235: "The experience of morality also reveals ways in which moral value, good or evil, may become rooted or ingrained in the subject. In this regard, the ethics of Aristotle and later that of Thomas Aquinas, as well as modern-day character studies, speak of habits (*de habitibus*) and also of moral proficiencies, of virtues and vices." See also Schmitz, *At the Center of the Human Drama*, 49. For an excellent introduction to virtue ethics (along with the role of grace and the gifts of the Holy Spirit in Christian ethics) and its ties to happiness/human fulfillment, see Servais Pinckaers, *The Sources of Christian Ethics*, trans. Mary Thomas Noble (Washington, D.C.: The Catholic University of America Press, 1995). For an introduction that is particularly useful in pedagogical contexts, see William C. Mattison III, *Introducing Moral Theology: True Happiness and the Virtues* (Grand Rapids, Mich.: Brazos, 2008).

61. See Mattison, *Introducing Moral Theology*, 105–6. Mattison corrects this image of one's conscience as a moral duality, explaining instead that conscience deals with "what we honestly and sincerely think to be right, despite any temptations, peer pressures, or other challenges. It is what we think in our gut, in our heart of hearts, is the right thing to do." This position is congruent with Wojtyła's.

square, in terms of "acting according to one's conscience." Conscience, by this account, carries a certain weight of responsibility or duty with it, and it is this latter usage that is closest to what Wojtyła intends.

While acknowledging the importance of the impression it makes upon a person's interiority, Wojtyła is quick to note that the experience of the conscience is necessarily wrapped up with the experience of perceiving the truth about the matter at hand. "The function of the conscience," he explains, "consists in distinguishing the element of moral good in the action and in releasing and forming a sense of duty with respect to this good."[62] Yet this sense of duty is nothing less than the "experiential form of the reference to (or dependence on) the moral truth."[63] Thus, in a given situation, one's conscience compels a certain action precisely because it manifests a recognition of the truth.

Conscience, therefore, is the experiential proof of the will's reliance upon the intellect in a conscious act. The student who, by the weight of his conscience, decides to forgo cheating on an exam has cognized the good inherent in doing his own work and the evil connected to copying the work of another. In such an act, the intellect's perception of the truth precedes the will's choice.[64] Thus, while the will is largely responsible for the fulfillment of the person, its acts must be informed by the intellect. As Wojtyła explains, "Nothing may be the object of will unless it is [first] known."[65]

True to his own method, Wojtyła has thus embraced the traditional metaphysical claims of the priority of the intellect and the convertibility of truth and goodness, though he has brought these claims to light by

62. Wojtyła, *Acting Person*, 156.

63. Ibid.

64. That the intellect's receptivity to the truth leads to the will's choice of a good demonstrates that not only are being and goodness convertible, but so are goodness and truth. See ST I, q. 16, a. 3. It should be pointed out that the "object" in question in a conscious act is not limited to a particular thing the person desires (e.g., a piece of fruit). Rather, as Michael Sherwin explains, the will's action can be distinguished by willing, intending, and choosing: "All these acts presuppose the presence of cognition. Willing presupposes cognition of something as simply good; intending presupposes cognition of a good understood as attainable through some means; choosing presupposes the cognitive judgment that a particular good is the best means to attaining an intended end." See Michael S. Sherwin, *By Knowledge and by Love: Charity and Knowledge in the Moral Theology of St. Thomas Aquinas* (Washington, D.C.: The Catholic University of America Press, 2005), 32.

65. Wojtyła, *Acting Person*, 114. On page 146 he adds, "The cognitive transcendence toward the object as known is the condition of the transcendence of the will in the action with respect to the object of the will." See also ST I-II, q. 6, a. 4; and St. Augustine, *De Trinitate* 10.1.

way of a common experience.[66] One's conscience is certainly an important and essential moral source; still, the conscience, in being faithful to its etymology (con/with–science/knowledge), is dependent on the truth about the good under consideration. In returning to the experience of human freedom as manifested in vertical transcendence, one can now say that the fulfillment a person seeks is not only contingent upon the goodness of a given object of the will, but on the truth of that object as cognized by the intellect as well. In Wojtyła's words, "The experience of fulfillment goes hand in hand with the experience of truth."[67]

Ultimately, then, the moment of deliberation in a conscious act is intimately bound up with a person's receptivity to the truth about the good. It may sound like a strange truth for modern liberal societies, but freedom alone is not the essence of happiness. Rather, it is the means to the truth about the good that forms happiness' inner core.[68] Wojtyła's look into the interiority of the person—his pausing at the moment of conscious decision—shows that objectivity is the necessary foundation for the fulfillment of the person. In the end, one's longing is contingent upon the external world, that which is other than oneself. Freedom and the fulfillment it promises are dependent on a "surrender to truth."[69]

The Act of Love: Fulfillment with Other Persons

Wojtyła's phenomenological and metaphysical exploration of the person describes how a human being comes to fulfill him- or herself in a

66. See Wojtyła, "On the Metaphysical and Phenomenological Basis of the Moral Norm," 80: "The good is the object of the will, whereas the cognitive apprehension of the good—its objectification—is, according to St. Thomas, an object of reason. Both of these faculties work closely together and with one another (utraque ad actum alterius operator): the will wills so that reason may know; reason, in turn, knows that the will wills and what the will wills. A result of this cooperation of reason and the will is that the good and the true somehow mutually include one another." See also ST I, q. 59, a. 2, ad. 3.

67. Wojtyła, Love and Responsibility, trans. H. T. Willets (San Francisco: Ignatius Press, 1981), 117. See also Deborah Savage, "The Subjective Dimension of Human Work: The Conversion of the Acting Person in Laborem Exercens," in Billias, Curry, and McLean, Karol Wojtyła's Philosophical Legacy, 199–220, especially 210–13.

68. See Wojtyła, Acting Person, 166: "Far from abolishing freedom, truth liberates it." See also Servais Pinckaers, "Freedom and Happiness," in Morality: The Catholic View, trans. Michael Sherwin (South Bend, Ind.: St. Augustine's Press, 2001), 65–81. For the political consequences of the differing conceptions of freedom, see Joseph A. Komonchak, "Vatican II and the Encounter between Catholicism and Liberalism," in Catholicism and Liberalism, ed. R. Bruce Douglas and David Hollenbach (Cambridge: Cambridge University Press, 1994), 76–99.

69. Wojtyła, Acting Person, 156.

conscious act. Still, one could justly say that, among the various acts of which a person is capable, it is the *act of love* that preoccupied the Polish scholar and pastor the most. Even as a young priest, Wojtyła had become fascinated by the human longing for love, both received and given, and he made it a point of emphasis in his pastoral ministry to teach young men and women how to answer their inner "vocation to love."[70] He was known for taking trips with such friends into the mountains for prayer and recreation, and it is not a stretch to imagine that on these journeys, in the many moments of listening to their hopes and longings, he began to cultivate a deeper awareness of the importance of human love.

As such, it is easier to understand why Wojtyła would eventually claim that, though any morally good act contributes to the actualization of the person and, thus, to his or her fulfillment, none is more fulfilling than the act of love. "The potential inherent in the person," he explained, "is most fully actualized through love. [Indeed,] the person finds in love the greatest possible fullness of being."[71] Certainly, other acts participate in the self-actualization of the person precisely because that person surrenders him- or herself to the truth about the good; but, in the act of love, the person can surrender him- or herself in such a way that he or she makes a total self-gift.[72]

Wojtyła's time in the mountains most certainly played a substantial role in bringing him to claim such preeminence for love. Even so, he stands as part of a long tradition that holds a central place for love in the lives of human beings. Indeed, Aristotle had claimed that love "is most necessary for our life. For no one would choose to live without friends even if he had all the other goods."[73] Such attention to love is undoubtedly rich and compelling for a modern world that does not cease to be fascinated by the longing to love and be loved; nevertheless, it raises certain questions that must be addressed if it is to be adequately reconciled with Wojtyła's earlier analysis of human persons

---

70. See the poignant reflections in John Paul II, *Crossing the Threshold of Hope*, 122–24 and 200.

71. Wojtyła, *Love and Responsibility*, 82.

72. Ibid., 95–100. More will be said about Wojtyła's concept of "self-gift" later.

73. Aristotle, *Nicomachean Ethics* 8.1. I have used the version found in Aristotle, *Introductory Readings*, trans. Terence Irwin and Gail Fine (Indianapolis: Hackett, 1996), 263. As Irwin and Fine note in the appended glossary, friendship (*philia*) and love (*philein*) share the same common Greek root.

and their fulfillment. Thus far, it has been possible to read Wojtyła's anthropology in purely individualistic terms. But (a) love necessitates other persons, and, indeed, (b) such persons bear an intrinsic, equal dignity to that of the lover. As such, the questions arise: Does the fullest self-actualization of the person require a loving relationship with other persons—in other words, community—to fulfill human existence? Furthermore, how can love be the most self-fulfilling act without regarding other persons as mere objects of fulfillment for the one who loves?

These questions form the remainder of the concerns of this chapter. In answering both it is helpful, once again, to recognize Wojtyła's reliance upon the thought of St. Thomas. In fact, in many ways, Thomas's analysis of love forms the foundation of Wojtyła's own understanding. Still, as was the case with the previous analysis, he augments Thomas's thought with a distinctly personalistic concern. For Wojtyła, as for the Angelic Doctor, love can be spoken of in terms of being a "complacency" or attraction, and it can involve both love of concupiscence and love of friendship. Yet, moving beyond Thomas, Wojtyła also speaks of the possibility of "betrothed love" as a particularly important manifestation of the "gift of self."

To begin, for Thomas love is, at its most basic level, a change wrought in a person by an object he or she has encountered as a good. Love is a *complacentia* in that object[74]—it is a certain "inclination" toward it, "the very first tug of attraction" felt in response to it.[75] From this complacency (*com*/with–*placentia*/pleasure), one is either moved to desire the object if it is not possessed or to take joy in it if it is. In a sense, then, love is the basic principle that underlies all action. "Every agent, whatever it be," Thomas notes, "does every action from love of some kind."[76] This implies that, for human beings, love requires a prior cognition by the

74. ST I-II, q. 26, a. 1. For the Latin text, I have used the University of Navarra's *Corpus Thomisticum*, http://www.corpusthomisticum.org/iopera.html. All subsequent references to the Latin will be from this source. While "complacency" in its normal English usage is marked by a certain imprudent self-contentment, *complacentia*, for St. Thomas, bespeaks an attraction for an object with no connection to such imprudence. As William Mattison explains, "The object of love effects a change on the lover, such that there is an aptitude in the lover toward 'complacency' in the beloved as something good." See Mattison's "Movements of Love: A Thomistic Perspective on *Agape* and *Eros*," *Journal of Moral Theology* 1, no. 2 (2012): 34.

75. See Sherwin, *By Knowledge and by Love*, 71; and James McEvoy, "The Other as Oneself: Friendship and Love in the Thought of St. Thomas Aquinas," in *Thomas Aquinas: Approaches to Truth*, ed. James McEvoy and Michael Dunne (Dublin: Four Courts, 2002), 21.

76. ST I-II, q. 28, a. 6 [713].

intellect in order for an object to effect this inclination.[77] One must first know or understand an object in some way before it can be desired or enjoyed.

In his book *Love and Responsibility*, Wojtyła inherits this understanding of love, though he refers to it simply as "love as attraction."[78] Although he is mainly concerned with the type of love that develops between a man and a woman, he nevertheless evidences the basic Thomistic structure noted earlier. Thus, love as attraction occurs when someone is "regarded as a 'good.'"[79] This recognition of the beloved likewise requires the knowledge procured by the intellect—in Wojtyła's words, "we discover in an attraction a certain cognitive commitment of the subject ... towards the object."[80] Furthermore, just as Thomas holds love as complacency to be the principle of all of the lover's acts, so too does Wojtyła claim this initial attraction to be at the source of human love: "Y's reaction to a particular value depends ... not only on the fact that it is really present in person *x*, but also on the fact that *y* is particularly sensitive to it, particularly quick to perceive and respond to it."[81] Ultimately, then, for both thinkers love has its root in a complacency/attraction that is caused when a person cognizes a particular object.

Attraction, however, is not the only aspect of love considered by St. Thomas.[82] Drawing upon the Augustinian distinction between "use" and "enjoyment," Thomas notes that one can experience both "love of

77. See Sherwin, *By Knowledge and by Love*, 71. It should be noted that, while love takes a certain form in rational animals, according to Thomas love is "present wherever appetition is to be found," meaning that "love is found in all beings, since all beings have some kind of striving, tendency, or inclination." Thus love occurs whether the appetite is natural, sensitive, or rational. See also David M. Gallagher, "Person and Ethics in Thomas Aquinas," *Acta Philosophica* 4, no. 1 (1995): 52, as well as ST I-II, q. 26, a. 1.

78. See Wojtyła, *Love and Responsibility*, 74–80. On page 76, he specifically refers to love as attraction as *amor complacentia*.

79. Ibid., 74.

80. Ibid., 75.

81. Ibid., 77. Both on this page and the preceding one, Wojtyła notes that "attraction is not just one of the elements of love, one of its components so to speak, but is one of the essential aspects of love as a whole."

82. St. Thomas's analysis of love certainly presents a "bewildering variety" of concepts, yet the "very richness of these concepts challenges his reader constantly to make sense of their intertwining." See Guy Mansini, "*Duplex Amor* and the Structure of Love in Aquinas," in *Thomistica*, supplement, vol. 1 of *Recherches de théologie ancienne et medievale* (1995): 196, and McEvoy, "The Other as Oneself," 19, respectively.

concupiscence" and "love of friendship."[83] Augustine had previously explained the distinction between enjoyment and use as the difference between loving something for its own sake and using something so as to apply it to the possession of that which should be enjoyed.[84] Thomas makes this distinction his own in article 4 of question 26 of the *Prima Secundae*:

The movement of love has a twofold tendency: towards the good which a man wishes to someone (to himself or to another) and towards that to which he wishes some good. Accordingly, man has *love of concupiscence* towards the good that he wishes to another, and *love of friendship* towards him to whom he wishes good.[85]

While, here, Augustine's distinction retains its force, later, in the same article, Thomas will establish specific directional tendencies, so to speak, for one type of love versus the other. Thus, in the previous text, both the good desired and the love of the friend can be directed toward the friend or to the self (the "friend" is the self in this latter case); but, in the reply to the first objection, Thomas claims that "a friend is, properly speaking, one to whom we wish good, while we are said to desire what we wish *for ourselves*."[86] This reply reveals an apparent tension in the analysis of these two distinct types of love, the tension between the self-fulfillment that is the driving force behind Thomas's own anthropology (and, as this chapter has shown, Wojtyła's as well) and the love of someone for his or her own sake.[87] It appears, in this second use, that love of concupiscence and love of friendship cannot coexist.

83. ST I-II, q. 26, a. 4.

84. See St. Augustine, *De Doctrina Christiana* 1.3: "To enjoy something is to hold fast to it in love for its own sake. To use something is to apply whatever it may be to the purpose of obtaining what you love." I have used the version *On Christian Teaching*, trans. R. P. H. Green (Oxford: Oxford University Press, 1997), 9. In 1.20 [16–17], Augustine exclaims that only eternal and unchangeable things (i.e., God) are to be enjoyed, while everything else, including humans, are to be used. His concern, therefore, is that humans find the satisfaction of their desire solely in God; everything else serves as a means to this end. Mansini, "Duplex Amor," 157–58, explains how St. Thomas appropriated Augustine's general distinction in 1.3, but freed it from the division between created and eternal things present in 1.20. For Thomas, it is possible for a person to love something for its own sake without finding his or her final rest in that thing.

85. ST I-II, q. 26, a. 4 [706]. Emphasis mine.

86. Ibid. Emphasis mine.

87. For an application of the love of concupiscence and love of friendship to modern readings on *eros* and *agape*, see Mattison, "Movements of Love," 31–60. Mattison raises the issue of this same tension by way of Anders Nygren, who claimed that *agape* and *eros* are fundamentally opposed. See Nygren's *Agape and Eros*, trans. Philip Watson (Philadelphia: Westminister Press, 1953).

One either wills another's good (love of friendship) or desires a good for oneself (love of concupiscence).

An initial step toward resolving this tension is found in one of Thomas's earlier works, his *Scriptum Super Sententiis*. The article in question concerns whether angels, apart from grace, would have loved God more than themselves, though its conclusions are applicable to the dynamic of human love already raised. For instance, in the second objection, Thomas notes that "nature is always curved back upon itself"— that is, any act of love by a subject must, by metaphysical necessity, be aimed toward a good for that subject.[88] The next objection follows suit, noting that only God's actions are truly free from necessity. For all others, every action "pursues some benefit for the agent himself."[89] In the replies to these objections, Thomas affirms the metaphysical principle underlying each but notes the significance of the agent's *intention*. Thus, in replying to the former objection, he explains that it is true that nature loves its own good; however, "it need not be the case that the lover's intention rests in the fact that the good is *his own*, but rather it can be the case that the intention rests in this, that it is *good*."[90] Likewise, in replying to the latter objection, he explains that, "even though from its action some benefit accrues to any created creature whatsoever, it need not be the case that that benefit be the object of intention, as is evident in the friendship of noble-minded people."[91] Both answers provide a type of psychological solution to the problem: one can intend the love of the beloved for the beloved's sake, while, metaphysically speaking, the act of love will nevertheless be self-fulfilling.[92] Even so, there is latent in this explanation a more metaphysical solution, and I believe

---

88. *Scriptum Super Sententiis* II, d. 3, q. 4. I have used the translation found in Thomas Aquinas, *On Love and Charity: Readings from the Commentary on the Sentences of Peter Lombard*, trans. Peter A. Kwasniewski, Thomas Bolin, and Joseph Bolin (Washington, D.C.: The Catholic University of America Press, 2008), 82.

89. Ibid.

90. Ibid., 85. Emphasis in the original.

91. Ibid.

92. See Thomas D. Williams, *Who Is My Neighbor? Personalism and the Foundations of Human Rights* (Washington, D.C.: The Catholic University of America Press, 2005), 172: "While friendship and benevolence do undoubtedly redound to the moral benefit of the one who practices them, they are not *sought* chiefly as self-perfecting goods. One does not set out to 'practice the virtue of friendship' but to love the other as a friend. The self-perfecting virtue of friendship *results from* loving the other principally for his own sake and not for one's own benefit" (emphasis in the original).

that this solution is brought to light more clearly elsewhere in the *Summa Theologiae*.

While two uses of the love of concupiscence/love of friendship distinction in the *Summa* have already been noted, Guy Mansini draws attention to a third use that, I propose, can serve to illuminate Thomas's observation of the friendship of "noble-minded people" in the *Scriptum Super Sententiis*. This third use is found in article 3 of question 27 of the *Prima Secundae*. In this article, Thomas explains how a likeness between the lover and the beloved can be a cause of love. Love of concupiscence is, thus, based on the "*potential* likeness of the lover to the beloved object," which is to say "its basis is a lack in the subject that the subject wants filled."[93] Love of friendship, on the other hand, is founded upon an *actual* likeness, which is to say it is based upon "some common possession of a positive determination."[94] Now the difference between love of concupiscence and love of friendship is placed upon the metaphysical ground of the potency/act distinction. As Mansini explains, this third use resolves the tension between love of other and love of self, for while love of concupiscence can be strictly self-regarding, love of friendship is based upon some perfection that is *shared*.

If love were solely of the first type, then "potters would quarrel among themselves," to use Thomas's own example, "because they hinder one another's gain" (i.e., they fight over their customers' business).[95] In other words, people are bound to fight over goods they lack, so long as those goods are finite. But, in a love of friendship, "there is a principle of universalizability . . . associated with the dictum that actual likeness is [its] foundation. . . . Likeness in these respects cannot, it is supposed, ever lead to the one person's impeding the good of the other."[96] Why is it that this actual likeness is able to overcome the divide between self-directed and other-oriented love? It is because, from a moral perspective, only a greater participation in the good can actualize the human person, and the goodness that is shared in this case—what might be termed *virtue*—is not finite but universal.[97] "Noble-minded

93. Mansini, "*Duplex Amor*," 185. Emphasis mine.
94. Ibid.
95. ST I-II, q. 27, a. 3 [708].
96. Mansini, "*Duplex Amor*," 187.
97. David Gallagher's comments in "Person and Ethics in Thomas Aquinas," 68, are worth quoting at length: "Precisely here, however, the theme of teleology and perfection enters. To

people" not only cognize such goodness as fulfilling for themselves, but cognize it precisely as good universally, such that it is also good for their friends. In such a friendship, "the affections of one tend to the other, as being one with him; and he wishes good to him as to himself."[98]

Thomas's theory of participation in the good is fully evidenced here. The love of friendship is possible because a person is able to transcend the desire for his or her own pleasure by recognizing that one's goodness is only part of a greater whole. "The objective order of goods holds sway over our love" such that we are able to recognize the good as *common*.[99] This common good, then, is able to embrace both the perfection

---

will the other's good presupposes that the other *has* a good, that there is for him a distinction between a better and worse state or between more perfect and less perfect conditions.... What occurs if this pre-given ordination to perfection is denied? First of all, the notion of good is changed, and instead of referring to the thing's perfection, it comes to mean simply that which is desired. Whatever a person desires is good for that person; the good becomes relative to each individual and it is no longer possible to draw a distinction between the true good—what is truly perfective of the person—and the apparent good—what a person simply desires. What would beneficence mean in this context? What would it mean to seek the other person's good? ... It seems that beneficence is radically changed. I can no longer seek a good for the other which the other himself does not take to be good, nor could I refuse him a desired good on the ground that it was not truly good for him. I cannot wish for him what is 'truly' good (benevolence) because this term has lost its content. As soon as we consider the benevolence and beneficence proper to persons such as parents or teachers, we glimpse how radical this view would be, if (as is seldom the case) it were consistently followed. But there is an even more fundamental question: is it at all possible to have a love of friendship if we remove teleology and so change the meaning of 'good'? If the good is what each person desires, it seems that the good can be said only with reference to the desiring individual, and only insofar as it satisfies the desire of that individual. Thus it seems that when the good is so understood, the only love possible for anything, including other persons, is a love of concupiscence ordered to one's own individual good" (emphasis in the original).

98. ST I-II, q. 27, a. 3 [708]. See also Russell Hittinger, *A Critique of the New Natural Law Theory* (Notre Dame, Ind.: University of Notre Dame Press, 1987), 54: "For Aquinas, the issue is not only the good as objectively fulfilling, but rather the morally appropriate kind of love with regard to various kinds of entities being loved. The appropriateness of love with regard to its objects sets the criteria for what is appropriately fulfilling, and, by nature, what is most fulfilling. In short, right reason requires attention not only to a good as it promises to fulfill the self, but also to the status of the beloved. Aquinas presupposes that the agent is situated in a world of hierarchical settings, and a recognition of this is crucial to the operation of right reason in a practical mode."

99. Manisini, "*Duplex Amor*," 161. See also ST II-II, q. 26, a. 3 [1290–91]: "The fellowship of natural goods bestowed on us by God is the foundation of natural love, in virtue of which not only man ... loves God above all things and more than himself, but also every single creature, each in its own way ... because each part naturally loves the common good of the whole more than its own particular good. This is evidenced by its operation, since the principal inclination of each part is towards common action conducive to the good of the whole. It may also be seen in civic virtues whereby sometimes the citizens suffer damage even to their own property and persons for the sake of the common good."

of the lover and that of the beloved simultaneously. In sum, then, for St. Thomas, the problem of harmonizing self-fulfillment and the love of other persons can be reconciled on both psychological and metaphysical grounds.

How does Wojtyła appropriate all of this? First, he inherits Thomas's distinction between love of concupiscence and love of friendship, calling them, for his own purposes, "love as desire" and "love as goodwill."[100] Love as desire he describes as "longing for some good for [the lover's] sake: 'I want you because you are good for me.'"[101] So, too, does Wojtyła appropriate the metaphysical foundation of this desiring love: such a love is caused by a potency, revealing that the "human person is a limited being, not self-sufficient and therefore ... [needing] other beings."[102] Ultimately, love as desire "originates in a need and aims at finding a good which it lacks."[103]

While love as desire is a regular and even necessary aspect of the love between human beings, Wojtyła notes that such a love, on its own, falls short of the dignity of the person. The beloved, like the lover, is a person endowed with intellect and will, and likewise the freedom of self-determination. As such, only love as goodwill is capable of acknowledging this dignity appropriately: "It is not enough to long for a person as a good for oneself; one must also, and above all, long for that person's good."[104] Love as goodwill, therefore, takes a distinct form: "Not 'I long for you as a good' but 'I long for your good,' 'I long for that which is good for you.'"[105] As was the case with love as desire, Wojtyła connects love as goodwill with its metaphysical foundation. Because the good of persons bears a distinctly moral quality, the "true essence of love is realized" when it is "directed to a genuine (not merely an apparent) good in the true way, or in other words, the way appropriate to the nature of that good."[106] Thus, because the proper perfection of human

---

100. Once again, Wojtyła makes reference to the Latin terms used by St. Thomas, *amor concupiscentia* and *amor benevolentiae*. See Wojtyła, *Love and Responsibility*, 80 and 83, respectively. Regarding the latter, although Thomas most commonly uses *amor amicitiae*, he also uses *amor benevolentiae* as its synonym. See, for instance, ST I-II, q. 27, a. 3: "Primus ergo similitudinis modus causat amorem amicitiae, seu benevolentiae."
101. Wojtyła, *Love and Responsibility*, 81.
102. Ibid., 80.
103. Ibid., 81.
104. Ibid., 83.
105. Ibid.
106. Ibid., 82–83.

beings is the virtuous good and is, therefore, universally available, love as goodwill is able to do "more than any other to perfect the person who experiences it," while simultaneously "[bringing] both the subject and the object of that love the greatest fulfillment."[107]

It is clear that, because Wojtyła has followed St. Thomas so closely, he finds no difficulty in reconciling the human drive for self-fulfillment with the love appropriate to persons—that is, a love directed toward them for their own sake. The metaphysical foundations of the potency/act distinction and the theory of participation in the good have, once again, shown their value for his project. Like Thomas, Wojtyła recognizes that a person's good is only a participation in the goodness that can be common to all. Because of this, "it is in the nature of love that desire and goodwill are not incompatible but, on the contrary, closely connected."[108]

Of course, in his affirmation of this compatibility, Wojtyła remains grounded in human experience, and here his pastoral knowledge shows through. Persons do desire other persons as goods. Not only is this often true of the start of romantic relationships, but it seems to be a dynamic that informs much of human life. Do not employers, in some sense, "use" their employees to accomplish the advancement of the company? Do not officers "use" soldiers in combat in order to attain their strategic goals?[109] Surely, in his time in the mountains with friends, Wojtyła often witnessed how *eros* initially drew lovers together, well before *agape* ever matured.[110] In such situations, Wojtyła recognizes that it is the *common good* that is able to furnish the ground from which love can authentically grow.[111] Employers and employees can both will

107. Ibid., 84.
108. Ibid., 83.
109. Ibid., 26 and 29–30. These are Wojtyła's own examples.
110. For the relation of *eros* and *agape* to love of desire and love of friendship, see Mattison's "Movements of Love," 31–60. *Eros* often denotes a desiring love, while *agape* is characterized as self-giving and, thus, is similar to love of friendship.
111. Ibid., 30: "Love, as we have said, is conditioned by the common attitude of people towards the same good, which they choose as their aim, and to which they subordinate themselves." See also Wojtyła, *Acting Person*, 339, where he speaks of the common good as the source of a person's ability to participate in a community: "Everybody expects that such communities of being ... will allow one to choose what others choose and because they choose it, and that his choice will be *his own good* that serves the fulfillment of *his own* person. At the same time, owing to the same ability of participation, man expects that in communities founded upon the common good his own actions will serve the community and help to maintain and enrich it" (emphasis in the original). For more on this aspect of Wojtyła's anthropology in relation to

a common goal, in which case neither will be reduced to merely their usefulness for the other. Likewise, officers and soldiers agree upon the same mission, enabling them to move past love as desire to encompass love as goodwill. Finally, lovers undoubtedly find their love budding as desire, but over time it flowers into the goodwill of wishing perfecting virtue for each other.[112] In each case, when the parties "so arrange their association that the common good which both serve becomes clearly visible, then the danger of treating a person as someone less than he really is will be reduced almost to nothing."[113] Because of the common good, love as desire can be subsumed under and raised up by love as goodwill—in more colloquial terms, use is taken up by love.[114]

Thus far, Wojtyła has remained in step with St. Thomas in his account of human love: Thomas's description of love as complacency and his distinction between love of concupiscence and love of friendship have all appeared in Wojtyła's account, though under different names. Nevertheless, for the Polish philosopher, there is a category of love that extends beyond the previous analysis, that of "betrothed love":

Betrothed love differs from all the aspects or forms of love analyzed hitherto. Its decisive character is the giving of one's own person (to another). The essence of betrothed love is self-giving, the surrender of one's "I." This is something different from and more than attraction, desire, or even goodwill. These are all ways by which one person goes out toward another, but none of them can take him as far in his quest for the good of the other as does betrothed love. "To give oneself to another" is something more than merely

---

Catholic Social Teaching, see Elzbieta Wolicka, "Participation in Community: Wojtyła's Social Anthropology," *Communio* 8, no. 2 (1981): 108–18.

112. Wojtyła, *Love and Responsibility*, 84: "The love of man for woman and woman for man cannot but be love as desire, but must as time goes by move more and more in the direction of unqualified goodwill, *benevolentia*." See also Benedict XVI, *Deus Caritas Est*, no. 7: "*Eros* and *agape*—ascending love and descending love—can never be completely separated. The more the two, in their different aspects, find a proper unity in the one reality of love, the more the true nature of love in general is realized. Even if *eros* is at first mainly covetous and ascending, a fascination for the great promise of happiness, in drawing near to the other, it is less and less concerned with itself, increasingly seeks the happiness of the other, is concerned more and more with the beloved, bestows itself and wants 'to be there for' the other. The element of *agape* thus enters into this love, for otherwise *eros* is impoverished and even loses its own nature." See Benedict XVI, *Deus Caritas Est*, Vatican translation (San Francisco: Ignatius Press, 2006), 24–25; AAS (2006): 217–52. Henceforth, DCE.

113. Wojtyła, *Love and Responsibility*, 29.

114. See Sherwin, *By Knowledge and by Love*, 75, where he explains that love of concupiscence and love of friendship are, in a certain sense, always involved in human love: "Human love always has two components, one of which is subordinated to the other."

t is good" for another—even if as a result of this another "I" were my own, as it does in friendship. Betrothed love is some-
ıt from and more than all the forms of love so far analyzed, both
:he individual subject, the person who loves, and as regards the
al union that it creates. When betrothed love enters into this in-
ter̲ relationship something more than friendship results: two people give themselves to each other.[115]

Here, Wojtyła offers a description of love as it is manifested in relationships of a particularly intimate type. Such a total "gift of self" seems to be most applicable to marriage and, he interestingly notes, to the love between a human being and God.[116] Briefly, the philosopher questions whether betrothed love exists, at least analogically, in such cases as the relationship between a doctor and his patients, a teacher and her pupils, and a pastor and the souls entrusted to his care. In these instances, it is certainly possible for a person to give of him- or herself in such a way that one would recognize an incredible amount of self-giving and, indeed, a vocation to give one's self to others. Yet, Wojtyła concludes, it would be difficult to affirm these as cases of betrothed love.[117] A spousal love seems to be what Wojtyła most has in mind—a love that is characterized by a complete surrender of the lover to the beloved. This surrender is so complete that, in it, "one's inalienable and non-transferable 'I' [becomes] someone else's property."[118]

Admittedly, this account of betrothed love raises several questions,

115. Wojtyła, Love and Responsibility, 96. Despite Wojtyła's characterization, it is perhaps too hasty to assume that this form of love has no foundation in St. Thomas's thought. Elsewhere, Wojtyła likens betrothed love to ekstasis (ecstasy) because "the lover 'goes outside' the self to find a fuller existence in another." Thomas himself had described love in terms of this ecstasy in ST I-II, q. 28, a. 3. Both David Gallagher and Michael Waldstein trace the notion of self-giving to this extasis in Thomas's thought. See Gallagher, "Person and Ethics in Thomas Aquinas," 67, footnote 62; and Michael Waldstein, "John Paul II and St. Thomas on Love and the Trinity (first part)" Anthropotes 18, no. 1 (2002): 128–29. See also DCE, no. 6.

It is possible to see an affinity between Wojtyła's explanation of betrothed love and the concept of "wedded" or "conjugal love" in the thought of Dietrich von Hildebrand, though Wojtyła never cites Hildebrand's work. See Hildebrand, Marriage: The Mystery of Faithful Love, trans. Emmanuel Chapman and Daniel Sullivan (Manchester, N.H.: Sophia Institute Press, 1984), 5: "Quite independently of sensuality, conjugal love in itself constitutes a completely new kind of love. It involves a unique mutual giving of one's self, which is the outstanding characteristic of this type of love. It is true that in every kind of love one gives oneself in one way or another. But here the giving is literally complete and ultimate."

116. Wojtyła, Love and Responsibility, 98.

117. Ibid.

118. Ibid., 97.

first, in that it appears that the dignity of the self-determining ego tha forms the heart of Wojtyła's philosophy has been ceded to the possibility of becoming someone else's "property." Connected to this, and perhaps more fundamentally, one must ask how betrothed love relates to the other loves previously described, especially in light of their metaphysical foundations. Is this form of love set apart from Wojtyła's previous considerations, particularly love as goodwill? Certainly, in his description of betrothed love cited previously, Wojtyła twice claims that it is "different from" and "more than" the other forms of love. It seems possible, then, that betrothed love can be said to stand in continuity with these loves, even while surpassing them. But what is the precise nature of the relationship between them?

In an article published fourteen years after this initial description of the spousal form of love in *Love and Responsibility*, Wojtyła offers some clarifications on the meaning of betrothed love, especially in light of critiques that had been raised by a fellow scholar concerning how a human being could make a complete "self-gift" to another person while remaining, to use the Thomistic term, *incommunicable*.[119] Wojtyła begins by relating all forms of love to what he calls the "law of the gift." According to this law, it is precisely because a human person is incommunicable that one can choose to give him- or herself to another person. In short, "only . . . a being that possesses itself can, likewise, give itself, which is to say, make itself a gift."[120] By giving oneself and therefore belonging to another person, one does not betray the incommunicability of the person. Rather, "through the gift of self . . . the person confirms in some profound way his self-possession and self-governance. Through the gift of self in a moral sense, the person loses nothing but enriches himself."[121] This helps clarify what Wojtyła had already stated in *Love and Responsibility*:

The person as such cannot be someone else's property, as though it were a thing. . . . But what is impossible and illegitimate in the natural order and in a physical sense, can come about in the order of love and in a moral sense. In this sense, one person can give himself or herself, can surrender entirely to

---

119. See ST I, q. 30, a. 4.

120. Wojtyła, "Sobre el Significado del Amor Conyugal (1974)," in *El don del amor: Escritos sobre la familia*, trans. Antonio Esquivias and Rafael Mora (Madrid: Ediciones Palabra, 2005), 206. Translations from this work are my own.

121. Ibid., 208.

another, whether to a human person or to God, and such giving of the self creates a special form of love which we define as betrothed love.[122]

A person's self-governance and self-possession, therefore, are the basis of that person's ability to give him- or herself to another. And yet this opens up into a second aspect of the law of the gift: not only is the self-possessing person able to give him- or herself to another, but in this self-gift, the person also finds more of him- or herself.[123] This idea is related to Wojtyła's analysis of human acts in The Acting Person. Such acts move the person from potency to act and therefore lead to fulfillment. Here, love becomes the most fulfilling of such acts because it manifests the law of the gift that is rooted in the very being of the person. For Wojtyła, the law is "inscribed in the being of the person as a principle from which flows the meaning of human existence, and in this way it describes the *actualization* of man in a very fundamental way."[124]

Betrothed love, then, can most completely manifest this law of the gift because the self-gift involved is total. As opposed to the loving acts he might perform for others in his life, in marriage the groom gives of himself completely to his bride (and the bride, likewise, to her groom). This completeness is marked by the fact that betrothed love is not only one act of love, or even a repeated set of acts, but a *lifelong vocation*. In this sense it is a stable platform, formed by a complete self-gift, that becomes the foundation from which many acts of love can occur. Wojtyła explains:

Basing himself on the law of the gift, man can realize an immediate act of love in which the gift of self, on occasion, reaches the heights of heroism (it is enough to recall the act of Blessed Maximilian in Auschwitz). [Yet,] also basing himself on it, man can choose a vocation that endures for the whole of life, [one] that will demand from him constant acts of love.[125]

As a vocation, betrothed love encompasses the entirety of a person's life. It is distinguished from all other forms of love because it takes into consideration the extent of the lover's self-giving as well as its hope for permanence.

122. Wojtyła, *Love and Responsibility*, 96–97.
123. Ibid., 207. Wojtyła roots this aspect of the law of the gift in the conciliar teaching of *Gaudium et Spes*, no. 24. Although his reflections are thus influenced by theology, he nevertheless moves in and out of philosophical reflection throughout the article.
124. Ibid. Emphasis mine.
125. Wojtyła, "Sobre el Significado del Amor Conyugal," 211.

Even so, we should remember that, by distinguishing betrothed love from other forms of love, he does not intend to sever it completely from them. The self-giving of betrothed love remains tied to the self-actualization that is the framework of Wojtyła's anthropology. There is no fundamental discontinuity between this love and the previous analyses of love in *Love and Responsibility*. Self-giving, written in the very being of persons, "is realized in diverse forms through *each* act of love. An act of any virtue is thoroughly an act of this type, because all virtues find in love their common root, their fullest meaning and expression."[126] Thus, "as is the case with an isolated act of love, so too in betrothed love, there operates the same *law of the gift*."[127] In this light one could say that, in betrothed love, Wojtyła is emphasizing a dynamic that is present in every form of love, indeed, in every act that brings a person to participate more fully in the good. One must always surrender him- or herself to the truth about the good, though this takes a heightened form in betrothed love.[128] Thus, I believe it is possible to say that each love analyzed by Wojtyła contains the forms of love that precede it. Love as desire is an expression of love of attraction; love as goodwill encompasses love as desire; and now betrothed love remains in continuity with love as goodwill, even while surpassing it. In this way betrothed love is "different from" and "more than" every other type of love.

Person and Community: Love's Necessity

Ultimately, these clarifications continue the constant theme of Wojtyła's concern for integrating metaphysics and phenomenology, with uniting the foundations of being with attention to human experience. If there is anything left to add to this discussion of love in Wojtyła's thought, it is found in ascertaining the precise role community—that which is formed by love—plays in the fulfillment of the person. Another way of addressing this issue is to ask the question: is the love of other persons *necessary* for the fulfillment of the human person? For Wojtyła, "that people fulfill themselves in and through community with others

126. Ibid., 210–11. Emphasis mine.
127. Ibid. Emphasis in the original.
128. See Wojtyła, *Love and Responsibility*, 100: "Betrothed love, though of its nature it differs from all the forms of love previously analyzed, can nevertheless not develop in isolation from them."

seems beyond doubt. But does this mean that we can somehow reduce the self-fulfillment of the person to community, or autoteleology to the teleology of one or more communities?"[129]

This is a question with no small implications. For instance, in recent years, some have questioned whether the emphasis of modern liberal societies on the individual and his or her rights is adequate to the communal nature of human life.[130] So, too, do the moral questions surrounding such issues as abortion, euthanasia, and the dignity of people with disabilities bring to light the tension between the autonomy of the self and the relationship, even dependence, of the self upon others.

One already finds a trace of the significance of this issue in the same article, mentioned earlier, in which Wojtyła addresses the critiques of betrothed love. There, he finds that, "in the context of these reflections the problem should be considered of that which ultimately constitutes the person: *substance* or *relation*."[131] In other words, what is it that is most basic to a human person? Is it that which belongs solely to the person and individuates him or her—the person's "substance," so to speak[132]—or the relationships the person has with other beings? In the Christian tradition, these terms are most notably found in the debates that led to the proper articulation of the nature of the three Persons of the Trinity.[133] As such, their theological significance will be addressed in chapter 4. But, for now, it is enough to point out Wojtyła's philosophical thoughts on the relationship between the person and community.

To begin, it is certainly true that, in the love of other persons, one

---

129. Wojtyła, "Person: Subject and Community," 240. See also Wojtyła, *Acting Person*, 175, where the author speaks of the person and his or her relation to the various kinds of objects that inform a conscious act: "All these relations are in one way or another meaningful for the happiness of man, but man's relation to other persons plays an especial and crucial role."

130. See, for instance, David L. Schindler, *Heart of the World, Center of the Church*: Communio *Ecclesiology, Liberalism, and Liberation* (Grand Rapids, Mich.: William B. Eerdmans, 1996).

131. Wojtyła, "Sobre el Significado del Amor Conyugal," 209 (emphasis mine). Still, he continues, "We cannot think of occupying ourselves with this analysis within the present work."

132. Etymologically speaking, "sub-stance" refers to that which "stands under" the other qualities that characterize a particular being. Thus, an individual dog is its own substance, though it has many qualities that are accidental to it (e.g., its size, color, etc.). The substance is what the object alone has (only that individual instance of the dog is that dog); the accidents are qualities that inhere in the substance and that, presumably, other beings may also have (its brown color may be shared by other dogs or other beings).

133. Grabowski's "Person: Substance and Relation" provides a helpful summary of some of the historical issues as well as modern attempts to address the roles of substance and relation in human persons.

experiences a certain union with those persons, a "doubling of the 'I,'" so to speak.[134] This characterization is significant for Wojtyła because a true community or, to use one of his preferred phrases, a *communio personarum* (communion of persons), is not found simply in any random grouping of individuals. Rather, community is found only where there exists an interpersonal dimension—each self-determining I recognizes the same dignity in every *thou*.[135] Certainly, as the number of subjects increases, one can move from referring to an I-*thou* relationship to a communal *we*, but even in such cases, the dignity of each individual person remains paramount. For Wojtyła, what is most significant in any given community is that each person must have the freedom to exercise his or her own self-governance and self-determination. Thus *communio*, "in the primary sense, refers to community as a mode of being and acting (in common, of course) through which the persons involved mutually confirm and affirm one another, a mode of being and acting that promotes *the personal fulfillment of each of them* by virtue of their mutual relationship."[136]

That a communion of persons is able to meet the "personal fulfillment of each" through mutual confirmation should not be read as a veiled argument for unbridled individualism. The self-governance and self-determination that make up human dignity are only properly exercised in relation to the truth about the good. And, in the coming together of two or more persons, this proper good, as has already been seen, is able to accommodate each one precisely because it is universal or common.[137] As a participant in a community, one chooses the common good not only to serve the "fulfillment of his own person" but to "serve the community and help to maintain and enrich it."[138]

---

134. Wojtyła, *Love and Responsibility*, 90. See also ST I-II, q. 28, a. 3.

135. See Wojtyła, "Person: Subject and Community," 236–46.

136. Karol Wojtyła, "The Family as a Community of Persons," in *Person and Community*, 321. Emphasis mine. In *Acting Person*, Wojtyła refers to this ability to fulfill oneself when acting together with others as "participation" (which should be distinguished from the Thomistic notion of participating in being/goodness mentioned in the earlier analysis of this chapter). See *Acting Person*, 317–57.

137. Wojtyła, *Acting Person*, 337: "We now see that the solution to the problem of the community and participation lies not in the reality itself of acting and existing 'together with others,' but is to be looked for in the common good." This, of course, does not mean that individuals and even groups of individuals do not often fall prey to intending common objects that are morally wrong. In such cases, the object of intention may be common, though it is certainly not good. Each person in the group would then, by such an acting together, move further into nonfulfillment.

138. Ibid., 339.

Here, Wojtyła's analysis of participation and the common good remains characteristically Thomistic, though, as is also typical of his thought, he augments Thomas's insights with his own personalism. At stake here is the notion of genuine community fulfilling individuals in a way that is inseparable from the community itself. Investors in a mutual fund, for instance, only seem to have a "common good"—the growth of the fund—but, ultimately, their goal is to cash out their earnings individually. Likewise, the mere "material fact" of people living and acting together is not enough to confirm the existence of a common good. Moviegoers, for example, might all be watching the same film, but it would be unusual to describe their pursuits as genuinely communal.[139]

Instead, Wojtyła recognizes along with the Angelic Doctor that authentic communities must have both *intrinsic* and *extrinsic* common goods.[140] Laborers digging a trench and students listening to a lecture have a common extrinsic good—the trench for the former and the truth for the latter—that cannot be divided individually. However, limiting the common good to an extrinsic goal is, for Wojtyła, "manifestly a cursory and superficial simplification."[141] To complete the picture, there must also be what St. Thomas identifies as the intrinsic common good, which is to say the social order of the community itself. Such an order would exist even if the community failed to achieve its extrinsic goals.

Wojtyła augments this second characteristic of the common good by incorporating the subjectivity of the persons involved. In a sense, he seeks to add the "flesh" of lived experience to Thomas's metaphysical foundation.[142] For Wojtyła, the intrinsic common good is experientially manifested only when the members of a community "abide in a mutual affirmation of the transcendent value of the person (a value that may also be called *dignity*) and confirm this by their acts."[143] Thus, the

139. See Wojtyła, "Person: Subject and Community," 138.

140. See ST I-II, q. 111, a. 5, ad. 1. For more on the role of intrinsic and extrinsic forms of the common good, see the excellent chapter of F. Russell Hittinger, "Toward an Adequate Anthropology: Social Aspects of the *Imago Dei* in Catholic Theology," in *Imago Dei*, ed. Thomas Albert Howard (Washington, D.C.: The Catholic University of America Press, 2013), 39–78.

141. Wojtyła, *Acting Person*, 338. Wojtyła himself uses the examples of laborers and students that, of course, resonate with his own personal experience during World War II.

142. See Wojtyła, "Person: Subject and Community," 239–40: "There must be a special value of community, one that I do not think should simply be identified with the common good. We discover this value by observing the co-existence and co-operation of people as if from the perspective of the personal subjectivity of each of them."

143. Ibid., 246. He continues, "Only such a relationship seems to deserve the name *communio*

totality of the common good is only achieved when each member recognizes the intersubjectivity of the entire community such that each freely participates, aiming at not only his or her own good but the good of the whole.

Of special note is the fact that this common good "represents a greater fullness of value than the individual good" of each separate person.[144] Its superiority comes from the fact that it is a good that can incorporate the many without being diminished and, yet, by this very fact, it also refutes any claims to negate individual dignity. Rather, the good of each person is "more fully expressed and more fully actualized in the common good" such that "the human I more fully and more profoundly discovers itself precisely in a human *we*."[145] This is not to deny that, to achieve this superior good, people will often choose to sacrifice certain individual goods—something evidenced, for instance, by a soldier storming the beach at Normandy or by the parent who rises from bed in the middle of the night to comfort a frightened child. But the character of these actions proves, for Wojtyła, that while the common good "is often a difficult good," it nevertheless is superior, conditioning individual goods of the members of a community and, in certain situations, even proving to be the foundation that allows individual goods to exist.[146]

Ultimately, Wojtyła's understanding of the relationship between the person and community skillfully navigates between two extremes, extremes that both deny the dignity of the person in their respective ways—Wojtyła names them "individualism" and "totalism." Individualism may affirm the self-governance and self-determination that forms a substantial part of human dignity; yet, it lacks a receptivity to the truth about the good as common. By positing the unbridled freedom of the individual, it remains unable to bear responsibility for others and, in the final analysis, is incapable of love.[147]

---

personarum" (emphasis in the original). Elsewhere, Wojtyła likens friendship to a *communio personarum*. See his "Participation or Alienation?," in *Person and Community*, 204.

144. Wojtyła, "Person: Subject and Community," 250.

145. Ibid.

146. Ibid. See also *Acting Person*, 339, where Wojtyła describes situations in which a person "will readily relinquish his individual good and sacrifice it to the welfare of the community. Since such a sacrifice corresponds to the ability of participation inherent in man, and because this ability allows him to fulfill himself, it is not 'contrary to his nature.'"

147. See Wojtyła, *Acting Person*, 330: "Individualism . . . isolates the person who is then

Totalism, on the other hand, suppresses the fulfillment of the individual for the supposed sake of the greater good. It feigns the affirmation of a good that is common but in reality seeks "protection from the individual, who is seen as the chief enemy of society and of the common good."[148] The self-governance and self-determination proper to human dignity are thus abandoned.

In the latter, one can sense the significance of Wojtyła's anthropology in light of the experience of Poland both during and after World War II. Totalitarian regimes, though claiming to act for the greater good of society, were an affront to the dignity of the person.[149] Yet, in the former, one can also sense, as one commentator notes, an implicit critique of the political liberalism and economic consumerism that occupy much of the West.[150] For Wojtyła, human dignity simultaneously enfolds the person's fulfillment while affirming fulfillment for other persons. His notion of community is, therefore, an extension of love as goodwill (or, in Thomistic terms, love of friendship) and, in some cases, betrothed love.[151]

This analysis allows for a return to the initial question concerning the necessity of community for human fulfillment, along with its underlying metaphysical basis in the concepts of substance and relation. To ask if community is necessary is essentially to ask whether love is necessary for personal fulfillment, and to this Wojtyła's answer is clear: self-fulfillment is a metaphysical and experiential necessity of the human person, and this "self-perfection proceeds side by side and step by step with love."[152] In fact, love is the most proper act of the will: "Love is the fullest realization of the possibilities inherent in man"; in an act of love, the person is "most fully actualized" and finds "the greatest possible fullness of being, of objective existence."[153] Love, therefore, as well as the communion of persons it forms, is necessary for human fulfillment.

---

conceived of solely as an individual concentrated on himself and on his own good, which is also regarded in isolation from the good of others and of the community."

148. Ibid., 331.

149. See Weigel, Witness to Hope, 177.

150. See Williams, Mind of John Paul II, 212. See also Wojtyła, "Thomistic Personalism," 174.

151. The latter most certainly includes the community of the family. See Wojtyła, "Family as a Community of Persons," 315–27.

152. Wojtyła, Love and Responsibility, 97.

153. Ibid., 82. See ST I-II, q. 28, a. 6 [713]: "Every agent, whatever it be, does every action from love of some kind."

This affirmation of community for human fulfillment should not, however, be confused with a claim of the priority of relation over substance in human beings[154]—for Wojtyła, such a claim would amount to the conflation of person with community. Rather, in a given community, the person "is always [the community's] proper substantial subject. The terms 'community,' like 'society' or 'social group,' are indicative of the accidental order."[155]

Wojtyła thus affirms the necessity of love for fulfillment and the priority of substance over relation in a human being. There is no contradiction here when one keeps in mind the metaphysical structure that undergirds the whole of his anthropology. Gilson's Thomistic distinction from the earlier part of this chapter is helpful in this regard: "The very first thing which 'to be' does, is to make its own essence to be, that is, 'to be a being.' This is done at once, completely and definitively.... But the next thing which 'to be' does, is to begin bringing its own individual essence somewhat nearer [to] its own completion."[156]

The first act of being, therefore, is that of existence, and this existence most certainly forms the substance of the human person—his or her individuality.[157] One's nature as a human being is complete and intact—even if, in various ways, it remains in potentiality—from the very first moment of existence. There is nothing incomplete about a human being in any given state, in the sense of lacking what belongs to human nature. The child, the adult, the elderly, and the disabled are all complete in this sense, maintaining the dignity that intrinsically stems from their humanity and freedom (whether this freedom is potential or actualized) by the very fact of their existence.

154. Ratzinger, for instance, writes in his "Concerning the Notion of Person," 452, that "relativity toward the other constitutes the human person. The human person is the event or being of relativity." Wojtyła and Ratzinger thus differ in this regard.

155. Wojtyła, Acting Person, 334. Emphasis in the original. See also Wojtyła, "Person: Subject and Community," 238: "Only the individual people—the personal subjects—who are members of this society are substantial subjects (supposita), each of them separately, whereas the society itself is simply a set of relations, and therefore an accidental being"; and 252: "All of this, in turn, confirms that the subject as a person has a distinctive priority in relation to community. Otherwise it would be impossible to defend not just the autoteleology of the human self, but even the teleology of the human being."

156. Gilson, Being and Some Philosophers, 184.

157. One could certainly speak of relation here, in the sense that existence is a result of creation by a Creator, thus establishing a relation between the human being and God. But as for human relations that form a communio personarum, for Wojtyła, these belong properly to the "second act" of existence.

The second act of being, then, encompasses the move from existence to completion. To combine Gilson's Thomistic terminology with that of Wojtyła: the second act is the act of fulfillment, and as such it is one that requires love. Love, of course, establishes relations with other beings, but even in this establishment, substance retains its priority: *operari sequitir esse*. The human person is, then, most properly a substance-in-relation.[158]

So, in one sense, community is accidental because the human person always maintains his or her dignity as a being of self-governance and self-determination—a person's substance cannot be assimilated into a group such that the group becomes the proper actor in human acts. However, it is precisely this self-governance and self-determination inherent in the being of the person that allow the person to make a gift of him- or herself.[159] Only in this self-gift of love does the person reach the pinnacle of self-actualization; thus, love is necessary as the primary act of personal fulfillment—indeed, the law of the gift is fulfillment's inner core. In a certain sense one could, therefore, speak of community as a "necessary accident."[160] Substance has priority over relation by way of the first act of being, while love (and the communal relations it brings) are necessary by way of the second.

Crossing the Threshold

Karol Wojtyła's philosophical anthropology proves to be both metaphysically robust and authentic to the nature of human experience. He has, by entering into the very subjectivity of this experience, shown both the need for the metaphysical foundations of the person and that

158. There is no one who has done more to highlight this conjunction between essence/existence and substance/relation than W. Norris Clarke. See Clarke's *Person and Being*, especially page 14: "It turns out, then, that relationality and substantiality go together as two distinct but inseparable modes of reality. Substance is the primary mode, in that all else, including relations, depend on it as their ground. But since 'every substance exists for the sake of its operations,' as St. Thomas has just told us, being as substance, as existing *in itself*, naturally flows over into being as relational, as turned *towards others* by its self-communicating action. To be fully is to be *substance-in-relation*" (emphasis in the original). The passage quoted from St. Thomas is from ST I, q. 105, a. 5. Clarke, in many ways, considers his own work as a development of Wojtyła's project. See Clarke, "The Integration of Personalism and Thomistic Metaphysics in Twenty-First-Century Thomism," in his *The Creative Retrieval of St. Thomas Aquinas: Essays in Thomistic Philosophy, New and Old* (New York: Fordham University Press, 2009), 226–31.

159. See Wojtyła, "Family as a Community of Persons," 318–19.

160. See ST I, q. 3, a. 6 [18]: "A substance is compared to its accidents as potentiality to actuality; for a subject is in some sense made actual by its accidents."

of the world in which the person finds him- or herself. He has, in a sense, affirmed reality in all of its dimensions.[161]

This chapter has traced this understanding of the human person, beginning with the inner workings of human consciousness, slowly working its way outward toward the objectivity of reality, and finally culminating in the communion of love that occurs between persons. Yet, at the heart of all of this lies the same dynamic: the transcendence of human freedom and the goal that this freedom seeks—truth and goodness.

It is ironic but no less true that, though Wojtyła's analysis has concentrated on the consciously willed act, he has nevertheless proven the human person to be ultimately *receptive before being active*. The praxis of human persons, by its very nature, demands an openness to the world, to others, and to all that is good and true. All moments of fulfilling self-determination are, therefore, predicated on a participation in the good and a "surrender to truth."[162] It is true that the experience of the senses rooted in the body, the cognition of the self and the world, and the power of the will all culminate in a decisive moment, the moment of freedom. But, in what is perhaps a phrase of inestimable value, Wojtyła explains that this moment "may be viewed as an instance of [a] *threshold that the person, as a person, has to pass on his way toward the good*."[163]

A person, therefore, has the capacity for transcendence precisely in order to pass this threshold. Wojtyła has shown that true fulfillment only comes by way of truth and goodness; yet, in every human act, one

---

161. If there is any doubt concerning Wojtyła's dedication to both the experiential and metaphysical dimensions of the person, then one could surely look to his remarks concerning his first encounter with the philosophy of St. Thomas, in the seminary, via a book on metaphysics by Fr. Kazimierz Wais: "Immediately I found myself up against an obstacle. My literary training, centered around the humanities, had not prepared me at all for the scholastic theses and formulas with which the manual was filled. I had to cut a path through a thick undergrowth of concepts, analyses, and axioms without even being able to identify the ground over which I was moving. After two months of hacking through this vegetation I came to a clearing, to the discovery of the deep reasons for what until then I had only *lived and felt*. When I passed the examination I told my examiner that, in my view, the new vision of the world that I had acquired in my struggle with that metaphysics manual was more valuable than the mark I had obtained. I was not exaggerating. *What intuition and sensibility had until then taught me about the world found solid confirmation*" (emphasis mine). See the interview with Pope John Paul II now published as André Frossard and Pope John Paul II, *"Be Not Afraid!" Pope John Paul II Speaks Out on His Life, His Beliefs, and His Inspiring Vision for Humanity*, trans. J. R. Foster (Garden City, N.Y.: Image, 1985), 17.
162. Wojtyła, *Acting Person*, 156.
163. Ibid., 127. Emphasis mine.

must travel beyond the self—across the threshold—to achieve this goal. Interestingly, for Wojtyła, the experience of personal transcendence stands as a sort of signpost on the journey that points all men and women toward what lies beyond: "The evidence of experience tells us that the spiritual life of man essentially refers to, and in its strivings vibrates with, the ... innermost attempts to reach truth, goodness, and beauty."[164] Every person is, in every conscious exercise of freedom, seeking these transcendental goals.

This is a truth the Christian tradition has often recognized, holding that every conscious exercise of choice is—if only implicitly—an attempt to reach the depths of God, the One who is Truth and Goodness itself.[165] In a sense, this same thought is immortalized in the words of Augustine:

I have learnt to love you late, Beauty at once so ancient and so new! I have learnt to love you late! You were within me, and I was in the world outside myself. I searched for you outside myself and, disfigured as I was, I fell upon the lovely things of your creation. You were with me, but I was not with you. The beautiful things of this world kept me far from you and yet, if they had not been in you, they would have had no being at all.[166]

Yet, even while recognizing the correlation between one's interior longing and its final transcendent resting place, the Christian tradition has also recognized the human person's inability to attain this goal in its fullness when left to his or her own devices. In the midst of the entirety of the cosmos, the human person remains finite—one therefore seemingly finds him- or herself in a sort of mysterious juxtaposition of realities, bearing a dignity surpassing the rest of creation, yet unable to attain the final goal of this transcendence.

Thus, the capacity for transcendence is an indication of that point where the human person touches what is beyond, infinite, and eternal. Yet, longing for the fullness of good—for union with it—what happens when the person realizes that he or she cannot obtain this goodness by

164. Ibid., 155–56. He continues, "We may thus safely speak of the role of these absolute modes of values that accompany the experience of ... personal transcendence." Interestingly, though Wojtyła mentions beauty as a transcendental here, his analysis focuses exclusively on truth and goodness, though presumably this is due to his attention to the roles of the intellect and the will as aimed precisely at truth and goodness.

165. See ST I-II, q. 1, a. 6.

166. Augustine, *Confessions* 10.27 [231–32].

his or her own powers? Longing for truth, what happens when reason recognizes its own limits? Is such a complete fulfillment possible? It seems only a movement from the outside could effect such a union.

This is a fact that does not go unnoticed by Wojtyła. As such, this study now turns to his thoughts on the human person when the person is reached by just such an in-breaking from the transcendent. It turns to the person as seen in the light of divine revelation.

Chapter 4

The Human Person in the Light of Jesus Christ

He is the image of the invisible God, the firstborn of all creation. For in him were created all things in heaven and on earth.... For in him the fullness was pleased to dwell, and through him to reconcile all things for him, making peace by the blood of his cross [through him], whether those on earth or those in heaven.

Colossians 1:15–16, 19–20

The desire for God is written in the human heart, because man is created by God and for God; and God never ceases to draw man to himself. Only in God will he find the truth and happiness he never stops searching for.

***Catechism of the Catholic Church*, no. 27**

By way of reason's vision, Karol Wojtyła's philosophical anthropology has provided an equally metaphysical and experiential look at the human person and the transcendence that stands at the heart of the human drive for fulfillment. Still, it is no secret that Wojtyła's insights were influenced in great part by what are ultimately theological sources. Even his main philosophical work, *The Acting Person*, was written during the Second Vatican Council, with the author finding in the conciliar discussions and documents insights that illuminated what he had come to know about humanity through his own experience and reflection.[1]

Indeed, Pope John Paul II's constant return to the Council's teaching became a hallmark of his pontificate. As others have noted, he continuously returned to two articles of the constitution *Gaudium et Spes* in particular—articles 22 and 24.[2] Both articles act as the culmination of the Council's teaching on the human person as the image of God. If article 12 of the same document had spoken of the *imago dei* in such a way that allowed for critique of its "flat" and purely philosophical vision of the person, the same cannot be said for these two articles, where one finds a more clearly Christian vision of humanity.[3]

Thus, where article 12 defines the image in terms of human freedom and dominion over creation, article 22 reveals the true image to be Jesus Christ:

> It is only in the mystery of the Word made flesh that the mystery of man truly becomes clear. For Adam, the first man, was a type of him who was to come, Christ the Lord. Christ the new Adam, in the very revelation of the mystery of the Father and of his love, fully reveals man to himself and brings to light his most high calling.[4]

Here the Council posits a vision of the human person that is distinctly Christological. Indeed, in framing the entire Constitution around the question of humanity's vocation, the Council fathers now present Christ as the answer to the human search for happiness—he is the fulfillment of all truly human desires.[5]

Likewise, article 12 speaks of the social dimension of human life by

---

1. See Wojtyła, *Acting Person*, 302, footnote 9, where the author writes of himself, "While writing this book (in the first, Polish version) the author attended the Second Vatican Council and his participation in the proceedings stimulated and inspired his thinking about the person. It suffices to say that one of the chief documents of the Council, the *Pastoral Constitution on the Church in the Modern World* (*Gaudium et Spes*), not only brings to the forefront the person and his calling, but also asserts the belief in his transcendent nature." See also Williams, *Mind of John Paul II*, 186.

2. For John Paul II's use of GS 22 in his writings, see William Newton, "John Paul II and *Gaudium et Spes* 22: His Use of the Text and Involvement in its Authorship," *Josephinum Journal of Theology* 17, no. 1 (2010): 168–93. For his use of GS 24 and its implications for a "theology of the gift," see Pascal Ide, "Une Théologie du Don: Les occurrences de *Gaudium et spes*, no. 24, §3 chez Jean-Paul II (première partie)," *Anthropotes* 17, no. 1 (2001): 149–78, as well as the *seconde partie* in *Anthropotes* 17, no. 2 (2001): 313–44.

3. See the section "The Human Person," of chapter 1.

4. *GS*, no. 22 [922].

5. Thus, the article continues, "All the truths mentioned so far should find in him their source and their most perfect embodiment."

expressing the necessity of communion with other persons—or *communio personarum*—for a person to reach his or her full potential: "For by his innermost nature man is a social being; and if he does not enter into relations with others he can neither live nor develop his gifts."[6] Yet article 24 transcends this philosophical claim in revealing the theological reason for this necessity:

Furthermore, the Lord Jesus, when praying to the Father "that they may all be one . . . even as we are one," has opened up new horizons closed to human reason by implying that there is a certain parallel between the union existing among the divine persons and the union of the sons of God in truth and love. It follows, then, that if man is the only creature on earth that God has wanted for its own sake, man can fully discover his true self only in a sincere giving of himself.[7]

Building upon article 22's claim that Christ is "the revelation of the mystery of the Father and of his love," the Council now grounds the *imago dei* in a trinitarian foundation: love is, in some way, the mark of the relationship between the Persons of the Trinity. The human person, then, as the image of the trinitarian God, is called to love—the communion created by such acts of self-gift thus becomes an image of trinitarian communion. In this light, what was once a seemingly flat description of the *imago dei* in article 12 is now, in articles 22 and 24, given a new and theological dimension.

These articles are, I believe, the key to interpreting the totality of the pontifical works of John Paul II, a position only reinforced by his constant reference to them. John Paul's use of article 22 in his magisterial writings numbers over two hundred times, and article 24 nearly one hundred.[8] The former, in the pope's own words, "serves as one of the constant reference points of my teaching."[9] It is, according to Edward T.

---

6. GS, no. 12 [913–14]: "But God did not create man a solitary being. From the beginning 'male and female he created them' (Gn 1:27). This partnership of man and woman constitutes the first form of communion between persons [*communionis personarum*]. For by his innermost nature man is a social being; and if he does not enter into relations with others he can neither live nor develop his gifts [*nec vivere nec suas dotes expandere potest*]." In the Latin text, found in AAS 58 (1966): 1034, what is here rendered in English as "gifts" is actually *potest*, meaning "potency" or "potential." This more closely parallels Wojtyła's Thomistic understanding of the person's nature being fulfilled by love and community.

7. GS, no. 24 [925]. See Jn 17:21–22.

8. Newton, "John Paul II and *Gaudium et Spes* 22," 177. See footnote 34 on the same page for some of the specific papal texts in which articles 22 and 24 are used.

9. FR, no. 60 [78].

Oakes, the "lodestar" of *Gaudium et Spes* and thus of the Council's presentation of the faith to the modern world.[10] Because of this, John Paul likewise made it the lodestar of his papacy, as was evidenced from his first call to "open wide the doors to Christ" in his inaugural homily to the claim that "the Redeemer of Man, Jesus Christ, is the center of the universe and of history" that opened his first encyclical.[11] In a speech given on the thirtieth anniversary of *Gaudium et Spes*, he expressed in further detail the importance of the Constitution—especially article 22's claim—and its relation to his own thought:

I must confess that *Gaudium et Spes* is particularly dear to me, not only for the themes it develops, but also because of my direct involvement in its drafting. In fact, as the young Archbishop of Kraków, I was a member of the subcommission responsible for studying "the signs of the times" and, from November 1964, I was asked to be part of the central subcommission in charge of drafting the text. It is precisely my intimate knowledge of the origin of *Gaudium et Spes* that has enabled me fully to appreciate its prophetic value and to make wide use of its content in my Magisterium, starting with my first encyclical, *Redemptor Hominis*. In it I took up the legacy of the conciliar Constitution and wished to confirm that the nature and destiny of humanity and of the world can be definitively revealed only in the light of the crucified and risen Christ.[12]

While *Gaudium et Spes* 22 clearly takes pride of place in the pope's thought, it is nevertheless my contention that it is only completely understood in relation to article 24. This latter article provides the key to understanding how John Paul conceives of the union with God in Christ that is mentioned in the first text. This is a discussion that I will take up later in the chapter. For now it is enough to reiterate the significance of article 22, especially in the context of the anthropological aims of both the Council and any hoped for evangelizing catechesis that would stem from its teaching.

Chapter 1 of this study recalled the conciliar aim of reuniting the

10. Edward T. Oakes, *Infinity Dwindled to Infancy: A Catholic and Evangelical Christology* (Grand Rapids, Mich.: William B. Eerdmans, 2011), 401. See also Weigel, *Witness to Hope*, 169: "In Wojtyła's interpretation of Vatican II, *Gaudium et Spes* 22 was the theological linchpin of the entire Council."

11. See John Paul II, "Homily of His Holiness John Paul II for the Inauguration of His Pontificate," and RH, no. 1.

12. The speech can be found in John Paul II, "Only Christ Can Fulfill Man's Hopes," *Communio* 23, no. 1 (1996): 122–28, with the quote appearing on pages 122–23.

Christian faith with life and especially the manifestation of this aim in *Gaudium et Spes*. How could the church effectively propose Jesus Christ as the fulfillment that modern men and women hoped for and, indeed, the fulfillment of all truly human designs? As noted earlier, one of the most important yet difficult points of debate in interpreting the final text is brought to the fore by the claim of Henri de Lubac—namely, that the *supernatural* union with God offered in the beatific vision is itself the *natural* end of human beings. In this regard, de Lubac's solution to reconciling faith and life is to posit the goal of union with Jesus Christ as inherent to the very definition of being human. The scholar of the early church believed that this idea, latent in the writings of the church fathers, could provide the remedy for a modern world that too easily conceived of humanity apart from God. Indeed, the poignant claim of *Gaudium et Spes* 22 can be found in germ in the earlier text of de Lubac's *Catholicism*, where he wrote, "By revealing the Father and by being revealed by him, Christ completes the revelation of man to himself."[13]

But how should this claim, reiterated by the Council, be interpreted? As mentioned earlier, for all of its admirable goals, de Lubac's solution faces the practical difficulty of the evangelizer calling forth a desire in the human heart that may, in fact, be unrecognized. In this light, I claimed that evangelization is better served by an account in which human nature can be affirmed by revelation, yet also corrected and ultimately transcended by it. In such an anthropology, the parts of human experience that can be affirmed by the Christian faith become a pathway by which modern men and women can reach the very Source of what makes that experience true, good, and beautiful in the first place. Human experience, then, maintains its integrity while ultimately being open to the transcendent—it is *sacramental*.

Here lies the crux of this chapter: I believe that John Paul II's theological anthropology conforms precisely to this sacramental account of the intersection of revelation and the human person. His is an anthropology that embraces the *via positionis*, the *via negationis*, and the *via eminentiae*. As such, John Paul II's view of the human person is able to reconcile the difficult (and seemingly contradictory) dual affirmation of

---

13. Henri de Lubac, *Catholicism: Christ and the Common Destiny of Man*, trans. Lancelot C. Sheppard and Elizabeth Englund (San Francisco: Ignatius Press, 1988), 339, a translation of *Catholicisme: Les aspects sociaux du dogme* (Paris: Cerf, 1938).

Gaudium et Spes—that human nature claims its own "autonomy," while nevertheless finding communion with God in Christ to be its "most high calling."[14]

The point in raising all of this, of course, is not to vindicate one side or the other in the debate on de Lubac's claim concerning human nature, but rather to get to the very heart of the reason he claimed it in the first place.[15] In this time of the New Evangelization, I believe that John Paul II's theological anthropology provides an important foundation for seeing precisely how the faith of the church can be related to human life. More boldly, it provides the blueprint for how the church can affirm human nature in its integrity and yet proclaim union with God in Jesus Christ as the end to which all human beings are called.

Here, there can be no attempt at a comprehensive answer to the question of the relationship of nature to grace that has proven to be one of the most foundational if elusive issues in the church's history. Furthermore, John Paul's thoughts on the matter are never worked out in a specific text or systematized in his writings to any large extent. Yet I do believe that his theological anthropology provides rudiments and insights that can contribute to the church's understanding of the issue and that can bear important fruit for the New Evangelization.

John Paul II's Theological Anthropology: Breadth and Scope

Before beginning to explore John Paul II's theological anthropology, it is important to offer a word concerning its breadth and scope. It is not uncommon to have the pope's anthropological thought solely associated with the catecheses he delivered concerning the role of the human body in theology, and even when doing so, to interpret these catecheses through the single lens of Catholic sexual ethics. This *Theology of the Body*, as it is more commonly known, does indeed form a substantial portion of the late Holy Father's thoughts on the human person, and its importance is captured in the oft-quoted line of George

---

14. GS, nos. 36 [935] and 22 [922], respectively.

15. Even so, if what I claim here is true, then John Paul's anthropology can be viewed as one that simultaneously embraces the reason for de Lubac's claim while remaining closer to the anthropology of his neo-Thomist interlocutors.

Weigel, that it "constitute[s] a kind of theological time bomb set to go off, with dramatic consequences, sometime in the third millennium of the Church."[16] Be that as it may, I agree with John Grabowski when he states that proponents and critics alike of the pope's thought "often [fail] to do justice to the many facets of his presentation on the human person," aspects such as "scripture, action theory, Christology, gift theory, and experience."[17] These aspects are found not only in the *Theology of the Body* but in the entirety of his magisterial corpus. Thus to limit John Paul II's theological anthropology to a certain set of catecheses or to see it solely in relation to Catholic sexual ethics and the realm of post-*Humanae Vitae* debate would be to take a myopic vantage point.

Better vision is most assuredly attained by approaching the center of his anthropology. There, the heart of his understanding of the human person becomes the unifying point by which all other aspects, including human sexuality, are bound together. This center is revealed by John Paul's continuous reliance upon *Gaudium et Spes* 22 and 24: the fulfillment of the human person as the image of God in Jesus Christ and the self-gift—first of the person of Christ, then of the human person in response—that makes that fulfillment possible. It is surely not a matter of coincidence that both parts of this center parallel John Paul's philosophical emphases on the *person* and the *act*.[18]

Only with this established can one truly understand the pope's anthropology and its implications for the various theological disciplines. And it is from the vantage of this unifying center that this study proceeds in its aim to appropriate a better anthropological foundation for the church's ministry of the Word.

As was the case in examining Wojtyła's philosophical anthropology, the present chapter begins with the dignity of the human person, though this time with a much more theological look at the concept of

16. Weigel, *Witness to Hope*, 343. The description is certainly impactful, though it is open to great misinterpretation in a post-9/11 world.

17. Grabowski, "Luminous Excess of the Acting Person," 120. He continues, "His multifaceted presentation generates a kind of excess which overflows shallow characterizations or reductions of his thought to preexisting positions."

18. See David Stagaman, "The Implications for Theology of *The Acting Person*," in McDermott, *The Thought of Pope John Paul II*, 217: "As one reads through *The Acting Person*, one cannot help but suspect that the person of Jesus Christ lurks between the lines on each page. For John Paul, Jesus Christ reveals not only who God is, but who the human person is and how that person ought to exist. Only he is the acting person fully alive, able to integrate all of his capabilities and energies in a deliberated act which is complete self-donation."

the person as the image of God. It does so especially by way of John Paul's interpretation of the Genesis texts concerning creation, placing this interpretation within the wider context of the doctrine of the *imago dei* as found in the Christian tradition. It then proceeds to examine this theme of the *imago dei* as found in the texts of *Gaudium et Spes* 22 and 24 and argues that John Paul's interpretation of the former is only complete by taking account of the latter. In this examination, John Paul's attention to the relationship between the person and his or her act will, once again, prove to be of inestimable value. In fact, I argue here that the act of faith is the most perfect manifestation of the person's self-transcendence—a claim that will have to be clarified in light of Wojtyła's philosophical understanding of love. Finally, the chapter returns to the crux of the matter—namely, the relationship between grace and nature and the way in which this relationship informs how the church relates to the modern world and the hopes and designs of modern men and women. Ultimately, it is this sacramental relationship, exemplified for John Paul in the relationship between faith and reason, that can serve as the paradigm from which catechesis for the New Evangelization can take its most effective shape.

The Dignity of the Human Person: The Image of God

Solitude

John Paul II's reflections on the creation of human beings in the image of God are scattered throughout his many writings; still, because of his central focus on what can be called a Christocentric anthropology, it could rightly be said that the doctrine of the *imago dei* plays a foundational role in all of his magisterial teaching. Even so, I would like to draw attention to the moments in which he specifically meditated on the doctrine; many of these moments are found in the course of his Wednesday general audiences on the Creed and the *Theology of the Body*.

In both sets of catecheses, John Paul's understanding of the *imago dei* stems largely from his reading of the creation accounts of Genesis given in its opening chapters—the first account tells of the seven days of creation and is more cosmological in nature; the second focuses on the creation of Adam and Eve in the garden and, with its narrative style, is clearly more anthropological in scope. In the pope's words, the first account is "objective" and, indeed, contains "hidden within itself a powerful metaphysical content."[19] He explains further that, "despite some detailed and plastic expressions in this passage, man is defined in it primarily in the dimensions of being and existing ('*esse*')," which is to say, "he is defined in a more metaphysical than physical way."[20] The second account, on the other hand, "has by its nature a different character"; because of its narrative form and the interpretive depth that this brings, it is "subjective in nature and thus in some way psychological."[21]

The pope makes further distinctions between the two accounts by drawing upon the work of modern biblical scholarship. He distinguishes between what is commonly known as the "priestly" account of Genesis 1 and the "Yahwist" account of Genesis 2 and even acknowledges that the second account most likely precedes the first in terms of its chronological provenance.[22] Interestingly, however, and in contrast with the methodology of many modern biblical scholars, he reads both accounts as a unity: "Taken together, the two descriptions complete each other."[23]

That the pope could make such a claim is due in large part to his method of reading the narrative parts of scripture in a uniquely meditative and prayerful way, indeed, through a sort of *lectio divina*. In this *lectio*, and using a method that imitates his own philosophical approach, John Paul enters into the subjective consciousness of biblical characters in hopes that their experience will reveal objective truths. Such a method necessitates a vivid understanding of the context in which the story takes place, and, in this way, it is not unlike the "composition of place" encouraged by St. Ignatius of Loyola.[24]

19. TOB 2:5 [136].
20. Ibid.
21. TOB 3:1 [137].
22. See John Paul II, *God, Father and Creator: A Catechesis on the Creed*, trans. *L'Osservatore Romano*, English ed. (Boston: Pauline Books and Media, 1996), 221–25, esp. 221–22; and TOB 2:2 [134].
23. John Paul II, *God, Father and Creator*, 221.
24. See, for instance, St. Ignatius of Loyola, *The Spiritual Exercises*, no. 47. The overall assessment of John Paul II's use of scripture by scholars varies. See, for example, the critiques of Luke Timothy Johnson, "A Disembodied 'Theology of the Body': John Paul II on Love, Sex, and Pleasure," *Commonweal*, January 26, 2001, 11–17, especially 13–14; and Charles E. Curran, "The Sources of Moral Truth in the Teaching of John Paul II," in *The Vision of John Paul II: Assessing His Thought and Influence*, ed. Gerard Mannion (Collegeville, Minn.: Liturgical Press, 2008), 128–43, especially 131–34; and the generally positive assessments by Michel Ségin, "The Biblical Foundations of the

When applied to the two creation accounts, this *lectio* provides a bridge between them—the subjective experience of Adam and Eve in the garden of Genesis 2 becomes revelatory of the objective truths stated in Genesis 1. More specifically, for John Paul, "When we compare the two accounts, we reach the conviction that this subjectivity [of the second account] corresponds to the objective reality of man created in the 'image of God' [in the first account]."[25]

The pope's explanation of this correspondence is rooted in both intratextual evidence and the Christian tradition. Thus, in reading Genesis 1, he finds that the triple use of the word "created" in verse 27, as well as the distinguishing remark that the creation of human beings is "very good" in verse 31, allow him to ask a metaphysical question of the text: what sets humans apart from the rest of creation?[26] In answer, he embraces the predominant reading of the Western Christian tradition already noted in the previous chapter, that "man ... bears in himself the reflection of God's power, which is manifested especially in the faculty of intelligence and free will."[27]

And yet, the second chapter of Genesis provides a subjective and psychological description of these same truths. "Although," the pope explains, "the account of Genesis 2 does not speak directly of the 'image' of God, it presents some of its essential elements—the capacity of self-knowledge, the experience of man's own being in the world, the need to fulfill his solitude, his dependence on God."[28] It is as if this second, though earlier account is the dramatic unfolding of the metaphysical claims made by its counterpart: its truths are reached by way of the persons of Adam and Eve and their actions in relation to God and the world.

Thus, Adam's loneliness amid the animals he is charged with naming—what John Paul refers to as "original solitude"—is an experiential indication of the uniqueness of humanity in the face of the rest of cre-

---

Thought of John Paul II on Human Sexuality," *Communio* 20, no. 2 (1993): 266–89; and William Kurz, "The Scriptural Foundations of Theology of the Body," in *Pope John Paul II on the Body: Human, Eucharistic, Ecclesial,* ed. John M. McDermott and John Gavin (Philadelphia: St. Joseph's University Press, 2007), 27–46.

25. TOB 3:1 [139].
26. See John Paul II, *God, Father and Creator,* 222.
27. Ibid., 223.
28. Ibid.

The Human Person in the Light of Jesus Christ

ation.[29] This metaphysical loneliness is a consequence not only of his intellectual powers but also of his body—in encountering each animal Adam recognizes that he is both like the rest of creation and yet set apart from it.[30] That he can find no suitable partner among creation, then, is the dramatic counterpart to the "very good" of Genesis 1. In the pope's words:

Self-knowledge goes hand in hand with knowledge of the world, of all visible creatures, of all living beings to which man has given their names to affirm his dissimilarity before them. Thus, consciousness reveals man as the one who *possesses the power of knowing* with respect to *the visible world.* With this knowledge, which makes him go in some way outside of his own being, man at the same time *reveals himself to himself in all the distinctiveness of his being.* . . . Man is alone because he is "different" from the visible world, from the world of living beings. When we analyze the text of Genesis, we are in some way witnesses of how man, with the first act of self-consciousness, "distinguishes himself" before God-Yahweh from the whole world of living beings (*animalia*), how he consequently reveals himself to himself and at the same time affirms himself in the visible world as a "person."[31]

Likewise, God's commandment not to eat from the tree of the knowledge of good and evil reveals the "aspect of choice and self-determination (that is, of free-will)" in human beings.[32] For the pope, the tree is a symbol for the freedom with which all humans are endowed. Taken together, these two moments from Adam's experience in the garden become the subjective proof of the transcendence (recalling Wojtyła's philosophical anthropology) of the human person that lies at the core of human knowing and willing. The traditional and metaphysical account of the image of God that John Paul gleans from Genesis 1 is, thus, affirmed in the narrative of Genesis 2.

Of course, as is characteristic of his philosophical anthropology, John Paul clearly finds the subjective account of Genesis 2 to be not only an affirmation of the metaphysical foundation of the person but also, in

29. See TOB 5–7 [146–56]. For John Paul II, such experiences are "original," not in the sense of being the first to appear in history, but in the sense that they are foundational to all human experience. On this, see TOB 11:1 [169–70].

30. See TOB 6:3 [152]. In TOB 7:1–2 [154], John Paul also notes that Adam's body allows him to recognize his uniqueness among the animals precisely because it is what allows him to be author of distinctly human activity in the world.

31. TOB 5:6 [150]. Emphasis in the original.

32. TOB 6:1 [151].

a particular way, an important addition to it. Adam's experience of the world, his subjectivity (his "self-knowledge" and "self-determination," to use the terms of the two preceding quotes), reveal him as a *person*. As was already underscored in chapter 3, this emphasis on personal existence is a means of capturing the unique dignity of *each* individual person. It is a way of expressing the worth of a given human being (in this case, Adam) even if, metaphysically speaking, all human persons share an equal dignity. The point should be made, once again, that this understanding of personhood does not contradict the metaphysical account but, in actuality, only exists because of it.[33] Ultimately, then, Adam's lived experience relies upon his nature as a rational being while, at the same time, it provides a view of his existence as uniquely "personal."

Communion

While this mining of Adam's experience—particularly the experience of his solitude—clearly displays the richness of John Paul's philosophical method for reading Genesis 2, it does not exhaust its fruitfulness. For, as seen in chapter 3, his anthropology begins with the "solitude" of the person but ultimately reaches its fulfillment in community. It is no surprise, then, that in the pope's reading of Genesis, Adam's solitude leads to unity, which is to say, *communion*.

This movement from solitude to communion occurs in two ways, each notably distinct from the other. First and foremost, for John Paul, original solitude is an indication of the human person's relationship with God. This truth is captured in the narrative of Genesis 2 by way of the relationship between God and Adam that is present from the moment God forms Adam from the earth and breathes life into him. In a certain sense, this initial communion is metaphysical (to use a nonbiblical though applicable term) because to be created and sustained in existence is necessarily to be thrust into relationship with the Creator. Yet it must be acknowledged that the same can be said of the rest of creation as well—all things from the sun, moon, and stars to the animals in the sea, in the sky, or on land claim the same relationship by way of their very existence.[34]

33. Wojtyła opposed the phenomenological reduction that would see "nature" solely as what is passively received in a human being and "person" as manifesting the active and freely determined aspect of the same being. See Wojtyła, *Acting Person*, 78–80.

34. St. Thomas describes this relation on the side of the creature as a "real" relation. Yet,

Thus, this initial passage from solitude to communion must also come through Adam's distinction from the rest of creation precisely as a person. This "personal" relationship between God and Adam is captured by John Paul's use of the words "covenant" and "gift" in describing creation. Adam is *"a subject of the covenant, that is, a subject constituted as a person, constituted according to the measure of [being a] 'partner of the Absolute.'"*[35] John Paul's reading implies that the covenant is a relationship that can only be constituted by persons.[36] It is not a mere contracting of obligations or an exchange of goods but, in its deepest sense, an exchange of persons, a mutual offering of self-gift.[37] Because creation is the establishment of a covenant between God and Adam, it thereby offers a vision in which all that exists is a manifestation of love:

Throughout the description of Genesis the heart can be heard beating. We have before us not a great builder of the world, a demiurge: we stand in the presence of the great heart! No cosmogony, no philosophical cosmology of the past, no cosmological theory of the present-day can express a truth like this truth. We can find it only in the inspired pages of Genesis: revelation of the love that pervades the whole earth to its very core, revelation of the Fatherhood which gives creation its full meaning, together with the covenant which gives rise to the creation of man in the image of God.[38]

In sum, "Love is the motive for creation and, consequently, love is the motive for the covenant."[39]

The pope further explains this vision of creation as a manifestation of love by way of reading Genesis through what he calls the "hermeneutics of the gift."[40] Once again, metaphysics has an important and foundational role to play: because Adam and, indeed, all creatures are

---

since God is complete in himself and has no need of creation, from the divine side the relation is merely "logical." See *Summa Contra Gentiles* II, ch. 12.

35. TOB 6:2 [151]. Emphasis in the original.

36. Personhood, of course, is used analogously of God. God is the ultimate Personal Being, and humans, because they are made in his image, are persons.

37. See Scott Hahn, "Covenant in the Old and New Testaments: Some Current Research (1994–2004)," *Currents in Biblical Research* 3, no. 2 (2005): 262–92, esp. 285: "The reductionist idea that covenant means only 'obligation' and is essentially one-sided has been largely abandoned. Most scholars contributing to the field recognize that the covenant always involves mutuality and relationship; indeed, even when the terms only express obligations for one party, there seems to be the assumption of reciprocal loyalty on both sides."

38. Wojtyła, *Sign of Contradiction*, trans. unknown (New York: Crossroad, 1979), 22.

39. Ibid., 21.

40. TOB 13:2 [179].

thrust into relationship with God and are dependent upon him for their very existence, they are contingent. Their very being, in this sense, is a gift. "The contingent being," Wojtyła explains, "is not a necessary being," and "the created world is not an absolute. But the goodness of the created world—created contingent and thus non-necessary—shows us that the motive for creation is love."[41] Thus, because God willingly created everything from nothing, "every creature bears within itself the sign of the original and fundamental gift."[42]

Furthermore, this concept of giving is able to express the relationship between God and human persons because, by its very nature, it implies both a receiver and a giver of the gift.[43] For John Paul, amidst the entirety of the cosmos, only human beings can perceive their existence and the existence of all things as a gift. And behind every gift must be someone who gives it. Thus, to marvel at the world and at one's transcendence over it is to have the capacity to recognize the Giver of existence. Though at first unforeseen, the rational nature of human beings—that which makes humans "alone" in the world—is able to bring forth an initial communion by allowing men and women to perceive themselves as the recipients of an act of love.[44]

Ultimately then, and returning to the narrative of Genesis 2, Adam's solitude is surprisingly revelatory of his relationship with God. Though he is "of the earth" like the animals he is charged with naming, he is also uniquely "alone" precisely because he is the one who bears the breath of God in him and because he alone is the one with whom God speaks. Adam experiences creation as a sign that he is made for more, and he is called to perceive and receive it as a gift. Bringing both creation accounts together—to be created and sustained in existence is to be thrust into relationship with the Creator; and to be created as a human person is to be conscious of the faculties that set one apart from the world precisely so that one can recognize the Creator. In the

41. Wojtyła, *Sign of Contradiction*, 21.
42. TOB 13:4 [180].
43. Ibid.
44. See TOB 13:4 [180–81]: "*Creation is a gift, because man appears in it, who, as an 'image of God,' is able to understand the very meaning of the gift in the call from nothing to existence....* Creation constitutes the fundamental and original gift: man appears in creation as the one who has received the world as a gift" (emphasis in the original). For more on this understanding of creation as a gift, see the helpful analogy of Carl Anderson and José Granados, in *Called to Love: Approaching John Paul II's Theology of the Body* (New York: Doubleday, 2009), 5–6.

end, for John Paul, a relationship with God is not accidental to human beings but is constitutive of human existence: *"Man is 'alone': this is to say that through his own humanity, through what he is, he is at the same time set into a unique, exclusive, and unrepeatable relationship with God himself."*[45] In this way, a foundational unity is written into the ontological fabric of human existence: a relationship with God is part of the very definition of being human.[46]

Still, there is a second communion that springs from Adam's solitude, and, in a certain sense, it is an extension of the first. For, if all of creation is a manifestation of love and bears a gift-character, then all beings must, in some way, be ordered to love or self-gift. John Paul therefore speaks of whether Adam "lived the world truly as a gift"—that is, whether he found in creation the "basic conditions that [made] it possible to exist in a relation of reciprocal gift."[47] The pope thus makes a query of the Genesis text based upon a metaphysical premise. God is the source of all goodness because he is goodness itself; and yet, as St. Thomas explains, *bonum est diffusivum sui*. This key Thomistic and Dionysian insight then becomes an important lens through which to view creation:

Bonum est diffusivum sui. It is indeed so: the God of infinite majesty—*Ipsum esse subsistens*—distributes in varying degrees of perfection the good of existence, and spreads it as he effects creation; spreads it because he is not only omnipotence but also love.[48]

All beings, then, precisely because they come from and participate in the God who is love, must bear the mark of love in themselves.

---

45. TOB 6:2 [150]. Emphasis in the original. See also John Paul II, *God, Father and Creator*, 233.

46. A play entitled *Radiation of Fatherhood*, which the pope had published in the Kraków monthly *Znak* in 1979 (though he had written it earlier as an archbishop), is in many ways a meditation on the creation of human beings in God's image. The title itself is indicative of this, as humans are called to accept the "radiation of [God's] Fatherhood" and "refract it as a prism refracts light." In the play, the character Adam (who, for the author, stands for "every man") sheds further light on this first implication of unity found in solitude: "I am afraid of the word 'mine,' though at the same time I cherish its meaning. I am afraid because this word always puts me face to face with You. An analysis of the word 'mine' always leads me to You. And I would rather give up using it than find its ultimate sense in You." See Wojtyła, *Radiation of Fatherhood*, in *The Collected Plays and Writings on Theater*, trans. Bolesław Taborski (Berkeley: University of California Press, 1987), 337. See also the pope's thoughts in *Crossing the Threshold of Hope*, 35–36: "One cannot think adequately about man without reference, which for man is constitutive, to God."

47. TOB 14:1 [181].

48. Wojtyła, *Sign of Contradiction*, 22. See also ST I, q. 5, a. 4, ad. 2, and ST II-I, q. 3, a. 2, ad. 3.

Though they cannot be love's equal—cannot be pure Act as God is pure Act—they are called to give of themselves, nonetheless, to the extent their natures allow. In the words of Norris Clarke, "All beings, by the very fact that they *are*, possess [the] natural dynamism toward self-communicative action [because] they are all diverse modes of participation in the infinite goodness of the one Source, whose very being is self-communicative love."[49]

John Paul II, in accord with this Thomistic insight, recognizes that all beings are self-communicative in this sense. But *human* beings, precisely because they are "persons" and are therefore expressions of the most perfect form of being, can only give of themselves in the fullest sense when this gift takes the form of the love of other persons.[50] This has immense implications for our understanding of both God and the human person. In terms of the former, if personal being is the highest form of existence and if humans are made in the image of God, then it is fitting that God—as Being itself—is a relationship of Persons. Thus, the metaphysical overflow from Creator to creature that marks all being as self-communicative is due not only to the economic action of God in creating, but also to God's own inner life as Father, Son, and Holy Spirit. The revelation of God as Trinity becomes the archetype of human love.[51] In terms of the latter, the content of the image of God is now expanded to horizons previously unforeseen: "Likeness to God ... is reflected not just in the *rational and free nature*—the spiritual nature—of the human person.... The human being's likeness to God [also] occurs *by reason of a relation that unites persons*."[52]

Here, then, is the deepest reason for Adam's loneliness amidst the animals. As the image of God, he cannot fully realize this image without another person to whom he can give himself. Solitude gives way to a second unity because Adam's inability to find a suitable partner points ahead to the creation of Eve. His longing for one who is like himself is expressed most powerfully in the words he utters in finding her. Eve

49. Clarke, *Person and Being*, 11. Emphasis in the original.

50. See ST I, q. 29, a. 3 [158]: "*Person* signifies what is most perfect in all nature."

51. In no way does John Paul II argue that God as a Trinity of Persons can be deduced from philosophical principles, nor from an interpretation of the Genesis creation accounts alone. Rather, as he explains in *Mulieris Dignitatem*, such can only be "a *prelude* to the definitive self-revelation of the Triune God: a living unity in the communion of the Father, Son, and Holy Spirit" (emphasis mine). See *Mulieris Dignitatem*, no. 7.

52. Wojtyła, "Family as a Community of Persons," 318. Emphasis in the original.

alone is, at last, "bone of my bones and flesh of my flesh"—she alone is the "suitable partner" for Adam.[53] In this way, "the meaning of original solitude enters and becomes part of the meaning of *original unity*."[54] Through Eve, God's words in the second creation story, "it is not good for man to be alone," become the anthropological counterpart to the first story's claim that "God created man in his image; in the divine image he created him; *male and female* he created them."[55] For John Paul II, the call to communion is part of being created in the image of God and is foundational to human personhood.[56]

Ultimately, original solitude—Adam's loneliness amidst the world—is profoundly connected to two unities. I believe it is important to emphasize once again that John Paul II finds one relationship (that between God and the human being) to be constitutive of the human person from the *beginning* while the other (between human persons) takes the form of an *end*—it is a calling or vocation that is only attained through human action.[57] The consistency with his philosophical an-

53. Gn 2:23 and 18, respectively.

54. TOB 8:1 [156]. Emphasis mine. See also TOB 14:2 [182]: "When God-Yahweh says, 'It is not good that the man should be alone' (Gn 2:18), he affirms that, 'alone,' the man does not completely realize this essence. He realizes it only by existing '*with someone*'—and, put even more deeply and completely, by existing '*for someone*.' . . . Communion of persons means living in a reciprocal 'for,' in a relationship of reciprocal gift. And this relationship is precisely the fulfillment of 'man's' original solitude" (emphasis in the original).

55. Gn 2:18 and 1:27. Emphasis mine. A precursor to this understanding of the image as communion is found in the work of the great Protestant theologian Karl Barth. See Barth's *Church Dogmatics*, ed. G. W. Bromiley and T. F. Torrance, trans. J. W. Edwards, O. Bussey, and H. Knight (Edinburgh: T. and T. Clark, 1958), 3:195: "Could anything be more obvious than to conclude from this clear indication that the image and likeness of the being created by God signifies existence in confrontation, i.e., in this confrontation, in the juxtaposition and conjunction of man and man which is that of male and female, and then to go on to ask against this background in what the original and prototype of the divine existence of the Creator consists?"

56. Once again, the body is not an afterthought in John Paul II's reflections—it is expressive of the original unity of which he speaks. For the pope, Adam's acclamation in Gn 2:23, "flesh of my flesh and bone of my bones," reveals that it is the perception of Eve's body that allows him to realize the possibility of communion with her. See TOB 9:4 [164]. For more on the ability of the body to manifest the image of God as communion, see Christopher M. Cullen, "Between God and Nothingness: Matter in John Paul II's *Theology of the Body*," in McDermott and Gavin, *Pope John Paul II on the Body*, 65–75.

57. See McDermott, "Response to 'The Nuptial Meaning of the Body,'" in McDermott and Gavin, *Pope John Paul II on the Body*, 132: "The philosophical tension between formal and final causalities finds a corresponding reflection in man's polar being, individual and social." Of course, this second form of communion, established by acts of love, is indicative of the final end of the human being, too—communion with God. Such a communion is the fulfillment of the first unity.

thropology is clear: the first unity concerns the "first act" of existence and thus determines human nature; the second unity is a result of personal acts and is related to the "second act" of existence that moves one to a greater participation in what is true and good. So, too, does the first unity speak of a human being's existence as a person endowed with the intellect and will, while the second unity—precisely because it is a calling and thus only results from personal acts—speaks of communal existence as "accidental," though necessary if one is to fulfill him- or herself.[58] Ultimately, there is an inherent congruence between Wojtyła's philosophical anthropology and the vision of human beings found in the Genesis narrative: a relationship with God forms Adam's very being whether he finds a suitable partner or not; but Adam must love another person, Eve, if he is to fulfill himself.

Disunity and Redemption

That this vision of communion is central to John Paul's anthropology is only confirmed further by the fact that he views both the Fall and redemption through the same lens. For the pope, the choice of the primordial couple to eat from the tree of knowledge is a rejection of the original meaning of creation as "gift" and "love."[59] At its core it is a deformation of both the communion of Adam and Eve with God and the communion between Adam and Eve. Indeed, one can say that, for John Paul, the hallmark of sin is its disruption of the relationship of the person with every aspect of reality.[60]

58. What was true for Wojtyła's philosophical anthropology is true here: though the substance of the human person (which can only exist by means of an ontological relationship with God) takes primacy over relation (with other creatures), love and the community it forms are still necessary for human nature to be perfected. That the second unity is "accidental" should not be read pejoratively; it only highlights an important metaphysical distinction. See TOB 9:2 [162]: "In his original solitude man reaches personal consciousness in the process of 'distinction' from all living beings, and at the same time, in this solitude, he opens himself toward a being akin to himself, defined by Genesis as 'a help similar to himself' (Gn 2:18, 20). This opening is no less decisive for man as a person; in fact, it is perhaps more decisive than the 'distinction' itself."

59. See TOB 26:4 [237].

60. See John Paul II, *Jesus, Son and Savior: A Catechesis on the Creed*, trans. L'Osservatore Romano, English ed. (Boston: Pauline Books and Media, 1996), 27, where the pope explains that Genesis' account of original sin presents "the fundamental and decisive implication of that event for man's relationship with God, and consequently for the interior 'situation' of man himself, for reciprocal relationships between people, and in general for man's relationship with the world." Though here I am mainly concerned with the disruption of communion between persons, the

That sin damages a person's fundamental communion with God is evident in Adam and Eve's hiding among the trees when the Lord God comes to look for them after the first sin.[61] They are ashamed before the One who created them, the One who holds them in existence and offers the world to them as a gift. This experience of shame then extends to the relationship of Adam and Eve with each other. What was once a scene characterized by Adam's joy in finding a suitable partner is now transformed into one marked by the sewing of fig leaves. In the moment of sin, the nakedness that was a sign of intimacy becomes an experience of "alienation" and "defenselessness."[62] Even the divine punishment imposed upon the couple manifests this disruption of communion: "The expression, 'Your desire shall be for your husband, but he will dominate you,' immediately indicates," John Paul explains, "*a lack of full unity . . . to which both were called.*"[63] In sum, through their sin, Adam and Eve cause damage to the communion that forms their very existence as human beings,[64] and they likewise damage the image that is formed in their communion with one another.[65] For the pope, because the *imago dei* extends beyond human rationality to in-

---

other forms are immensely important and deserve further study. In the same work on page 50, John Paul highlights the damage sin does to the relationship between a person and the world by way of Rom 8:19–22 and Gn 3:17–19: "St. Paul says that as a result of man's sin 'creation was subjected to futility,' and for this reason also 'the whole creation has been groaning in travail together until now' until it will be 'set free from its bondage to decay.' This lack of balance of creation has its influence on the destiny of man in the visible world. The labor by which he acquires the means of sustenance is carried out 'in the sweat of his face,' and is linked with toil." Finally, John Paul explains the disruption of communion within oneself as the alienation of the soul from the body in TOB 28:2. In using the trees to hide from God and a loincloth to hide from his wife, Adam reveals that he has in some sense distanced himself, through sin, from his own body. This is a theme Benedict XVI would take up in DCE, no. 5.

61. See TOB 27:1 [238]; and Gn 3:8–10.

62. TOB 27:2 [239] and 27:4 [242], respectively. In TOB 26:5 [238], John Paul identifies the experience of shame as the subjective experience of the objective reality that is broken communion.

63. TOB 30:2 [250]. Emphasis in the original. See Gn 3:16. John Paul II further explores the impact of sin on communion with other persons in *Reconciliatio et Paenitentia*, nos. 15 and 16, where he speaks of the connection between "personal sin" and "social sin." See John Paul II, *Reconciliatio et Paenitentia*, Vatican trans. (Boston: Pauline Books and Media, 1984), 34–39; AAS 77 (1985): 185–275.

64. TOB 27:2 [239]: "What shows itself through 'nakedness' [after the Fall] is man deprived of participation in the Gift, man alienated from the Love that was a source of the original gift." The experience that captures this broken communion is described by John Paul in TOB 28:1 [243] as "cosmic shame."

65. TOB 28:1 [243].

clude the call to communion, the marring of that image must necessarily lead to disunity or alienation.

If sin is both a rejection of the love that establishes creation and a failure in the human vocation to love, then redemption must be a healing of these two rifts. It must be a reconciliation that restores communion among human beings and between creation and God. Accordingly, John Paul sees the advent of Christ as the coming of Love itself into human history. He who is the self-gift of God in his very person is the living revelation that God is love: "In man's history this love and mercy has taken a form and a name: that of Jesus Christ."[66]

By his coming, Christ restores the link between creation and its divine source: "As this link was broken in the man Adam, so in the Man Christ it was reforged."[67] This healing of nature by grace then extends to the plane of human action as a calling that can be answered with divine help:

Redemption is therefore the new creation in Christ. It is a gift of God—grace—and at the same time it implies *a call directed to man*. Man must cooperate with the work of spiritual liberation accomplished in him by God by means of Christ.... Certainly man cannot attribute to himself salvation, that saving liberation which is a gift of God in Christ. Yet at the same time one must see in these gifts the origin of a constant *exhortation to act* in such a way as to be worthy of such a gift.[68]

This call or exhortation forms what John Paul calls the "ethos of redemption," the full expression of which is found in the communion that is restored through grace-filled acts of love.[69] Thus, the restoration of nature overflows into a call to act—the healing of one unity compels the healing of the other. In sum, through redemption human beings are "called to grace [and] called to love."[70]

Clearly, one can see the influence of *Gaudium et Spes* upon this interpretation of the creation, Fall, and redemption of humanity, particularly in its teaching on the *communio personarum*. John Paul II even

66. RH, no. 9 [18]. See also John Paul II, *Jesus, Son and Savior*, 426.
67. RH, no. 8 [15].
68. John Paul II, *Jesus, Son and Savior*, 404. Emphasis mine.
69. Ibid., 404–5. Here the pope draws upon Eph 2:14–16 in its expression of the unity Christ brings between Israel and the nations. He then extends this restoration of communion to "everyone without exception or difference."
70. RH, no. 9 [17].

acknowledges his debt to the Council in this regard.[71] The pope's interpretation of the Pastoral Constitution is central to his understanding of the human person as seen in the light of revelation. Still, before moving to the pope's interpretation of the conciliar texts themselves, I believe it will be helpful to place this interpretation of the image of God in the greater context of the Christian tradition.

The Image of God in Tradition: Ontic and Ethical, Natural and Supernatural Aspects of the Image

John Paul II's reading of the creation accounts embraces the predominant interpretation of the *imago dei* in the Western Christian tradition by seeing the image as consisting, in part, in rational human nature. This reading has deep roots in St. Augustine who, in his *De Trinitate*, offers several trinitarian analogies in his attempt to locate the image of God as Trinity in human beings, most notably the mind and its ability to know and to love. For Augustine, such images serve as earthly symbols by which human beings can ascend to the knowledge of God; they are part of the upward path that leads to knowing and loving the Father, Son, and Holy Spirit. His use of these so-called psychological analogies is, therefore, not merely for the purpose of identifying triads that could helpfully explain orthodox trinitarian doctrine (something akin to the legend of St. Patrick and the shamrock) but is rather an exploration of the epistemology of faith.[72] In other words, Augustine meditates upon the faculties of rational human nature precisely because he is seeking an understanding of how humans come to know and love God. For Augustine, if humans are able to know and love the Trinity, then there must be a trinitarian structure within human knowing and loving.

This helps explain the reason for his first analogy in book 8 of *De Trinitate*, in which the Trinity is mirrored in human love. Only because

---

71. See TOB 9:2 [162].

72. Khaled Anatolios offers an excellent overview of the purpose and structure of *De Trinitate*, including an explanation of this Christological ascent of the mind to the vision of the trinitarian God, in his *Retrieving Nicaea: The Development and Meaning of Trinitarian Doctrine* (Grand Rapids, Mich.: Baker Academic, 2011), 241–80. As he states on page 258, "Augustine's explanation of what he considers to be the scriptural sense of 'image' alerts us again to the fact that the kind of trinitarian knowledge he is looking for is not a simple or punctiliar transaction between a given set of propositions and their objective referent in divine being but rather an all-encompassing way of imitation, purification, and ascent."

"God is love," as 1 John 4:8 proclaims, is a trace of the Trinity found in a lover, the beloved, and the love between them.[73] While one might be tempted to see here an early source of Vatican II's teaching on the *communio personarum*, it is noteworthy that Augustine later claims that one should *not* hold that a community of human persons (he specifically mentions a family consisting of father, mother, and son) is an image of God precisely because the biblical witness testifies to the image being in *each* person and because three separate human persons cannot claim the consubstantiality of orthodox trinitarian faith.[74] The scriptures and the doctrinal formulations that flow from them are, for the bishop of Hippo, the norms by which any analogy can be measured.[75]

This leads Augustine to look inward in his analogy of the mind and its abilities to know and to love, a triad that he further expresses in terms of memory, intellect, and will.[76] By focusing on how the image is present in a single person and by holding the unity of the mind to be the ground of its remembering, knowing, and loving, Augustine is able to offer an analogy that conforms to both the biblical witness and Nicene faith. And it is precisely in this analogy that he sets a trajectory that will be furthered in the Western tradition, as evidenced by the acceptance of the Augustinian doctrine in the scholastic period by both St. Thomas and St. Bonaventure.[77]

Still—and to once again recall his overall purpose—though Augustine believes he must leave behind his social analogy for a more interiorly gazing one, it would be incorrect to see this new consideration as confined solely to the realm of human consciousness, a sort of precursor to the Cartesian inward turn. Augustine does not hold that introversion is the path by which one reaches the vision of God; rather, the interior faculties of the person have an outward, extroverted purpose. In his words, "This trinity of the mind is not [only] the image of God

73. See *De Trinitate* 8.10.14: "Now love is of someone who loves, and something is loved with love. So then there are three: the lover, the beloved, and the love.... It remains to ascend even from here and to seek for those higher things, insofar as it is granted to man." I have used the translation found in St. Augustine, *The Trinity*, trans. Stephen McKenna (Washington, D.C.: The Catholic University of America Press, 1963), 266.

74. See *De Trinitate* 12.6.8–12.7.9. Following Augustine, St. Thomas calls this idea of the image in several persons "manifestly absurd." See ST I, q. 93, a. 6, ad. 2 [474].

75. See Anatolios, *Retrieving Nicaea*, 261.

76. See *De Trinitate* 9.5.8 and 10.11.18.

77. See, for example, ST I. q. 93, a. 1–9 and Bonaventure's *Itinerarium Mentis in Deum* 3.5.

because the mind remembers *itself*, understands *itself*, and loves *itself*, but because it can also remember, understand, and love *Him* by whom it was made."[78] Thus, the mind is more properly an image when it is turned toward God—ultimately, "it is His image by the very fact that it is *capable of* Him, and can be a *partaker of* Him."[79]

This point clears the way for what is possibly the most striking aspect of *De Trinitate*, for, as John Cavadini notes, Augustine ultimately finds that his analogies—if considered only human attempts to understand God—must fail.[80] True, the mind and its remembering, knowing, and loving are an image of God in and of themselves, but this is only in some lesser sense. They are more properly the image only when they remember, know, and love the Trinity—a task inhibited by human sinfulness and one that is ultimately impossible apart from grace. Augustine, appropriately named the *Doctor Gratiae*, recognizes the need for divine help in the mind's ascent. As he explains toward the end of *De Trinitate*, "When [the mind] rightly remembers its Lord . . . it feels with absolute certainty . . . that it can only raise itself by the affection which He freely gives, and could only have fallen by the defection which it freely committed."[81] Augustine thus finds in his exploration of the mind's ascent to God that the climb is only accomplishable by faith in Jesus Christ, the mediator who purifies human nature by taking it upon himself.

It is the grace-empowered vision of faith, then, that is able to overcome sin on the mind's path to God. Augustine is clear that this faith and the vision it offers are not a matter of a single moment, such as that provided by baptism and its washing away of sin, but is a continual purification that only reaches its perfection in the beatific vision. The journey of the mind, while grounded in the sacrament of regeneration, bears the character of the already-not yet:

This renewal is not brought about in the one moment of conversion itself, as in Baptism that renewal is brought about in one moment by the remission

---

78. *De Trinitate* 14.12.15 [432]. Emphasis mine. For further insight on how Augustine's interior gaze at the mind ultimately manifests the person's extroversion toward God, see Anatolios, "Interiority and Extroversion in Biblical Trinitarian Faith in Augustine's *De Trinitate*," *Letter and Spirit* 7 (2011): 173–90.

79. *De Trinitate* 14.8.11 [426]. Emphasis mine.

80. See John Cavadini, "The Structure and Intention of Augustine's *De trinitate*," *Augustinian Studies* 23 (1992): 103–23.

81. *De Trinitate* 14.15.21 [439–40].

of all sins. . . . But just as it is one thing to be free from fevers, and another thing to recover from the weakness which has resulted from the fevers; and similarly, just as it is one thing to remove a spear that has been driven into the body, and another thing to heal the wound that has been made by it through the treatment that follows, so the first step in a cure is to remove the cause of the disease, which is done through the remission of all sins; the second is to heal the disease itself, which is done gradually by making progress in the renewal of this image.[82]

The ascent, then, is only truly accomplished in the eschatological future, though here, in its earthly existence, the mind begins the process of purification by which it will eventually be able to see God. This gradual renewal of the mind proceeds, Augustine explains, "day by day," and it is hard-won in the happenings and vicissitudes of daily life.[83] It proceeds until that point in which the person, by holding fast to faith in Christ, is ultimately received into heavenly glory and, at the eschaton, is given an incorruptible body. Only then is the ascent completed: "For the likeness to God in this image will then be perfect when the vision of God will be perfect."[84]

Though brief, this look at the source of the traditional understanding of the *imago dei* in Augustine brings to light a significant correspondence with Pope John Paul II (and, indeed, Vatican II). At first glance it seems that, in leaving behind his social analogy for a more interior one, Augustine has closed the door to an understanding of the image of God as the *communio personarum*.[85] But, upon closer inspection, he provides a significant bridge by which to see a proper development in this regard.

It is true that the bishop of Hippo ultimately rejects his own social analogy for the Trinity on grounds of the inability of human commu-

---

82. *De Trinitate* 14.17.23 [444].

83. *De Trinitate* 14.17.23 [444–45]. Augustine quotes 2 Cor 4:16 in this regard: "Even though the outer man is decaying, yet our inner man is being renewed day by day."

84. *De Trinitate* 14.17.23 [445]

85. Ratzinger actually faults Augustine for this inward turn because it disassociates human persons (individual substances) from divine Persons (relations), though he places greater blame on St. Thomas. See his "Concerning the Notion of Person," 447. In the East, the social or familial analogy of the Trinity emerged in the thought of Gregory of Nazienzen and posed less of a problem, since, according to the Cappadocians, human beings communed in the same substance. On this, see Lionel Gendron, "La famille: Reflet de la communion trinitaire," in *La famille chrétienne dans le monde d'aujourd'hui: Réflexions et témoignages*, ed. Christian Lépine, 127–48 (Montreal: Bellarmin, 1994).

nion (a unity of individual substances) to correlate with divine communion (three relations that are consubstantial), but neither is John Paul's understanding of the *communio personarum* based upon such an ontological foundation. For John Paul, substance is only predicated of the individual person within a given human community. In upholding the dignity of each individual person, he rejects an understanding of community in which the community itself is considered a substantial actor—only individual persons in a community can be substantial subjects of conscious action. Thus, a communion of persons is the product of the relations brought about by consciously willed human acts. Such acts do not define the nature of the person who is acting—they do not equate to his or her substance—though they flow from it. Ultimately, then, John Paul II agrees with Augustine that the consubstantiality of divine communion is unique to the Trinity and is not shared by the coming together of separate, individual substances in human communion. The analogy that legitimizes the *communio personarum* as an image of God must be based upon something other than a correlation of "substance."

Is it to "relation," then, that one must turn to establish human communion as an image of the Trinity? It is true that, in a certain sense, one could speak of relation as at least *partially* constitutive of the human person, for the de facto existence of a person demands relationship to other beings, beginning with one's family and extending outward to the community, the human race, and even to the rest of the created world.[86] Even so, the person, as a real being, ultimately remains a substance at his or her innermost core—there must be some "thing" that is related to other beings, even in this ontological sense. The etymology of the word "substance"—that which "stands under"—speaks just as much.[87]

But more important here is the fact that the ontological "communion" afforded by such relations is not what John Paul II means when

86. Ratzinger's "Concerning the Notion of Person," as a whole, argues that the human person, like the divine, is constituted by relation. Ratzinger does not, however, identify the role of substance in this relational anthropology. See also Adrian J. Walker, "Personal Singularity and the *Communio Personarum*: A Creative Development of Thomas Aquinas' Doctrine of *Esse Commune*," *Communio* 31, no. 3 (2004): 457–79, who, in a similar vein, argues that human singularity is constituted in communion by creatively reinterpreting St. Thomas's notion of *esse commune*.

87. See Clarke, "To Be Is to Be Substance-in-Relation," in *Explorations in Metaphysics* (Notre Dame, Ind.: University of Notre Dame Press, 1994), 104–5.

speaking of the *communio personarum*.[88] For the pope, the *communio personarum* is not a constituent of nature but is the result of conscious acts of self-gift. In the biblical narrative, he finds that solitude "leads to" unity, that it is properly characterized as "opening toward and waiting for" communion.[89] In this way, substance precedes and is the basis for relation. Men and women are indeed "created for unity," but this unity *"has from the beginning the character of a union that derives from a choice."*[90]

Thus, John Paul does not see this second understanding of relation as constitutive of human personhood but as its fulfillment. The beginning of his anthropology in the axiom *operari sequitir esse* begins to see its full flowering here. Not only does operation follow being, but it is the actualization of it—a substance exists for its operations; the potency inherent in human nature is unleashed in human acts of love. In view of Genesis, Adam's solitude is not the mere remoteness of his individual substantiality but is a sign that he is made for communion. That he experiences himself as alone is the proof of precisely this fact. Relations formed in communion are, in this sense, the *telos* of the human substance.

From this dynamic understanding of being and operation, or substance and act, emerges a link between Augustine's traditional account of the image and John Paul II's understanding of the *communio personarum*. The common ground between Augustine and John Paul is found in the former's distinction between the mind as the image of God in itself and the mind's remembering, knowing, and loving as the image of God when the person acts in accord with divine help. For Augustine, the mind, even when "impaired and disfigured by the loss of its participation in God . . . remains nonetheless an image of God"; and, yet, one can grow in "likeness to God in this image" by living a life informed by grace.[91] Augustine thus provides an important distinction between

88. One could perhaps speak of such relations in Aristotelian terms as potencies waiting to be actualized in communion. See Grabowski, "Public Moral Discourse on Abortion: The Contribution of Theology," *Irish Theological Quarterly* 64, no. 4 (1999): 365.

89. TOB 9:2 [162].

90. TOB 10:3 [168]. Emphasis in the original.

91. *De Trinitate* 14.8.11 [426] and 14.17.23 [445], respectively. So too does Augustine, like John Paul II, ground this growth into the image in the initial metaphysical communion between God and a given human being that is formed simply by way of the person's existence. See *De Trinitate* 14.12.16 [434]: "Humanity's great wretchedness, therefore, is not to be with Him, without whom we cannot exist. For undoubtedly we are not without Him in whom we are, and yet if we do not remember Him nor understand Him nor love Him, then we are not with Him."

the *imago dei* as part of what can be termed human *nature* and the perfected image as the result of graced human *acts*.[92] Similarly, John Paul II claims that the image of God is found in the transcendence of human rationality; and yet this transcendence is ordered to the image found in the act of love, that act which is the most fulfilling a person can make and that establishes relations with other persons.

Latent in Augustine's theology, then, is this importance of the role of act, or to put it more richly, love. While he began his social analogy from the consideration of the Johannine statement "God is love," Augustine ultimately rejected the analogy on the metaphysical grounds of substance's inability to bridge divine and human communion. But John Paul II, aided by an Aristotelian-Thomistic metaphysic, is able to bring out the fruitfulness of relation for bridging the gap by pointing to its foundation in act. Because God is love, humans, as the image of God, are called to love. Thus, the analogy that allows the *communio personarum* to be an image of God is not based upon the direct correlation of divine relations with human substances but, rather, upon the correlation of divine and human acts of love.

As with all analogies between what is divine and human, dissimilarity must outweigh similarity. Only in God can the act of love itself constitute another Person. For humans, persons exist even before they give themselves to another; the relations they form can only be a product of the "second act" of existence, a product of the acts by which the substance of the person seeks its perfection. Nevertheless, love proves to be the bridge between divine and human forms of communion. One could even say that relation succeeds where substance fails, as long as the concept of relation is undergirded by a robust understanding of act. In this light, John Paul's (and, indeed, the Council's) understanding of the image as *communio personarum* can rightly be seen as a development of the traditional and Augustinian doctrine. "Very ancient themes," Wojtyła once wrote, "here take on a genuinely new aspect."[93]

92. See Cavadini, "Structure and Intention of Augustine's *De trinitate*," 108: "For what is necessary now is not so much an uninterrupted consideration of the image but a 'renewal' of the image. And this consists not in the static regard of an essentially unchanging intellect or in the eschatological cleansing of that image from extrinsically accrued bodily taint at death, but in the genuine 'growth' of the image itself in, as Augustine puts it, a 'gradual,' 'day by day' 'progress,' one which is accomplished 'holding fast to the faith of the Mediator.'"

93. Wojtyła, *Sources of Renewal*, 62.

Finally, it should be pointed out that what ultimately lies at the heart of this correspondence between Augustine's and John Paul II's understanding of the image of God is not only the philosophical relationship between nature and personal acts but, even more, the person of Jesus Christ, he who is, as the beginning of this chapter recalls, the "image of the invisible God" and the "firstborn of all creation."[94] Christ is the perfect image of God, and he is the one from whom all of creation, and especially human beings, take their form. Not only this, but after the sin of Adam, he is the one who restores the image to fallen human beings. According to this Pauline theology of the image, "all of us, gazing with unveiled face on the glory of the Lord, are being transformed into the same image from glory to glory, as from the Lord who is the Spirit."[95]

The implication of this theology is that the Christian life is one of "growing into" the image of God, a growth made possible by the redemption of Christ and the gift of his Spirit.

John Paul often refers to this possibility of growth as a "call" or "vocation," words that reveal the underlying metaphysical structure of the "second act" in its movement from potentiality to actuality. For the pope:

The truth about man created in the image of God does not merely determine man's place in the whole order of creation, but it already speaks even of his link with the order of salvation in Christ, who is the eternal and consubstantial "image of God" (2 Corinthians 4:4)—the image of the Father. Man's creation in the image of God, from the very beginning of the book of Genesis, bears witness to his call. This call is fully revealed in the coming of Christ. Thanks to the action of the "Spirit of the Lord," there opens up the perspective of the full transformation in the consubstantial image of God, which is Christ (cf. 2 Corinthians 3:18). Thus the "image" of the book of Genesis (1:27) reaches the fullness of its revealed significance.[96]

This understanding of the image, while in accord with Augustine, is found throughout the writings of the church fathers, and it quite often comes by way of an interpretation of Genesis 1:26 that focuses upon the text's use of the two terms "image" and "likeness."[97] By viewing the

---

94. Col 1:15. See also Rom 8:29, 1 Cor 11:7 and 15:49, 2 Cor 3:18, Eph 4:24, and Col 3:10.
95. 2 Cor 3:18.
96. John Paul II, God, Father and Creator, 225. Emphasis mine.
97. See Erhueh, Vatican II: Image of God in Man, 5; and Hans Urs von Balthasar, Theo-Drama: Theological Dramatic Theory, trans. Graham Harrison (San Francisco: Ignatius Press, 1990), 2:319, who note the consensus of modern biblical scholars that the two terms are nearly synonymous.

Old Testament in light of the New, the fathers were able to read into the seemingly small space offered by the distinction between these terms a much larger theological truth: that there is an aspect of divine dignity (image) that remains constant in human beings even after the Fall while, nevertheless, there is one (likeness) that is lost through sin and must be recovered through a life lived in the grace of Jesus Christ. Thus, it is not uncommon to find the patristic distinction made between "image" and "likeness" such as that found in Irenaeus:

> In earlier times it was said that man was created in the image of God, but it was not a manifest truth, for the Word according to whose image man was created was invisible, and so the likeness was easily lost. But the Word, becoming flesh, firmly established both: it demonstrated the truth of the image by becoming precisely what its image was and restored the likeness by assimilating man to the invisible Father through the mediation of the now invisible Word.[98]

The distinction between the terms is not unanimously strict and systematically made in the fathers, even when one reads the same author.[99] Still, the meaning behind it remains consistent, and this, as Hans Urs von Balthasar relates, "can crudely be described as [the distinction] between the ontic and ethical aspects of the image."[100] To use a more Thomistic and Wojtyłan turn of phrase, a distinction can be made between the quality of the image that belongs to human *nature* and that which belongs to the realm of *personal acts* that move a person to greater participation in the good.

Still, as Irenaeus's quote makes clear, the distinction between the ontic and the ethical does not exhaust the content of the patristic interpretation of the image of God. Rather, it provides the foundation for a further distinction, which Balthasar explains as that "between an essential constituent of man's nature, which cannot be lost in the sinner ... and the gift of the Pneuma."[101] In terms of modern theology, this is

98. St. Irenaeus, *Adversus Haereses* 5.16.2, as quoted in Balthasar, *Theo-Drama*, 2:324–25. See also Origen's *On First Principles* 3.6.1: "Man received the honour of God's image in his first creation, whereas the perfection of God's likeness was reserved for him at the consummation," in *Origen: On First Principles*, trans. G. W. Butterworth (Gloucester, Mass.: Peter Smith, 1973), 245, as quoted in R. R. Reno, *Genesis* (Grand Rapids, Mich.: Brazos, 2010), 51.

99. See Balthasar, *Theo-Drama*, 2:325; and Erhueh, *Vatican II: Image of God in Man*, 30.

100. Balthasar, *Theo-Drama*, 2:324.

101. Ibid., 325. See also Erhueh, *Vatican II: Image of God in Man*, 32: "According to the Fathers, the image consists in man's metaphysical reality, while the likeness [consists] in the grace of God himself [given] to man."

none other than the distinction between nature and "supernature," or nature and grace.[102]

The fathers, then, were quite accustomed to building an important theological relationship upon the foundation of a philosophical one when interpreting the image of God—the relation of nature to grace was somehow bound up with that between human nature and personal acts. This union of distinctions is offered in its most succinct form in the words of St. Athanasius: "[God], indeed, assumed humanity that we might become God."[103] Speaking from within this tradition, John Paul II offers this same union of distinctions when he explains that Christian thought has seen in the *image of God* that "man is ... capable of knowledge and freedom," while it has "perceived in man's *'likeness' to God* the foundation of man's call to participate in the interior life of God—his opening to the supernatural."[104] For the pope, "the revealed truth about man, created 'in the image and likeness of God,' contains not only all that is '*humanum*' in him, and therefore essential to his humanity, but potentially also what is '*divinum*' and therefore gratuitous."[105]

Thus, as both John Paul II and the church fathers demonstrate, a Christological reading of the *imago dei* is able to unite the philosophical distinction between the ontic and the ethical with the theological relationship between nature and grace. It is of secondary though still great importance that this affirmation allows us to see in John Paul—whose philosophy so heavily relies upon the anthropology of St. Thomas (even while augmenting it)—the continuity that exists between Thomas's anthropology and that of the fathers, with both finding a foundation in the biblical theology of the image of God. Yet, more importantly for our purposes here, I believe this Christological understanding of the image of God provides an important key for understanding the path of

102. Balthasar, *Theo-Drama*, 2:325: "Of course, the Fathers do not make the distinction between nature and supernature that is made in modern technical theology; yet it is not at all clear why, from the vantage point of the latter, people should engage in polemics against analyzing the 'image' into a 'natural' and a 'supernatural' element."

103. *De Incarnatione Dei Verbi* 8.54, in Athanasius, *On the Incarnation*, 93. In Eastern patristic thought, Athanasius's words summarize the doctrine of human deification or divinization. See also Maximus the Confessor, *Ambigua ad Iohannem* 41: "The one deified through grace receives for himself everything that God possesses, apart from the identity of substance," as quoted in Christoph Schönborn, *From Death to Life: The Christian Journey*, trans. Brian McNeil (San Francisco: Ignatius Press, 1995), 48.

104. John Paul II, *God, Father and Creator*, 235. Emphasis mine.

105. Ibid.

evangelization set forth for the church in *Gaudium et Spes*—it provides the hermeneutical lens by which to see how union with God in Jesus Christ is the fulfillment of all that is truly human.

John Paul II's Interpretation of *Gaudium et Spes*

The Fulfillment of the Human Person: The Image of God in *Gaudium et Spes*

All that has been said opens the way for a more fruitful approach to the crux of the matter—the proper interpretation of *Gaudium et Spes* 22. Because it is the culmination of the Council's argument in presenting the faith to the modern world—a presentation in which anthropology is the primary framework and the *imago dei* plays a central role—its interpretation takes on the greatest significance. How, then, should we interpret its claim that Jesus Christ, as the true image of God, "reveals man to himself and brings to light his most high calling"?[106] For in this text, Wojtyła claims, lies the key to answering the "question" of human existence.[107] Indeed, such an answer, because it includes "all the encounters between God and the world," is theology in its "most integral form."[108]

Some scholars, David Schindler and Paul McPartlan among them, believe that John Paul's reliance upon article 22 should be read through a de Lubacian lens.[109] In such an interpretation, a human person's na-

---

106. *GS*, no. 22 [922].

107. See Wojtyła, *Sources of Renewal*, 75.

108. John Paul II, *Crossing the Threshold of Hope*, 59.

109. See Schindler's "Religious Freedom, Truth, and American Liberalism: Another Look at John Courtney Murray," *Communio* 21, no. 4 (1994): 704–5; "Christology and the *Imago Dei*," 172–75; and "Reorienting the Church on the Eve of the New Millennium," *Communio* 24, no. 4 (1997): 729–39; as well as McPartlan, "John Paul II and Vatican II," in *The Vision of John Paul II*, 45–61, esp. 49–51. Indeed, writings by both de Lubac and John Paul II indicate that they were acquainted with and appreciative of each other's work. De Lubac, *At the Service of the Church*, 171, wrote about their collaboration at Vatican II: "We worked side by side.... It did not take long observation to discover in him a person of the very highest qualities. He knew my works, and we were soon on good terms." John Paul II, in *Rise, Let Us Be on Our Way*, trans. Walter Ziemba (New York: Warner, 2004), 165, also wrote, "Another Frenchman with whom I established a close friendship was the theologian Henri de Lubac, S.J., whom I myself, years later, made a cardinal. The Council was a privileged period for becoming acquainted with bishops and theologians, above all in the individual commissions. When Schema 13 was being studied (later to become the Pastoral Constitution on the Church in the Modern World, *Gaudium et spes*), and I spoke on personalism, Father de Lubac came to me and said, encouragingly: 'Yes, yes, yes, that's the way forward,' and this meant a great deal to me, as I was still relatively young." Nevertheless, John Paul was also well acquainted with the great antagonist of the *nouvelle théologie*,

ture paradoxically desires, even apart from grace, what is supernatural to it.[110] The mission of the church, as expressed in *Gaudium et Spes*, would then be to present the Gospel as the end that all persons naturally desire, whether consciously or not.[111]

But, as I believe the previous analysis of his teaching on the *imago dei* shows, John Paul interprets *Gaudium et Spes* in accord with his own anthropological vision, one that maintains the integrity of human nature (and its own rightful ends) and yet sees communion—even with God—as the result of personal acts of love. In accord with his earlier philosophy, John Paul holds an Aristotelian-Thomistic concept of nature, one in which nature "refers to what is specific to man as such, that is, points to what is essentially human" and also denotes "the manner of acting open" to a being that possesses it.[112] In such an understanding, nature is so inseparable from its finality or end that it necessarily demands the means to achieve it.[113] Thus to claim that the innate end of human nature is supernatural union with God is, in the Thomistic analysis, a contradiction in terms, for the beatific vision belongs to God alone to supply.

For John Paul, and contrary to de Lubac's paradoxical claim, the Aristotelian-Thomistic understanding of nature need not be sacrificed to posit that all human beings are ordered to God in Jesus Christ. Rather, the ontological duty de Lubac hangs upon *nature* can be better accomplished by the dynamism of *person*. In other words, whether a per-

---

Réginald Garigou Lagrange, as the Dominican priest was his dissertation director when Wojtyła wrote on John of the Cross at the Angelicum. Ultimately, on the issue of whether Wojtyła agreed with de Lubac's view of human nature, the biographical information is inconclusive. But based upon the claims of his teaching and scholarship as outlined in this chapter, I believe Wojtyła would agree with de Lubac's intention, but not with the substance of his argument.

110. See de Lubac, *Mystery of the Supernatural*, 167.

111. Mansini, in "The Abiding Theological Significance of Henri de Lubac's *Surnaturel*," *Thomist* 73, no. 4 (2009): 616, claims that evangelization under de Lubac's anthropology would then look like "mystagogical catechesis."

112. Wojtyła, *Acting Person*, 77. In pages 76–85 Wojtyła analyzes the relation of *nature* to *person*, including a discussion of the phenomenological reduction that would see nature as an experience of passivity and person as one of conscious action. Ultimately, he concludes, experience confirms that nature is the source of all human dynamism, both acts that seem to occur apart from the exercise of the will and those that occur because of it. Nature and person are thus always integrated, with the former providing the potential for all actions of the latter.

113. As an analogy, a can opener has the nature of being a can opener because it can, barring dysfunction, accomplish the end of opening cans (even if the "nature" of a can opener is accidental or imposed). The end determines nature, and nature must be able to accomplish the end.

son is fallen, redeemed, or glorified in Christ, he or she still retains human nature. Yet what term can encompass the change that occurs in the passage from one state to another? "Person" is able to capture this reality, for, the person and his or her "lived experience," to use John Paul's term—his or her experience of virtue and vice, greater and lesser participation in the good, sin and redemption—is unique in each individual instance. As Guy Mansini explains:

I would distinguish *person* and *nature*. I think it true to say that we are not *who we are* without the ordination to God, without the grace he has offered, without the promise of vision. Who we are is something dramatically constituted; it is something we become according as we are related to other persons, make moral decisions, and especially, according as we are engaged with the God revealed to us by Christ, whose Spirit dwells in our hearts. But *what we are*—that is another question. What we are can be the same, indeed, is the same, whether we are called to grace and glory or not. Sharing in the divine nature does not give us another nature. Deification does not make us no longer men.[114]

John Paul's earlier philosophy had maintained this distinction in its own way, distinguishing between the nature that is universal to all human beings and is present from the first act of their existence and the person who, in lived experience, incrementally moves him- or herself by second acts to either fulfillment or nonfulfillment. Granted, such acts of a person are always rooted in human nature, finding in it their source of dynamism; but personhood for John Paul must also include one's lived experience, that which is unique to each person, including the conscious acts one chooses to do.[115] The distinction is helpful in that it allows us to say that, while human nature does not claim union with God as its innate end, persons in their de facto existence are nevertheless called by God to this union (with some attaining it and some presumably not).[116] While such a claim extends beyond the explicit as-

114. Mansini, "Abiding Theological Significance," 606–7. Emphasis mine. See also White, "'Pure Nature' of Christology," 297.

115. See Wojtyła, *Acting Person*, 84: "The efficacy of the human ego pertaining to action reveals the transcendence of the person, without, however, separating the person from nature." See also ST III, q. 20, a. 1, ad. 2 [2131]: "Now to act is not attributed to the nature as agent, but to the person. . . . Nevertheless action is attributed to the nature as to that whereby the person or hypostasis acts."

116. See McDermott, "The Theology of John Paul II: A Response," in McDermott, *Thought of Pope John Paul II*, 63–64: "The pope's strong Christocentrism is never grounded in a necessity of nature. Like Christ, the truth of faith comes directly from God to man; it does not rise from

sertions of any of John Paul II's writings, it is clear that his anthropology, as described earlier, provides a firm basis for it.

It is also worthwhile to point out that this distinction between nature and person likewise manifests itself in the pope's understanding of communion. As noted previously, only consciously chosen acts of self-gift are able to form a *communio personarum*. Participation, to use the words of his earlier philosophy, is always personal. "Participation in the humanity of other people," Wojtyła wrote, "does not arise primarily from an understanding of the essence 'human being.' . . . Rather, [it] arises from consciously becoming close enough to the human being as a concrete I."[117] As pope he reaffirmed that, in communion, each individual human being "is not only a passive object . . . and in this way determined 'by nature.' On the contrary . . . each of them is 'given' to the other as a unique and unrepeatable subject, as 'I,' as a person."[118] Thus, for John Paul II, human personhood always includes the nature that is universal to all human beings and that offers the potential for human acts; nevertheless, human nature cannot capture the uniqueness that belongs to a given person and the particular acts he or she has chosen to perform.

Because this distinction between nature and person undergirds John Paul II's anthropology, it is clear that his reading of *Gaudium et Spes* cannot be taken in de Lubacian terms. Rather, it seems to me that, for the pope, the poignant claim of article 22—that Christ "reveals man to himself and brings to light his most high calling"—is only fully understood in relation to article 24's claim that "man can fully discover his true self

---

creation. The underlying Thomistic paradox of the natural desire for the supernatural is adequately explained neither by the 'velleity' of Garrigou-Lagrange and Maritain nor by transcendental Thomism's natural dynamism, which ultimately leads to the postulation of a fundamental paradox. For Wojtyła the abstractly known natures can apparently guarantee the distinction of natural and supernatural but man's personal transcendence demands the God of grace revealed in Christ. That may be called a 'natural desire for God,' but in *The Acting Person* man's transcendental dynamism is always described in personal terms. Insofar as nature and person condition each other, St. Thomas's language may be employed, but Wojtyła prefers to speak of a personal dynamism and openness to God rather than of a natural dynamism and openness."

117. Wojtyła, "Participation or Alienation?," 201. Emphasis in the original. He adds, "Relationship does not emerge from having a universal concept of the human being, a concept that embraces all people without exception. The I-*other* relationship is not universal but always interhuman, unique and unrepeatable in each and every instance" (emphasis in the original).

118. TOB 20:5 [208]. See also Andrew N. Woznicki, *A Christian Humanism: Karol Wojtyła's Existential Personalism* (New Britain, Conn.: Mariel, 1980), 5.

only in a sincere giving of himself."[119] Though the articles occur in different chapters of the Constitution, the latter completes the theology of the image of God that is found in the former. This completion is anchored in the same dynamic anthropology put forth by the fathers and reiterated by John Paul in his teaching on the *imago dei*: a human being is, by nature, the image of God, and yet the fulfillment of the image only occurs through acts of self-gift that are empowered by grace.[120]

Just as article 22 explains that Christ is the revelation of humanity and its most high calling, article 24 adds that this calling—this ability to find one's "true self"—is only achieved by way of love. Here is where Wojtyła's "law of the gift" that undergirds all human fulfillment becomes most fully illuminated. Indeed, in his first encyclical, that which is emblematic of the direction of his entire pontificate, John Paul ties articles 22 and 24 together in explaining:

Man cannot live without love. He remains a being that is incomprehensible for himself, his life is senseless, if love is not revealed to him, if he does not encounter love, if he does not experience it and make it his own, if he does not participate intimately in it. This, as has already been said, is why Christ the Redeemer "fully reveals man to himself."[121]

It is in this drawing together of both passages that we reach the very heart of John Paul's understanding of the image of God in human beings: because Christ is love—because he is the self-gift of the Father given in the Holy Spirit[122]—human beings, as those made in his image, are *called* to love. They cannot become their fullest selves without it.

And yet, in perhaps what is the most crucial point, the pope is clear that this imaging is not limited to a human imitation of divine love. True, by loving one another, humans reach a sort of fulfillment through the communion this brings. But even more so—and here John Paul echoes Augustine's claim—it is in loving God in Jesus Christ that humans most fully find themselves and reach the greatest fulfillment:

119. GS, no. 22 [922] and 24 [925], respectively.

120. See *Mulieris Dignitatem*, no. 7: "Being a person means striving towards self-realization (the Council text speaks of self-discovery), which can only be achieved 'through a sincere gift of self.' The model for this interpretation of the person is God himself as Trinity, as a communion of Persons. To say that man is created in the image and likeness of God means that man is called to exist 'for' others, to become a gift" (emphasis in the original).

121. RH, no. 10 [18].

122. See John Paul II, *God, Father and Creator*, 148; and *Dominum et Vivificantem*, nos. 9 and 10.

The man who wishes to understand himself thoroughly—and not just in accordance with immediate, partial, often superficial, and even illusory standards and measures of his being—he must with his unrest, uncertainty, and even his weakness and sinfulness, with his life and death, draw near to Christ. He must, so to speak, enter into him with all his own self, he must "appropriate" and assimilate the whole of the reality of the Incarnation and Redemption in order to find himself.[123]

This self-gift is none other than the act of faith, which *Dei Verbum* describes as the commitment of "the entire self to God."[124] Such a description moves faith beyond the realm of the intellect alone to encompass the will, and indeed the whole person. In fact, John Paul describes such faith as that which "allows individuals to give consummate expression to their own freedom. . . . Men and women can accomplish no more important act in their lives than the act of faith."[125] Nevertheless, viewing faith in this way requires some important clarifications: first, because the theological tradition has always distinguished among the three theological virtues of faith, hope, and charity (along with the acts that each of the three make possible); and second, because Wojtyła's earlier philosophy had claimed that love, and not faith, was the most fulfilling act of the person.

So how can faith now, theologically speaking, be the most important act a human person can make? Several points can help clarify how John Paul can make such a claim in light of his earlier philosophy. First, in defining faith, the pope is reliant upon the definition from *Dei Verbum*, in which faith is characterized biblically by "obedience," an obedience in which "man commits his entire self to God," including the "full submission of his intellect and will."[126] This biblical way of understanding the act of faith would be confirmed by the later tradition: St. Thomas, for instance, while properly situating faith as residing in the intellect, nev-

123. RH, no. 10 [18]. See also *Veritatis Splendor*, no. 19: "This is not a matter only of disposing oneself to hear a teaching and obediently accepting a commandment. More radically, it involves holding fast to the very person of Jesus, partaking of his life and his destiny, sharing in his free and loving obedience to the will of the Father"; in John Paul II, *Veritatis Splendor*, Vatican trans. (Boston: Pauline Books and Media 1993), 32; AAS 85 (1993): 1133–1228. Henceforth, VS.

124. DV, no. 5 [752].

125. FR, no. 13 [23]. The pope adds, "Put differently, freedom is not realized in decisions made against God. For how could it be an exercise of true freedom to refuse to be open to the very reality which enables our self-realization?"

126. DV, no. 5 [752]. The conciliar passage refers to Rom 16:26 as its biblical source for the definition of faith.

ertheless claims that the will always moves the intellect to its assent.[127] Thus, in the act of faith, both the intellect and the will play their respective roles.

Second, it is important to remember that *all* human acts are characterized by love. "Every agent," St. Thomas writes, "does *every action from love of some kind*."[128] Love, Josef Pieper explains, is not one attribute among others in volition but the "primal act of the will"; it is "the fundamental principle of all volition and the imminent source of every manifestation of the will."[129] Love is that which compels every human act, because any act of volition is first a complacency in (or in Wojtyła's words, an attraction to) the object being willed. This attraction then manifests in either a love of concupiscence (in which one loves an object for the sake of a friend or oneself—Wojtyła refers to this as love as desire) or a love of friendship (in which one loves a friend him- or herself—for Wojtyła, love of goodwill). In this way, even the theological act of faith is, philosophically speaking, an act of love because the will's affirmation of the beloved—in this case, God—remains present within faith's act.

Properly speaking, the act of faith belongs to the intellect. Still, the will specifies the object of this act by drawing the intellect's attention to its beloved: "Toward what does the believer direct his will when he believes? Answer: Toward the warrantor and witness whom he affirms, loves, 'wills'—insofar as he accepts the truthfulness of what the witness says, accepts it on his mere word."[130] Thus, without taking away from the intellect's role in assenting to the truths of divine revelation or, more properly, to God as the First Truth, it is still true that this assent demands

127. See ST II-II, q. 2, a. 9. Sherwin's *By Knowledge and By Love* is indispensable for understanding this interrelation between the intellect and will, both in natural and supernatural human acts. As he says on page 152, "Reason commands all the will's acts, except the will's first act, which is instilled in it by nature, while the will moves the intellect to engage in all its acts except the intellect's first act, which is instilled in it by nature.... [Similarly], faith has priority in one way, charity has priority in another." One difficulty with Sherwin's comparison between natural and supernatural acts of knowledge and love is that, on the level of grace, it implies that faith requires charity in order to fulfill its rightful act. Nevertheless, the tradition has consistently claimed that a person can have faith and yet lack charity, whether through mortal sin or because, as Jas 2:17 explains, without works it is "dead."

128. ST I-II, q. 28, a. 6 [713]. Emphasis mine.

129. Josef Pieper, *Faith, Hope, Love*, trans. Richard Winston, Clara Winston, and Sister Mary Frances McCarthy, SND (San Francisco: Ignatius Press, 1997), 39. Tellingly, this explanation of the will's primal act serves as part of Pieper's description of the act of faith.

130. Ibid. On the next page, Pieper quotes Cardinal Newman: "We believe because we love."

the volition of the will and is therefore fueled by love. St. Thomas's love of friendship, therefore, necessarily undergirds the act of faith.[131]

Third, with this in view, one can now adequately differentiate between what we can more generally refer to as *love* and the theological virtue of *charity*. Any act of volition is an act of love, but charity is the virtue by which one loves God and neighbor. Because it is strictly a gift, as is the case with all three theological virtues, charity cannot simply be the result of a person's natural capacity to love. It is a participation in God's own love. Furthermore, it should not be confused with that act of the will just mentioned by which faith's object is specified. Even a person with faith can lack charity.[132] Rather, Aquinas holds that the specification of the object of faith's act happens by God moving the person's will through a divine *instinctus* [prompting].[133] Even so, though charity does not necessarily *precede* faith, it still must *proceed from* faith if it is to make that faith living or meritorious before the eyes of God. As James 2:17 says, severed from charity, faith is "dead." Similarly, for faith to live it must, Paul claims, work "through love."[134]

I believe it is precisely this "living faith" of which John Paul II speaks when he claims that faith is the most important act a person can make. Such a faith is vivified by charity, and, in this way, it maintains continuity with his prior philosophical claim that love is the most fulfilling of human acts. It is quite possible that he first encountered this understanding of living faith in the writings of John of the Cross while, during the Nazi occupation, he huddled in the apartment of the mystic Jan Tyranowski to study the texts of the Carmelite doctor. There, in the midst of Poland's "Dark Night," Wojtyła found in St. John's spiritual poems and treatises an exposition of the self-gift of faith that would leave an enduring mark upon him.

The impact of this encounter with the Mystical Doctor is evidenced by Wojtyła's doctoral dissertation on St. John's doctrine of faith, written under the direction of the noted Thomist Réginald Garrigou-Lagrange.[135]

131. For Wojtyła, faith is undergirded by the love of goodwill or, even further, betrothed love. See the section "The Act of Love: Fulfillment with Other Persons," in chapter 3.

132. See ST II-II, q. 4, a. 7, ad. 5, and II-II, q. 5, a. 2, ad. 2.

133. See Sherwin, *By Knowledge and By Love*, 140–44.

134. Gal 5:6. See *Scriptum Super Sententiis* III., d. 23, q. 3, a. 1.

135. Wojtyła's first doctoral dissertation, "Doctrina de fide apud S. Joannem a Cruce," was an exploration of the metaphysical and experiential aspects of faith in the saint's writings. Reference information for the English translation of the dissertation, *Faith according to St. John*

For St. John, faith is, before all else, a gift bestowed by God. It is only by God's gifts—namely, the theological virtues—that one becomes a "partaker of the divine nature" and is thus able to give him or herself in return to God.[136] Wojtyła also recognized in the writings of the Mystical Doctor that this self-gift draws upon the power of the intellect, but further, it is an act in which faith is "vivified by charity."[137] With the aid of the Doctor of Fontiveros, Wojtyła found that his philosophical anthropology was now raised to the theological level. By partaking in the divine nature through the virtue of faith and by participating in the love of God through the virtue of charity, one's self-offering to God takes on a divine character: "Since God gives himself with a free and gracious will, so too the soul … gives to God, God himself in God; and this is a true and complete gift of the soul to God."[138]

As pope, John Paul reaffirmed his reliance upon this doctrine of faith, holding that St. John's teaching was perennially relevant, for it

---

of the Cross, is found in the introduction of this volume. For more on Wojtyła's appropriation of the Mystical Doctor, see Alvaro Huerga, "Karol Wojtyła, comentador de San Juan de la Cruz," Angelicum 56, no. 2–3 (1979): 348–66.

136. See 2 Pt 1:4.

137. Wojtyła, Faith according to St. John of the Cross, 250. Wojtyła bolsters his claim that faith is vivified by charity by connecting it to St. John's teaching on the "Dark Night of the Soul." For St. John, the light afforded by revelation is so bright that it overwhelms and, in this sense, blinds the intellect. The will is required to cross the threshold of darkness and, thus, as Wojtyła observes on page 255, "St. John of the Cross never speaks about faith alone or unformed faith, but always about faith vivified by charity" (emphasis mine). See The Ascent of Mount Carmel II.3.1, in St. John of the Cross, The Collected Works of Saint John of the Cross, rev. ed., trans. Kieran Kavanaugh and Otilio Rodriguez (Washington, D.C.: Institute of Carmelite Studies Publications, 1991), 157: "Faith, the theologians say, is a certain and obscure habit of the soul. It is an obscure habit because it brings us to believe divinely revealed truths that transcend every natural light and infinitely exceed all human understanding. As a result the excessive light of faith bestowed upon a soul is darkness for it; a brighter light will eclipse and suppress a dimmer one. The sun so obscures all other lights that they do not seem to be lights at all when it is shining, and instead of affording vision to the eyes, it overwhelms, blinds, and deprives them of vision since its light is excessive and unproportioned to the visual faculty. Similarly, the light of faith in its abundance suppresses and overwhelms that of the intellect. For the intellect, by its own power, extends only to natural knowledge, though it has the potency to be raised to the supernatural act whenever our Lord wishes."

True to form, Wojtyła considered this overcoming of the darkness to be an experiential or "psychological" addition to the scholastic metaphysics that undergirds John of the Cross's teaching. As Rocco Buttiglione points out, Garrigou-Lagrange, while also an admirer of the Mystical Doctor, critiqued his pupil's dissertation for too often retaining St. John's experiential language, rather than translating it into more objective, scholastic form. Still, Wojtyła "tended to develop the subjective side of the problem, while seeing it not as autonomous but as tightly bound to the objective side." See Buttiglione, Karol Wojtyła, 47.

138. St. John of the Cross, The Living Flame of Love III.79, in Collected Works, 706.

offered a vision of a living faith, the adult faith called for by the Second Vatican Council—"a *personal faith*, free and convicted, embraced with one's entire being; an *ecclesial faith*, confessed and celebrated in the communion of the Church, a *prayerful and adoring faith*, matured in the experience of communion with God; a *faith of solidarity and commitment*, manifested in a moral coherence of life and in a dimension of service."[139] In this way, the pope explained, faith is central to "carrying out the new evangelization."[140]

Ultimately then, while Wojtyła's earlier philosophy had claimed that love was the most fulfilling act of a person, his theological anthropology now builds upon that claim by seeing the act of faith as one that requires the self-gift of grace-filled love. Such a living faith is the most perfect of personal acts because it unites the horizontal and vertical dimensions of what Wojtyła called human transcendence. Beyond a greater participation in the good that is achieved by moral human acts— what if one could choose the very Source of this vertical participation by making it the object of the will? Is this not the new reality that opens up before human beings when they encounter the divine self-gift that is revelation? The in-breaking of the eternal into the temporal, of the vertical plane into the horizontal, offers them just this possibility.

Faced with God's self-revelation, faith emerges as a grace-empowered response, and in it one can, as St. John claims, give God, as it were, back to God. When we return to the claim that (contrary to initial appearances) John Paul develops his understanding of the *communio personarum* along Augustinian lines, we must now add that he does so via the thought of John of the Cross. Augustine's interpretation of the *imago dei* as concerning not only human nature but the act of knowing and loving God is developed further by way of St. John's doctrine of living faith. By standing within this tradition, John Paul is able to see that it is self-gift and the communion it brings that are the very heart of the image of God in human beings.

In this vision of the *imago dei*, the communion of divine Persons that the Trinity is, and the communion of human persons that men and women are *called* to form, are not meant to be divided by an uncrossable

---

139. John Paul II, *Maestro en la Fe*, no. 7. Emphasis in the original. Translations from the original Spanish version found on the Vatican's website are my own.
140. John Paul II, *Maetstro en la Fe*, no. 3.

chasm. For the pope, a communion of communions is accomplished by the self-offering of Christ in revelation and the returning gift of the human person in living faith. By partaking of the divine nature offered in Christ, the person's natural capacity for self-gift is elevated to supernatural heights. In this way the person's self-gift becomes an insertion into Christ's very Body—the church—and thus it becomes an insertion into the love that is shared by the members of the Trinity. Human love, joined with divine love, then reaches its pinnacle in God, in the *communio personarum* that is the Source of all being and existence. If Adam's solitude had been indicative of two unities—one foundational, the other vocational—here both find their ultimate fulfillment. Thus, the *exitus* and *reditus* of every person (and through the person, all of creation) are accomplished in Jesus Christ. He is, rightfully, the revealer of God and the human person.

Once again, and to return to the heart of the matter, the continuity and distinction between nature and grace in John Paul's analysis become clear. For the pope, there must be a distinction because the person's eschatological fulfillment, in a certain sense, excludes earthly forms of communion—here John Paul quotes Matthew 22:30: "In the resurrection they take neither wife nor husband."[141] And yet, there is still a fulfillment of the human vocation to communion because the person enters into the communion of the Trinity. But the continuity does not end there, for this fulfilling communion, in turn, allows for the rediscovery in God of "the whole 'world' of relations that are constitutive of the world's perennial order ('cosmos')," including those persons brought together in the "communion of saints."[142] Grace, in this sense, proves to be a surpassing fulfillment of human nature.

To proclaim this fulfillment is, for John Paul II, the mission of the church. Love can, through Christ, reach divine heights—indeed, it can reach to Love itself. In David Meconi's words, "The good news of Christianity is that the *communio personarum* is now extended to the human-divine encounter. One's fullest self is discovered in union with Je-

---

141. See TOB 68:1–69:4 [394–401]. In 69:3 [398] the pope states, "Christ points out man's identity, although this identity *is realized in a different way in eschatological experience than in the experience of the very 'beginning' and all of history. And nevertheless, man will always be the same, just as he came forth from the hand of his Creator and Father*" (emphasis in the original).

142. TOB 68:4 [395–96].

sus Christ, whose divine presence transforms and completes us for-ever."[143]

The Text in Light of John Paul II's Vision of the Person

With John Paul II's interpretation of *Gaudium et Spes* 22 (with the aid of article 24) now in place, it is possible to return to the text of the Constitution more fruitfully and to see how this interpretation sheds light on the greater context of the Council's argument. In returning to the actual text, I believe it is helpful to begin with article 24, since, for John Paul, it provides the key to reading article 22.

Gaudium et Spes 24 begins with simple yet emphatic statement that "all, in fact, are destined to the very same end, namely God himself," and roots this claim in the creation of human beings in God's image and likeness.[144] By way of Romans 13:9–10 and 1 John 4:20, it then speaks of the unity of love of God with love of neighbor, reiterating the biblical teaching that the former cannot be accomplished without the latter. Yet, the core of its argument for the communitarian vocation of humanity lies in its use of the great "high priestly prayer" of Jesus in John 17, in which John offers a glimpse of the intimacy shared by Jesus with the Father. Here, Jesus prays for his disciples, present and future:

I pray not only for them, but also for those who will believe in me through their word, so that they may all be one, as you, Father, are in me and I in you, that they also may be in us, that the world may believe that you sent me. And I have given them the glory you gave me, so that they may be one, as we are one, I in them and you in me, that they may be brought to perfection as one, that the world may know that you sent me, and that you loved them even as you loved me.[145]

One could rightly call this prayer one of the main scriptural sources of the church's understanding of *communio*: Jesus prays that his disciples

---

143. David V. Meconi, "Deification in the Thought of John Paul II," *Irish Theological Quarterly* 71, no. 1–2 (2006): 133. The importance of the human-divine communion is further evidenced by Wojtyła/John Paul II's tracing of the term "communion" to its theological source in the celebration of the Eucharist. The Eucharist is the source and the summit of the union of humans with the Father, through the Son, in the Holy Spirit. See Wojtyła, "Family as a Community of Persons," 320. In fact, to my knowledge, the only passage in which John Paul II explicitly cites both articles 22 and 24 of *Gaudium et Spes* together occurs in *Dominum et Vivificantem*, no. 62, where he meditates upon the Eucharist's ability to manifest and effect the communion of human beings with God and each other.

144. GS, no. 24 [925].

145. Jn 17:20–23.

would be united with one another, and he links this hope to the union that he and the Father share. Even those who have not yet heard the Word of God, by communing with the current disciples, can commune with Jesus and the Father. The result of this glimpse into the inner dialogue of the Trinity is the opening up of "new horizons" whereby one sees "a certain parallel between the union existing among the divine persons and the union of the sons of God in truth and love."[146] This vision offered by the priestly prayer of Christ is, indeed, that of a *communion of communions*: Jesus is united with the Father, his disciples to each other and to him, and those who will hear the Word to Christ through the disciples who proclaim him. Earlier in the Gospel, Jesus had mentioned that, by the gift of the Spirit of truth, his followers would always know that "I am in my Father, and you are in me, and I in you," thereby giving the Holy Spirit a central role in this vision.[147] Ultimately, because human communion finds its source in trinitarian love, the Council can proclaim, "If man is the only creature on earth that God has wanted for its own sake, man can fully discover his true self only in a sincere giving of himself."[148]

For his part, Joseph Ratzinger had claimed that this insight offered by the high priestly prayer of Jesus demands a rethinking of the theological category of personhood. That the word "person" had been applied equivocally to the relations of the Trinity and to the individual substance that is a human being was already a part of the tradition in the time of Augustine, as has already been seen. But, Ratzinger believed, it was St. Thomas, in his attempt to preserve the analogy between human and divine personhood while still holding to the Boethian definition of person, who had committed Catholic theology to a disagreeable path.[149] Thomas, of course, could not easily apply Boethius's formulation (*naturae rationalis individua substantia*) to the persons of the Trinity, for they each shared the same divine substance. The analogy is further complicated by the Christological issue of Christ's divine and human natures belonging to the same person. The Angelic Doctor's solution was to claim a more general—and one might add, existential—meaning for personhood in which "person" signifies that which *subsists* in a given

---

146. GS, no. 24 [925].

147. Jn 14:20.

148. GS, no. 24 [925], referencing Lk 17:33: "Whoever seeks to preserve his life will lose it, but whoever loses it will save it."

149. See Ratzinger, "Concerning the Notion of Person," 449, but especially 454, footnote 12.

rational nature. By drawing out this larger category of "subsistence," he could now claim that the relations in the Trinity were Persons, that individual humans were likewise, as was the person of Christ who subsists in both human and divine natures.[150] In sum, for Thomas, while the Persons of the Trinity are subsisting relations, human persons are, to use Norris Clarke's term, substances-in-relation.[151]

Yet, for Ratzinger, Thomas's misstep was in not allowing the theological and existential definition of person to transform the philosophical meaning inherited from Boethius, particularly in regard to the role of *relation*. Human persons, in the end, remained substances and therefore too narrowly individualistic, leaving the person-as-relation of divine personhood to be a "theological exception."[152] Rather, in Ratzinger's own reading of John 17, "it is part of the existence even of the disciples that man does not posit the reservation of what is merely and properly his own, does not strive to form the substance of the closed self, but enters into pure relativity toward the other and toward God."[153] For the cardinal, it is ultimately "relativity toward the other [that] constitutes the human person. The human person is the event or being of relativity."[154]

For all the continuity that exists between Wojtyła/John Paul II and Ratzinger/Benedict XVI, it is clear that, on this issue, they part ways. As has been seen, John Paul consistently holds that the human person is an individual substance called to relationship, a position he claimed in his earlier philosophy and reiterated during his papacy. Yet, while John Paul willingly embraces Thomas's anthropology and thus the primacy of substance in human persons, his anthropology is nevertheless thoroughly "relational." The pope overcomes the danger of individualism by recognizing that all substances are ordered to their operations. Relations, in this sense, as essential to communion, are the very *telos*

150. St. Thomas develops the argument in succession in ST I, q. 29, a. 1–4. In preserving the analogy he appropriately adds in a. 4, ad. 4, "So it does not follow that . . . the word *person* is used in an equivocal sense. Though neither is it applied univocally, since nothing can be said univocally of God and creatures." For a helpful explanation of the development of Thomas's argument, see McDermott, "Response to 'The Nuptial Meaning of the Body,'" 144–47.

151. See Clarke's "To Be Is to Be Substance-in-Relation," 102–22.

152. Ratzinger, "Concerning the Notion of Person," 449.

153. Ibid., 445.

154. Ibid., 452. As pope, Benedict XVI reiterated this claim in *Caritas in Veritate*, no. 55, though in a more cautious manner: "The Christian revelation of the unity of the human race presupposes a *metaphysical interpretation of the 'humanum' in which relationality is an essential element*" (emphasis in the original). See also Lambino, *Freedom in Vatican II*, 79–80.

of the person. Even if considered metaphysically "accidental," they are always necessary if the person is to fulfill him- or herself. Thus, a more John-Pauline reading of John 17 would bring out the theology of vocation that is latent there. Christ prays that his disciples "*may be* one" as he and the Father "*are* one."

The implication of his petition is that God allows human freedom to reject or to accept the divine will. The discovery of one's true self undoubtedly requires love and the relations it brings, but it is a calling that may or may not be fulfilled. A failure to love is a possibility in John Paul's reading—the conscious and dramatic choice to give oneself to others and to God must be played out in the life of each individual human person.

This pivotal role played by the vocation to love in human fulfillment thereby becomes an important lens by which to read *Gaudium et Spes* 22. If I am correct that John Paul's distinction between nature and personal act—and thus between the image as human nature and the fulfillment of the image in the graced self-gift of love—is the correct framework for interpreting the passage, then such a reading must be tested against the greater context of the article. Already, such an interpretation lends itself to new emphases in the central claim of the Constitution: Jesus, as the "revelation of the Father *and of his love,* fully reveals man to himself and brings to light his most high *calling*."[155] If love is necessary for men and women to fulfill themselves, as article 24 proclaims, then article 22 clarifies that the greatest fulfillment is found in giving oneself to the source of love that is Jesus Christ. This fulfillment in Christ, though unforeseen by nature apart from grace, is nevertheless a calling of the person—it must be answered on the existential level.

This call to love and the role personal acts play in answering are now able to shed more light on the rest of article 22. After proclaiming Christ to be the fulfillment of the human person, the Council fathers turn to the biblical and patristic theology of the *imago dei* that, as noted previously, was inherited and developed by John Paul: "He who is the '*image* of the invisible God' is himself the perfect man who [restores] in the children of Adam that *likeness* to God which had been disfigured ever since the first sin."[156] This patristic distinction between the ontic and ethical

---

155. *GS*, no. 22 [922].

156. Ibid., referencing Col 1:15. Emphasis mine. While Flannery translates the Latin *restituit* as "has restored," it can also simply mean "restores." See AAS 58 (1966): 1024.

dimensions of the image then flows into a discussion of the effects of the Incarnation and Redemption on humanity. Here, too, the Council's Christocentrism distinguishes between human nature and the plane of personal existence. For the Council, "human nature, by the very fact that it was assumed, not absorbed, in [Christ], has been raised in us also to a dignity beyond compare."[157] And yet Jesus "worked with human hands, he thought with a human mind. He acted with a human will, and with a human heart he loved.... As an innocent lamb he merited life for us by his blood.... By suffering for us he not only gave us an example so that we might follow in his footsteps, but *he also opened up a way.*"[158]

The Council's anthropology, therefore, clearly parallels John Paul's concern for seeing the human person in terms of both the person's metaphysical foundations and his or her personal acts. Ratzinger, while differing in his own anthropology, is nevertheless able to draw out the implications of article 22 in a way that accords with John Paul's reading:

The human nature of all men is one; Christ's taking to himself the one human nature of man is an event which affects every human being; consequently human nature in every human being is henceforward Christologically characterized. This idea is then extended to the real plane of actual concrete human existence. Human action, thought, willing, and loving have become the instrument of the Logos; what is first present on the *plane of being* also gives new significance to the *plane of action*, to the actual accomplishment of human personal life.[159]

Ratzinger even finds that this conciliar teaching brings to mind the personal character of the call of Christ: "Christ is not a great super-ego into which the I-monads are organized, but a most individual human being who looks at me personally. He enters into a personal conversation of love; he has something to say to me alone, which no one else knows.... Christ no longer appears as a merely general form to which human existences are conformed. His exemplarity means the concrete summons to follow him."[160]

John Paul II's theology of the *imago dei* thus proves to be a fruitful hermeneutic for the anthropological argument of *Gaudium et Spes*. From this analysis I believe that one could rightfully claim that John Paul's

157. GS, no. 22 [922–23].
158. GS, no. 22 [923]. Emphasis mine.
159. Ratzinger, "Part I: The Church and Man's Calling," 160. Emphasis mine.
160. Ibid., 160–61.

theology of the image is inseparable from a *theology of love* and likewise a *theology of vocation*.[161] Because "God created man in his own image and likeness, calling him to existence *through love*," the pope explains, "he called him at the same time *for love*. . . . Love is therefore the fundamental and innate vocation of every human being."[162]

The heart of the Council's teaching—and thus, the heart of the New Evangelization—is, for John Paul, found in this call of all human persons to offer themselves to God with a living faith. This faith is prompted by the self-gift of God in revelation, but accepting this revelation must amount to more than the intellectual acceptance of knowledge. It must lead to the commitment of one's entire self to God in Jesus Christ:

The essence of faith resides not only in knowledge, but also in vocation, in the *call*. For what in the last analysis is this obedience of faith by which man displays "a total submission of his intelligence and will to the God who reveals himself"? It is not simply hearing the Word and listening to it (in the sense of obeying it): it also means responding to a call, to a sort of historical and eschatological "Follow me!" uttered both on earth and in heaven. To my mind, one must be very conscious of this relation between knowledge and vocation inherent in the very essence of faith if one is to decipher correctly the extremely rich message of Vatican II.[163]

Indeed, the failure to answer this call was the error of the rich young man of Matthew's gospel.[164] Even his knowledge and keeping of the commandments were not enough to heed the call to follow Jesus. In the end, the "most high calling" of all human persons is a matter of both "truth and love."[165]

The Epistemology of Nature and Grace: Faith and Reason

If there is anything left to be added to this account of John Paul II's metaphysical and personalistic approach to the Council's anthropology,

---

161. For some implications of *Gaudium et Spes* for a theology of vocation, see Erhueh, *Vatican II: Image of God in Man*, 153–56.

162. John Paul II, *Familiaris Consortio*, no. 11, Vatican translation (Boston: Pauline Books and Media, 1981), 22; AAS 74 (1982): 81–191. Henceforth, FC. Emphasis in the original.

163. Frossard and John Paul II, "*Be Not Afraid!*," 65. Emphasis in the original.

164. See VS, nos. 19–22, and Mt 19:16–22.

165. GS, nos. 22 [922] and 24 [925].

it is that it must necessarily carry with it an epistemological character if it is to be applied to the church's mission of evangelization. The pope's reading of *Gaudium et Spes* may provide a solid anthropological framework, but what does this mean for the concrete ways men and women actually come to know God in Jesus Christ and hear his summons to follow him? For the pope, the relationship between nature and grace finds its epistemological counterpart in the relationship between reason and faith.

Another return to a text of the *Doctor Gratiae* can be of some use here. In what is perhaps the most celebrated line of Augustine's corpus, he confesses to God, "Thou hast made us for Thyself, and our hearts are restless till they rest in Thee."[166] This idea of the heart's desire for God is so supremely important for the mission of the church that the Catechism takes it up as its opening theme: "The desire for God is written in the human heart, because man is created by God and for God; and God never ceases to draw man to himself. Only in God will he find the truth and happiness he never stops searching for."[167] And yet, if this stunning claim is not to be read through a de Lubacian understanding of nature, how should it be interpreted?

Interestingly, John Paul II reflects on this Augustinian claim and its meaning for the human person in several of his papal writings. One of the most significant times occurs in his *Letter to Families* in which he relates the quote to the Council's claim in *Gaudium et Spes* 24 that God wills a human being for his or her own sake while nevertheless calling that person to a share in the divine life. The pope asks, "Does affirming man's ultimate destiny not conflict with the statement that God wills man 'for his own sake'? If he has been created for divine life, can man truly exist 'for his own sake'?"[168] Augustine's quote becomes the resolution to this apparent contradiction:

What then is the relationship between the life of the person and his sharing in the life of the Trinity? Saint Augustine provides us with the answer in his celebrated phrase: "Our heart is restless until it rests in you." This "restless

---

166. *Confessions* 1.1.1. Here, I have broken from my previous use of the Pine-Coffin translation for the more oft-quoted translation of Frank Sheed. See St. Augustine, *Confessions*, 2nd ed., trans. Frank Sheed (Indianapolis: Hackett, 2006), 3.

167. CCC, no. 27 [13].

168. *Letter to Families*, no. 9 [23], in John Paul II, *Letter to Families*, Vatican translation (Boston: Pauline Books and Media, 1994), 46; AAS (1994): 868–925.

heart" serves to point out that between the one finality and the other there is in fact no contradiction, but rather a relationship, a complementarity, a unity. By his genealogy, the person created in the image and likeness of God, exists *"for his own sake"* and reaches fulfillment precisely *by sharing in God's life.*[169]

The pope's reference to the bond between natural and supernatural finalities as "a relationship, a complementarity, a unity" does not by itself provide the theological distinction necessary to definitively determine his understanding of the workings of nature and grace.[170] Even so, his references to the person, the doctrine of image and likeness, and fulfillment all bear the marks of his anthropology outlined earlier.

A clearer picture emerges in *Redemptor Hominis*, in which John Paul explains in more detail the meaning of the restless heart: "In this creative restlessness beats and pulsates what is *most deeply human*—the search for truth, the insatiable need for the good, hunger for freedom, nostalgia for the beautiful, and the voice of conscience."[171] Here, the finality desired by the human heart is undoubtedly God, but it is God as he is found by the means of human nature: reason's desire for truth; the will's thirst for goodness; the memory's "nostalgia" for beauty; and in good personalist fashion, the hunger for freedom and the voice of conscience. Yet the question arises: has the infinite breadth of Augustine's restless heart been truncated and confined to the earthly realm, to what can be achieved by human powers alone?

It seems clear to me that the pope's intent in this encyclical—indeed, in his anthropology as a whole—is to present communion with God in Christ as the fulfillment of these natural desires, even as nature has its own ends.[172] Obviously, my claim must be parsed out to avoid contradiction. But I think a return to *Dei Verbum*'s Christological vision of creation and the role faith and reason play in it can be of some ser-

169. Ibid. Emphasis in the original.

170. In the Latin text of AAS (1994): 880, it reads that, between the two finalities there is "vero vinculum, compositionem, congruentiam maximam."

171. *RH*, no. 18 [45]. Emphasis mine.

172. See D. C. Schindler's "The Redemption of *Eros*: Philosophical Reflections on Benedict XVI's First Encyclical," *Communio* 33, no. 3 (2006), where on page 377, the author explains that "the novelty of Christianity must be a novelty that heals and fulfills even as it raises up; as the old scholastic dictum has it, grace perfects and elevates nature, it does not destroy it. What this means is that the redemption brought by grace must bring to light the deepest truth of nature in its essence, and not simply add something to it that was not previously there. If we emphasize the discontinuity of grace without continuity, or we emphasize continuity with nature without any discontinuity, we will have falsified what is essential about Christianity."

vice here. In chapter 1, I noted that in article 6 of the Constitution, the Council fathers reiterated Vatican I's distinction between, on the one hand, reason's ability to know of God and, on the other, the supernatural revelation that allows humans to know him and the decrees of his will. In commenting on this passage, Ratzinger explains that, while Vatican II had reaffirmed this teaching, it presented it in the reverse order: "It develops revelation from its Christological center, in order then to present the inescapable responsibility of human reason as one dimension of the whole."[173] The Council's epistemology, therefore, sees reason and faith as distinct in their nature yet united in their ultimate goal. Thus, while reason seeks for God in the form of truth, revelation reveals that such truth finds its source in the *Logos* who is truth itself. What faith and reason seek is in this sense the same, though each does so in its own way.

Faith and reason, then, are two parts of one Christological whole or, as John Paul explains, "two wings on which the human spirit rises to the contemplation of the truth."[174] Because of this relationship, the restless heart of humanity and its longing for what is authentically true become a path by which the church can proclaim Jesus Christ as the Way, the Truth, and the Life. This is the argument John Paul develops in *Fides et Ratio*, in which he affirms that the search for truth is "deeply rooted in human nature."[175] Furthermore, though still on the level of nature, humans grow through relationship, with family and society playing indispensable roles in allowing persons to entrust themselves to other persons and the truths they proclaim, truths that cannot always be verified by experience but are received nonetheless by inherited tradition or by trust.[176] "Human perfection," explains the pope, "consists not simply in acquiring an abstract knowledge of the truth, but in a dynamic relationship of self-giving with others."[177]

In this way, all human persons "are on a journey of discovery which is humanly unstoppable—a search for the truth and a search for a per-

173. Ratzinger, "Chapter I: Revelation Itself," 180.
174. FR, preface [7]. The pope continues, "And God has placed in the human heart a desire to know the truth—in a word, to know himself—so that, by knowing and loving God, men and women may also come to the fullness of truth about themselves."
175. FR, no. 28 [41].
176. See FR, no. 31–32 [43–44].
177. FR, no. 32 [44].

son to whom they might entrust themselves," and it is precisely on this journey where the church's faith can meet them:

Christian faith [offers] the concrete possibility of reaching the goal which they seek. Moving beyond the stage of simple believing, Christian faith immerses human beings in the order of grace, which enables them to share in the mystery of Christ, which in turn offers them a true and coherent knowledge of the Triune God. In Jesus Christ, who is the Truth, faith recognizes the ultimate appeal to humanity, an appeal made in order that what we experience as desire and nostalgia may come to its fulfillment.[178]

The *logos* of human reason is thus met by the *Logos* made flesh. This is the way in which John Paul, following the Council, envisions the evangelization of the modern world.

Ultimately, by recognizing this relationship between faith and reason, John Paul is able to simultaneously affirm that sharing in the divine life is, indeed, the final end of all human persons, while human nature nevertheless retains its own ends. This is no contradiction or paradox. It is as if—by way of analogy—one could, by one's own powers, recognize the appealing and wondrous gifts of a lover yet unknown. In this case reason could, through these gifts, even recognize the existence of the lover, and yet, again by its own power, also recognize that it could never truly know the lover apart from the lover's own self-revelation. But, in the utterly gratuitous self-revelation of the lover—the lover's words and deeds—what reason once knew as true now becomes fulfilled by a person.[179] For John Paul, Christ is the utterly gratuitous self-revelation of God. He is the Giver behind every good gift and the one who fulfills, in his very person, all that is rightfully sought by human nature.[180]

While *Fides et Ratio* purposely limits its scope to the human pursuit of truth, John Paul's reading of Augustine's restless heart implies that this same dynamic extends to the human "need for the good" and "nostalgia for beauty"—to all that is authentically human.[181] For the pope:

---

178. FR, no. 33 [46–47]. See also no. 25.

179. Even after encountering the self-gift that is revelation, one must still use his or her reason to understand the self-gift and to embrace it. See FR, no. 73; and Clarke, "John Paul II: The Complementarity of Faith and Philosophy in the Search for Truth," *Communio* 26, no. 2 (1999): 563.

180. Or, to put it differently, "The God of creation is also the God of salvation history." See FR, no. 34 [47].

181. RH, no. 18 [45].

Although man instinctively loves life because it is a good, this love will find further inspiration and strength, and new breadth and depth, in the divine dimensions of this good. Similarly, the love which every human being has for life cannot be reduced simply to a desire to have sufficient space for self-expression and for entering into relationships with others; rather, it develops in a joyous awareness that life can become the "place" where God manifests himself, where we meet him and enter into communion with him. The life which Jesus gives in no way lessens the value of our existence in time; it takes it and directs it to its final destiny.[182]

In this way, and in keeping with the Council's teaching in *Gaudium et Spes*, John Paul's affirmation of human nature extends to the totality of human experience in its interior and exterior dimensions—to the signs of the times that manifest present history and to the human intentions and actions that give this history its shape: "History therefore becomes the arena where we see what God does for humanity. God comes to us in the things we know best and can verify most easily, the things of our everyday life, apart from which we cannot understand ourselves."[183] It is the role of the church, then, to affirm human nature where it attains what is true, good, and beautiful; to correct human nature where, due to sin, it fails to attain these ends; and to transcend human nature by proclaiming Jesus Christ as the fulfillment of these ends in God. In sum, revelation, handed on by the church, has a "sacramental character."[184]

Toward Catechesis for the New Evangelization

The exposition of the relationship between nature and grace is no easy theological task, though it in some way affects all theology and, further still, lies at the heart of the church's mission of presenting the faith to the modern world. In a sense, John Paul II's own conception of this re-

182. *Evangelium Vitae*, no. 38, in John Paul II, *Evangelium Vitae*, Vatican translation (Boston: Pauline Books and Media, 1995), 65; AAS 87 (1995): 401–522.

183. FR, no. 12 [21].

184. FR, no. 13 [23]. See also Stephen Fields, "Nature and Grace after the Baroque," in *Creed and Culture: Jesuit Studies of Pope John Paul II*, ed. Joseph W. Koterski and John J. Conley (Philadelphia: Saint Joseph's University Press, 2004), 233: "In short, for John Paul revelation is the sacrament of reason's integrity. Graciously incarnating the divine in history, it is an outward sign that manifests to reason its limit and its boldness, which reason can nonetheless discern through a critical self-examination. Moreover, revelation is an efficacious sign, because it answers the question of ultimate meaning that reason's limit generates, even as it expands reason's bold capacity to know universally true propositions about wisdom."

lationship is sympathetic to the concerns of Henri de Lubac and yet is grounded in the anthropology of de Lubac's neo-Thomist interlocutors. John Paul's theological anthropology is no rehashing of the two-tiered scholastic worldview decried by the *nouvelle theologie*, nor is it the conflation of nature and grace. Rather, by first distinguishing between nature and personal acts and then, in turn, by showing the epistemological relationship between faith and reason, he has found a way to affirm both the integrity of human nature and the claim that all are called to share in the divine life of the Trinity.

For John Paul, the one who gave the New Evangelization its name and rooted it in the teachings of the Second Vatican Council, this fundamental relationship between nature and grace is best examined by way of the person. And yet, because humans are created *ad imago dei*, the human person is only fully understood in relation to Jesus Christ, he who is truly the image of God. This chapter has shown that while John Paul fully inherits the Christian tradition that relates the image to human rationality, he nevertheless sees in the conciliar teaching on the *communio personarum* a development of this tradition: "Very ancient themes here take on a genuinely new aspect."[185] In its full trinitarian breadth, the *imago dei* is now found in *communio*, that which the Trinity is and that human beings are called to be. Because God is love, humans are called to love, and only in this love will they truly find themselves. And when this communion bridges the human and the divine, it becomes the deepest meaning of that claim of *Gaudium et Spes* that stands as the lodestar of the Council, that Christ "reveals man to himself and brings to light his most high calling."[186]

Thus, John Paul recognizes the human need so prevalent in every age—the need to love and to be loved. And yet, through the Council's teaching, he discovers the path by which this restlessness of the human heart can be met by the faith of the church. Even on the level of reason alone, love is what most actualizes a person's potential. But, by appropriating the self-gift that is the revelation of God, by participating in it through word and sacrament, human love is able to reach new heights: it can commune with Love itself. The act of faith, when vivified by charity, is therefore the greatest act of human transcendence—it is the vo-

185. Wojtyła, *Sources of Renewal*, 62.
186. GS, no. 22 [922].

cation of every human being, for it helps the intellect and will and the entire person attain to their ultimate goal, God himself.

The proclamation of revelation that calls forth this living faith, in accord with the theology of revelation put forth in *Dei Verbum* and *Gaudium et Spes*, is an in-breaking into human experience, for as Paul says, quoting the prophet Isaiah, "What eye has not seen, and ear has not heard, and what has not entered the human heart, what God has prepared for those who love him—this God has revealed to us through the Spirit."[187] And yet it is able to draw into itself all that is authentically human: human experience itself—when it is true, good, beautiful, and freed from the corruption of sin—thus becomes the place of encounter with God.

I believe that this conciliar teaching on the relation of revelation and experience, grace and nature, and faith and reason, brought to light more clearly by John Paul II's anthropology, provides the proper framework for the church's mission in the present. All that has been said up to this point thus prepares the way for the final part of this study, in which I hope to draw the contours of the church's ministry of catechesis in this time of the New Evangelization. It is to this task that this study now turns.

187. 1 Cor 2:9; Is 64:3.

Chapter 5

Catechesis for the New Evangelization

What we have seen from the beginning, what we have heard, what we have seen with our eyes, what we looked upon and touched with our hands concerns the Word of life—for the life was made visible; we have seen it and testify to it and proclaim to you the eternal life that was with the Father and was made visible to us—what we have seen and heard we proclaim now to you, so that you too may have fellowship with us; for our fellowship is with the Father and with his Son, Jesus Christ.

1 John 1:1–3

When the fullness of time had come God sent his Son, Jesus Christ, to humanity. He brought to the world the supreme gift of salvation by accomplishing his redemptive mission in a manner which continued the "pedagogy of God," with the perfection found in the newness of his Person.

General Directory for Catechesis, no. 140

The late Johannes Hofinger had compared the work of the modern catechetical movement to the construction of a house. And yet, as one of its primary architects, he also believed that the construction was unfinished. The work of the anthropological phase of catechesis and its concern for human experience had failed to connect itself to the proclamation of Christ that is the very heart of catechesis and the scriptures and doctrines that give voice to this proclamation. "The promoters of the human approach provided us with a fine roof; but unfortunately, instead of placing the roof upon the walls, they constructed the roof on the grounds beside the edifice."[1]

Thus far, this study has examined Vatican II's teaching on revelation and human experience in order to ground the New Evangelization in the conciliar documents; it then traced the development of the catechetical renewal that both spurred and developed from the Council's teachings; and it probed the thought of Karol Wojtyła/Pope John Paul II in order to discover the way in which the late pope himself interpreted the Council and, in doing so, paved the way for the New Evangelization. And now, in this final chapter, it seeks to illuminate what this fourth phase of renewal that Hofinger envisioned must look like. By synthesizing and drawing from what has been said in the previous chapters, I hope to offer some theological and catechetical thoughts about an evangelizing catechesis, one that places the roof upon the walls, so to speak.

The point of focus for this chapter is John Paul II's post-synodal apostolic exhortation, *Catechesi Tradendae*.[2] As a document stemming from the 1977 Synod of Bishops it is, in a certain sense, a fruit of Vatican II. By its nature, it does not spell out its teachings theologically at any great length, but I do believe one can find in it a clear confirmation of John Paul's Christological and anthropological way of reading the Council, as well as the way forward for catechesis that he believed the Council indicated. As such, what follows can be considered a commentary on the document, though one that fills out John Paul's teachings with the philosophical and theological reflections of the previous chapters as well as my own thoughts on how those reflections can best be applied to the church's mission. Since the goal of this chapter is to articulate the shape of catechesis for the New Evangelization, the commentary does not proceed according to the document's own structure, but according to the framework of the catechetical renewal as articulated by Hofinger and examined in chapter 2 of this book. Thus, this chapter proposes a consideration of catechesis in its propositional, kerygmatic, and anthropological aspects that integrates the fruits of the catechetical renewal

1. Hofinger, "Looking Backward and Forward," 356.
2. Bibliographical information for the document is given in chapter 1.

with the pope's interpretation of the Council and his Christocentric anthropology. I intend to show how his vision of the human person as ontologically and existentially fulfilled in Christ is able to garner what is best from the catechetical movement while alleviating many of its weaknesses. In doing so, I hope to affirm the work of the renewal while developing it along the lines suggested by Hofinger.

The work of the current chapter is necessarily more synthetic and creative than those before it. As such, I hope that my contributions toward tracing the contours of catechesis in the New Evangelization prove to be of some small service to those engaged in the ministry and study of the Word, and I know full well how indebted I am to those whose thoughts upon which I now build.

Situating John Paul II's Thoughts on Catechesis in Our Time

Though one could hardly doubt that John XXIII's spirit imbued the entirety of Vatican II's proceedings, it was Paul VI who led the church during the majority of the Council, overseeing the final three of its four sessions. From his experience of the collegial nature of the Council, Paul established the Synod of Bishops as a body that would meet every few years to advise him in his shepherding of the universal church.[3] Synods, in this sense, are a result of the Council.

If synods are a fruit of the Council, then post-synodal exhortations like *Catechesi Tradendae* are the magisterial fruit of these synods. They are authoritative declarations in which the pope gathers the synodal input from the world's bishops and, after discerning their suggestions, offers his own teaching that becomes a part of the ordinary magisterium.[4] It is noteworthy that *Catechesi Tradendae* was only the second such document to be promulgated after the Council, the first being Paul VI's *Evangelii*

3. For a description of the three types of synods that the pope can call to order, see J. Michael Miller, "Introduction to the Post-Synodal Apostolic Exhortations," in *The Post-Synodal Exhortations of John Paul II*, ed. J. Michael Miller (Huntington, Ind.: Our Sunday Visitor, 1998), 18–21.

4. Though this is now the case, these exhortations are in part a matter of happenstance. The fathers of the 1974 synod on evangelization could not, in fact, agree upon the drafting of a concluding document. As such, they asked Paul VI to intervene, with the end result being the promulgation of *Evangelii Nuntiandi*. A new precedent had begun, if unexpectedly. See Miller, "Introduction to the Post-Synodal Apostolic Exhortations," 24.

Nuntiandi, which was briefly covered in chapter 2.[5] For Paul VI, that document was his attempt to identify the very heart of Vatican II, "the objectives of which are definitively summed up in a single one: to make the Church ... ever better fitted for proclaiming the Gospel"; even more strongly, he wrote, "Evangelizing is in fact the grace and vocation proper to the Church, her deepest identity."[6] By identifying the heart of the Council and the all-encompassing mission of the church as evangelization, Paul VI set the precedent by which his successors would place the New Evangelization at the forefront of the church's consciousness.

Catechesi Tradendae is an extension of this same evangelistic impulse. In its opening lines it dispels any misconceptions of catechesis as a mere exercise in the memorization of information or as something that pertains solely to the classroom, whether in a school or a parish. Rather, it grounds the mission of catechesis in Christ's commissioning of his apostles to make disciples. For John Paul, Jesus Christ is the ultimate source of the church's mission of handing on the Word, and this mission is born from the apostles' tangible encounter with him: Christ "entrusted them with the mission and power to proclaim to humanity what they had heard, what they had seen with their eyes, what they had looked upon and touched with their hands."[7] The use of this opening line in the first Johannine letter is characteristic of John Paul's methodology. It is the experiential counterpart to the grand metaphysical introduction to John's gospel in which the Word is proclaimed to be God, to have been with God, and to have dwelt among us. In John's first letter, the objective reality of what was proclaimed in his gospel becomes something willingly received and experienced by the apostles, and it thus becomes a new beginning, a place for action aimed at fulfillment or, in the words of the letter, acts that fulfill until one's "joy may be complete." That the apostles' mission began with their encounter with Christ confirms John Paul's consistent attention to the

---

5. The first Ordinary Synod took place in 1967, and it led to the establishment of the International Theological Commission and the drafting of principles for the revision of Canon Law. The second took place in 1971, and Paul VI gave his approval to the synod's official statements on the priesthood and justice in the world. It was only after the third Ordinary Synod of 1974 that he promulgated *Evangelii Nuntiandi*, and though he presided over the fourth, it was ultimately left to John Paul II to write and promulgate the post-synodal exhortation. See Miller, "Introduction to the Post-Synodal Apostolic Exhortations," 18–19.

6. EN, nos. 2 [157] and 14 [161].

7. CT, no. 1 [3], referencing 1 Jn 1:1.

fact that receptivity to the truth always precedes action—to put it in terms of Wojtyła's philosophy, only in the encounter with the objective reality beyond themselves could the apostles act in the freedom of self-determination so as to fulfill their very being. In total, the implication is that the apostles encountered their Lord in a powerfully experiential way, received the word of life and the power to hand it on from him, and are now entrusted with the task of making disciples. Catechesis, then, continues this mission. Even in the opening paragraph of *Catechesi Tradendae*, a myopic understanding of catechesis is shattered.[8]

For John Paul, following Paul VI, catechesis is one part of the church's overall mission of evangelization, though it is a part that is particularly "remarkable":

> *Evangelii Nuntiandi* . . . rightly stressed that evangelization—which has the aim of bringing the Good News to the whole of humanity so that all may live by it—is a rich, complex, and dynamic reality, made up of elements, or one could say moments, that are essential and different from each other, and that must all be kept in view simultaneously. Catechesis is one of these moments—a very remarkable one—in the whole process of evangelization.[9]

This contextualization of the church's teaching ministry changes the terms by which the ministry of the Word was previously understood. The 1971 *General Catechetical Directory* had envisioned evangelization solely in terms of the initial proclamation of the faith to non-Christians and catechesis as the period of instruction to follow.[10] Such a division runs the danger of severing instruction in the faith from the church's proclamation of Christ as Savior of the world, leaving the former solely as a

---

8. In several places, John Paul continues this shattering of superficial understandings of catechesis. See, for instance, CT, no. 13 [12]: "Catechesis is intimately bound up with the whole of the Church's life. Not only her geographical extension and numerical increase, but even more, her inner growth and correspondence with God's plan depend essentially on catechesis"; and no. 15 [13]: "The more the Church, whether on the local or the universal level, gives catechesis priority over other works and undertakings the results of which would be more spectacular, the more she finds in catechesis a strengthening of her internal life as a community of believers and of her external activity as a missionary Church."

9. CT, no. 18 [17]; and EN, nos. 17–24. In the same section, John Paul identifies some of the other moments as "the initial proclamation of the Gospel or missionary preaching through the *kerygma* to arouse faith, apologetics or examination of the reasons for belief, experience of Christian living, celebration of the sacraments, integration into the ecclesial community, and apostolic and missionary witness."

10. See GCD, no. 17. Even so, in the next paragraph, the GCD recognizes that "according to circumstances, evangelization can precede or accompany the work of catechesis proper." See GCD, no. 18 [23].

diminished cognitive endeavor. Here, however, catechesis is conceived as a way in which the church makes and deepens this first proclamation. It is the remarkable moment during the process of evangelization given to deepening the hearer's initial encounter with the Word so that he or she may know Christ and his teachings more deeply and entirely. In John Paul's words, "Within the whole process of evangelization, the aim of catechesis is to be the teaching and maturation stage."[11]

John Paul elaborates on this definition of catechesis by way of a beautiful image, that of the gradual transfiguration of the person through the light of Christ. In the official Latin text of *Catechesi Tradendae*, the pope writes that catechesis seeks a deeper understanding of the "mystery of Christ" that the "entire man might be permeated" by his light; by catechesis one can therefore be "transfigured" into a "new creature."[12] Such words bring to mind the powerful context of Mt. Tabor, in which the glory of the transfigured Christ permeated his humanity. Catechesis aims to imbue its hearers with this same light. Interestingly, the Vatican's English translation of the text implies a different metaphor, that of human pregnancy. Catechesis takes the "seed" sown at the initial proclamation and develops it "so that the whole of a person's humanity is impregnated by that word."[13] Here, the image is deeply Marian: like she who first received the Word himself in faith, catechesis nourishes the proclaimed word in an organic and systematic way to the point in which Christ can be born within each person. Mary's vocation is thus emblematic for every Christian: to bear forth Christ to the world. In both cases, the goal is the same: by catechesis, the Christian is gradually transformed into an image of Christ, learning "more and more within the Church to think like him, to judge like him, to act in conformity with his commandments, and to hope as he invites us to."[14]

Most striking in this account of the nature of the catechetical ministry is how thoroughly Christocentric it is—Christ is the source of the ministry, he is its objective content, and its ending point is the fullness

11. CT, no. 20 [18].

12. See AAS 71 (1979): 1294: "Catechesis igitur eo spectat, ut intellectum mysterii Christi, verbo affulgente, promoveat, cuius luce homo totus imbuatur. Qui gratia transfiguratus in novam creaturam."

13. CT, no. 20 [18]. It is unclear what accounts for this uniqueness in translation, though several of the Vatican's official modern language translations—Spanish, Italian, French—follow suit. The presumed original Polish, however, is similar to the Latin text.

14. Ibid.

of Christian maturity that can only be found in him. While more will be said about this Christocentrism later, for now it is possible to establish three significant points regarding how John Paul views the ministry of catechesis, drawn from this Johannine origin. First, because the source of the ministry is the apostles' encounter with their Lord, catechesis must always remain connected to the church's overall mission of evangelization—that is, to the call Jesus gave to the apostles to make disciples by teaching others and drawing them sacramentally into the church's communion. Evangelization is here construed not only as an initial missionary proclamation but as the church's efforts to bring all people into the fullness of communion with God in Jesus Christ. Thus, catechesis, while distinct from the initial proclamation, is nevertheless organically linked to it. By remaining connected to a person's initial encounter with the risen Lord, it is and must remain evangelizing.[15] Only in this way can it meet the demands of the New Evangelization, to call forth and nourish the faith of those who, though found in traditionally Christian societies, are, as John Paul says, "really catechumens."[16]

Second, catechesis is fundamentally grounded in divine revelation. The apostles first received the Word in person and, in communion with him, teach the Word of God to others. Yet, if catechesis is essentially founded upon divine revelation, then activities of purely human origin cannot be the true ground of the catechetical endeavor. For the pope, educational theories, the use of written and visual media, and different educational and ministerial settings are all important yet secondary characteristics of catechesis. It is Jesus Christ who is the ministry's source, and it is the same Christ who is, as Vatican II taught, the fullness of revelation. Thus, John Paul explains that the "primary and essential object" of catechesis is "the mystery of Christ,"—it is to "reveal in the Person of Christ the whole of God's eternal design reaching fulfillment in that Person."[17] Accordingly, "it is on the basis of revelation that catechesis will try to set its course, revelation as transmitted by the universal magisterium of the Church."[18]

---

15. See CT, no. 18 [16]: "There is no separation or opposition between catechesis and evangelization. Nor can the two be simply identified with each other. Instead, they have close links whereby they integrate and complement each other."

16. CT, no. 44 [36].

17. CT, no. 5 [6].

18. CT, no. 52 [42].

Stemming from this second point is the third: because catechesis is based upon divine revelation, its normative pedagogy is not of human origin. Human pedagogies such as those derived from educational, psychological, and sociological study are useful to the church's ministry only to the extent to which they conform to the irreducible pedagogy of faith:

Pedagogy of faith is not a question of transmitting human knowledge, even of the highest kind; it is a question of communicating God's revelation in its entirety. Throughout sacred history, especially in the Gospel, God himself used a pedagogy that must continue to be a model for the pedagogy of faith. A technique is of value in catechesis only to the extent that it serves the faith that is to be transmitted and learned; otherwise it is of no value.[19]

It is this affirmation of the existence of a divine pedagogy that allows one to more clearly assess the modern catechetical movement. For John Paul, the normativity of God's own pedagogy given in divine revelation is the rule by which the movement's advances and regressions can be measured. While more will be said about this pedagogy of God later, it is clear that the pope's reception of the catechetical renewal is measured because of his understanding of it. In *Catechesi Tradendae* he echoes the 1977 synod fathers in recognizing that "renewal is sometimes unequal in value," thus applauding the "undeniable advance in the vitality of catechetical activity" brought about by the renewal while still acknowledging the "limitations or even 'deficiencies' in what has been achieved to date."[20] It is to the various stages of the catechetical renewal, seen in light of the pope's exhortation, that this study now turns.

Doctrinal Catechesis

As noted in chapter 2, the modern catechetical movement emerged from a context in which catechesis was primarily doctrinal and child-based. Post-Tridentine reforms had emphasized the role of the catechism, and the proliferation of doctrinal compendiums helped solidify the unity of the Catholic faith after the Reformation. Even so, the rising secularism spurred by the Enlightenment had altered the culture outside the home. By the start of the twentieth century many religious

19. CT, no. 58 [48].
20. CT, no. 17 [14–15].

educators began to claim that the neo-scholastically influenced form of handing on the faith was unable to curtail the rising secular tide. The content of the faith, they claimed, was not the problem; rather, it was the method of communicating it.

Granting that catechesis for the New Evangelization cannot take the sole form of the memorization of propositions, the question still remains: what role does doctrinal catechesis play in the vision of John Paul II? Clearly, his approach cannot be characterized by the so-called law of the pendulum that would pit doctrine against human experience. His philosophical and theological works all champion experience as the necessary path by which one reaches objectivity. At the same time, he is the pope who, among other things, is remembered by the promulgation of the first universal catechism since the Council of Trent, the *Catechism of the Catholic Church*. Thus, he is plainly not averse to the teaching of doctrine and, in fact, finds it essential to the craft of catechesis.

Indeed, in *Catechesi Tradendae*, he writes that catechesis must be systematic and sufficiently complete. It is marked especially by "the teaching of Christian doctrine imparted, generally speaking, in an organic and systematic way, with a view to initiating hearers into the fullness of Christian life."[21] Elsewhere in the document he writes that the integrity of this type of catechesis is demanded not only by the need to present the fullness of the faith (without getting bogged down by the minutest of details) but by the "right" of the catechized to receive the faith, "not in mutilated, falsified, or diminished form but whole and entire, in all its rigor and vigor."[22] Here, that which the renewal considered traditional is ironically argued in strikingly modern terms. When emphasizing this organic and systematic catechesis that is owed to the faithful by right, John Paul likewise does not shy away from the distinctive marks of post-Tridentine catechesis: he encourages the development of catechisms for instruction and even recalls the value of memorizing principal truths of the faith.[23]

21. CT, no. 18 [16]. See also CT, no. 21.
22. CT, no. 30.
23. See CT, nos. 50 and 55, respectively. Elsewhere, in *God, Father and Creator*, 18, John Paul II even links the older method of organizing the catechism into questions and answers to anthropological concerns: "Often, the formulas of catechisms, with a series of questions and answers, have expressed concretely and practically the fundamental structure of catechesis, which can be defined as the meeting between man's question and God's response."

Ultimately, then, John Paul embraces the doctrinal aspects of catechesis that marked the milieu from which the catechetical renewal emerged. Maturing in one's faith requires an understanding of the church's teachings, not in a random or haphazard way, but in such a way that everything is connected to the central truths of Christianity and, through these, to the person of Christ who communes with the Father in the Spirit.

Still, this embrace of the catechetical tradition should not be read as a call to return to the older form of catechesis undergirded by a purely propositional understanding of revelation. John Paul is well aware of the work of the pioneers of the renewal, desiring both to affirm its strengths and to correct its weaknesses. Thus, he unmistakably stands in accord with the kerygmatic phase in grounding doctrine in the person of Jesus Christ. Catechesis is, at its heart, Christocentric. In the introduction and chapter 1 of this book I recalled that the teachings of Christ were inseparable from his person. Corresponding to this, the pope holds that faith has a "double reference"—that is, it refers "to the person and to the truth; to the truth in consideration of the person who enjoys special claims to credibility."[24] Accordingly, in *Catechesi Tradendae* he writes that being a Christian means "saying 'yes' to Jesus Christ, but let us remember that this 'yes' has two levels: it consists in surrendering to the word of God and relying on it, but it also means, at a later stage, endeavoring to know better and better the profound meaning of this word."[25] Catechesis, because it remains rooted in this initial surrender even as it continues to nourish faith with greater knowledge, must always remain kerygmatic.

Perhaps one of the clearest examples of this kerygmatic rooting of doctrine is found in John Paul's encyclical on the church's moral teaching, *Veritatis Splendor*. In its widely celebrated first chapter, the document views the Christian life through the lens of the Gospel encounter of the rich young man with Jesus. Though he has, by his own assessment, kept the commandments, the man possesses an incomplete moral life, for there remains one thing he still lacks. As Jesus explains in Matthew 19:21, if he wishes to be perfect, he must sell all his possessions, give the money to the poor, and, ultimately, "Come, follow me." For

24. John Paul II, *God, Father and Creator*, 31.
25. CT, no. 20 [18].

John Paul, the Christian life "is not a matter only of disposing oneself to hear a teaching and obediently accepting a commandment" but is "holding fast to the very person of Jesus."[26] More recently, Pope Francis has echoed this grounding of doctrine in the person of Christ in his own way: "Christian doctrine is ... living, is able to unsettle, is able to enliven. It has a face that is supple, a body that moves and develops, flesh that is tender: Christian doctrine is called Jesus Christ."[27]

Not only does John Paul ground doctrine in its Christological source, but he sees it as open to the anthropological concerns of the catechetical renewal as well. In fact, for the pope, it is precisely when catechesis is doctrinal that it can most effectively address the experience of the human person. Only if catechesis is integral, he explains, can it be "open to all the other factors of Christian life."[28] This was something Jungmann had recognized even as he pushed the renewal to return to the kerygma. Jungmann, in fact, did not reject the usefulness of catechisms; nor did he disavow the neo-scholastic theology upon which they were based, though he was often accused of doing so. Rather, he claimed that the more thoroughly a teacher knows the faith—systematically, organically, integrally—the more capable he is of addressing hearers from any and all experiential backgrounds. Such knowledge "would enable him to utilize the full treasure of eternal truth in a thoroughly vital way for the changeable needs of the time and the varying requirements of the community. In fact, the deeper the analysis has gone, the further it has penetrated to basic elements, the greater should be the freedom and flexibility with which the bearer of God's message brings forth from the store of doctrine that which can furnish the real answer to the questions and longings of the erring children of men."[29] For both Jungmann and John Paul, the integrity of the church's doctrine yields what would be a surprising consequence for the practitioners of the third phase of renewal: rather than crowding out human experience, the organic nature of the church's faith makes it possible to address the experiences of all men

26. VS, no. 19 [32]. John Paul even italicizes the section on "holding fast ... to Jesus" in the original.

27. Francis, "Meeting with the Participants in the Fifth Convention of the Italian Church, 10 November 2015," Vatican, http://w2.vatican.va/content/francesco/en/speeches/2015/november/documents/papa-francesco_20151110_firenze-convegno-chiesa-italiana.html.

28. CT, no. 21 [19].

29. Jungmann, *Good News Yesterday and Today*, 32.

and women. The integrity of doctrinal teaching and openness to human experience are directly related, rather than inversely.

The same logic is on display when *Catechesi Tradendae* lauds the Roman *Catechism* and, at the same time, recommends the creation of local catechisms by episcopal conferences.[30] It is the universality of the faith that allows it to be communicated effectively to people of different places and cultures. Thus, when the Synod of 1985, under John Paul's direction, recommended the creation of a new universal catechism, it was incorrectly seen by many theologians and catechetical scholars as a move toward Roman and papal centralization. Instead, as the synod's general secretary Walter Kasper noted, the call for the *Catechism of the Catholic Church* came from the peripheries.[31] The bishops of the various language groups recognized that to successfully hand on the faith to their own people demands communion with a unifying source. In sum, then, the concerns of the modern catechetical movement are not displaced by a doctrinal emphasis in catechesis but are, when integrated well, addressed more effectively.

Catechetical Method

By the turn of the twentieth century, the catechetical milieu of instructing from the catechism eventually gave way to new advances in teaching methodology. Catechists began to develop their doctrinal lessons from stories, often biblical ones, that they believed could more powerfully call forth understanding in the minds of their hearers. Thus the first phase of the catechetical renewal began, with the Munich Method being the most prominent example of this development.

In its attention to method, the first phase is, in a certain sense, the forerunner of the more completely anthropological catechesis that dominated after Vatican II. As such, I will leave my more detailed remarks on the role of experience in catechesis when addressing the third phase later on. But, for now, it is important to offer a few brief thoughts regarding the role of teaching methodology in *Catechesi Tradendae*. In the first place, John Paul recognizes that a certain creativity is needed for catechesis to be effective for modern men and women. New circum-

30. See CT, nos. 13 and 50.
31. See Pedraza, "Catholic Disagreements and the Catechism's 25th Anniversary."

stances may demand new methods, and John Paul's famous description of the New Evangelization as "new in its ardor, in its methods, and in its expression" is emblematic of this.[32] Yet, at the same time, this creativity must be harnessed well, "with the required vigilance" that is demanded by the integrity of divine revelation.[33] The freedom of the teacher to find new ways to reach his or her audience, then, is bound by fidelity to the Christian tradition.

Yet, is such a binding an affront to the freedom of the catechist? John Paul's anthropology has already shown that an examination of the intentional acts of a person reveals a reliance upon truth, the truth about the good that one intends.[34] "Freedom," Wojtyła wrote, "carries within itself the surrender to truth."[35] As pope he put it even more emphatically: "Worship of God and a relationship with truth are revealed in Jesus Christ as the deepest foundation of freedom."[36]

This claim, which echoes the teaching of Christ in John 8:32, opens up what is, perhaps, the most important teaching of *Catechesi Tradendae* concerning catechetical methodology. John Paul certainly recognizes things seemingly more pertinent to methodological considerations— the need for the church to harness new media in its efforts to preach the Gospel and the adaptation of the teaching of the faith to various contexts (youth groups, Bible studies, missions, pilgrimages). But one of the most significant teachings of his exhortation is the claim that *method is always at the service of content*. "Reasons of method or pedagogy," he writes, "suggest that the communication of the riches of the content of catechesis should be organized in one way rather than in another"; yet, the validity of the methodological choice is determined not by "more or less subjective theories or prejudices stamped with a certain ideology" but by "the humble concern to stay closer to a content that must remain intact."[37]

Modern educators may find these words troubling. Is not the notion

---

32. John Paul II, "Discurso del Santo Padre Juan Pablo II a la Asamblea del CELAM, 9 March 1983," Vatican, https://w2.vatican.va/content/john-paul-ii/es/speeches/1983/march/documents/hf_jp-ii_spe_19830309_assemblea-celam.html. Translations from the original Spanish text found on the Vatican website are mine.

33. CT, no. 4 [5].

34. See the section "Transcendence: Freedom Directed toward Fulfillment," in chapter 3.

35. Wojtyła, Acting Person, 156.

36. VS, no. 87 [108]. Indeed, *Veritatis Splendor* can, in certain sense, rightfully be considered an extended meditation on the relationship between freedom and truth.

37. CT, no. 31 [27].

of some sort of content to be handed on from teacher to student an outmoded one? Instead, today, Socratic education seeks to draw out what the learner already knows inherently, and liberating models of education eschew "banking methods" in which teachers transmit content (i.e., make deposits) into their students' minds.[38]

To be sure, the church's ministry of the Word would be an exercise in futility if it failed to address the experience of its hearers and especially if it did not open up the path of true freedom for the catechized. John Paul recognizes the value and necessity of human experience as well as the transcendence of self-determination that stands at the heart of this experience. But key, here, is the recognition that it is experience itself that begs for something outside of the subject—that is, outside of the one who experiences. The fulfillment the person seeks, which can only come by way of the operation of his or her freedom, is dependent on that which is other than the person. "The tendency toward the fulfillment of oneself," Wojtyła wrote, "shows that this self is somehow incomplete."[39] Thus, it is only in surrendering to the truth about the good that one can find this fulfillment, thereby growing in knowledge and freedom. While this holds for any form of genuine education, secular or religious, it is particularly manifested in catechesis in which the content of divine revelation is, by definition, always from the outside, so to speak. So, too, is it especially manifest as the metaphysical ground of what Wojtyła termed the "law of the gift"—namely, that it is in giving oneself to another that one truly finds him- or herself.

Thus, the object of the self-gift of the catechized will always be twofold: catechesis evokes surrender to the truth about the good but also to *persons*, indeed a *community of persons*, who manifest this truth and goodness. Human fulfillment can only be pursued in community—the community stands not only as the necessary context for this fulfillment but, in its own way, is its goal. In this way, the common good of the ecclesial community is not some shared material object but the church's participation in Jesus Christ. This is the law of the gift most fully on display: the person gives him- or herself in faith to join the communion of persons that is the church and thereby is ushered into the *communio personarum* that is the Blessed Trinity.

38. See Freire, *Pedagogy of the Oppressed*, 72.
39. Wojtyła, "Person: Subject and Community," 232–33.

Returning nearer to the matter at hand, catechetical method is necessarily the servant of content not because John Paul has imposed some sort of stifling uniformity upon the church's endeavors. Rather, the church is only truly attentive to the catechized when it proposes the full objectivity of the content of the faith. A freedom severed from this truth is only a supposed freedom. Likewise, to call upon human experience without recognizing its yearning for fulfillment in God and the truth he has proclaimed would leave the catechetical endeavor incomplete. Fidelity to the content of the faith thereby opens up the greatest freedom for the evangelizing catechist, enabling him or her to harness methods new and old to advance the ministry of the Word. In this vision, something as time-honored as memorization is not opposed to the world of social media, and the catechist might, in fact, find the need to utilize or even integrate both. Whatever the case, the experience of the past decades has shown, the pope notes, that methods devoid of content are "in danger—a danger that has unfortunately proved only too real—of disappointing their members and also the Church."[40] In the end, the experience of modern men and women should never be simply pitted against the content of divine revelation. An honest look at this experience discloses the need for this revelation if the person is ever to reach the fulfillment for which he or she longs.

All this being said, John Paul recognizes that the master catechist is one who knows how to be creative with methodology so that the content of the faith is effectively communicated to people in all of their diversity. In *Catechesi Tradendae*, he dedicates several paragraphs to the various age groups to which catechesis is aimed, beginning with infancy and proceeding to childhood, adolescence, young adulthood, and, finally, adulthood. Within this range he includes the necessity of adapting catechesis to youth culture, those who have disabilities, those who lack religious support from their families or communities, and those who have lost the living sense of their faith.[41] So, too, does he recommend the use of modern media, a multitude of catechetical settings, homilies, catechisms, and other forms of catechetical literature to help transfigure the catechized into images of Jesus Christ.[42] Ultimately, the

40. CT, no. 47 [39].
41. See CT, nos. 35–45.
42. See CT, nos. 46–50.

catechist's methods can vary as much as the people he or she wishes to catechize, and this variety is, for John Paul, a "sign of life" in the church so long as it is "not harmful to the unity of the teaching of the one faith."[43]

The Kerygma and an Evangelizing Catechesis

In the second phase of the catechetical movement, Jungmann, followed by his disciple Hofinger, claimed that attention to method alone could not renew catechesis in the way necessary to advance the church's mission in the modern world. Neither was fidelity to the content of the church's teachings—though both men were adamant this was necessary—the sole remedy for what ailed the ministry. Rather, the church must return to the very *person* of Jesus Christ to effectively reach the modern world. Jungmann referred to this as *Christocentrism*, a term taken up by John Paul to describe catechesis in its essence.

Jungmann explained that this Christocentrism is both objective and subjective. Objectively, Christ is the center of salvation history and of the church's doctrine such that he is the point of convergence of the entire Christian faith:

Christ is the pivotal point of all God's ways—those by which his mercy descends to his creation and those by which the creature mounts back to its Source. All dogmatic treatises converge about Christ. His person and work form the true core of the Christian message of salvation. In this sense, Christ may rightly be called the center of all doctrine, in fact, of all theological disciplines. All of theology is, then, Christocentric.[44]

However, Jungmann noted, this Christocentrism must be perceived subjectively by the human person if he or she is to truly understand the faith in a way that transforms the whole of life and sets him or her firmly on the *sequela Christi*. Jungmann thus emphatically called for a return to the proclamation of the *kerygma* as the heart of the catechetical endeavor.

Given the foundation of this call in the objective Christocentrism of the Christian faith, the kerygma, for Jungmann, is not simply a prepackaged collection of statements that propose to the unevangelized a

43. CT, no. 51 [42].
44. Jungmann, *Good News Yesterday and Today*, 9–10.

summary of their sinful state and the redemption offered by the sacrifice of Christ—though, of course, it may and often does take this form. More deeply and comprehensively, it is the proclamation of the truth that Christ is the fulfillment of God's plan for the salvation of all humankind. He is the center, the converging point of all that was promised before and all that will come to be upon his return and full ushering-in of the kingdom of God. In this we discover why Jungmann followed Augustine so closely in stressing the importance of the *narratio*, the telling of salvation history, so that the catechized might see Jesus as its apex and main protagonist. So, too, did the catechetical pioneer emphasize the sacraments and their liturgy as the very place where one can enter into this history and touch the resurrected Christ, becoming incorporated into him and receiving the salvation he promised.

For his part, John Paul takes up this "Christocentricity" and places it at the heart of his understanding of catechesis: "At the heart of catechesis we find, in essence, a Person, the Person of Jesus of Nazareth."[45] For the pope, catechesis is Christocentric in a double sense, corresponding with the twofold object of the act of faith—to believe in the person and in what the person reveals.

Regarding the first, because the primary and essential object of the ministry is the "mystery of Christ," it must "reveal in the Person of Christ the whole of God's eternal design reaching fulfillment in that Person."[46] Here John Paul echoes Jungmann's foundational Augustinian insight. Following from this, the end goal of the ministry is described in similarly personalistic terms. In what is one of the most striking lines of *Catechesi Tradendae*, John Paul writes, "The definitive aim of catechesis is to put people not only in touch but *in communion, in intimacy,* with Jesus Christ."[47] The pope's characteristic Thomistic Personalism is here matched by a catechetical personalism. As with the former, this personalism remains firmly rooted in objectivity—in this case, the objectivity of the person of Christ. Yet, in a likewise similar fashion, this objectivity must be appropriated by the acting subject. It must be experienced such that the person of Christ is not only encountered by the senses, so to speak (in the myriad ways he is present in his church), but

---

45. CT, no. 5 [6].
46. Ibid.
47. Ibid. Emphasis mine.

is also chosen. Was this not the way Wojtyła, as archbishop of Krakow, had interpreted the evangelizing mission of the Council, as "an enrichment of the content of faith … but also, originating from that content, an enrichment of the whole existence of the believing member of the Church"?[48] For Wojtyła, "this enrichment of faith in the objective sense … is at the same time an enrichment in the subjective, human, existential sense, and it is from the latter that realization of the Council is most to be hoped for."[49] Thus, communion with Christ—including its subjective experience as intimacy—is the overarching aim of catechesis for the New Evangelization.[50]

While this first consideration views the Christocentricity of catechesis by way of its object and its subjective appropriation, the second concerns the teacher of the faith and what is to be taught. John Paul echoes the gospels in claiming that Christ alone is the true teacher and that his teaching is inseparable from himself: "Christocentricity in catechesis also means the intention to transmit not one's own teaching or that of some other master, but the teaching of Jesus Christ, the truth that he communicates or, to put it more precisely, the truth that he is."[51] Likewise, "it is Christ alone who teaches—anyone else teaches to the extent that he is Christ's spokesman, enabling Christ to teach with his lips."[52] The fact that Jesus is the true teacher impresses upon the catechist a humbling deference while, at the same time, nurturing him or her with a comforting reassurance.[53] The deference is especially manifest when the catechist recognizes that one is not there to win the affections of one's hearers to his or her own person or opinions. Instead, echoing Jesus, the catechist should say, "My teaching is not mine, but his who sent me."[54]

48. Wojtyła, *Sources of Renewal*, 18.

49. Ibid.

50. One should not, however, read John Paul as saying the *feeling* of intimacy is the true gauge of this subjective appropriation. As he learned so long ago studying John of the Cross in Tyranowski's apartment, union with Christ does not always manifest itself in consoling feelings. The dark night proves this to be true. For John Paul, the subjective appropriation is grounded in the act—the choice to give oneself over to Christ. In this self-gift one could say the intimacy is always *experienced* but not always *felt* as consolation.

51. CT, no. 6 [6–7]. Here, John Paul II references Jn 14:6, though in no. 8 he cites Mt 23:8.

52. Ibid.

53. See CT, no. 8 [8], where the pope writes that "this image of Christ the Teacher is at once majestic and familiar, impressive and reassuring."

54. CT, no. 6 [7], quoting Jn 7:16.

Yet, in these very words, the catechist also finds assurance and a reminder, the assurance that the fruitfulness of the ministry does not rely on human efforts alone and a reminder that the kingdom of God grows in hidden ways, seeming at first to be a mustard seed but eventually revealed as the large plant where birds of all kinds can find rest.[55] To use another biblical image, humans can plant and water, but it is God who provides the increase.[56] Because Jesus is the true teacher and, thus, the only one who can bring about conversion and spiritual maturity in the catechized, the lone path by which catechists can be fruitful in their ministry opens up: by ever deepening communion with him. "Only in deep communion with him," John Paul writes, "will catechists find light and strength for an authentic, desirable renewal of catechesis."[57]

The other dimension signified by this second meaning of Christocentrity is that the teaching of Christ, now handed on in the church, is inseparable from his person. This is not to deny that, in practice, this is in fact what often happens. Those who criticized the "older" or "more traditional" form of catechesis based upon memorization of the catechism had grown tired of a lifeless presentation of doctrine and moral commands cut off from their Source. One can recall the words of Jungmann when he described preconciliar Christianity as a hollowed-out tree: the remaining bark of custom gave the appearance of strength, but the inner strands of life had withered through separation from Christ.[58] Pope Francis has raised the same issue more recently in *Evangelii Gaudium*, where he links the unity of the church's doctrine and moral practice to the classical teaching on the unity of the virtues.[59] For Francis, "each truth is better understood when related to the harmonious totality of the Christian message," the centrality of which is found in "the God of love who saves us" and the "response of love" prompted

---

55. See Mk 4:30–32. On this more hidden aspect of the New Evangelization, see Ratzinger, "Intervento del Cardinale Joseph Ratzinger durante il convegno dei catechisti e dei docent religione, 10 Dicembre 2000," Vatican, http://www.vatican.va/roman_curia/congregations/cfaith/documents/rc_con_cfaith_doc_20001210_jubilcatechists-ratzinger_it.html.

56. See 1 Cor 3:7.

57. *CT*, no. 9 [9].

58. See Jungmann, "Adult Christian," 6.

59. This classic thesis, advanced by those such as Plato, Aristotle, St. Augustine, and St. Thomas Aquinas, holds that one cannot possess any of the virtues without possessing all of them. For more on this claim and its relationship to Francis's thoughts on evangelization, see Andrew Kim, "The Unity of the Virtues in a Missionary Key," in *Pope Francis and the Event of Encounter*, ed. John C. Cavadini and Donald Wallenfang (Eugene, Ore.: Pickwick, 2018), 146–65.

by evangelization.[60] Without this foundation, the church's teaching is "a house of cards," ready to topple by the lightest wind or touch.[61]

Catechesis for the New Evangelization, then, cannot content itself with such a dubious edifice. Doctrine must be systematic, organic, and integral—yes—but even the most uniform of structures will fall without a firm foundation. In catechesis, the foundation is God, and God is most fully revealed and is solely accessed by way of the person of Jesus Christ. "We must therefore say," John Paul proclaims, "that in catechesis it is Christ, the Incarnate Word and Son of God, who is taught—everything else is taught with reference to Him."[62] The supreme duty of catechists is, therefore, to root their teachings in the person of Christ. It is perhaps the common failure of the past to highlight a doctrine of the church, to even cover it thoroughly, and yet to fail to connect that doctrine to life in Christ. One can speak of the sacrament of confession, painstakingly going through its various elements, but if it is not placed within the framework of Christ's redemption and merciful love, the lesson is like a resounding gong. It is condemned to become the facts of trivia, like the names and dates of a history book that are often forgotten in a short while.[63] But, connected to Christ, doctrines become entry points to a greater understanding of the mystery of God and signposts for the spiritual life. Rather than being cordoned off from the actual lives of Christians, they become, as the Catechism states, "lights along the path of faith; they illuminate it and make it secure."[64] In total, the Christocentricity of catechesis means, for John

60. See EG, no. 39 [32].

61. Ibid.

62. CT, no. 6 [7].

63. See Pedraza, "Participation over Imitation," 33: "In this light I often use the analogy of someone telling me about my wife to explain the necessity of reconnecting doctrine to the person of Christ. If I had never met my wife, the simple facts about her—her eyes, the color of her hair—could be spoken to me such that they entered my mind but did nothing to move my heart. But, in knowing her and experiencing the beauty of her person, the fact that her eyes are green or her hair is brown has the power to captivate me. Every truth about her is another reason to love her more. In a similar way, then, every truth about Christ must be more than a passing fact—it must become another reason to love him more. What we as catechists teach is 'not a body of abstract truths. It is the communication of the living mystery of God' (Catechesi Tradendae, no. 7)."

64. CCC, no. 89 [28]. St. John Chrysostom, in one of his catechumenal instructions, makes a remark that beautifully ties together both aspects of this second form of Christocentricity. Commenting on the etymology of the word "catechesis," he begins the lesson by asking his hearers for proof of their internalization of his last lesson: "First I have come to ask your loving

Paul, that the church's "teaching is not a body of abstract truths. It is the communication of the living mystery of God."[65]

Catechesi Tradendae affirms another dimension of Jungmann and Hofinger's proposal, indeed, the one by which their phase of the renewal received its name. For both Jesuit scholars, the return to the person of Christ in catechesis demands a return to the apostolic way of proclaiming him as the converging point of salvation history and, in fact, all reality—it demands a return to the kerygma.

As mentioned earlier, John Paul conceives of catechesis as the maturation of what was first received in seed by a person's acceptance of this initial proclamation. He likewise recognizes that, in the context of the New Evangelization, catechesis must often be kerygmatic in form, concerning itself "not only with nourishing and teaching the faith, but also with arousing it unceasingly with the help of grace, with opening the heart, with converting, and with preparing total adherence to Jesus Christ on the part of those who are still on the threshold of faith."[66] In both cases, catechesis remains thoroughly kerygmatic, either by deepening the initial acceptance of the proclamation or by delivering the kerygma within the context of catechetical instruction.

John Paul's defense of this kerygmatic nature of catechesis in Catechesi Tradendae seems especially aimed at those who would see the ministry as a lifeless, rationalistic endeavor:

Through catechesis the Gospel kerygma (the initial ardent proclamation by which the person is one day overwhelmed and brought to the decision to entrust himself to Jesus Christ by faith) is gradually deepened, developed in its implicit consequences, explained in language that includes an appeal to reason, and channeled towards Christian practice in the Church and the world. All this is no less evangelical than the kerygma, in spite of what is said by certain people who consider that catechesis necessarily rationalizes, dries up, and eventually kills all that is living, spontaneous, and vibrant in the kerygma.

---

assembly for the fruits of my recent discourse. For I do not speak only that you may hear, but that you may remember what I said and give me proof of it by your deeds; rather, you must give proof to God, who knows your secret thoughts. This is why my discourse is called a catechesis, so that even when I am not here my words may echo in your minds." See Baptismal Instruction 12.1, in St. John Chrystosom, Baptismal Instructions, trans. Paul W. Harkins (Mahwah, N.J.: Paulist Press, 1963), 173. Catechesis "echoes," then, the teaching of Christ and resounds in the lives of the catechized.

65. CT, no. 7 [7].
66. CT, no. 19 [18].

The truths studied in catechesis are the same truths that touched the person's heart when he heard them for the first time. Far from blunting or exhausting them, the fact of knowing them better should make them even more challenging and decisive for one's life.[67]

More recently, Pope Francis has reiterated his predecessor's thoughts:

On the lips of the catechist the first proclamation must ring out over and over: "Jesus Christ loves you; he gave his life to save you; and now he is living at your side every day to enlighten, strengthen and free you." This first proclamation is called "first" not because it exists at the beginning and can then be forgotten or replaced by other more important things. It is first in a qualitative sense because it is the principal proclamation, the one which we must hear again and again in different ways, the one which we must announce one way or another throughout the process of catechesis, at every level and moment.[68]

Indeed, for Francis, "we must not think that in catechesis the kerygma gives way to a supposedly more 'solid' formation. Nothing is more solid, profound, secure, meaningful and wisdom-filled than that initial proclamation. All Christian formation consists of entering more deeply into the kerygma, which is reflected in and constantly illumines the work of catechesis."[69] For both popes, while the material content of the kerygma and catechesis may differ, their formal content is, in some sense, the same. The Christocentricity of catechesis demands that it be so.

Before concluding this section, it is important to consider a question that arises in regard to what I have called John Paul's catechetical

---

67. CT, no. 25 [21–22]. He adds, "This broad meaning of catechesis in no way contradicts but rather includes and goes beyond a narrow meaning which was once commonly given to catechesis in didactic expositions, namely, the simple teaching of the formulas that express faith." An examination of John Paul's younger years reveals that this insight was born from experience. In an article in which he reflected upon the influence of the tailor and mystic Jan Tyranowski on his life, he wrote about the time when the catechist first called together a group of youth of which Wojtyła was a part: "When he spoke for the first and the second time at a meeting of the group ... all of the young people present had great reservations about him. This was caused in part by the obvious age difference (Jan's hair was then decidedly graying, even though he was barely forty), and much more so by his manner of formulating the issues, a manner that seemed overly pious, too much from the catechism, in no way original." Even so, Wojtyła would eventually come to see Tyranowski as a creative and captivating formator, as evidenced by the title of the article, "The Apostle." See Wojtyła, "The Apostle," in *The Making of the Pope of the Millennium: Kalendarium of the Life of Karol Wojtyła*, ed. Adam Boniecki (Stockbridge, Mass.: Marian Press, 2000), 66.

68. EG, no. 164 [116–17].

69. EG, no. 165 [117].

personalism. With all of this attention to intimacy, the kerygma, and personal encounter, is the magisterium pushing the church to leave its time-honored communal understanding of the faith? Is not the "Catholicity" of the church one of its characteristic marks? One can see this issue at play, for instance, in the discussion between George Weigel and John Cavadini regarding the former's book, *Evangelical Catholicism*.[70] For Weigel, the church of the twenty-first century must take up the papal call to evangelization by promoting personal encounters with Jesus Christ, with friendship with him becoming one of the primary determinants of the degree of communion by which one belongs to the church. In Cavadini's review, the esteemed Augustinian scholar lauds the book's emphasis on evangelization but criticizes its implied ecclesiology: "The communion of the Church does not arise from personal friendship with the Lord Jesus," he writes, "but from Christ's undeserved, atoning love which, mediated by the sacraments, makes the Church. The Church is the bond of communion, whether it is consciously known in a subjective friendship or not."[71] Because integration into Christ's Body is effected by the sacrament of baptism, "there is no amount of subjective friendship that can replace or add anything substantial in comparison with this utter gift."[72] Though Cavadini goes on to explain that Weigel never explicitly embraces such a problematic sacrament-less ecclesiology, his concern remains an important one for the catechist who wishes to take up John Paul's call for the church to remain rooted in personal encounter with its Lord.

A first step in unpacking this issue is found in revisiting the recent papal magisterial teachings concerning a personal friendship with Jesus Christ. While I have already referenced some of John Paul and Francis's remarks on the matter in terms of the kerygma, we can add to these the opening invitation of *Evangelii Gaudium*: "I invite all Christians, everywhere, at this very moment, to a renewed personal encounter with Jesus Christ, or at least an openness to letting him encounter them; I ask all

---

70. Weigel, *Evangelical Catholicism: Deep Reform in the 21st-Century Church* (New York: Basic, 2013). Cavadini reviewed the book in "Church as Sacrament," *First Things*, August 2013, https://www.firstthings.com/article/2013/08/church-as-sacrament, and Weigel responded in "Evangelical Catholicism: Response to Cavadini," *First Things*, October 17, 2013, https://www.firstthings.com/web-exclusives/2013/10/evangelical-catholicism-response-to-cavadini.

71. Cavadini, "Church as Sacrament." Emphasis in the original.

72. Ibid.

of you to do this unfailingly each day. No one should think that this invitation is not meant for him or her."[73] So, too, should one include the thoughts of another renowned Augustinian, Pope Benedict XVI. Benedict's first papal document, *Deus Caritas Est*, shocked uninformed critics of his election who worried that the former head of the Congregation for the Doctrine of the Faith would simply be a dogmatic curmudgeon. The title of the document alone might be enough to dispel such a misconception, but, for our purposes, the encyclical's first paragraph reveals something of the essence of Benedict's pontificate. "Being Christian," the pope explains, "is not the result of an ethical choice or a lofty idea, but the encounter with an event, a person, which gives life a new horizon and a decisive direction."[74] Later in 2011, before the bishops of the Philippines, he exclaimed, "Above all, to keep God at the center of the life of the faithful, the preaching of you and your clergy must be personal in its focus so that each Catholic will grasp in his or her innermost depths the life-transforming fact that God exists, that he loves us, and that in Christ he answers the deepest questions of our lives. Your great task in evangelization is therefore to propose a personal relationship with Christ as key to complete fulfilment."[75]

Yet, in true Augustinian fashion, Benedict reveals the nature of this personal encounter, which can only occur through the presence of Christ that is the church: "He encounters us ever anew, in the men and women who reflect his presence, in his word, in the sacraments, and especially in the Eucharist. In the Church's Liturgy, in her prayer, in the living community of believers, we experience the love of God, we perceive his presence and we thus learn to recognize that presence in our daily lives. He has loved us first and he continues to do so."[76] Here, Benedict reveals the breadth of Augustine's conception of the *Totus Christus*. Ascended into heaven, the Lord remains in history through his Body the church, and together the head and the body make up the whole Christ. This is only the Doctor of Grace's way of recounting Paul's

73. EG, no. 3 [5–6].
74. DCE, no. 1 [7]. Benedict's trilogy of nonmagisterial books on Jesus of Nazareth should, I believe, be read within this same reference.
75. Benedict XVI, "Address of His Holiness Benedict XVI to the Bishops of the Episcopal Conference of the Philippines on their 'Ad Limina' Visit, 18 February 2011," Vatican, https://w2.vatican.va/content/benedict-xvi/en/speeches/2011/february/documents/hf_ben-xvi_spe_20110218_bishops-philippines.html.
76. DCE, no. 17 [42].

central ecclesiological insight gained when, knocked to the ground, he learned the identity of the One who existed in the Christians he had been persecuting.[77] By persecuting the followers of Jesus of Nazareth he had, in fact, been persecuting Christ himself, for the church is his body. This incorporation is undoubtedly sacramental, but no one familiar with Paul's conversion, or Augustine's for that matter, would deny the significance of the subjective appropriation of this objective, sacramental reality and the fruitfulness brought about by a lived faith, a faith "vivified by charity," to use Wojtyła's phrase.[78]

Thus, while catechesis seeks to foster and deepen one's personal encounter with Jesus Christ, it is and must always remain ecclesial in scope. Christ is, in his person, the sacrament of the encounter between human beings and God, but the church is, John Paul notes, the "sacrament of Christ's presence."[79] Is this not, after all, the very heart of John Paul's anthropology? The human person stands as an individual made unto the image of God and supreme in dignity amidst the other earthly creatures, and yet, patterned after the *communio personarum* of the Trinity, he must, by grace, give himself to another, entering into communion, in order to restore his likeness to God. As bishop of Krakow, Wojtyła read the Council's ecclesiology in this way, seeing in the church the point where the human person's vertical and horizontal axes of transcendence converge.[80] The Council, Archbishop Wojtyła wrote, taught that the church "possesses the nature of a communion (*communio*) in which, by means of mutual services, in different ways and in various relationships, 'that sincere giving of himself' takes place in which man can fully discover his true self."[81] But because the church is the Body of Christ, to give oneself over in faith to its communion is not merely to give oneself over to other Christians—it is to give oneself to the person of Jesus Christ, who communes with the Father and the Holy Spirit. Thus, "as faith advances, it will always have in view, as its ultimate reality and model, the *communio personarum* of God himself in the Trinity of Persons."[82]

77. See Acts 9:5.
78. Wojtyła, *Faith according to St. John of the Cross*, 250.
79. *CT*, no. 29 [25]. See also *CT*, no. 24 [21]: "A person who has given adherence to Jesus Christ by faith and is endeavoring to consolidate that faith by catechesis needs to live in communion with those who have taken the same step."
80. See Wojtyła, *Sources of Renewal*, 114.
81. Ibid., 120, referencing *GS*, no. 24.
82. Ibid., 121. It is important to add here that, as seen in chapter 1's analysis of *Dei Verbum*,

With this in mind we are able to return to the poignant text of *Catechesi Tradendae* in which John Paul speaks of the aim of catechesis in such strong personalistic terms. Because catechesis is Christocentric it is thereby ecclesial, and because it is ecclesial it must bring about an encounter with the person of Christ. "The definitive aim of catechesis," John Paul reveals, "is to put people not only in touch but in communion, in intimacy, with Jesus Christ." Yet, he adds, "only he can lead us to the love of the Father in the Spirit and make us share in the life of the Holy Trinity."[83]

The Role of Experience in Catechesis

The kerygmatic renewal brought new life to the church's teaching ministry in the middle of the twentieth century, and Jungmann's prominent role as *peritus* at Vatican II stands as one of the many confirmations of the Council's embrace of the return to the sources of tradition as a way to bring renewal to the church in the modern world. Even so, attempts to interpret the Council as a break with this tradition, one designed to accommodate the world, along with the scholarly establishment of the historical-critical method as the seemingly sole way of reading the scriptures, quickly derailed the kerygmatic way of handing on the faith. The Council sought to open the doors and windows of the church so as to let the Gospel out that the world might be "Christified," but, as can happen with such an opening, many read it as a sign that the church was finally "letting the world in." With the ramparts of post-Tridentine neo-scholasticism breached, the order of the day was to read the "signs of the times" in order to find what God might be saying through present history, to see God's revelation not only as addressed to human experience but as found within it. Catechetically, the second phase of the movement gave way to the third. Theologically and pastorally, the church had seemingly made an anthropological turn.

Much of this turn to experience is laudable, though some of it had

---

the church's emphasis on doctrine is ecclesial and communal as well. Doctrine helps to unite all Christians in the universal communion of the church, and it is, by nature, the expression of the faith of the church as it has been handed on in history by the Christians of earlier ages, helping us to stand in communion with them. A catechesis that was not doctrinal would therefore be decidedly uncommunal.

83. CT, no. 5 [6].

devastating effects on the church's mission and especially its desire to implement the teachings of the Council. The Synod of 1985 and the creation of the Catechism, then, surely add a new chapter to catechetical history, and, more recently, the papal call for a New Evangelization advances this history to the present. Yet, should these new "chapters" be read as an affirmation of preconciliar doctrinal catechesis and the kerygmatic phase while being a repudiation of the anthropological turn?

Such a claim would be superficial at best and would deny genuine aspects of the teaching of the Council, particularly those that, while not equating the church's faith with the experience of the modern world, sought to address this experience and even find seeds of the Gospel within it. So, too, should we remember that John Paul identified the Council's teaching as the source and inspiration of the New Evangelization. Because he aimed this New Evangelization at regions once evangelized that have lost a living sense of the faith, one of the "new" characteristics of this mission must undoubtedly be the cultural and social context of the people living in those places. What the practitioners of the third phase of the catechetical movement termed "anthropology" is, therefore, an essential consideration for the church's mission in the present age. The relationship between divine revelation and human experience—brought to light from the first moment of the church's emergence in the Roman Empire—once again becomes a paramount point of focus.

Chapter 2's analysis distinguished between two subsections of the third phase of the catechetical movement, the first concerning human experience in its individual, interior form and the second in its social form, with special attention to present history and the liberating praxis of communities. These coincided with chapter 1's analysis of the teaching of *Gaudium et Spes*, in which the Council sought to bring the Gospel to the experience of the modern world by appealing to the inner longings of the human person and to the "signs of the times." One of the conclusions from the study week at Medellín is emblematic of both elements of the third phase: "Contemporary catechesis, in agreement with a more adequate theology of revelation, recognizes in the historical situations and in authentic human aspirations, the first sign to which we must be attentive in order to discover the plan of God for the men of today. Such situations therefore are an indispensable part of the content of catechesis."[84]

This conclusion rightly assumes that both subsections of the third phase are linked. To speak of the signs of the times is not simply to refer to history in itself but history as viewed by human beings. The theological phrase *signa temporum* implies the voice of the age as heard by the people of that age, those who not only hear the *vox temporis* but give shape to it by their actions. Yet, this dynamic can have devastating consequences when the *vox temporis* is equated with the *vox dei*. The analysis of the first two chapters of this book revealed that this is precisely what happened in various sectors of the church, both theological and pastoral.

The danger in such a conception is that divine revelation loses its essence. No longer coming "from above" or "from the outside," it is discovered within. And when I find it within myself I soon become tempted to think my actions are necessarily a manifestation of it. *Vox temporis vox dei*. The voice of the age becomes the voice of God. To claim that God is already present in the horizon of human consciousness, as the catechetical movement eventually did, will necessarily lead to the claim that God is indiscriminately active in the actions of a given community.

With such a theology of revelation as the backdrop, catechists of the third phase began to critique older forms of catechesis, whether doctrinal or kerygmatic. Gabriel Moran's opposition to "a set of truths that are self-interpretive and are imposed from the outside" is characteristic of much of catechesis in the first two decades after the Council.[85] And, yet, if catechesis for the New Evangelization is to rightfully consider human experience in its interior and historical dimensions, how can the Council's true theology of revelation be practically applied to the ministry of the Word? *Catechesi Tradendae* offers rudiments of the solution that I hope to flesh out here.

In the first place, John Paul offers a general observation regarding this issue in a section of the document entitled "Catechesis and Life Experience." His words are strong in this regard:

---

84. Conclusion 11, from "General Conclusions of the International Study Week," in *Medellín Papers*, 217.

85. Moran, *Catechesis of Revelation*, 46.

It is useless to play off orthopraxis against orthodoxy: Christianity is insep-
arably both.... It is also quite useless to campaign for the abandonment of
serious and orderly study of the message of Christ in the name of a method concentrating on life experience.... Nor is any opposition to be set up
between a catechesis taking life as its point of departure and a traditional
doctrinal and systematic catechesis. Authentic catechesis is always an orderly
and systematic initiation into the revelation that God has given of himself to
humanity in Christ Jesus.... This revelation is not, however, isolated from life
or artificially juxtaposed to it. It is concerned with the ultimate meaning of
life, and it illumines the whole of life with the light of the Gospel, to inspire
it or to question it.[86]

The "uselessness" of such opposition is also apparent in other sections
of the document— for instance, when the pope recommends the creation of catechetical literature that can offer the faith in its integrity
while nevertheless being "linked with the real life of the generation to
which they are addressed" and speaking "a language comprehensible"
to that generation.[87]

Beyond these general yet forceful statements, John Paul offers a
more nuanced understanding of the meeting of revelation and experience in paragraph 29, one that corresponds with *Gaudium et Spes's*
genuine theology concerning the Gospel's ability to scrutinize human
experience. Recalling the analysis of chapter 1, this discerning illumination has a triple effect: the *via negationis*, the *via positionis*, and the *via
eminentiae*. John Paul begins with the second of these effects when he
claims that the catechist should be able to tell anyone the same words
Paul spoke at the Areopagus: "What you worship as unknown, this I
proclaim to you."[88] And yet this affirmation of experience does not
have the only word. It was, for Paul, the entryway for a proclamation of
Christ as the fulfillment of that experience, a fulfillment that surpassed
and challenged the expectations of his hearers by calling them to repent
and to embrace the resurrected Lord. John Paul makes this strategy his
own, explaining that "it is important to explain that the history of the
human race, marked as it is by grace and sin, greatness and misery, is

86. CT, no. 22 [19–20].
87. CT, no. 49 [41]. What John Paul applies here to generations he also applies to peoples,
nations, and races in CT, no. 8 [8], where he writes of Jesus being called the Teacher: "One can
understand why people of every kind, race, and nation have for 2000 years in all the languages
of the earth given him this title with veneration."
88. CT, no. 29 [24–25], citing Acts 17:23.

taken up by God in his Son Jesus."[89] The Gospel thus makes demands "that involve self-denial but also joy," a joy that can be experienced "as life in the world but lived in accordance with the beatitudes and called to an extension and transfiguration hereafter."[90] For the pope, the Gospel affirms genuine human experience, yes, but also negates what is sinful in it and raises what it affirms into the transcendence of God's own life.[91]

The same triplefold effect is present later in the document when John Paul considers the form the church's teaching must take when addressing people of different cultures.[92] For the pope, inculturation cannot simply be reduced to the translation of the Gospel into another language, though it should of course include this. Rather, catechesis must "seek to know these cultures and their essential components; it will learn their most significant expressions; it will respect their values and riches. In this manner it will be able to offer these cultures the knowledge of the hidden mystery and help them to bring forth from their own living tradition original expressions of Christian life, celebration, and thought."[93] At the same time, however, catechists should keep in mind two principles: first, the Gospel does not spontaneously spring from a given culture's soil. It is rooted in its first cultural milieu, that of Jesus of Nazareth, and is necessarily connected to the various cultures in which it has already been expressed throughout history. Catechesis, then, takes place within a certain dialogue of cultures that spans millennia. Second, "the power of the Gospel," John Paul reminds the church, "everywhere transforms and regenerates. When that power enters into a culture, it is no surprise that it rectifies many of its elements. There would be no catechesis if it were the Gospel that had

89. CT, no. 29 [25].

90. Ibid.

91. The same paragraph of the document concludes by noting that catechesis extends from this transfiguration of the person into social consequences as expressed in the church's social doctrine, thus addressing an important aspect of the renewal's third phase.

92. Note that culture, for John Paul, has more than geographical significance and is not limited to peoples of a certain language or place. Culture is not monolithic, and one place or group of people may participate in a number of cultures—for instance, youth culture, the culture of social media, etc. An extensive study on John Paul II's theology of culture is made by the late Francis E. George, in *Inculturation and Communion: Culture and Church in the Teaching of Pope John Paul II* (Rome: Urbaniana University Press, 1990).

93. CT, no. 53 [43].

to change when it came into contact with the cultures."[94] Following the true Teacher, catechesis must, in other words, "take flesh" in the various cultures of the catechized, though the effects of the Incarnation will similarly apply.[95] Sin will be rectified, and humanity will not only be embraced but lifted up to become a partaker of the divine nature.

It is precisely the Christocentricity of catechesis, then, that allows human experience to be appropriately integrated into the church's ministry of the Word. Like us in all things but sin, Jesus is the one who incorporates what is genuinely human into his person, purifying that humanity of things incompatible with his divine presence while providing the way for it to commune with God.[96] It is in this light that we can see how the practitioners of the third phase, by rejecting the second, had unwittingly cut off the branch upon which their own rightful concerns sat. Without a hermeneutic of tradition that embraces continuity on the fundamental level, one eventually separates oneself from the historical communion of the church's teaching, life, and worship. In this case, to use Hofinger's words, the movement had built a roof, but apart from the foundation and walls.

Near the end of chapter 2 I observed that modern catechetics has witnessed a recurring swing of the pendulum in which the ministry of the Word has oscillated between the content of the faith and its reception in human experience. For John Paul, both ends of the pendulum's arc are indeed important, but they find their union in the person of Jesus Christ. *Gaudium et Spes*, no. 22's affirmation that Christ is the revealer of God and the human person is the leitmotif of the pope's thought, is present in his teaching on catechesis, as well: Christ is "the Teacher who reveals God to man and man to himself, the Teacher who saves, sanctifies, and guides, who lives, who speaks, who rouses, moves, redresses, judges, forgives, and goes with us day by day on the path of history, the Teacher who comes and will come in glory."[97] Thus, the faith is not merely propositional or taught "from above," nor is it merely anthropological and discovered "from below." It is, at its heart, Christological, and through Christ it introduces persons into trinitarian com-

94. Ibid. John Paul applies the same principles to the use of popular devotions in catechesis in CT, no. 54.

95. CT, no. 53 [44].

96. See Heb 4:15.

97. CT, no. 9 [9].

munion. Jesus Christ is the one who reveals both God and humanity in his very being.

Catechesis and the Pedagogy of God

To conclude this chapter I would like to return to an important concept raised earlier that can help bring into greater relief what John Paul is suggesting here regarding the Christological meeting point of revelation and human experience in the Incarnation. Paragraph 58 of *Catechesi Tradendae* suggested that catechesis has a unique pedagogy because, within divine revelation, "God himself used a pedagogy that must continue to be a model for the pedagogy of faith."[98] A closer look at this pedagogy can, I believe, illuminate John Paul's vision of catechesis given previously.

Both the 1971 *General Catechetical Directory* and its 1997 revision, the *General Directory for Catechesis*, refer to this pedagogy of God as normative for catechesis.[99] Both documents build upon the claim of *Dei Verbum* that the books of the Old Testament, even before the coming of Christ, "show us authentic divine teaching [*paedagogiam*]."[100]

That God himself could claim a specific pedagogy is a remarkable idea, but it has its roots in the teaching of Paul and the theology of the fathers.[101] In Galatians, Paul uses the Greek word *paidagogos* to make a distinction between the Old Law and the coming of Christ:

Before faith came, we were held in custody under law, confined for the faith that was to be revealed. Consequently, the law was our disciplinarian [*paidagogos*] for Christ, that we might be justified by faith. But now that faith has come, we are no longer under a disciplinarian [*paidagogos*]. For through faith you are all children of God in Christ Jesus.[102]

In Paul's time a pedagogue was not, as we might suppose, a teacher but a disciplinarian—he was a guardian, often a trusted slave, who watched

---

98. CT, no. 58 [48].

99. See GCD, no. 33; and GDC, nos. 38, 112, 129, and 139–47.

100. DV, no. 15 [759].

101. Thomas Groome calls the idea "a rather amazing proposal, and, perhaps, [the GDC's] most memorable one." See Groome's "Total Catechesis/Religious Education: A Vison for Now and Always," in *Horizons and Hopes: The Future of Religious Education*, ed. Thomas H. Groome and Harold Daly Horell (Mahwah, N.J.: Paulist Press, 2003), 26.

102. Gal 3:23–25.

over sons while standing in the stead of the father of the household.[103] The pedagogue would lead the child to and from school (and therefore to and from education by teachers) but, ultimately, his role was to discipline the child until he reached the point of maturity. For Paul, therefore, the Law is the pedagogue who leads the People of God to the teacher, Jesus Christ; and by faith in Christ, one shares in his sonship, coming to full maturity and being made an heir to that which Christ is heir.[104] The Law, in this sense, is a preparation for the Gospel.

The fathers took this Pauline metaphor and applied it to the relationship of the church with the surrounding society and culture. In what ways could these surroundings also provide a preparation for the Gospel for the men and women of their time? And imitating Paul's own attempts to preach to the Gentiles, how could the church find *logoi spermatikoi* or *rationes seminales* in these surroundings that could allow for an effective preaching of Christ as their fulfillment?[105] Justin Martyr, in his *Second Apology*, wrote, "Everything that the philosophers and legislators discovered and expressed well, they accomplished through their discovery and contemplation of some part of the *Logos*"; likewise the writers, Stoics, poets, and historians of his time, "seeing, through [their] seminal participation in the Divine Word, what was related to it, spoke very well.... The truths which men in all lands have rightly spoken belong to us Christians."[106] Clement of Alexandria, citing the Pauline passage from Galatians noted earlier, adds, "Perchance, too, philosophy was given to the Greeks directly and primarily, till the Lord should call the Greeks. For this was a schoolmaster to bring 'the Hellenic mind,' as the law [for] the Hebrews, 'to Christ.'"[107]

---

103. See Richard N. Longenecker, "The Pedagogical Nature of the Law in Galatians 3:19–4:7," *Journal of the Evangelical Theological Society* 25, no. 1 (1982): 53–61; David J. Lull, "'The Law Was Our Pedagogue': A Study in Galatians 3:19–25," *Journal of Biblical Literature* 105, no. 3 (1986): 481–98; Norman H. Young, "*Paidagogos*: The Social Setting of a Pauline Metaphor," *Novum Testamentum* 29, no. 2 (1987): 150–76; and Michael J. Smith, "The Role of the Pedagogue in Galatians," *Bibliotheca Sacra* 163, no. 650 (2006): 197–214.

104. See Eph 4:15–16.

105. In addition to Paul's famous speech in Acts 17:22–31 at the Areopagus, Paul and Barnabas make a similar but smaller speech at Lystra in Acts 14:15–17.

106. St. Justin Martyr, *Second Apology* 10 and 13, in *The Fathers of the Church*, vol. 6, *The Works of Saint Justin Martyr*, trans. Thomas B. Falls (Washington, D.C.: The Catholic University of America Press, 1948), 129 and 133–34, respectively. However, in chapter 13 [133], Justin cautions that the teachings of the philosophers and those of Christ are "not in every way similar."

107. Clement of Alexandria, *Stromata* 1.5, in *The Ante-Nicene Fathers*, vol. 2, *Fathers of the Second Century*, trans. W. L. Alexander (New York: Charles Scribner's Sons, 1905), 305. Along with

Latent in this Patristic theology of the "seeds of the Word" is the theology of revelation put forth in *Gaudium et Spes* regarding the proper discernment of the signs of the times. To recall a significant passage from that document already highlighted in chapter 1, the church:

profits from the experience of past ages, from the progress of the sciences, and from the riches hidden in various cultures, through which greater light is thrown on the nature of man and new avenues to truth are opened up. The Church learned early in its history to express the Christian message in the concepts and language of different peoples and tried to clarify it in the light of the wisdom of their philosophers: it was an attempt to adapt the Gospel to the understanding of all men and the requirements of the learned, insofar as this could be done. Indeed, this kind of adaptation and preaching of the revealed Word must ever be the law of all evangelization.[108]

As we have already seen, it would be incorrect to take this type of "adaptation" to be a mere translation of the Gospel into the "language" of another culture. As the previous analysis of the Council's theology of revelation has shown, the discernment of the signs of the times is a part of tradition's ongoing development, where realities that are true, good, and beautiful, while at first outside the church's walls, are received and brought within, becoming a part of its treasury of faith. It is the church's way of participating in God's own pedagogy whereby he reveals himself to his people gradually, accommodating this revelation to their present experience and current state, while always providing the way forward for further "maturation" in understanding his identity and plan of salvation.[109] There is, of course, a necessary distinction between the pedagogy of scripture of which Paul speaks—for scripture is the inspired Word of God—and the pedagogy that the church now practices in reading the signs of the times, yet both find their unity in the way God concretely works in the one *narratio* of salvation history.

Irenaeus's *Adversus Haereses*, Clement's trilogy of *Protrepticus*, *Paedagogus*, and *Stromata* is foundational for understanding the patristic concept of the divine pedagogy.

108. GS, no. 44 [946]. See the section "Signs of the Times" in chapter 1 of this volume.

109. This aspect of the divine pedagogy is summarized well in GDC, no. 139 [137], when it states that God "assumes the character of the person, the individual, and the community according to the conditions in which they are found. He liberates the person from the bonds of evil and attracts him to himself by bonds of love. He causes the person to grow progressively and patiently towards the maturity of a free son, faithful and obedient to his word. To this end, as a creative and insightful teacher, God transforms events in the life of his people into lessons of wisdom, adapting himself to the diverse ages and life situations."

The church now, as in every age, is charged with the task of discerning God's speaking and acting in the world, and, in doing so, it becomes the mediator of this speaking and acting. It is the great "sacrament of salvation," as *Lumen Gentium* put it.[110] There is a monumental union in the Council's thought, therefore, in which the traditional and ever-demanding inquiry into the sacramental relationship between nature and grace is integrated with the modern concern of history and its cultural manifestations. As John O'Malley explains, "The persistent Catholic impulse to reconcile 'nature and grace' is, when raised to the level of social institutions, an impulse to reconcile the Church with human culture in all its positive dimensions—with sin excepted and the gospel affirmed."[111]

As the receiving subject of revelation, the church uses the deposit it has already received to discern present realities, incorporating what is authentically human, correcting what is sinful and errant, and showing forth the ultimate fulfillment of all that is good in Jesus Christ. By this discernment, not only does tradition make progress incrementally, as the Council put it, but the church also walks the path of evangelization, one that proclaims the Gospel as affirming, purifying, and fulfilling Good News.

Evangelizers—lay, religious, and ordained—therefore have a significant role to play in the advance of the Gospel. They must be astute observers of the culture, even as they live in it and are affected by its soil. Simultaneously, they must be thoroughly inhabited by the Gospel, constantly meditating on the Word of God as found in scripture and church teaching and putting that word into action in their lives. The balance is difficult, for it is all too easy to denounce the world in favor of the church or to ignore the church in favor of the world. Yet, as Cardinal George explained:

Our culture is as much in us as we are in it. Religious critics of the culture can imagine a bad system opposed by good people. But that distinction is too easy. If our social system and culture are at least in part evangelically deficient or corrupt, so are we all. The evangelizer begins by taking responsibility for the culture that has to be evangelized. But separating the good from the bad in a culture's values and way of life, its institutional patterns, its goals and ac-

110. LG, no. 48 [407].
111. O'Malley, "Developments, Reforms, and Two Great Reformations," 406.

complishments demands a principle of discernment. What is good and what is bad? And when the Catholic looks for such a principle, he or she reaches for the gospel as interpreted by the faith of the Church.[112]

The pedagogy of God allows for no oversimplified dichotomies. It is an incremental path in which the light of the church's faith affirms, negates, and fulfills the experience of the world. In John Paul II's words, "The presentation of Jesus Christ as the only Savior needs to follow a *pedagogy* which will introduce people step by step to the full appropriation of the mystery."[113] The consequence of this divine pedagogy for evangelization is:

a continuous, permanent conversion which, while requiring an interior detachment from every evil and an adherence to good in its fullness, is brought about concretely in steps which lead us ever forward.... Therefore an educational growth process is necessary, in order that individual believers, families, and peoples, even civilization itself, by beginning from what they have already received of the mystery of Christ, may patiently be led forward, arriving at a richer understanding of this mystery in their lives.[114]

Such a theology of revelation put forth by the Council and affirmed here in the New Evangelization recognizes the necessary interplay of divine revelation and human experience. But what I would also like to point out, as O'Malley suggests, is the significance of grounding this conciliar approach to history and culture in the ontological realties of nature and grace. Even in the dynamic movements of history, the sacramental structure of revelation remains—history always remains rooted to the ontology of creation, and salvation history likewise.

A helpful way of approaching this ontology is by examining it through the lens of the divine pedagogy as manifested in Christ's own teaching. In particular, I have in mind his use of parables.

112. See Francis Cardinal George, "Evangelizing Our Culture," in *The New Evangelization: Overcoming the Obstacles*, ed. Steven Boguslawski and Ralph Martin (New York: Paulist Press, 2008), 44–45.

113. John Paul II, *Ecclesia in Asia*, no. 20, Vatican, http://www.vatican.va/holy_father/john_paul_ii/apost_exhortations/documents/hf_jp-ii_exh_06111999_ecclesia-in-asia_en.html. AAS 92 (2000): 449–528. Emphasis in the original. The entire paragraph is an extended reflection on the divine pedagogy and its application to the evangelization of Asia.

114. *FC*, no. 9 [20–21]. See also no. 8 [19]: "The whole Church is obliged to a deep reflection and commitment, so that the new culture now emerging may be evangelized in depth, true values acknowledged, the rights of men and women defended, and justice promoted in the very structures of society. In this way the 'new humanism' will not distract people from their relationship with God, but will lead them to it more fully."

In the story of his conversion, John Henry Newman wrote of his encounter with the works of Clement and Origen, where he came to the realization that "the exterior world, physical and historical, [is] but the manifestation to our senses of realities greater than itself. Nature [is] a parable."[115] In a parable, a teacher enters into human experience in order to affirm it, subvert it, and harness it to convey a message that extends beyond it. Parables are effective pedagogy precisely because of the sacramental structure of reality.

Along the same lines, John Paul II's own consideration of the divine pedagogy as seen in the teaching of Jesus highlights its parabolic nature:

Catechesis poses some problems of pedagogy. From the Gospel texts we know even Jesus had to face them. In his preaching to the crowds he used parables to communicate his teaching in a way that suited the intelligence of his listeners. In teaching his disciples he proceeded gradually, taking into account the difficulty they had in understanding.... We note also that, in his most detailed dialogues, he communicated his revelation by answering the questions of his listeners and using language their mentality easily understood.[116]

Parables are representative of the law of evangelization precisely because of their ability to show the interplay of the worldly and the transcendent, of nature and grace. Likewise, they are an icon that provides insight into the way the church can harness human experience, correcting what is sinful and affirming what is good, incrementally moving people more deeply into the mystery of God.

Joseph Ratzinger also meditated upon this ability of the parable to mediate revelation to human experience. For Ratzinger, too, the parable was the very structure of revelation.[117] In mediating revelation, he explained, parables have a tripartite function:

[First], they transcend the realm of creation in order, by this transcendence, to draw it above itself to the Creator. [Second], they accept the past historical

---

115. John Henry Newman, *Apologia Pro Vita Sua* (London: Longman, Green, 1908), 27.
116. John Paul II, *God, Father and Creator*, 21.
117. See Ratzinger, *Principles of Catholic Theology*, 344: "Jesus taught consistently in the form of parables—and the parable was obviously not, in this case, just a pedagogical trick that could be eliminated without loss. In his farewell words, Jesus states explicitly that the parable was the way in which knowledge of the faith is to be realized in this world (Jn 16:25); in the Synoptics, too, the parable appears as the structure by which access is to be had to the mystery of the kingdom of God (Mk 4:10–11)."

experience of faith, that is, they prolong the parables that have grown up with the history of Israel. We should, perhaps, add here a third point: they also interpret the simple world of everyday life in order to show how a transcendence to what is more than human stereotype occurs in it. On the one hand, the content of the faith reveals itself only in parables, but, on the other hand, the parable makes clear the core of reality itself. This is possible because reality itself is a parable. Hence, it is only by way of parable that the nature of the world and of man himself is made known to us.[118]

Thus, the parable is the pedagogical extension of reality's sacramental structure. Parables unite revelation with human experience in order to bear fruit in conversion. Jesus used them precisely for this reason, at once telling the crowds to recall their experience of losing a coin or a sheep, or even to place themselves in the role of a servant who comes home from a hard day's work only to have to serve a meal to his master.[119] Taking this last teaching as an example, it is evident that Jesus uses such experience as a doorway to a greater mystery. The lesson of this encounter on its lowest level is that servants are obliged to obey their masters, even when a nod of thanks is withheld. But in Jesus' teaching it is clear that experience must be transcended, at times even exploded, to convey a deeper truth yet. Parables use experience to convey something that is greater than experience. Thus, a lesson on another level emerges: though a Christian is exhausted by the strains of ministry, he or she must continue to serve without need of acknowledgment, for love demands as much.

But even in this new level Jesus' lesson is not complete. In the fullness of revelation that is himself, there is an ever greater "more," a transcendence that will always call men and women through the heart of their experience to a continual conversion that exceeds a person's capacities and history.[120] Thus, at the end of his life, Jesus would be the one to don the clothes of the servant, and in offering himself, he would provide a meal and even wash the feet of those who imagined themselves to be at his beck and call. He would become the most perfect revelation of obedience and self-gift. It is precisely in the locus of the

118. Ibid.

119. See Lk 15:8–10, Mt 28:12–14, and Lk 17:7–10, respectively.

120. Ratzinger relates this "more" to St. Ignatius's *Deus semper maius*. See Ratzinger, *Principles of Catholic Theology*, 345. Though I have no evidence of their collaboration on the matter (though it clearly happened quite often), John Paul's catechesis in *God, Father and Creator*, 21–22, parallels the flow of Ratzinger's argument.

earthy, temporal, sometimes joyful, sometimes sorrowful experience of life that one learns that truth is greater than experience, even as it embraces it.

This ever greater "more" of revelation raises three final points. First, the church would do well to reexamine the transition between the second and third phases of the catechetical movement. At Bangkok, those gathered for the study week found in the lesson of the early church's catechumenate the need for what they termed "pre-evangelization." Based on the precatechumenal period in which inquirers first encountered the church (most likely through Christians in their community), the significance of this term is found in the fact that, while acknowledging human experience, it does not yet equate it with the Gospel.[121]

While, as Edward Yarnold notes, "we have little indication how this period was conducted in the early church," patristic texts offer some important clues as to how differing inquirers came upon the church.[122] In the fourth century, for instance, Cyril speaks of "a man . . . wishing to pay court to a [Christian] woman, and on that account come hither; and the same applies to women likewise; again, a slave often wishes thus to please his master, or one friend another."[123] In the following century, Augustine writes of those who approach the church by means of signs or personal revelation, as a "result of a warning or dread inspired from

121. A major influence at Bangkok, Alfonso Nebrada helped initiate the move to the third stage of renewal. Yet he recognized the inherent dangers. See Nebrada, "Some Reflections," 95: "It would be distressing if, by the all-too-natural law of the pendulum, we swung too wide to another extreme. It is one thing to move now from the unacceptable past tendency of insisting on indoctrination and teaching of 'Christian truths' as the main task of religious education. It is another matter to go to the opposite pole of watering things down to the point of declaring ourselves satisfied with stressing human experience and human values under the claim that objectively they are Christian anyhow and there is thus no need to spell out their Christian specificity or explore its full-blossomed Christian implications. . . . It is one thing not to separate; quite another thing altogether is to identify to the point of confusion."

122. Yarnold, *Awe-Inspiring Rites of Initiation*, 2.

123. *Protocatechesis* 5, as found in St. Cyril of Jerusalem, *Lectures on the Christian Sacraments*, trans. R. W. Church, ed. F. L. Cross (Crestwood, N.Y.: St. Vladimir's Seminary Press, 1977), 43. Cyril masterfully uses the Matthean parable of the man caught improperly dressed for the wedding feast to stir the consciences of the candidates, whatever their motivations. On his use of this parable and Cyril's other ways of using the scriptures, see Pamela Jackson, "Cyril's Use of Scripture in Catechesis," *Theological Studies* 52, no. 3 (1991): 431–50. Along with EG, nos. 135–59, and the USCCB's recent document on preaching (Committee on Clergy, Consecrated Life, and Vocations, *Preaching the Mystery of Faith: The Sunday Homily* [Washington, D.C.: United States Conference of Catholic Bishops, 2012]), Jackson's article provides excellent food for thought for the study of homiletics.

on high," and still others who learned of Christianity from their education, being "moved to that decision by books, whether the canonical Scriptures or those of good writers."[124] In all cases, it was the "stuff" of the inquirers' human experience—relationships, truths acquired, even inner movements of the soul—that eventually cried out for fulfillment in the communion of the church.

Such varied experiences serve to remind the church today that pre-evangelization is an important if all too often forgotten stage of preaching the Gospel.[125] The precatechumenate exemplifies its significance. Before Christ is preached or accepted, evangelizers must discern the seeds of the Word present in their communities, seeds that can eventually grow to full maturity in the church. Such seeds become the vehicle for the preaching of the kerygma.[126]

This also means that, in pre-evangelization, the lay faithful have an irreplaceable role to play. For quite often it is the witness of Christians, those who are a part of the same cultures and communities as the unevangelized, that becomes the initial locus of sacramental revelation.[127] And even when inquirers approach the church by other means,

124. Augustine, *De Catechizandis Rudibus* 6.10 and 8.12, respectively, as found in *First Catechetical Instruction*, 26 and 30–31. One gets the sense that Augustine speaks from personal experience on both counts.

125. Sherry Weddell's *Forming Intentional Disciples: The Path to Knowing and Following Jesus* (Huntington, Ind.: Our Sunday Visitor, 2012) is a helpful pastoral guide to the steps leading to the proclamation of the kerygma and its acceptance, and it is becoming increasingly recognized by dioceses in the United States and beyond. Weddell describes the stages of evangelization as trust, curiosity, openness, seeking, and intentional discipleship.

126. See George, "Evangelizing Our Culture," 45.

127. See EN, no. 21 [164–65]: "Above all the Gospel must be proclaimed by witness. Take a Christian or a handful of Christians who, in the midst of their own community, show their capacity for understanding and acceptance, their sharing of life and destiny with other people, their solidarity with the efforts of all for whatever is noble and good. Let us suppose that, in addition, they radiate in an altogether simple and unaffected way their faith in values that go beyond current values, and their hope in something that is not seen and that one would not dare to imagine. Through this wordless witness these Christians stir up irresistible questions in the hearts of those who see how they live: Why are they like this? Why do they live in this way? What or who is it that inspires them? Why are they in our midst? Such a witness is already a silent proclamation of the Good News and a very powerful and effective one. Here we have an initial act of evangelization. The above questions will ask, whether they are people to whom Christ has never been proclaimed, or baptized people who do not practice, or people who live as nominal Christians but according to principles that are in no way Christian, or people who are seeking, and not without suffering, something or someone whom they sense but cannot name. Other questions will arise, deeper and more demanding ones, questions evoked by this witness which involves presence, sharing, solidarity, and which is an essential element, and generally the first one, in evangelization"; and no. 70 [187]: "Lay people, whose particular

their conversion will eventually demand communion with members of Christ's Body who witness to the truth of the Gospel by their lives.[128]

Second, the *semper maius* of the pedagogy of God demands the self-gift of faith as its corollary. If self-gift is the corresponding response to God's gradual self-revelation, then it, too, must grow in stages. Faith is simultaneously a human act and a gift of the Holy Spirit, and as a virtue, it continually grows according to the openness one has to the Spirit's workings.[129] At the initial stages of one's encounter with God's reveal-ing Word, self-gift will look different than it will in the later stages of mature discipleship. This act of faith calls upon both the intellect and the will, indeed the entire person. As the church incrementally takes in what is authentically human, hearers of the word must repeatedly give themselves over to the God who reveals himself. For, the only way we can move beyond our own experience—the only way one can grow in the true sense of conversion—is by encountering that which is an "oth-er" and giving oneself over to it. In the New Testament, conversion, or *metanoia*, literally means to go beyond or above one's mind. Conversion requires the crossing of the threshold of our subjectivity in love. And love, Wojtyła/John Paul II has shown, is always preceded by a perception

vocation places them in the midst of the world and in charge of the most varied temporal tasks, must for this very reason exercise a very special form of evangelization. Their primary and im-mediate task is not to establish and develop the ecclesial community—this is the specific role of the pastors—but to put to use every Christian and evangelical possibility latent but already present and active in the affairs of the world."

128. See Roch Kereszty, "'*Sacrosancta Ecclesia*': The Holy Church of Sinners," *Communio* 40, no. 4 (2013): 676–78: "If we interview those who have found Christ, we discover, in a great vari-ety of ways, some form of ecclesial mediation. Even those who had come to Christ by a spiritual experience apart from any visible ecclesial setting began to search afterward for a Christian community where they could find the Christ whom they had encountered in a private experi-ence. . . . In other cases, the encounter with holy Christians gave the first impetus to the process of conversion. For instance, searching for God or for some ultimate meaning in their lives, they met a person or a community that radiated goodness, peace, joy, and a readiness to forgive and love. Such an encounter has the potential to draw the one searching to discover the 'secret' that makes such a life possible. . . . Thus, in both types of conversion outlined above we find two kinds of causes, an inner and an external one: the inward experience of grace and a visible en-counter with the Church through some of her members or her communities. In each encounter with the Church it is essential that the searchers find Christ present in that Church member or Church community. In other words, the searchers must encounter the holy Church."

129. See DV, no. 5 [752], where the Council teaches that the same Spirit who gives the person faith, also "constantly perfects faith by his gifts." See also CCC, no. 1253 [319]: "The faith required for Baptism is not a perfect and mature faith, but a beginning that is called to develop"; and no. 1254 [320]: "For all the baptized, children or adults, faith must grow *after* Baptism" (emphasis in the original).

of truth. Teaching the faith, as in all teaching endeavors, is most fully effective when it brings the hearer to the frontier that extends beyond the borders of his or her previous experience. An encounter with truth always brings the hearer to this threshold—to the very point of decision.

This is where, I believe, one can see one of the most lasting contributions John Paul II makes to the church's mission in the New Evangelization—the significance of *self-gift*. Here, his thought can inform the ministry of the Word both in its academic and pastoral settings. Even with the unfortunate split between spiritual and moral theology, the value of this contribution remains: self-gift is the height of *ex-tasis* that brings a soul into communion with God; the conscious act of virtue (the form of which is love) is one that fulfills the person and, in this sense, the more one gives oneself away the more one finds oneself.[130] It informs fundamental theology in its examination of revelation as self-gift and faith as a returning gift of the human person. It informs systematic and dogmatic theology in showing a foundational link between anthropology and Christology, reaching even further to trinitarian theology at its roots.

This contribution is summed up by and in fact is the re-echoing of Christ's unique teaching: "Whoever wishes to come after me must deny himself, take up his cross, and follow me. For whoever wishes to save his life will lose it, but whoever loses his life for my sake will find it."[131]

All education, in the real sense, must call upon this unique role played by self-gift: the student must give him- or herself to a new reality to truly grow in mind and spirit. There is always, to quote the title of a book by Luigi Giussani, a "risk" involved.[132] In terms of catechesis, the ultimate risk is not merely to give oneself over to a doctrine—though doctrine is indeed necessary—but to give oneself over to the One who reveals himself through doctrine and, indeed, through every aspect of the church. It is to give oneself over to Jesus Christ, who gave himself for us.

---

130. Thus, though John Paul never propounds his own understanding of virtue ethics in any comprehensive fashion, it is clear that it undergirds his anthropology.

131. Mt 16:24–25.

132. Luigi Giussani, *The Risk of Education: Discovering Our Ultimate Destiny*, trans. Rosanna M. Giammanco Frongia (New York: Crossroad, 2001). For Giussani, the risk is on the side of the educator who must, at the appropriate time, allow the student to choose in freedom. But I believe this risk has a corresponding form on the side of the student who must now, in freedom, consciously choose (or disown) the meaning of reality that is offered by the teacher.

Thus, the incremental nature of the divine pedagogy draws upon the sacramental nature of reality and its ability to mediate revelation, yet it also calls upon the moral formation of human beings through its call to give oneself over to the good in greater and greater ways. In ancient times, the pedagogue was a disciplinarian more than a teacher, and the educational notion of *paideia*—whether in its pagan or Christian form—meant a formation of the entire person through not only knowledge but *practice* so as to incorporate that person fully into a community. Catechesis, then, must take the form of an integral initiation and apprenticeship in the Christian life.[133]

This *paideia* and the progressive growth it fosters are captured in the tradition of the church known as the baptismal catechumenate, the ancient practice renewed by the Second Vatican Council, in which adult converts are received into the church by stages.[134] The catechumenate manifests this gradual nature of the divine pedagogy through its stages of pre-evangelization, proclamation, and initial inquiry; acceptance and catechetical instruction; more focused instruction, prayer, and fasting; initiation into the church through the sacraments; and post-baptismal reflection on the sacraments, known as *mystagogy*.[135]

The catechumenate as practiced by the early church was global in scope—at the same time communal, experiential, scriptural, liturgical,

133. This notion of practice and its formative power, fundamental to the patristic and medieval understanding of virtue, has only recently found renewal in Christian formation, both Catholic and Protestant. For its role in Catholic ministry, see Robert Barron, *The Strangest Way: Walking the Christian Path* (Maryknoll, N.Y.: Orbis, 2002), and James C. Pauley, *Liturgical Catechesis in the 21st Century: A School of Discipleship* (Chicago: Liturgy, 2017). From the Reformed tradition, see James K. A. Smith, *Desiring the Kingdom: Worship, Worldview, and Cultural Formation* (Grand Rapids, Mich.: Baker Academic, 2009), and the same argument in more popular form, *You Are What You Love: The Spiritual Power of Habit* (Grand Rapids, Mich.: Brazos, 2016).

134. See *Sacrosanctum Concilium*, no. 64. In the United States, the revised Rite of Christian Initiation of Adults is the fruit of this conciliar reform. See *Rite of Christian Initiation of Adults*, study ed. (Collegeville: Minn.: Liturgical Press, 1985).

135. We know of the various stages especially through the writings of the fourth-century bishops Cyril of Jerusalem, Ambrose of Milan, Theodore of Mopsuestia, and John Chrysostom. A helpful introduction to these writings is found in Yarnold's *Awe-Inspiring Rites of Initiation*. It should be noted that mystagogy, while referring to the specific form of post-initiation catechesis, can also refer to the entire catechumenal process as an "initiation into the mysteries," as its etymology suggests. On this, see Enrico Mazza, *Mystagogy: A Theology of Liturgy in the Patristic Age*, trans. Matthew J. O'Connell (New York: Pueblo, 1989), 1–2. Mazza's work is an intriguing study of mystagogy as a form of liturgical theology. Especially important are his insights into the typological connections between the scriptures and the sacraments as found in the mystagogues noted previously.

and doctrinal.[136] Its source was the faith of the church and its end, the living faith, rooted in the sacraments, of the newly initiated Christian. As such, at the 1977 Synod of Bishops, the synod from which *Catechesi Tradendae* would emerge, the bishops proposed that the catechumenate become the "model for all catechesis," a proposal likewise taken up by the *General Directory for Catechesis*.[137] Such a suggestion seems to be well-suited for the mission of the New Evangelization, in which many baptized Christians bear a strong resemblance to the unbaptized.[138]

The key to heeding the directory's suggestion lies not in fitting every ministerial endeavor into the catechumenate's stages,[139] but in following its way of seeing catechesis as a "process of formation" and "true school of faith."[140] In *Evangelii Gaudium*, Pope Francis also reflects upon this type of formation and urges the church to return to a mystagogical form of catechesis, one marked by two things: "a progressive experience of formation involving the entire community and a renewed appreciation of the liturgical signs of Christian initiation."[141] Such a formation facilitates "insertion into a broader growth process and the integration of every dimension of the person within a communal journey of hearing and response."[142] Such growth is both intellectual and volitional: it involves the self-gift of the person to greater knowledge of the truth and to practices that form one in the virtues and habits necessary

---

136. Aidan Kavanagh offered one of the most vivid portrayals of the early church's catechumenate in a story he told as part of a lecture he delivered at Holy Cross Abbey in Colorado in 1977. It is reprinted as "Appendix: Part One: A Rite of Passage," in Gabe Huck, *The Three Days: Parish Prayer in the Paschal Tradition*, rev. ed. (Chicago: Liturgy, 1981), 171–75.

137. See the Synod Fathers' *Message to the People of God*, no. 7, reprinted as "Message to the People of God," *Living Light* 15 (1978): 91; and GDC, no. 59.

138. Whereas prior to the legalization of Christianity, initial conversion may have preceded baptism, afterward, the catechumenate became one of the primary means of conversion. See Paul F. Bradshaw, *The Search for the Origins of Christian Worship: Sources and Methods for the Study of Early Liturgy*, 2nd ed. (Oxford: Oxford University Press, 2002), 218–19.

139. See GDC, no. 91. Among the scholars who emphasize this point are Catherine Dooley, "Liturgical Catechesis: Mystagogy, Marriage or Misnomer?," *Worship* 66, no. 5 (1992): 386–97, and "Baptismal Catechumenate: Model for All Catechesis," *Louvain Studies* 23, no. 2 (1998): 114–23; Veronica Rosier, "The Baptismal Catechumenate in the *General Directory for Catechesis* (1997)," *Worship* 73 (1999): 98–124; and Mary Ann Clarahan, "Mystagogy and Mystery," *Worship* 83, no. 6 (2009): 502–23.

140. GDC, no. 91 [83–84]. In the same paragraph, the Directory explains what it means by calling the catechumenate a school of faith: its "comprehensiveness and integrity of formation; its gradual character expressed in definitive stages; its connection with meaningful rites, symbols, biblical, and liturgical signs; its constant references to the Christian community."

141. EG, no. 166 [118].

142. Ibid.

for mature Christian life. In short, a catechesis based on self-gift is a pedagogy, in the most classic sense of the word.

The first two conclusions have shown that the incremental nature of the divine pedagogy applies both to the nature of revelation and to the self-gift of faith, with both demanding that a person give him- or herself to truth and goodness that always surpass the experience of the person. The third and final conclusion brings us to the reason this must be so, to the archetype of revelation and self-gift. It brings us to Jesus Christ, who is *Logos* made flesh, truth and love incarnate, or as John says, "the way, the truth, and the life."[143] Christ is, as Paul taught, the end or *telos* of the divine pedagogy, and, as good metaphysics shows, the end determines the nature of a given reality. When the disciples on the road to Emmaus expressed their experience in all its joy and sadness, the hidden Christ drew their attention to the already received revelation of the community of faith, allowing it to correct their experience and to unveil the ways in which he had been present, in seed, within it the entire time. Yet it was only when they encountered him in the fullness of his resurrected glory in the Eucharist that their experience was most fully purified and transfigured and the faith handed on in their community's tradition enlivened.[144]

John Paul contextualizes catechesis within a Christocentric vision because Jesus is the true Teacher and the truth that is taught. In this time of the New Evangelization, the church must return to Christ in order to properly "place the roof upon the walls." The great work of the catechetical reformers is only properly seen by his light. Doctrine must be grounded in his person to reclaim its life-giving role in the church's ministry; he must be proclaimed as the fulfillment of God's plan and as the incarnation of divine love for all of humanity; and the light of his Incarnation and Paschal Mystery becomes the path by which the church can draw all that is good in human experience to itself. Only by looking to him can the church take what is best from all three phases of the catechetical movement, and only in communion with and fidelity to him can it truly accomplish its mission during this time of the New Evangelization.

---

143. Jn 14:6.
144. See Lk 24:13–35.

Conclusion

Truth and Love: Jesus Christ, Revealer of God and the Human Person

In our time, truth is often mistaken for the opinion of the majority. In addition, there is a widespread belief that one should use the truth even against love or vice versa. But truth and love need each other.... Do not accept anything as the truth if it lacks love. And do not accept anything as love which lacks truth!

Pope John Paul II, Canonization of Edith Stein, 1998

Jesus Christ is the answer to the question posed by every human life.

Pope John Paul II, Apostolic Journey to the United States, 1995

The central claim that guides the previous chapters has been that the anthropology of Karol Wojtyła/Pope John Paul II provides a sound theological and philosophical foundation for catechesis in the New Evangelization—that it provides a Christological way of understanding the union of divine revelation with human experience that can both correct and develop the work of the modern catechetical movement in a way that accords with the teaching of the Second Vatican Council. In order to prove this claim, chapter 1 explored the teaching of the Council on revelation and human experience with the purpose of formulating norms by which to measure the achievements of the catechetical renewal. Chapter 2 then traced the history of the renewal, noting its accomplishments as well as its weaknesses, especially the lack of integration of the third and final stage with the previous stages. Chapters 3 and 4 examined Wojtyła/John Paul II's philosophical and theological understandings of the person, drawing upon his own interpretation of the Council in order to show a way forward for catechesis in the postconciliar era. Finally, Chapter 5 proposed a reading of *Catechesi Tradendae* that could more fully illuminate the way in which the late pope's anthropology can effectively integrate the best insights of the catechetical movement while developing the ministry to be more effective for the New Evangelization.

I would like to end by returning to where this book began, with reflections on the nature of the Christian faith as a unity of truth and love, though this time in light of John Paul's Christocentric anthropology. For the late pope, the dichotomy between the truths of the faith and experience is overcome by recognizing the necessity of the union of both truth and love for the fulfillment of the human person. Christ himself, of course, embodies this union perfectly—he is the loving self-gift of the Father, and he is *Logos* made flesh. And yet, as one commentator explains, "Life and dogma are convertible only in Christ, in whom sovereign truth and life coincide."[1] For human persons, truth retains a certain priority in the order of action.[2] John Paul's exploration of human experience shows this clearly: by entering into the very subjectivity of experience, one discovers that all genuine human praxis is first initiated by a surrender to truth.

And yet, though knowledge precedes love, it nevertheless needs love to bear fruit in human life and in the world. *Logos* must always become flesh, and the truth must always become a way. That is the only

---

1. Romanus Cessario, "*Duplex Ordo Cognitionis*," in *Reason and the Reasons of Faith*, ed. Paul J. Griffiths and Reinhard Hütter (New York: T. and T. Clark, 2005), 337. See also FR, no. 15 [26]: "The truth made known to us by revelation is neither the product nor the consummation of an argument devised by human reason. It appears instead as something gratuitous, which itself stirs thought and seeks acceptance as an expression of love."

2. Cessario, "*Duplex Ordo*," 337–38: "Even in the saints, the difference obtains between sovereign truth and the need for conformity to that sovereign truth. Dogma articulates divine truth that *ought* to be the foundation for holy lives" (emphasis in the original). See also the reflections of Cardinal Ratzinger in his "Eucharist, Solidarity, and Communion, 2 June 2002," Vatican, http://www.vatican.va/roman_curia/congregations/cfaith/documents/rc_con_cfaith_doc_20020602_ratzinger-eucharistic-congress_en.html.

way the person reaches the perfection for which he or she is intended. "Faith finds its fullness of life," the pope explained, "in love. It is in love that the confident surrender to God acquires its proper character."[3] This key to John Paul's anthropology was also a key to his interpretation of the Council:

The essence of faith resides not only in knowledge, but also in the vocation, in the call.... It is not simply hearing the Word and listening to it (in the sense of obeying it): it also means responding to a call, to a sort of historical and eschatological "Follow me!" uttered both on earth and in heaven. To my mind, one must be very conscious of this relation between knowledge and vocation inherent in the very essence of faith if one is to decipher correctly the extremely rich message of Vatican II.[4]

Jesus Christ, as the fullness of revelation, is the truth that fulfills the desires of the human person, and he is the love that embodies the person's perfection—only in union with him can we give of ourselves to the fullest extent. United to him, we enter into his simultaneous self-gift to the Father and to all of humanity, allowing us to love God and neighbor in ways that transcend our own means.

The primacy of Jesus Christ, therefore, is the foundation of John Paul II's anthropology, and, as such, his anthropology is Christocentric to its core. For John Paul, the encounter with the person of Christ is the only seed from which the life of the church can grow. Efforts to hand on the faith since the Council for too long have stressed either the teachings of the faith *or* the experience of human persons, accepting one to the detriment of the other. To overemphasize the truths of the faith without attention to their reception by men and women in need of evangelization is to become a "resounding gong," as Paul put it.[5] It is a form of the fortress Catholicism that the Council wished to do away with, for the deposit of the church's faith is not a treasury meant to be stored for safe-keeping; its riches are meant to be received by the world as the fulfillment of all authentic human hopes and desires. Similarly, to capitulate to the experience of the world in hopes of making the Gospel more palatable to modern men and women is to domesticate the message of Jesus Christ, rendering it incapable of moving hearts to conversion.

3. Frossard and John Paul II, "*Be Not Afraid!*," 63.
4. Ibid., 65.
5. 1 Cor 13:1.

Evangelization is not a matter of picking sides, either the truths of the faith or the present experience of men and women. To use an image that emerged from the 2014 Synod of Bishops, the church is both a lighthouse and a torch.[6] That the church is like a lighthouse reminds us that the faith of the church is a sure guide in the midst of life, for it is fixed on the rock that is Christ. Even in the throes of life's storms, the lighthouse's beacon can act as a guide for all men and women. The proclamation of the faith must be a reflection of the light of Christ, one that symbolizes the place where all can find refuge and place their feet upon solid ground. And yet, the church must also be a torch, for a torch stays with a person in his or her present situation (and it may even show the pitfalls of that situation), always lighting the next steps forward. Both lights are necessary: for those in darkness, the torch alone offers no final refuge;[7] the lighthouse alone gives no initial steps to reach its shelter.[8]

Though secular and religious media may often serve to heighten a perception of polarity between the two, I hope that this book's attention to the theology of revelation put forth by the Council helps to show the true intersection of faith and experience as manifested in God's own pedagogy. The Council certainly did not intend to retreat to a position of disengagement from the world; nor did it simply accommodate the faith to the world. Its real purpose, as Bishop Robert Barron often says, was to "Christify the world."[9]

To Christify the world, Christians must live in the place of "tension." By nature, human beings want to resolve tension: Catholics do so either by favoring either the lighthouse or the torch.[10] But that place

6. Extraordinary General Assembly of the Synod of Bishops, *Relatio Synodi*, no. 28. The Vatican translation of the synodal text is from http://www.vatican.va.

7. Thus, Pope Francis calls upon evangelizers to learn the "art of accompaniment," while recognizing that its practice cannot be "a sort of therapy supporting [others'] self-absorption" but must always be "a pilgrimage with Christ to the Father." See EG, no. 170 [121].

8. See EG, no. 169 [120]: "The pace of this accompaniment must be steady and reassuring, reflecting our closeness and our compassionate gaze which also heals, liberates, and encourages growth in the Christian life." See Antonio Spadaro, "A Church on a Synodal Journey," *Americamagazine.org*, November 7, 2014, http://americamagazine.org/church-synodal-journey, where the author speaks of both images, but ultimately privileges the torch over the beacon.

9. See, for instance, Barron, *Eucharist*, 59. In more popular talks and presentations, Barron often uses the phrase to clarify the Council's intention of *aggiornamento*.

10. See Christopher J. Ruddy, "Responses to Synod 2014: A Journey of Accompaniment," *Americamagazine.org*, October 27, 2014, http://americamagazine.org/content/all-things/responses -synod-2014-journey-accompaniment, where the author insightfully states, "Accompaniment

where we love others *and* invite them to the fullness of life is the hardest place to be in. Yet it is the only place where the New Evangelization can occur. The church must shine forth its light—the *Lumen Gentium* who is Christ—so that others may see its brightness amidst the storm, and it must accompany all men and women, becoming a torch that lights the way forward incrementally.

In his first encyclical after succeeding John Paul as pope, Benedict XVI wrote, "Being Christian is not the result of an ethical choice or a lofty idea, but the encounter with an event, a person, which gives life a new horizon and a decisive direction."[11] In his words the unity of truth and love in the person of Christ offer the necessary path for the church and the world in this and in every age. The real meeting of faith and the modern world can only occur when one encounters the person of Jesus Christ, for, as the Council taught, he is the revealer of God *and* the human person. If we live in a context "where entire groups of the baptized have lost a living sense of the faith, or even no longer consider themselves members of the church, and live a life far removed from Christ and his Gospel," then it is with Christ that the New Evangelization must begin and end.[12] As John Paul II put it, "Jesus Christ is the answer to the question that is every human life."[13]

---

need not entail accommodation, nor truth intolerance. We cannot collapse this Christic tension, however demanding and discomfiting it may be."

11. DCE, no. 1 [7].

12. RM, no. 33 [46].

13. Pope John Paul II, "Homily of His Holiness John Paul II, Oriole Park at Camden Yards, Baltimore, Sunday, 8 October, 1995," Vatican, http://w2.vatican.va/content/john-paul-ii/en/homilies/1995/documents/hf_jp-ii_hom_19951008_baltimore.html.

Bibliography

Primary Sources

Frossard, André, and Pope John Paul II. *"Be Not Afraid!" Pope John Paul II Speaks Out on His Life, His Beliefs, and His Inspiring Vision for Humanity*. Translated by J. R. Foster. Garden City, N.Y.: Image, 1985.

John Paul II. "Homily of His Holiness John Paul II for the Inauguration of His Pontificate." 1978. Vatican. http://www.vatican.va/holy_father/john_paul_ii/ homilies/1978/documents/hf_jp-ii_hom_19781022_inizio-pontificato_en.html.

————. *Catechesi Tradendae*. Translated by L'Osservatore Romano. English ed. Boston: St. Paul Editions, 1979. AAS 71 (1979): 1277–1340.

————. *Redemptor Hominis*. Vatican translation. London: Catholic Truth Society, 1979. AAS 71 (1979): 257–324.

————. *Familiaris Consortio*. Vatican translation. Boston: Pauline Books and Media, 1981. AAS 74 (1982): 81–191.

————. "Discurso del Santo Padre Juan Pablo II a la Asamblea del CELAM, 9 March 1983." Vatican. https://w2.vatican.va/content/john-paul-ii/es/speeches/1983/ march/documents/hf_jp-ii_spe_19830309_assemblea-celam.html.

————. *Reconciliatio et Paenitentia*. Vatican translation. Boston: Pauline Books and Media, 1984. AAS 77 (1985): 185–275.

————. *Mulieris Dignitatem*. Vatican. 1988. http://w2.vatican.va/content/john-paul-ii/ en/apost_letters/1988/documents/hf_jp-ii_apl_19880815_mulieris-dignitatem .html. AAS 80 (1988): 1653–1729.

————. *Maestro en la Fe*. Vatican. 1990. http://www.vatican.va/holy_father/john_paul_ ii/apost_letters/1990/documents/hf_jp-ii_apl_19901214_juan-de-la-cruz_sp.html.

————. *Redemptoris Missio*. Vatican translation. Boston: Pauline Books and Media, 1990. AAS 83 (1991): 249–340.

————. *Veritatis Splendor*. Vatican translation. Boston: Pauline Books and Media 1993. AAS 85 (1993): 1133–1228.

————. *Fidei Depositum*. Vatican translation. In *Catechism of the Catholic Church*, 1–6. AAS 86 (1994): 113–18.

————. *Gratissimam Sane*. Vatican translation. Boston: Pauline Books and Media, 1994. AAS (1994): 868–925.

————. *Letter to Families*. Vatican translation. Boston: Pauline Books and Media, 1994).

———. *Evangelium Vitae.* Vatican translation. Boston: Pauline Books and Media, 1995. AAS 87 (1995): 401–522.

———. "Homily of His Holiness John Paul II, Oriole Park at Camden Yards, Baltimore, Sunday, 8 October, 1995." Vatican. http://w2.vatican.va/content/john-paul-ii/en/homilies/1995/documents/hf_jp-ii_hom_19951008_baltimore.html.

———. *God, Father and Creator: A Catechesis on the Creed.* Translated by *L'Osservatore Romano*, English edition. Boston: Pauline Books and Media, 1996.

———. *Jesus, Son and Savior: A Catechesis on the Creed.* Translated by *L'Osservatore Romano*. English ed. Boston: Pauline Books and Media, 1996.

———. "Only Christ Can Fulfill Man's Hopes." *Communio* 23 (1996): 122–28.

———. "Homily of John Paul II for the Canonization of Edith Stein, Sunday, 11 October, 1998." Vatican. http://w2.vatican.va/content/john-paul-ii/en/homilies/1998/documents/hf_jp-ii_hom_11101998_stein.html.

———. *Fides et Ratio.* Vatican translation. Boston: Pauline Books and Media, 1998. AAS 91 (1999): 5–88.

———. "The Mystery of the Church." In *Springtime of Evangelization: The Complete Texts of the Holy Father's 1998 ad Limina Addresses to the Bishops of the United States,* edited by Thomas D. Williams, 45–52. San Diego: Basilica Press; San Francisco: Ignatius Press, 1999.

———. *Springtime of Evangelization: The Complete Texts of the Holy Father's 1998 ad Limina addresses to the Bishops of the United States.* Edited by Thomas D. Williams. San Diego: Basilica Press; San Francisco: Ignatius Press, 1999.

———. *Ecclesia in Asia.* Vatican. http://www.vatican.va/holy_father/john_paul_ii/apost_exhortations/documents/hf_jp-ii_exh_06111999_ecclesia-in-asia_en.html. AAS 92 (2000): 449–528.

———. *Crossing the Threshold of Hope.* Translated by Jenny McPhee and Martha McPhee. New York: Alfred A. Knopf, 2001.

———. "Address of John Paul II to the International Catechetical Congress Held to Observe the 10th Anniversary of the Publication of the Catechism of the Catholic Church, 11 October, 2002." Vatican. http://www.vatican.va/holy_father/john_paul_ii/speeches/2002/october/documents/hf_jp-ii_spe_20021011_congresso-catechistico_en.html.

———. *Rise, Let Us Be on Our Way.* Translated by Walter Zięmba. New York: Warner, 2004.

———. *Memory and Identity: Conversations at the Dawn of a Millennium.* Translator unknown. New York: Rizzoli, 2005.

———. *Man and Woman He Created Them: A Theology of the Body.* Translated by Michael Waldstein. Boston: Pauline Books and Media, 2006.

Wojtyła, Karol. *The Acting Person.* Translated by Andrzej Potocki. Boston: D. Reidel, 1979. Originally published as *Osoba I czyn* [The Person and the Act]. Krakow: Polskie Towarzystwo Teologiczne, 1969.

———. *Sign of Contradiction.* Translator unknown. New York: Crossroad, 1979.

———. *En Esprit et en Vérité: Recueil de textes 1949–1978.* Translated by Gwendoline Jarczyk. Paris: Le Centurion, 1980.

———. "Nature et perfection." In *En Esprit et en Vérité: Recueil de textes 1949–1978,* translated by Gwendoline Jarczyk, 116–19. Paris: Le Centurion, 1980.

———. *Sources of Renewal: The Implementation of the Second Vatican Council.* Translated by P.S. Falla. San Francisco: Harper and Row, 1980.

————. *Faith according to St. John of the Cross.* Translated by Jordan Aumann. San Francisco: Ignatius Press, 1981.

————. *Love and Responsibility.* Translated by H. T. Willets. San Francisco: Ignatius Press, 1981.

————. *The Way to Christ: Spiritual Exercises.* Translated by Leslie Wearne. San Francisco: HarperSanFrancisco, 1984.

————. *Radiation of Fatherhood.* In *The Collected Plays and Writings on Theater,* translated by Collected Plays Taborski, 334–64. Berkeley: University of California Press, 1987.

————. "The Family as a Community of Persons." In Wojtyła, *Person and Community,* 315–27. 1993.

————. "On the Metaphysical and Phenomenological Basis of the Moral Norm." In Wojtyła, *Person and Community,* 73–94. 1993.

————. "Participation or Alienation?" In Wojtyła, *Person and Community,* 197–207. 1993.

————. *Person and Community: Selected Essays.* Translated by Theresa Sandok. New York: Peter Lang, 1993.

————. "The Person: Subject and Community." In Wojtyła, *Person and Community,* 219–61. 1993.

————. "Subjectivity and the Irreducible in the Human Being." In Wojtyła, *Person and Community,* 209–17. 1993.

————. "Thomistic Personalism." In Wojtyła, *Person and Community,* 165–75. 1993.

————. "In Search of the Basis of Perfectionism in Ethics." In Wojtyła, *Person and Community,* 45–56. 1993.

————. "The Apostle." In *The Making of the Pope of the Millennium: Kalendarium of the Life of Karol Wojtyła,* edited by Adam Boniecki, 66–70. Stockbridge, Mass.: Marian Press, 2000.

————. "Sobre el Significado del Amor Conyugal (1974)." In *El don del amor: Escritos sobre la familia,* translated by Antonio Esquivias and Rafael Mora, 205–26. Madrid: Ediciones Palabra, 2005.

Other Sources

Albacete, Lorenzo. "The Praxis of Resistance." *Communio* 21, no. 4 (1994): 612–30.

Alberich, Emilio. "Is the Universal Catechism an Obstacle or a Catalyst in the Process of Inculturation?" *Concilium* 204, no. 4 (1989): 88–97.

Alberigo, Giuseppe. "The Christian Situation after Vatican II." In *The Reception of Vatican II,* edited by Giuseppe Alberigo, Jean-Pierre Jossua, and Joseph A. Komonchak, 1–24. Washington, D.C.: The Catholic University of America Press, 1987.

————. "The Announcement of the Council: From the Security of the Fortress to the Lure of the Quest." In *History of Vatican II,* edited by Giuseppe Alberigo and Joseph A. Komonchak, 1:1–54. Maryknoll, N.Y.: Orbis, 1995.

————. "Vatican II et son heritage." In *Vatican II and Its Legacy,* edited by M. Lamberigts and L. Keni, 1–24. Leuven: Leuven University Press, 2002.

Amalorpavadass, D. S. "Workshop on Recent Developments in Catechetics." *Teaching All Nations* 4 (1967): 377–79.

————. "Guidelines for the Production of Catechetical Material." In Hofinger and Sheridan, *Medellin Papers,* 93–109. 1969.

————. "Catechesis as a Pastoral Task of the Church." In Warren, *Sourcebook for Modern Catechetics,* 1:339–60. 1983.

Ambrose of Milan, St. *De Sacramentis*. Translated by James Walsh, with slight emendations by Edward Yarnold. In *The Awe-Inspiring Rites of Initiation: The Origins of the RCIA*, by Edward Yarnold, 100–49. 2nd ed. Collegeville, Minn.: Liturgical Press, 1994.

Anatolios, Khaled. "Interiority and Extroversion in Biblical Trinitarian Faith in Augustine's De Trinitate." *Letter and Spirit* 7 (2011): 173–90.

———. *Retrieving Nicaea: The Development and Meaning of Trinitarian Doctrine*. Grand Rapids, Mich.: Baker Academic, 2011.

Anderson, Carl, and José Granados. *Called to Love: Approaching John Paul II's Theology of the Body*. New York: Doubleday, 2009.

Aquinas, St. Thomas. *Summa Theologiae*. Translated by the Fathers of the English Dominican Province. Allen, Tex.: Christian Classics, 1948.

———. *Summa Theologiae*. Corpus Thomisticum. Fundación Tomás de Aquino, 2013. http://www.corpusthomisticum.org/iopera.html.

Aristotle. *Introductory Readings*. Translated by Terence Irwin and Gail Fine. Indianapolis: Hackett, 1996.

———. *On Love and Charity: Readings from the Commentary on the Sentences of Peter Lombard*. Translated by Peter A. Kwasniewski, Thomas Bolin, and Joseph Bolin. Washington, D.C.: The Catholic University of America Press, 2008.

Athanasius, St. *On the Incarnation*. Translated and edited by a Religious of CSMV. Crestwood, N.Y.: St. Vladimir's Seminary Press, 1993.

Au, Wilkie. "Holistic Catechesis: Keeping Our Balance in the 90s." *Religious Education* 86, no. 3 (1991): 347–60.

Audinet, Jacques. "Catechetical Renewal in the Present Situation." In Hofinger and Sheridan, *Medellín Papers*, 55–67. 1969.

Augustine, St. *The First Catechetical Instruction*. Translated by Joseph P. Christopher. New York: Newman, 1946.

———. *Confessions*. Translated by R. S. Pine-Coffin. New York: Penguin, 1961.

———. *The Trinity*. Translated by Stephen McKenna. Washington, D.C.: The Catholic University of America Press, 1963.

———. *On Free Will*. Translated by J. H. S. Burleigh. In *Philosophy in the Middle Ages: The Christian, Islamic, and Jewish Traditions*, 2nd ed., edited by Arthur Hyman and James J. Walsh, 33–64. Indianapolis: Hackett, 1973.

———. *On Christian Teaching*. Translated by R. P. H. Green. Oxford: Oxford University Press, 1997.

———. *Confessions*. 2nd ed. Translated by Frank Sheed. Indianapolis: Hackett, 2006.

Baierl, Joseph J., Rudolph G. Bandas, and Joseph Collins. *Religious Instruction and Education*. New York: Joseph F. Wagner, 1938.

Balthasar, Hans Urs von. *Theo-Drama: Theological Dramatic Theory*. Vol. 2. Translated by Graham Harrison. San Francisco: Ignatius Press, 1990.

———. *Razing the Bastions*. Translated by Brian McNeil. San Francisco: Ignatius Press, 1993.

Barker, Kenneth R. *Religious Education, Catechesis, and Freedom*. Birmingham, Ala.: Religious Education Press, 1981.

Barron, Robert E. *The Strangest Way: Walking the Christian Path*. Maryknoll, N.Y.: Orbis, 2002.

———. *Eucharist*. Maryknoll, N.Y.: Orbis, 2008.

Barth, Karl. *Church Dogmatics*. Vol. 3. Edited by G. W. Bromiley and T. F. Torrance.

Translated by J. W. Edwards, O. Bussey, and H. Knight. Edinburgh: T. and T. Clark, 1958.

Baum, Gregory. "Vatican II's Constitution on Revelation: History and Interpretation." *Theological Studies* 28, no. 1 (1967): 51–75.

Benedict XVI. "First Message of His Holiness Benedict XVI at the End of the Eucharistic Concelebration with the Members of the College of Cardinals in the Sistine Chapel, 20 April, 2005." Vatican. http://www.vatican.va/holy_father/benedict_xvi/messages/pont-messages/2005/documents/hf_ben-xvi_mes_20050420_missa-pro-ecclesia_en.html.

———. *Deus Caritas Est.* Vatican translation. San Francisco: Ignatius Press, 2006. AAS (2006): 217–52.

———. *Jesus of Nazareth: From the Baptism in the Jordan to the Transfiguration.* Translated by Adrian J. Walker. New York: Doubleday, 2007.

———. "A Proper Hermeneutic for the Second Vatican Council." In *Vatican II: Renewal within Tradition*, edited by Matthew L. Lamb and Matthew Levering, ix–xv. Oxford: Oxford University Press, 2008.

———. *Caritas in Veritate.* Vatican, 2009. http://www.vatican.va/holy_father/benedict_xvi/encyclicals/documents/hf_ben-xvi_enc_20090629_caritas-in-veritate_en.html. AAS 101 (2009): 641–709.

———. *Verbum Domini.* Vatican translation. Boston: Pauline Books and Media, 2010. AAS 102 (2010): 681–787.

———. "Address of His Holiness Benedict XVI to the Bishops of the Episcopal Conference of the Philippines on their 'Ad Limina' Visit, 18 February 2011." Vatican. https://w2.vatican.va/content/benedict-xvi/en/speeches/2011/february/documents/hf_ben-xvi_spe_20110218_bishops-philippines.html.

———. "Address of His Holiness Benedict XVI to Participants in the Plenary Assembly of the Pontifical Council for Promoting the New Evangelization, 30 May, 2011." http://www.vatican.va/holy_father/benedict_xvi/speeches/2011/may/documents/hf_ben-xvi_spe_20110530_nuova-evangelizzazione_en.html.

Berkeley, George. *"Principles of Human Knowledge" and "Three Dialogues."* Edited by Howard Robinson. Oxford: Oxford University Press, 1996.

Billias, Nancy Mardas, Agnes B. Curry, and George F. McLean. *Karol Wojtyła's Philosophical Legacy.* Washington, D.C.: Council for Research in Values and Philosophy, 2008.

Bournique, Joseph. "Les Congrès de Manille." *Catéchèse* 29 (1967): 512–15.

———. "The Word of God and Anthropology." *Teaching All Nations* 4 (1967): 371–376.

Bovenmars, John. "Vatican II and the Motivation of the Missionary Apostolate." *Teaching All Nations* 4 (1967): 313–16.

Boys, Mary C. *Biblical Interpretation in Religious Education: A Study of the Kerygmatic Era.* Birmingham, Ala.: Religious Education Press, 1980.

Bradshaw, Paul F. *The Search for the Origins of Christian Worship: Sources and Methods for the Study of Early Liturgy.* 2nd ed. Oxford: Oxford University Press, 2002.

Bryce, Mary Charles. "Evolution of Catechesis from the Catholic Reformation to the Present." In *A Faithful Church: Issues in the History of Catechesis*, edited by John H. Westerhoff III and O. C. Edwards Jr., 204–16. Wilton, Conn.: Morehouse-Barlow, 1981.

———. *Pride of Place: The Role of the Bishops in the Development of Catechesis in the United States.* Washington, D.C.: The Catholic University of America Press, 1984.

Burkard, John J. "*Sensus Fidei*: Theological Reflection Since Vatican II (1965–89)." *Heythrop Journal* 34, no. 1 (1993): 41–59 and 123–36.

———. "*Sensus Fidei*: Recent Theological Reflection (1990–2001) Part I." *Heythrop Journal* 46, no. 4 (2005): 450–75.

———. "*Sensus Fidei*: Recent Theological Reflection (1990–2001) Part II." *Heythrop Journal* 47, no. 1 (2006): 38–54.

Buttiglione, Rocco. *Karol Wojtyła: The Thought of the Man Who Became Pope John Paul II.* Translated by Paolo Guietti and Francesca Murphy. Grand Rapids, Mich.: William B. Eerdmans, 1997.

Calle, José M. "Catechesis for the Seventies." *Teaching All Nations* 7 (1970): 91–113.

———. "Catechesis for the Seventies Part II." *Teaching All Nations* 7 (1970): 225–40.

Catechism of the Catholic Church. 2nd ed. Washington, D.C.: United States Catholic Conference–Libreria Editrice Vaticana, 1997.

Cavadini, John. "The Structure and Intention of Augustine's *De trinitate.*" *Augustinian Studies* 23 (1992): 103–23.

———. "Continuing the Conversation." In Imbelli, *Handing on the Faith*, 207–20. 2006.

Cessario, Romanus. "*Duplex Ordo Cognitionis.*" In *Reason and the Reasons of Faith*, edited by Paul J. Griffiths and Reinhard Hütter, 327–38. New York: T. and T. Clark, 2005.

Chauvet, Louis-Marie. *Symbol and Sacrament: A Sacramental Reinterpretation of Christian Existence.* Translated by Patrick Madigan and Madeleine Beaumont. Collegeville, Minn.: Liturgical Press, 1995.

Cechin, Antonio, "Evangelizing Men as They Are." In Hofinger and Sheridan, *Medellín Papers*, 131–36. 1969.

Chesterton, G. K. *Orthodoxy.* London: Image, 1959.

Clarahan, Mary Ann. "Mystagogy and Mystery." *Worship* 83, no. 6 (2009): 502–23.

Clarke, W. Norris. *Explorations in Metaphysics: Being—God—Person.* Notre Dame, Ind.: University of Notre Dame Press, 1994.

———. "John Paul II: The Complementarity of Faith and Philosophy in the Search for Truth." *Communio* 26, no. 2 (1999): 557–70.

———. *Person and Being.* Milwaukee: Marquette University Press, 2004.

———. "The Integration of Personalism and Thomistic Metaphysics in Twenty-First-Century Thomism." In *The Creative Retrieval of St. Thomas Aquinas: Essays in Thomistic Philosophy, New and Old*, 226–31. New York: Fordham University Press, 2009.

Clement of Alexandria. *Stromata.* In *The Ante-Nicene Fathers*, vol. 2, *Fathers of the Second Century*, translated by W.L. Alexander, 299–568. New York: Charles Scribner's Sons, 1905.

Committee on Clergy, Consecrated Life, and Vocations. *Preaching the Mystery of Faith: The Sunday Homily.* Washington, D.C.: United States Conference of Catholic Bishops, 2012.

Congregation of the Clergy. *General Catechetical Directory.* Vatican translation. In *The Catechetical Documents*, edited by Martin Connell, 11–77. Chicago: Liturgy Training Publications, 1996.

———. *General Directory for Catechesis.* Washington, D.C.: United States Catholic Conference, 1997.

Collins, Mary, and Berard L. Marthaler. Preface. In Marthaler, *Introducing the Catechism of the Catholic Church*, v–viii. 1994.

Colomb, Joseph. *Aux Sources du Catéchisme: Histoire Sainte et Liturgie.* Vol. 1. 2nd ed. Paris: Société de Saint Jean L'Évangéliste, 1949.

———. "Teaching Catechism as a Message of Life." In *Readings in European Catechetics*, ed. G. Delcuve and A. Godin, trans. unknown, 119–38. Brussels: Lumen Vitae, 1962.

Colosi, Peter J. "The Uniqueness of Persons in the Life and Thought of Karol Wojtyła/ Pope John Paul II, with Emphasis on His Indebtedness to Max Scheler." In *Karol Wojtyła's Philosophical Legacy*, edited by Nancy Billias, Agnes B. Curry, and George F. McLean61–99. Washington, D.C.: The Council for Research in Values and Philosophy, 2008.

Congar, Yves. *Tradition and Traditions* [*La Tradition et les Traditions*]. Translated by Michael Naseby and Thomas Rainborough. New York: Macmillan, 1967.

Conley, John J. "The Philosophical Foundations of the Thought of John Paul II: A Response." In McDermott, *Thought of Pope John Paul II*, 23–28. 1993.

Connell, Martin, ed. *The Catechetical Documents: A Parish Resource*. Chicago: Liturgy, 1996.

Corbett, John. "Pinckaers et le nouveau catechism." Translated by Giovanna Brianti. In *Renouveler toutes choses en Christ*, edited by Michael S. Sherwin and Craig Steven Titus, 173–89. Fribourg: Academic Press, 2009.

Crowe, Frederick E. "The Development of Doctrine and the Ecumenical Problem." *Theological Studies* 23, no. 1 (1962): 27–46.

Cullen, Christopher M. "Between God and Nothingness: Matter in John Paul II's Theology of the Body." In McDermott and Gavin, *Pope John Paul II on the Body*, 65–75. 2007.

Curran, Charles E. "The Sources of Moral Truth in the Teaching of John Paul II." In *The Vision of John Paul II: Assessing His Thought and Influence*, edited by Gerard Mannion, 128–43. Collegeville, Minn.: Liturgical Press, 2008.

Cyril of Jerusalem, St. *The Fathers of the Church*. Vol. 70, *The Works of Saint Cyril of Jerusalem*. Translated by L. P. McCauley and A. A. Stephenson. Washington, D.C.: The Catholic University of America Press, 1969.

———. *Lectures on the Christian Sacraments*. Translated by R. W. Church. Edited by F. L. Cross. Crestwood, N.Y.: St. Vladimir's Seminary Press, 1977.

Daley, Brian. "A Mystery to Share In: The Trinitarian Pperspective of the New Catechism." *Communio* 21, no. 3 (1994): 408–36.

———. "The Nouvelle Théologie and the Patristic Revival: Sources, Symbols, and the Science of Theology." *International Journal of Systematic Theology* 7, no. 4 (2005): 362–82.

D'Ambrosio, Marcellino. "Ressourcement, Aggiornamento, and the Hermeneutics of Tradition." *Communio* 18, no. 4 (1991): 530–54.

Delcuve, George. "A Few Suggestions for Renewal in Catechetics after Vatican II." *Teaching All Nations* 4 (1967): 277–82.

———. "Some Reflections on Dialogue as Used in Pre-Evangelization." *Teaching All Nations* 4 (1967): 346–47.

De Lubac, Henri. *La Révélation Divine*. 3rd ed. Paris: Les Éditions du Cerf, 1983.

———. *Catholicism: Christ and the Common Destiny of Man*. Translated by Lancelot C. Sheppard and Elizabeth Englund. San Francisco: Ignatius Press, 1988. Originally published as *Catholicisme: Les aspects sociaux du dogme*. Paris: Cerf, 1938.

———. *The Mystery of the Supernatural* [*Le mystère du surnaturel*]. Translated by Rosemary Sheed. New York: Crossroad, 1998.

———. *Surnaturel: Études historiques*. Paris: Desclée de Brouwer, 1991.

———. *At the Service of the Church*. Translated by Anne Elizabeth Englund. San Francisco: Ignatius Press, 1993.

————. *The Splendor of the Church*. Translated by Michael Mason. San Francisco: Ignatius Press, 1999.

De Mey, Peter. "The Relation between Revelation and Experience in *Dei Verbum*: An Evaluation in the Light of Postconciliar Theology." In *Vatican II and Its Legacy*, edited by M. Lamberigts and L. Keni, 95–105. Leuven: Leuven University Press, 2002.

Denis, Léopold. "Advantages and Difficulties of Modern Methods in Mission Catechesis." In Hofinger, *Teaching All Nations*, 95–107. 1961.

Descartes, René. *Meditations on First Philosophy*. 3rd ed. Translated by Donald A. Cress. Indianapolis: Hackett, 1993.

Dewey, John. "Religious Education as Conditioned by Modern Psychology and Pedagogy." *Religious Education* 69, no. 1 (1974): 6–11.

Di Noia, J. Augustine, Gabriel O'Donnell, Romanus Cessario, and Peter John Cameron. *The Love That Never Ends: A Key to the Catechism of the Catholic Church*. Huntington, Ind.: Our Sunday Visitor, 1996.

Dooley, Catherine. "Liturgical Catechesis: Mystagogy, Marriage or Misnomer?" *Worship* 66, no. 5 (1992): 386–97.

————. "Baptismal Catechumenate: Model for All Catechesis." *Louvain Studies* 23, no. 2 (1998): 114–23.

————. "The Religious Education Curriculum in Catholic Schools." In *The Catholic Character of Catholic Schools*, edited by James Youniss, John J. Convey, and Jeffrey A. McLellan, 156–76. Notre Dame, Ind.: University of Notre Dame Press, 2000.

Dulles, Avery. *Revelation Theology: A History*. New York: Herder and Herder, 1969.

————. "The Meaning of Revelation." In *Dynamics in Christian Thought*, edited by Joseph Papin, 52–80. Villanova, Pa.: Villanova University Press, 1970.

————. "Faith and Revelation." In *Systematic Theology: Roman Catholic Perspectives*, vol. 1, edited by Francis Schüssler Fiorenza and John P. Galvin, 89–128. Minneapolis: Augsburg Fortress, 1991.

————. *Models of Revelation*. Maryknoll, N.Y.: Orbis, 1992.

Duncan, Roger. "Lublin Thomism." *Thomist* 51, no. 2 (1987): 307–24.

Elsbernd, Mary, and Reimund Bieringer. "Interpreting the Signs of the Times in the Light of the Gospel: Vision and Normativity of the Future." In *Scrutinizing the Signs of the Times in the Light of the Gospel*, edited by Johan Verstraeten, 43–98. Leuven: Leuven University Press, 2007.

Erdozain, Luis. "The Evolution of Catechetics: A Survey of Six International Study Weeks on Catechetics." In Warren, *Sourcebook*, 86–109.

Erhueh, Anthony O. *Vatican II: The Image of God in Man*. Rome: Urbaniana University Press, 1987.

Extraordinary General Assembly of the Synod of Bishops. "Relatio Synodi." Vatican. http://www.vatican.va/roman_curia/synod/documents/rc_synod_doc_20141018_relatio-synodi-familia_en.html.

Farey, Caroline, Waltraud Linnig, and M. Johanna Paruch, eds. *The Pedagogy of God*. Steubenville, Ohio: Emmaus Road, 2011.

Feingold, Lawrence. *The Natural Desire to See God according to St. Thomas Aquinas and His Interpreters*. 2nd ed. Naples, Fla.: Sapientia Press of Ave Maria University, 2010.

Fields, Stephen. "Nature and Grace after the Baroque." In *Creed and Culture: Jesuit Studies of Pope John Paul II*, edited by Joseph W. Koterski and John J. Conley, 223–39. Philadelphia: Saint Joseph's University Press, 2004.

Flannery, Austin, ed. *Vatican Council II*. Vol. 1, *The Conciliar and Postconciliar Documents.* Northport, N.Y.: Costello, 1998.

Flynn, Gabriel, and Paul D. Murray, eds. *Ressourcement: A Movement for Renewal in Twentieth-Century Catholic Theology.* Oxford: Oxford University Press, 2012.

Ford, John T. "Revelation and Catechesis as Communication." *Living Light* (1972): 21–38.

Francis, Pope. *The Joy of the Gospel: Evangelii Gaudium.* Vatican translation. New York: Image, 2013. AAS 105 (2013): 1019–1137.

———. "Meeting with the Participants in the Fifth Convention of the Italian Church, 10 November 2015." Vatican. http://w2.vatican.va/content/francesco/en/ speeches/2015/november/documents/papa-francesco_20151110_firenze -convegno-chiesa-italiana.html.

Freire, Paulo. *Pedagogy of the Oppressed.* 30th Anniversary ed. Translated by Myra Bergman Ramos. New York: Continuum, 2006.

Gallagher, David M. "Person and Ethics in Thomas Aquinas." *Acta Philosophica* 4, no. 1 (1995): 51–71.

Garrigou-Lagrange, Réginald. "La nouvelle théologie où va-t-elle?" *Angelicum* 23, no. 3–4 (1946): 126–45.

Gatterer, M., and F. Krus. *The Theory and Practice of the Catechism.* Translated by J. B. Culemans. New York: Frederick Pustet, 1914.

Gendron, Lionel. "La famille: Reflet de la communion trinitaire." In *La famille chrétienne dans le monde d'aujourd'hui: Réflexions et témoignages,* edited by Christian Lépine, 127–48. Montreal: Bellarmin, 1994.

George, Francis E. *Inculturation and Communion: Culture and Church in the Teaching of Pope John Paul II.* Rome: Urbaniana University Press, 1990.

———. "Evangelizing Our Culture." In *The New Evangelization: Overcoming the Obstacles,* edited by Steven Boguslawski and Ralph Martin, 43–58. New York: Paulist Press, 2008.

Gilson, Étienne. *Being and Some Philosophers.* 2nd ed. Translator unknown. Toronto: Pontifical Institute of Medieval Studies, 1952.

Giussani, Luigi. *The Risk of Education: Discovering Our Ultimate Destiny.* Translated by Rosanna M. Giammanco Frongia. New York: Crossroad, 2001.

Gleeson, Thomas F. "History and Present Scene in Religious Education." *Teaching All Nations,* 2 (1974): 67–84.

Goldbrunner, Josef. "Catechetical Method as Handmaid of Kerygma." In Hofinger, *Teaching All Nations,* 108–21. 1961.

Gorman, Robert T. *The Church That Was a School: Catholic Identity and Catholic Education in the United States since 1790.* Washington, D.C.: United States Catholic Conference, 1987.

Grabowski, John S. "Person: Substance and Relation." *Communio* 22, no. 1 (1995): 139–63.

———. "Public Moral Discourse on Abortion: The Contribution of Theology." *Irish Theological Quarterly* 64, no. 4 (1999): 361–77.

———. "The Luminous Excess of the Acting Person: Assessing the Impact of Pope John Paul II on American Catholic Moral Theology." *Journal of Moral Theology* 1, no. 1 (2012): 116–47.

Gracias, Valerian Cardinal. "Concluding Address." In Hofinger, *Teaching All Nations,* 376–84.

Groome, Thomas. *Christian Religious Education: Sharing Our Story and Vision*. San Francisco: Harper and Row, 1980.

———. "Old Task: Urgent Challenge." *Religious Education* 78, no. 4 (1993): 492–96.

———. "Remembering and Imaging." *Religious Education* 98, no. 4 (2003): 511–20.

———. "Total Catechesis/Religious Education: A Vison for Now and Always." In *Horizons and Hopes: The Future of Religious Education*, edited by Thomas H. Groome and Harold Daly Horell, 1–30. Mahwah, NJ: Paulist Press, 2003.

Gutiérrez, Gustavo. *A Theology of Liberation: History, Politics, and Salvation*. Revised ed. Translated and edited by Caridad Inda and John Eagleston. New York: Orbis, 1988.

Hahn, Scott. "Covenant in the Old and New Testaments: Some Current Research (1994–2004)." *Currents in Biblical Research* 3, no. 2 (2005): 262–92.

Healy, Nicholas J. "Henri de Lubac on Nature and Grace: A Note on Some Recent Contributions to the Debate." *Communio* 35, no. 4 (2008): 535–64.

Hildebrand, Dietrich von. *Marriage: The Mystery of Faithful Love*. Translated by Emmanuel Chapman and Daniel Sullivan. Manchester, N.H.: Sophia Institute Press, 1984.

Hittinger, F. Russell. *A Critique of the New Natural Law Theory*. Notre Dame, Ind.: University of Notre Dame Press, 1987.

———. "Toward an Adequate Anthropology: Social Aspects of the *Imago Dei* in Catholic Theology." In *Imago Dei*, edited by Thomas Albert Howard, 39–78. Washington, D.C.: The Catholic University of America Press, 2013.

Hofinger, Johannes, ed. *Teaching All Nations: A Symposium on Modern Catechetics*. Revised and translated by Clifford Howell. New York: Herder and Herder, 1961.

———. "Contemporary Catechetics: A Third Phase?" *Chicago Studies* 2, no. 3 (1963): 257–68.

———. "Evangelizing Catechesis: Basic Principles." *Living Light* 11 (1974): 338–47.

———, "J. A. Jungmann (1889–1975): In Memorian." *Living Light* 13 (1976): 350–59.

———. "The Catechetical Sputnik." In *Modern Masters of Religious Education*, edited by Marlene Mayr, 9–32. Birmingham, Ala.: Religious Education Press, 1983.

———. "Looking Backward and Forward: Journey of Catechesis." *Living Light* 20, no. 4 (1984): 348–57.

Hofinger, Johannes, and Francis J. Buckley. *The Good News and Its Proclamation: Post–Vatican II Edition of The Art of Teaching Christian Doctrine*. Notre Dame, Ind.: University of Notre Dame Press, 1968.

Hofinger, Johannes, and Terence J. Sheridan. *The Medellin Papers: A Selection from the Proceedings of the Sixth International Study Week on Catechetics Held at Medellin, Columbia, August 11–17, 1968*. Manila: East Asian Pastoral Institute, 1969.

Hoge, Dean R., William D. Dinges, Mary Johnson, and Juan L. Gonzalez Jr. *Young Adult Catholics: Religion in the Culture of Choice*. Notre Dame, Ind.: Notre Dame University Press, 2001.

Houtart, François. "Reflections on the New Thinking in Latin America." In Hofinger and Sheridan, *Medellin Papers*, 72–74. 1969.

Huerga, Alvaro. "Karol Wojtyła, comentador de San Juan de la Cruz." *Angelicum* 56, no. 2–3 (1979): 348–66.

Hyman, Arthur, and James J. Walsh. "Thomas Aquinas." In *Philosophy in the Middle Ages: The Christian, Islamic, and Jewish Traditions*, 2nd ed., edited by Arthur Hyman and James J. Walsh, 503–8. Indianapolis: Hackett, 1973.

Ide, Pascal. "Une Théologie du Don: Les occurrences de *Gaudium et spes*, n. 24, § 3 chez Jean-Paul II (premiére partie)." *Anthropotes* 17, no. 1 (2001): 149–78.

———. "Une Théologie du Don: Les occurrences de *Gaudium et spes*, n. 24, § 3 chez Jean-Paul II (seconde partie)." *Anthropotes* 17, no. 2 (2001): 313–44.

Imbelli, Robert P., ed. *Handing on the Faith: The Church's Mission and Challenge*. New York: Herder and Herder, 2006.

Irenaeus, St. *Adversus Haereses*. In *The Ante-Nicene Fathers*. Vol. 1, *The Apostolic Fathers with Justin Martyr and Irenaeus*, American ed., edited and translated by Alexander Roberts and James Donaldson, 315–567. New York: Charles Scribner's Sons, 1903.

Jackson, Pamela. "Cyril's Use of Scripture in Catechesis." *Theological Studies* 52, no. 3 (1991): 431–50.

Jaeger, Werner. *Early Christianity and Greek Paideia*. Cambridge, Mass.: Belknap Press of Harvard University Press, 1961.

John XXIII. *Humanae Salutis*. Translated by Austin Vaughn. In *The Encyclicals and Other Messages of Pope John XXIII*, edited by the staff of *The Pope Speaks* Magazine, 386–96. Washington, D.C.: TPS, 1964. AAS 54 (1962): 5–13.

———. "Opening Address to the Council." Translated by H. E. Winstone. In *The Encyclicals and Other Messages of Pope John XXIII*, edited by the staff of *The Pope Speaks* Magazine, 423–35. AAS 54 (1962): 786–96.

———. *Pacem in Terris*. AAS 20 (1963): 257–304.

———. *The Encyclicals and Other Messages of Pope John XXIII*. Edited by the staff of *The Pope Speaks* Magazine. Washington, D.C.: TPS, 1964.

John Chrysostom, St. *Baptismal Instructions*. Translated by Paul W. Harkins. Mahwah, N.J.: Paulist Press, 1963.

John of the Cross, St. *The Collected Works of Saint John of the Cross*. Rev. ed. Translated by Kieran Kavanaugh and Otilio Rodriguez. Washington, D.C.: Institute of Carmelite Studies Publications, 1991.

Johnson, Mary. "Religious Education in Its Societal and Ecclesial Context." In Imbelli, *Handing on the Faith*, 13–29. 2006.

Jungmann, Josef A. "The Pastoral Effect of the Liturgy." *Orate Fratres* 23, no. 11 (1949): 481–91.

———. "An Adult Christian." *Worship* 27, no. 1 (1952): 5–11.

———. "Christ's Place in Catechesis and Preaching." *Lumen Vitae* 7 (1952): 533–42

———. "Liturgy and the History of Salvation." *Lumen Vitae* 10 (1955): 261–68.

———. *The Mass of the Roman Rite: Its Origins and Development*. Translated by F. A. Brunner. London: Burns and Oates, 1959.

———. "Religious Education in the Late Medieval Times." In *Shaping the Christian Message: Essays in Religious Education*, edited by Gerard Sloyan, 38–62. New York: Macmillan, 1959.

———. *The Good News Yesterday and Today*. Edited and translated by William A. Huesman. New York: W. H. Sadlier, 1962. Abridged and translated version of *Die Frohbotschaft und unsere Glaubensverkündigung*. Regensburg: Friedrich Pustet, 1936.

———. *Handing on the Faith: A Manual of Catechetics*. Translated by A. N. Fuerst. New York: Herder and Herder, 1962.

———. *Announcing the Word of God*. Translated by Ronald Walls. New York: Herder and Herder, 1967.

———. "Theology and Kerygmatic Teaching." In Warren, *Sourcebook*, 213–17. 1983.

Kasper, Walter. *Theology and Church.* Translated by Margaret Kohl. New York: Cross-road, 1989.

———. "The Theological Anthropology of *Gaudium et spes.*" *Communio* 23, no. 1 (1996): 129–40.

Justin Martyr, St. *Second Apology.* In *The Fathers of the Church,* vol. 6, *The Works of Saint Justin Martyr,* translated by Thomas B. Falls, 113–36. Washington, D.C.: The Catholic University of America Press, 1948.

Kavanagh, Aidan. "Appendix: Part One: A Rite of Passage." In *The Three Days: Parish Prayer in the Paschal Tradition,* revised ed., edited by Gabe Huck, 171–75. Chicago: Liturgy, 1981.

Kelly, Francis D. *The Mystery We Proclaim: Catechesis for the Third Millennium.* 2nd ed. Huntington, Ind.: Our Sunday Visitor, 1999.

Kereszty, Roch. "Why a New Evangelization? A Study of Its Theological Rationale." *Communio* 21, no. 4 (1994): 594–611.

———. "'*Sacrosancta Ecclesia*': The Holy Church of Sinners." *Communio* 40, no. 4 (2013): 663–79.

Kevane, Eugene. Introduction to *Teaching the Catholic Faith Today: Twentieth Century Catechetical Documents of the Holy See.* Boston: Daughters of St. Paul, 1982.

———. "Augustine's *De doctrina christiana*: A Treatise on Christian Education." *Recherches augustiniennes* 4 (1966): 97–129.

Kim, Andrew. "The Unity of the Virtues in a Missionary Key." In *Pope Francis and the Event of Encounter,* edited by John C. Cavadini and Donald Wallenfang, 146–65. Eugene, Ore.: Pickwick, 2018.

Komonchak, Joseph A. "Christ's Church in Today's World: Medellin, Puebla, and the United States." *Living Light* 17 (1980): 108–20. "Vatican II and the Encounter between Catholicism and Liberalism." In *Catholicism and Liberalism,* edited by R. Bruce Douglas and David Hollenbach, 76–99. Cambridge: Cambridge University Press, 1994.

———. "Modernity and the Construction of Roman Catholicism." *Cristianesimo nella Storia* 18, no. 2 (1997): 353–85.

Kupcak, Jarosław. *Destined for Liberty: The Human Person in the Philosophy of Karol Wojtyła/John Paul II.* Washington, D.C.: The Catholic University of America Press, 2000.

Kurz, William. "The Scriptural Foundations of Theology of the Body." In McDermott and Gavin, *Pope John Paul II on the Body,* 27–46. 2007.

Labelle, Jean-Paul. "An Appraisal of the Catechetical Situation in Southeast Asia," *Teaching All Nations* 4 (1967): 283–93.

Ladaria, Luis. "Humanity in the Light of Christ at the Second Vatican Council." In *Vatican II: Assessment and Perspectives,* edited by René Latourelle, 2:386–401. New York: Paulist Press, 1989.

Lamb, Matthew L., and Matthew Levering, eds. *Vatican II: Renewal within Tradition.* Oxford: Oxford University Press, 2008.

Lamberigts, M., and L. Keni, eds. *Vatican II and Its Legacy.* Leuven: Leuven University Press, 2002.

Lambino, Antonio B. *Freedom in Vatican II: The Theology of Liberty in Gaudium et spes.* Manila: Loyola School of Theology, 1974.

Latourelle, René. *Theology of Revelation.* Translator unknown. Staten Island, N.Y.: Alba House, 1966.

Lawler, Michael G., and Todd A. Salzman. "Human Experience and Catholic Moral Theology." *Irish Theological Quarterly* 76, no. 1 (2011): 35–56.

Lewis, C. S. *Miracles: A Preliminary Study.* New York: Macmillan, 1947.

Liégé, Pierre-André. "The Ministry of the Word: From Kerygma to Catechesis." In Warren, *Sourcebook*, 1:313–28. 1983.

Loewe, William P. "Revelation: Dimensions and Issues." *Living Light* (1979): 155–67.

Long, Stephen A. "On the Possibility of a Purely Natural End for Man." *Thomist* 64, no. 2 (2000): 211–37.

Longenecker, Richard N. "The Pedagogical Nature of the Law in Galatians 3:19–4:7." *Journal of the Evangelical Theological Society* 25, no. 1 (1982): 53–61.

Lull, David J. "'The Law Was Our Pedagogue': A Study in Galatians 3:19–25." *Journal of Biblical Literature* 105, no. 3 (1986): 481–98.

Maggiolini, Alessandro. "Magisterial Teaching on Experience in the Twentieth Century: From the Modernist Crisis to the Second Vatican Council." *Communio* 23, no. 2 (1996): 225–43.

Mannion, Gerard, ed. *The Vision of John Paul II: Assessing His Thought and Influence.* Collegeville, Minn.: Liturgical Press, 2008.

Mansini, Guy. "*Duplex Amor* and the Structure of Love in Aquinas." In *Thomistica*, supplement vol. 1 of *Recherches de théologie ancienne et medievale* (1995): 137–96.

———. "The Abiding Theological Significance of Henri de Lubac's *Surnaturel*." *Thomist* 73, no. 4 (2009): 593–619.

———. "Experiential Expressivism and Two Twentieth-Century Catholic Theologians." *Nova et Vetera* 8, no. 1 (2010): 125–41.

Maréchal, Joseph. *Le point de départ de la métaphysique.* Vol. 5. 2nd ed. Paris: Desclée de Brouwer, 1949.

Marthaler, Berard L. *Catechetics in Context: Notes and Commentary on the General Catechetical Directory Issued by the Sacred Congregation for the Clergy.* Huntington, Ind.: Our Sunday Visitor, 1973.

———. "The Modern Catechetical Movement in Roman Catholicism: Issues and Personalities." In Warren, *Sourcebook*, 275–89. 1983.

———. "Catechetical Directory or Catechism? *Une Question Mal Posée*." In *Religious Education and the Future*, edited by Dermot A. Lane, 55–70. New York: Paulist Press, 1986.

———. "The Ecclesial Context of the Catechism." In Marthaler, *Introducing the Catechism of the Catholic Church*, 5–17. 1994.

———, ed. *Introducing the Catechism of the Catholic Church: Traditional Themes and Contemporary Issues.* New York: Paulist Press, 1994.

———. *The Catechism Yesterday and Today: The Evolution of a Genre.* Collegeville, Minn.: Liturgical Press, 1995.

Martin, Francis. "Revelation and Its Transmission." In *Vatican II: Renewal within Tradition*, edited by Matthew L. Lamb and Matthew Levering, 55–75. Oxford: Oxford University Press, 2008.

Mattison, William C. III. *Introducing Moral Theology: True Happiness and the Virtues.* Grand Rapids, Mich.: Brazos, 2008.

———. "Movements of Love: A Thomistic Perspective on *Agape* and *Eros*." *Journal of Moral Theology* 1, no. 2 (2012): 31–60.

Mazza, Enrico. *Mystagogy: A Theology of Liturgy in the Patristic Age.* Translated by Matthew J. O'Connell. New York: Pueblo, 1989.

McDermott, John M. "The Theology of John Paul II: A Response." In McDermott, *Thought of Pope John Paul II*, 55–68. 1993.

———, ed. *The Thought of Pope John Paul II: A Collection of Essays and Studies*. Rome: Editrice Pontificia Università Gregoriana, 1993.

———. "Response to 'The Nuptial Meaning of the Body.'" In McDermott and Gavin, *Pope John Paul II on the Body*, 121–53. 2007.

McDermott, John M., and John Gavin, eds. *Pope John Paul II on the Body: Human, Eucharistic, Ecclesial*. Philadelphia: St. Joseph's University Press, 2007.

McEvoy, James. "The Other as Oneself: Friendship and Love in the Thought of St. Thomas Aquinas." In *Thomas Aquinas: Approaches to Truth*, edited by James McEvoy and Michael Dunne, 16–37. Dublin: Four Courts, 2002.

McLean, George F. "Karol Wojtyła's Mutual Enrichment of the Philosophies of Being and Consciousness." In Billias, Curry, and McLean, *Karol Wojtyła's Philosophical Legacy*, 15–29. 2008.

McPartlan, Paul. "John Paul II and Vatican II." In *The Vision of John Paul II: Assessing His Thought and Influence*, edited by Gerard Mannion, 45–61. Collegeville, Minn.: Liturgical Press, 2008.

Meconi, David V. "Deification in the Thought of John Paul II." *Irish Theological Quarterly* 71, no. 1–2 (2006): 127–41.

Metz, Johann Baptist. *Faith in History and Society: Toward a Practical Fundamental Theology*. Translated by David Smith. New York: Crossroad, 1980.

Metz, Johann Baptist, and Edward Schillebeeckx. "Editorial." *Concilium* 204, no. 4 (1989): 3–6.

Milbank, John. *The Suspended Middle: Henri de Lubac and the Debate Concerning the Supernatural*. Grand Rapids, Mich.: Eerdmans, 2005.

Miller, J. Michael. "Introduction to the Post-Synodal Apostolic Exhortations." In *The Post-Synodal Exhortations of John Paul II*, edited by J. Michael Miller, 9–45. Huntington, Ind.: Our Sunday Visitor, 1998.

Moeller, Charles. "Pastoral Constitution on the Church in the Modern World: History of the Constitution." In *Commentary on the Documents of Vatican II*, translated by W. J. O'Hara, edited by Herbert Vorgrimler, 5:1–76. New York: Herder and Herder, 1969.

Molnar, Paul D. "Can We Know God Directly? Rahner's Solution from Experience." *Theological Studies* 46, no. 2 (1985): 228–61.

Mongoven, Anne Marie. "The Directories as Symbols of Catechetical Renewal." In *The Echo Within: Emerging Issues in Religious Education*, edited by Catherine Dooley and Mary Collins, 131–44. Allen, Tex.: Thomas More, 1997.

———. *The Prophetic Spirit of Catechesis: How We Share the Fire in Our Hearts*. New York: Paulist Press, 2000.

Moran, Gabriel. "What Is Revelation?" *Theological Studies* 25, no. 2 (1964): 217–31.

———. *Catechesis of Revelation*. New York: Herder and Herder, 1966.

———. *Theology of Revelation*. New York: Herder and Herder, 1966.

———. *Vision and Tactics: Toward an Adult Church*. New York: Herder and Herder, 1968.

———. *Design for Religion: Toward Ecumenical Education*. New York: Herder and Herder, 1970.

———. *The Present Revelation: The Search for Religious Foundations*. New York: Herder and Herder, 1972.

———. "The Intersection of Religion and Education." In *Who Are We? The Quest for* a *Religious Education*, edited by John H. Westerhoff, 235–49. Birmingham, Ala.: Religious Education Press, 1978.

———. *Believing in a Revealing God: The Basis of the Christian Life*. Collegeville, Minn.: Liturgical Press, 2009.

Nebrada, Alfonso. *Kerygma in Crisis?* Chicago: Loyola University Press, 1965.

———. "Special Commission on International Cooperation." In Hofinger and Sheridan, *Medellin Papers*, 206–9. 1969.

———. "Fundamental Catechesis." In Hofinger and Sheridan, *Medellin Papers*, 26–54. 1969.

———. "Some Reflections on Father Gleeson's Paper on History and Present Scene in Religious Education." *Teaching All Nations* 11 (1974): 85–98.

———. "East Asian Study Week on Mission Catechetics: 1962." In Warren, *Sourcebook*, 40–53. 1983.

Neusner, Jacob. *A Rabbi Talks with Jesus*. Montreal: McGill-Queen's University Press, 2000.

Newman, John Henry. *Apologia Pro Vita Sua*. London: Longman, Green, 1908.

———. *An Essay on the Development of Christian Doctrine*. 6th ed. Notre Dame, Ind.: University of Notre Dame Press, 1989.

Newton, William. "John Paul II and *Gaudium et Spes* 22: His Use of the Text and Involvement in Its Authorship." *Josephinum Journal of Theology* 17, no. 1 (2010): 168–93.

Nichols, Aidan. "Thomism and the Nouvelle Théologie." *Thomist* 64 (2000): 1–19.

Nitorreda, Teresita E. "The Search for New Meanings." In Hofinger and Sheridan, *Medellin Papers*, 68–71. 1969.

Nygren, Anders. *Agape and Eros*. Translated by Philip Watson. Philadelphia: Westminster, 1953.

Oakes, Edward T. *Infinity Dwindled to Infancy: A Catholic and Evangelical Christology*. Grand Rapids, Mich.: William B. Eerdmans, 2011.

O'Collins, Gerald. *Foundations of Theology*. Chicago: Loyola University Press, 1971.

———. *Retrieving Fundamental Theology*. New York: Paulist Press, 1993.

O'Malley, John W. "Developments, Reforms, and Two Great Reformations: Towards a Historical Assessment of Vatican II." *Theological Studies* 44, no. 3 (1983): 373–406.

Origen. *Origen: On First Principles*. Translated by G. W. Butterworth. Gloucester, Mass.: Peter Smith, 1973.

Paul VI, Pope. *Evangelii Nuntiandi*. Vatican translation. In *The Catechetical Documents*, edited by Martin Connell, 157–99. Chicago: Liturgy Training Publications, 1996. AAS 68 (1976): 5–76.

Pauley, James C. *Liturgical Catechesis in the 21st Century: A School of Discipleship*. Chicago: Liturgy, 2017.

Pedraza, Brian. "Reform and Renewal in Catechesis: The Council, the Catechism, and the New Evangelization." *Josephinum Journal of Theology* 19, no. 1 (2012): 141–71.

———. "Participation over Imitation: Communion in Christ and Catechesis for the New Evangelization." *Church Life: A Journal for the New Evangelization* 2, no. 1 (2013): 27–34.

———. "*Gaudium et Spes* and the Pedagogy of God: Conciliar Roots of the New Evangelization." *Josephinum Journal of Theology* 22, no. 1–2 (2015): 249–71.

Piaget, Jean. *Science of Education and the Psychology of the Child*. Translated by D. Coltman. New York: Viking Press, 1971.

———. *Insights and Illusions in Philosophy*. Translated by W. Mays. London: Routledge and Kegan Paul, 1972.

Piaget, Jean, and Bärbel Inhelder. *The Psychology of the Child.* Translated by H. Weaver. New York: Basic Books, 1969.

Pieper, Joseph. *Faith, Hope, Love.* Translated by Richard Winston, Clara Winston, and Sister Mary Frances McCarthy, SND. San Francisco: Ignatius Press, 1997.

Pinckaers, Servais. *The Sources of Christian Ethics.* Translated by Mary Thomas Noble. Washington, D.C.: The Catholic University of America Press, 1995.

———. *Morality: The Catholic View.* Translated by Michael Sherwin. South Bend, Ind.: St. Augustine's Press, 2001.

———. "The Natural Desire to See God." *Nova et Vetera* 8, no. 3 (2010): 627–46.

Pius X. *Lamentabili Sane Exitu. Acta Sanctae Sedis* 40 (1907): 469–79.

Piveteau, Didier-Jacques, and J. T. Dillon. *Resurgence of Religious Instruction: Conception and Practice in a World of Change.* Notre Dame, Ind.: Religious Education Press, 1977.

Pontifical Biblical Commission. *The Interpretation of the Bible in the Church.* Translated by John Kilgallen and Brendan Byrne. Boston: Pauline Books and Media, 1993.

Rahner, Karl. *Foundations of Christian Faith: An Introduction to the Idea of Christianity.* Translated by William V. Dych. New York: Crossroad, 1978.

Rahner, Karl, and Joseph Ratzinger. *Revelation and Tradition.* Translated by W. J. O'Hara. New York: Herder and Herder, 1966.

Ranwez, Pierre. "General Tendencies in Contemporary Catechetics." In *Shaping the Christian Message: Essays in Religious Education,* edited by Gerard Sloyan, 112–27. New York: Macmillan, 1959.

Ratzinger, Joseph. *Theological Highlights of Vatican II.* Translated by Henry Traub, Gerard C. Thormann, and Werner Barzel. New York: Paulist Press, 1966.

———. "Chapter I: Revelation Itself." In *Commentary on the Documents of Vatican II,* translated by W. J. O'Hara, edited by Herbert Vorgrimler, 3:170–80. New York: Herder and Herder, 1969.

———. "Chapter II: The Transmission of Divine Revelation." In *Commentary on the Documents of Vatican II.* Translated by W. J. O'Hara, edited by Herbert Vorgrimler, 3:181–98. New York: Herder and Herder, 1969.

———. "Part I: The Church and Man's Calling, Introductory Article and Chapter I." In *Commentary on the Documents of Vatican II,* translated by W. J. O'Hara, edited by Herbert Vorgrimler, 5:115–63. New York: Herder and Herder, 1969.

———. *Principles of Catholic Theology: Building Stones for a Fundamental Theology.* Translated by Mary Frances McCarthy. San Francisco: Ignatius Press, 1987.

———. *The Theology of History in St. Bonaventure.* Translated by Zachary Hayes. Chicago: Franciscan Herald Press, 1989.

———. "Concerning the Notion of Person in Theology." *Communio* 17, no. 3 (1990): 439–54.

———. *Introduction to Christianity.* Translated by J. R. Foster. San Francisco: Ignatius Press, 1990.

———. *Milestones: Memoirs 1927–1977.* Translated by Erasmo Leiva-Merikakis. San Francisco: Ignatius Press, 1998.

———. "Intervento del Cardinale Joseph Ratzinger durante il convegno dei catechisti e dei docent religione, 10 Dicembre 2000." Vatican. http://www.vatican.va/roman_curia/congregations/cfaith/documents/rc_con_cfaith_doc_20001210_jubilcatechists-ratzinger_it.html.

———. *The Spirit of the Liturgy.* Translated by John Saward. San Francisco: Ignatius Press, 2000.

————. "Eucharist, Solidarity, and Communion, 2 June 2002," Vatican. http://
www.vatican.va/roman_curia/congregations/cfaith/documents/rc_con_cfaith_
doc_20020602_ratzinger-eucharistic-congress_en.html.

————. "Current Doctrinal Relevance of the Catechism of the Catholic Church,
9 October, 2002." Vatican. http://www.vatican.va/roman_curia/congregations/
cfaith/documents/rc_con_cfaith_doc_20021009_ratzinger-catechetical
-congress_en.html.

————. "Handing on the Faith and the Sources of the Faith." In *Handing on the Faith
in an Age of Disbelief*, by Joseph Ratzinger, Dermot J. Ryan, Godfried Danneels,
and Franciszek Macharski, translated by Michael J. Miller, 13–40. San Francisco:
Ignatius Press, 2006.

Ratzinger, Joseph, with Vittorio Messori. *The Ratzinger Report*. Translated by Salvator
Attanasio and Graham Harrison. San Francisco: Ignatius Press, 1985.

Ratzinger, Joseph, and Cristoph Schönborn. *Introduction to the Catechism of the Catholic
Church*. San Francisco: Ignatius Press, 1995.

Reimers, Adrian J. *Truth about the Good: Moral Norms in the Thought of John Paul II*. Ave
Maria, Fla.: Sapientia Press, 2011.

Reno, R. R. *Genesis*. Grand Rapids, Mich.: Brazos, 2010.

Rice, Joseph. "On the 'Proper Weight of a Man': Re-examining the Poetic Foundations
of Wojtyła's Theory of Participation." In Billias, Curry, and McLean, *Karol Wojtyła's
Philosophical Legacy*, 297–324. 2008.

Rite of Christian Initiation of Adults. Study ed. Collegeville: Minn.: Liturgical Press, 1985.

Rosier, Veronica. "The Baptismal Catechumenate in the *General Directory for Catechesis*
(1997)." *Worship* 73 (1999): 98–124.

Ruddy, Christopher J. "*Ressourcement* and the Enduring Legacy of Post-Tridentine Theology." In *Ressourcement: A Movement for Renewal in Twentieth-Century Catholic Theology*,
edited by Gabriel Flynn and Paul D. Murray, 185–201. Oxford: Oxford University
Press, 2012.

————. "Responses to Synod 2014: A Journey of Accompaniment." *Americamagazine.
org*. October 27, 2014. http://americamagazine.org/content/all-things/responses
-synod-2014-journey-accompaniment.

Ruff, Daniel M. "From *Kerygma* to Catechesis: Josef A. Jungmann's *Good News Yesterday
and Today*." *Living Light* 39, no. 1 (2002): 62–73.

Ryan, Mary Perkins. "The Identity Crisis of Religious Educators." *Living Light* (1969):
6–18.

Ryba, Thomas. "Action at the Moral Core of Personhood: Transcendence, Self-
Determination, and Integration in the Anthropology of John Paul II." In Billias,
Curry, and McLean, *Karol Wojtyła's Philosophical Legacy*, 243–64. 2008.

Rymarz, Richard M. "Who Is This Person Grace? A Reflection on Content Knowledge
in Religious Education." *Religious Education* 102, no. 1 (2007): 62–74.

Savage, Deborah. "The Subjective Dimension of Human Work: The Conversion of the
Acting Person in *Laborem Exercens*." In Billias, Curry, and McLean, *Karol Wojtyła's
Philosophical Legacy*, 199–220. 2008.

Schenk, Richard. "Officium Signa Temporum Perscrutandi: New Encounters of Gospel and Culture in the Context of the New Evangelization." In *Scrutinizing the Signs
of the Times in the Light of the Gospel*, edited by Johan Verstraeten, 167–203. Leuven:
Leuven University Press, 2007.

Schindler, D. C. "The Redemption of Eros: Philosophical Reflections on Benedict XVI's First Encyclical." *Communio* 33, no. 3 (2006): 375–99.

Schindler, David L. "Religious Freedom, Truth, and American Liberalism: Another Look at John Courtney Murray." *Communio* 21, no. 4 (1994): 696–741.

———. "Christology and the Imago Dei: Interpreting *Gaudium et Spes*." *Communio* 23, no. 1 (1996): 156–84.

———. *Heart of the World, Center of the Church: Communio Ecclesiology, Liberalism, and Liberation.* Grand Rapids, Mich.: William B. Eerdmans, 1996.

———. "Reorienting the Church on the Eve of the Millennium: John Paul II's 'New Evangelization.'" *Communio* 24, no. 4 (1997): 729–79.

Schmitz, Kenneth L. "Selves and Persons: A Difference in Loves?" *Communio* 18, no. 2 (1991): 183–206.

———. *At the Center of the Human Drama: The Philosophical Anthropology of Karol Wojtyła/ Pope John Paul II.* Washington, D.C.: The Catholic University of America Press, 1993.

Schönborn, Christoph. *From Death to Life: The Christian Journey.* Translated by Brian McNeil. San Francisco: Ignatius Press, 1995.

Schoonenberg, Piet. "Revelation and Experience." In Warren, *Sourcebook*, 303–12. 1983.

Secretariat for Evangelization and Catechesis. *Doctrinal Elements of a Curriculum Framework for the Development of Catechetical Materials for Young People of High School Age.* Washington, D.C.: United States Conference of Catholic Bishops, 2008.

Ségin, Michel. "The Biblical Foundations of the Thought of John Paul II on Human Sexuality." *Communio* 20, no. 2 (1993): 266–89.

Seifert, Josef. "Karol Cardinal Wojtyła (Pope John Paul II) as Philosopher and the Cracow/Lublin School of Philosophy." *Aletheia* 2 (1981): 130–99.

Sheridan, Terrence J. "The Occasion." In Hofinger and Sheridan, *Medellin Papers* 9–12. 1969.

Sherwin, Michael S. *By Knowledge and by Love: Charity and Knowledge in the Moral Theology of St. Thomas Aquinas.* Washington, D.C.: The Catholic University of America Press, 2005.

Simon, Maurice. *Un Catéchisme Universel Pour L'Église Catholique: Du Concile de Trente à Nos Jours.* Leuven: Leuven University Press, 1992.

Simpson, Peter. *On Karol Wojtyła.* Belmont, Calif.: Wadsworth, 2001.

Slipko, Tadeusz. "Le développement de la pensée éthique du Cardinal Karol Wojtyła." *Collectanea theologica* 50, special issue (1980): 61–87.

Sloyan, Gerard S., ed. *Shaping the Christian Message: Essays in Religious Education.* New York: Macmillan, 1959.

———. "Catechetical Crossroads." *Religious Education* 59, no. 2 (1964): 148–49.

———. *Speaking of Religious Education.* New York: Herder and Herder, 1968.

Smith, James. K. A. *Desiring the Kingdom: Worship, Worldview, and Cultural Formation.* Grand Rapids, Mich.: Baker Academic, 2009.

———. *You Are What You Love: The Spiritual Power of Habit.* Grand Rapids, Mich.: Brazos, 2016.

Smith, Michael J. "The Role of the Pedagogue in Galatians." *Bibliotheca Sacra* 163, no. 650 (2006): 197–214.

Spadaro, Antonio. "A Church on a Synodal Journey." *Americamagazine.org*, November 7, 2014, http://americamagazine.org/church-synodal-journey.

Spalding, J. L. A Catechism of Christian Doctrine Prepared and Enjoined by Order of the Third Plenary Council of Baltimore. New York: Catholic Publication Company, 1885.

Stagaman, David. "The Implications for Theology of The Acting Person." In McDermott, Thought of Pope John Paul II, 213–20. 1993.

Stone, Theodore G. "The Bangkok Study Week." Worship (1963): 184–90.

Swiezawski, Stefan. "Karol Wojtyła at the Catholic University of Lublin." In Wojtyła, Person and Community, ix–xvi. 1993.

Tanner, Norman P., ed. Decrees of the Ecumenical Councils. Vol. 2. Washington, D.C.: Sheed and Ward and Georgetown University Press, 1990.

Taylor, Jameson. "The Acting Person in Purgatory: A Note for Readers of the English Text." Logos 13, no. 3 (2010): 77–104.

Tillman, Klemens. "Origin and Development of Modern Catechetical Methods." In Hofinger, Teaching All Nations, 81–94. 1961.

Titus, Craig Steven. "Servais Pinckaers and the Renewal of Catholic Moral Theology." Journal of Moral Theology 1, no. 1 (2012): 43–68.

Tracy, David. "World Church or World Catechism: The Problem of Eurocentrism." Concilium 204, no. 4 (1989): 28–37.

Tracy, David, Hans Küng, and Johann B. Metz. Toward Vatican III: The Work That Needs to Be Done. New York: Seabury, 1978.

Tranzillo, Jeffrey. John Paul II on the Vulnerable. Washington, D.C.: The Catholic University of America Press, 2013.

Verstraeten, Johan, ed. Scrutinizing the Signs of the Times in the Light of the Gospel. Leuven: Leuven University Press, 2007.

Vorgrimler, Herbert, ed. Commentary on the Documents of Vatican II. Vol. 3. Translated by W. J. O'Hara. New York: Herder and Herder, 1969.

———, ed. Commentary on the Documents of Vatican II. Vol. 5. Translated by W. J. O'Hara. New York: Herder and Herder, 1969.

Waldstein, Michael. "John Paul II and St. Thomas on Love and the Trinity (first part)" Anthropotes 18, no. 1 (2002): 113–38.

Walker, Adrian J. "Personal Singularity and the Communio Personarum: A Creative Development of Thomas Aquinas' Doctrine of Esse Commune." Communio 31, no. 3 (2004): 457–79.

Warren, Michael. "Introductory Overview." In Warren, Sourcebook, 23–29. 1983.

———. "Jungmann and the Kerygmatic Theology Controversy." In Warren, Sourcebook, 193–98. 1983.

———, ed. Sourcebook for Modern Catechetics. Winona, Minn.: St. Mary's Press, 1983.

Weddell, Sherry. Forming Intentional Disciples: The Path to Knowing and Following Jesus. Huntington, Ind.: Our Sunday Visitor, 2012.

Weigel, George. Witness to Hope: The Biography of Pope John Paul II. New York: Cliff Street, 1999.

———. "Rescuing Gaudium et Spes: The New Humanism of John Paul II." Nova et Vetera 8, no. 2 (2010): 251–67.

———. Evangelical Catholicism: Deep Reform in the 21st-Century Church. New York: Basic, 2013.

White, Thomas Joseph. "The 'Pure Nature' of Christology: Human Nature and Gaudium et Spes 22." Nova et Vetera 8, no. 2 (2010): 283–322.

Wicks, Jared. "Six Texts of Prof. Joseph Ratzinger as Peritus before and during Vatican Council II." Gregorianum 89, no. 2 (2008): 233–311.

————. "Further Light on Vatican Council II." *Catholic Historical Review* 95, no. 3 (2009): 546–69.

————. "Vatican II on Revelation: From Behind the Scenes." *Theological Studies* 71, no. 3 (2010): 637–50.

————. "A Note on 'Neo-Scholastic' Manuals of Theological Instruction, 1900–1960." *Josephinum Journal of Theology* 18, no. 1 (2011): 240–46.

Willey, David James P. (Petroc). *Philosophical Foundation for a Catechesis in the Light of the Pedagogy of God: Excerptum theseos ad Doctoratum in Philosophia*. Rome: Pontificia Università Lateranense, 2010.

————. "An Original Pedagogy for Catechesis," "The Pedagogue and the Teacher," and "The Pedagogy of God: Aim and Process." In *The Pedagogy of God*, edited by Caroline Farey, Waltraud Linnig, and M. Johanna Paruch, 15–79. Steubenville, Ohio: Emmaus Road, 2011.

————. "The Catechism of the Catholic Church and the New Evangelization." In *The New Evangelization: Faith, People, Context, and Practice*, edited by Paul Grogan, 209–20. New York: Bloomsbury, 2015.

Williams, George Huntston. *The Mind of John Paul II: Origins of His Thought and Action*. New York: Seabury, 1981.

Williams, Thomas D. *Who Is My Neighbor? Personalism and the Foundations of Human Rights*. Washington, D.C.: The Catholic University of America Press, 2005.

Wippel, John F. *The Metaphysical Thought of Thomas Aquinas: From Finite Being to Uncreated Being*. Washington, D.C.: The Catholic University of America Press, 2000.

Wolicka, Elzbieta. "Participation in Community: Wojtyła's Social Anthropology." *Communio* 8, no. 2 (1981): 108–18.

Woznicki, Andrew N. *A Christian Humanism: Karol Wojtyła's Existential Personalism*. New Britain, Conn.: Mariel, 1980.

Wrenn, Michael J. *Catechisms and Controversies: Religious Education in the Postconciliar Years*. San Francisco:Ignatius Press, 1991.

Yarnold, Edward. *The Awe-Inspiring Rites of Initiation: The Origins of the RCIA*. 2nd ed. Collegeville, Minn.: Liturgical Press, 1994.

Young, Norman H. "*Paidagogos*: The Social Setting of a Pauline Metaphor." *Novum Testamentum* 29, no. 2 (1987): 150–76.

Index

Abraham (prophet), 33

Acts of the Apostles, 83n47, 269n88, 273n105

Adam, 43n92, 62, 66n170, 82n45, 146, 149, 188, 194, 196–206, 212, 214, 227, 231

aggiornamento, 21, 23–24, 54n130, 73, 81n41, 114, 130, 136

Albacete, Lorenzo, 101n125

Alberigo, Giuseppe, 11n29, 23nn16–18

Amalorpavadass, D. S., 78, 96n104, 99n116

Ambrose of Milan, St., 283n135

Anatolios, Khaled, 207n72

anthropology of Wojtyła/John Paul II, 10, 13–14, 16, 138; *actus humanus*, 153n37, 154n38, 157n52; betrothed love, 164, 172–76; Boethius's definition of person, 146–48; common good, 171–72, 178–81; *communio personarum*, 178–83, 189, 202–3, 206, 208, 210–13, 220–21, 226–27, 239, 254, 265; conscience, 160–62, 235; disunity, 204–7; and *Gaudium et Spes*, 189–94, 217–33, 271; and *imago dei* in tradition, 207–17, 221, 231; incommunicability, 174; individualism and totalism, 180–81; integration, 155n43; law of the gift, 174–76, 221, 254; lived experience, 147n21, 148, 149n25, 219; love as attraction, desire, goodwill, 164–72, 223; metaphysics and phenomenology, 143–51, 184n161; nature and person, 218–20; *operari sequitur esse*, 151–52, 154n38, 183, 212; original solitude, 194–201, 203, 212, 227; original unity, 201–4, 212, 227;

participation, Thomistic, 158–59, 171, 219; participation with others, 158n54, 178–81, 220; potency and act, 153–54, 156–59, 171, 175, 182–83, 212; reflective and reflexive consciousness, 149n26; second act of existence, 157, 183, 204, 214, 219; self-gift, 172–76, 189, 193n18, 199, 201, 206, 212, 220–22, 225–27, 231, 233, 236, 239, 254, 281–85; and St. John of the Cross, 224–26; substance and relation, 177, 182–83, 204n58, 211, 213, 230–31; *Theology of the Body*, 192–94; Thomistic Personalism, 151; transcendence, 154–55, 184–85, 187, 194, 197, 265; virtue ethics, 160n60

Aristotle, 156, 160n60, 163, 259n59

Athanasius, St., 65n166, 216

Audinet, Jacques, 98, 100n119, 102n133

Augustine, St., 5–6, 17, 18nn1–3, 158, 166, 185, 207–14, 221, 229, 234–35, 237, 259n59, 264–65, 279, 280n124; use vs. enjoyment, 165–66; and trinitarian image of God, 207–14

autonomy, 60, 65

Avicenna, 156

Bacon, Francis, 148n22

Baierl, Joseph J., 77, 79n34

Balthasar, Hans Urs von, 22, 214n97, 215, 216n102

Baltimore Catechism, 7, 12, 74, 131

Bandas, Rudolph G., 77, 79n34

Barker, Kenneth R., 104n138

Barron, Robert, 289
Barth, Karl, 203n55
Baum, Gregory, 34n52, 36n62
Benedict XVI, Pope, 2, 4n6, 5–6, 9–11, 13,
    21n13, 24, 27, 29nn37–38, 32–33, 36n62,
    37n67, 38n73, 39n79, 41n86, 42n91,
    43n92, 51n119, 51n121, 53, 54n130,
    61–62, 72, 109n155, 121n203, 130n217,
    132, 135n235, 172n112, 182n154, 205n60,
    210n85, 211n86, 229–30, 232, 236, 264,
    277, 278n118, 278n120, 290
Berkeley, George, 145
Boethius, 146–47, 229–30
Bonaventure, St., 33, 208, 22n14, 29n37
Bovenmars, John, 97n106
Boys, Mary C., 84n54, 91n85, 103n135
Bryce, Mary Charles, 77n24, 87n70, 102,
    108nn153–54
Buttiglione, Rocco, 225n137

Casel, Odo, 84n55
catechesis: adult as normative, 94, 110;
    defined, 2–3, 245–46; catechism based,
    74–76, 78–80, 126, 135, 248, 251–52, 255,
    259, 262n67; Christocentric, 10, 107,
    123, 246–47, 250–51, 256–66, 271, 285;
    experiential, 12, 71, 72n5, 85, 88n73,
    91–107, 114–16, 118–19, 124, 126–27,
    133–34, 138, 142, 144–45, 241, 252,
    254–55, 266–72; kerygmatic, 8n20, 72n5,
    80–90, 93–96, 102–5, 107, 115–16, 123,
    125–27, 133–34, 137–38, 250–51, 256–68;
    modern catechetical movement, 71–109,
    113–14, 123–28, 130–35, 138, 142, 241–42,
    248, 250–52, 287; praxis based, 12, 98,
    100–102, 103n135, 112, 115, 145, 269; and
    revelation, 19–20, 46, 70–71, 73, 104
Catechism of the Catholic Church, 1, 3, 12–13, 79,
    109n155, 129–30, 136–40, 149, 187, 249,
    252, 260, 267
catechumenate, baptismal, 94–95, 247,
    279–80, 283–84
Cavadini, John, 128, 209, 213, 263
Cessario, Romanus, 287nn1–2
Chenu, Marie-Dominique, 22, 62n156
Chesterton, G. K., 68n172
charity, 222–25, 239, 265
church, nature of, 47, 54n129, 55, 65, 113,
    140, 244, 263–65

Clarke, Norris, 157n48, 158n54, 183n158,
    202, 230
Clement of Alexandria, 273, 277
Colomb, Joseph, 88n73, 92
Colosi, Peter J., 150n27
Colossians, 62n152, 187, 214n94, 231n156
communion, 29, 46, 47n109, 54, 55, 58, 60,
    67, 123, 127, 184, 198–206, 210–12, 220,
    226–30, 235, 238, 247, 252, 257, 259, 263,
    265–66, 271, 280–82
Congar, Yves, 22, 43n92
Congregation for the Clergy, 19, 20n8, 102
Congregation for the Doctrine of the Faith,
    3, 264
Counter-Reformation, 22, 75–76
creation, 32–33, 39–40, 56, 60, 62, 65, 113,
    194–207, 214, 227, 276
creed, 128, 138, 194, 208; Credo, 1, 6
Crowe, Frederick E., 42n90
culture, 2, 18, 55–56, 94–96, 102, 270–71,
    273–76, 280
Cyril of Jerusalem, St., 136n237, 279,
    283n135

Daniélou, Jean, 22
Darwinism, 92n86
De Finance, Joseph, 147n20
Dei Filius, 25–26
Dei Verbum, 14, 19–21, 25–37, 38–48, 53,
    55–57, 64, 67, 71, 105n141, 110, 132, 137,
    140, 222, 235, 272n100, 281n129
Delcuve, George, 88n73, 97
De Lubac, Henri, 22, 26, 27n30, 28n34,
    35–36, 54n129, 58–59, 62–64, 117n191,
    191–92, 217–18, 220, 234, 239
De Mey, Peter, 39n77
Deogratias, 17
deposit of faith, 24n21, 26, 30–31, 37, 45, 71,
    78, 89, 132, 135–36, 275
Descartes, René, 31, 146, 148, 153
Deus Caritas Est, 172n112, 264, 290n11
development of doctrine, 31, 42, 136n238
Dignitatis Humanae, 140
doctrine, 3, 24n21, 27–28, 39, 42–43, 56–57,
    61, 68, 71, 74–75, 78, 80, 82, 84–85, 88,
    90, 104, 106, 109–11, 116, 118, 119n196,
    122–26, 128–31, 135, 137, 141, 208, 242,
    248–52, 256, 259, 266n82, 282, 284–85
Dooley, Catherine, 131, 132n224

Leo XII, Pope, 22n14
Léopold, Denis, 89n78
Levada, William, 3
Lewis, C. S., 65n165
liberation theology, 98–101, 112–13, 125
Liégé, Pierre André, 71, 93, 112n167
liturgy, 42–43, 47n109, 56–57, 68, 80, 84,
    105–6, 112, 125–26, 131–32, 135n235,
    245n9, 257, 264, 283
Loewe, William, 74
Loisy, Alfred, 30n42
Long, Stephen, 63, 65n167
Luke, Gospel of, 4, 83n47, 229n147
Lumen Gentium, 13n34, 21n12, 47, 54–55,
    69n173, 140, 275, 290
Luther, Martin, 74n9

Maggiolini, Alessandro, 44n96, 45
Magisterium, 15, 45–46, 68, 106n144,
    125–27, 136, 190, 243, 263
Mansini, Guy, 62n157, 64n162, 121n203, 168,
    169n99, 218n111, 219
Maréchal, Joseph, 117
Maritain, Jacques, 220n116
Mark, Gospel of, 1, 4n5, 83n47, 277n117
Martha of Bethany, 86–87
Marthaler, Berard, 73, 74n9, 75n15, 86n62,
    88n73, 102, 108, 110n159, 115, 130n217
Martin, Francis, 29n37, 32, 37
Marxism, 76, 148, 152n36
Mary of Bethany, 86–87, 246
mass. See liturgy
Matthew, Gospel of, 4n5, 50, 51n120, 52,
    83n47, 227, 233, 250, 258n51, 279n121,
    282n131
Mattison, William C., III, 160n61, 164n74,
    166n87
Maximus the Confessor, St., 216n103
Mazza, Enrico, 283n135
McBride, Alfred, 130–31
McDermott, John M., 203n57, 219n116
McPartlan, Paul, 217
Meconi, David, 227, 228n143
media, modern, 112, 253, 255
Melchizedek, 35
Metz, Johann-Baptist, 100n120, 130
ministry of the Word, 2, 14, 18–19, 21, 70n1,
    72, 77, 85, 110, 254–55, 271, 282
Modernist heresy, 21, 30–31, 36, 43–45

modernity, 31, 49
Moeller, Charles, 47n110
Mongoven, Anne Marie, 88n73, 95n101, 107,
    111n164
Moran, Gabriel, 12, 44n96, 73, 103n135,
    104–5, 114–22, 125–26, 268
Moses (prophet), 33, 35, 104
Munich Method, 18, 76–77, 80, 86, 90, 107,
    124, 252
mystery, theological, 27, 29–30, 34, 40, 46,
    55, 84n55, 136, 140n3, 247, 257, 260, 276,
    278; Paschal Mystery, 42, 133, 285

narratio, 18n3, 84, 257, 274
Nebrada, Alfonso, 87, 93, 94n97, 95n100,
    102n131, 103–4, 115–16, 134n234, 279n121
neo-scholasticism, 22, 25, 31, 39, 44, 58, 64,
    71, 74, 77–78, 80–81, 83n47, 89–90, 110,
    116, 123, 135–36, 249, 251, 266
Neusner, Jacob, 4n6
New Evangelization, 2, 3, 6, 9–10, 12–14, 21,
    50, 72, 74, 114, 122, 131, 134–35, 137–38,
    141–43, 192, 194, 226, 233, 239–40, 242–
    44, 247, 249, 253, 258, 259n55, 260–61,
    267–68, 276, 282, 284–87, 290
Newman, John Henry, St., 223n130, 277
Newton, William, 189n8
nouvelle théologie, 22, 73, 81, 125, 136n238,
    217n109, 239

Oakes, Edward T., 190
O'Collins, Gerald, 4n7, 26n29, 36n6, 46,
    56n135
O'Malley, John, 10n26, 11n31, 275–76
O'Malley, William, 130–31
"Opening Address to the Council" (John
    XXIII), 11n27, 23n20, 47n107–8, 132n226
Origen, 215n98, 277

Pacem in Terris, 50
Pascendi Dominici Gregis, 31n42
Patrick, St., 207
Paul VI, Pope, 108, 111–13, 243–45
Paul (apostle), 5, 27, 29, 38, 61n149, 66n170,
    71–72, 240, 265, 269, 272–73, 286, 288
paideia, 18, 283
pedagogy, 18, 87, 88n73, 91–92, 107, 119,
    123–24, 253; divine, 19, 34, 36, 50, 67,
    71–72, 122, 241, 248, 272–85

person: theological origin, 29n38; substance and relation, 177, 181–83

Peter (apostle), 4, 13n34, 82

Piaget, Jean, 91, 92n86

Pichler, Willhelm, 76

Pieper, Joseph, 223

Pinckaers, Servais, 160n60

Pius X, Pope, 31n42, 36–37

Plato, 259n59; Platonism, 5–6

pluralism, 97–98, 101, 113, 122, 131

pre-evangelization, 93–94, 138, 279–80, 283

Rahner, Karl, 22, 36n62, 39n77, 44, 62n156,
100n120, 117, 119, 118n192, 121n203

Ranwez, Pierre, 76n17

Ratzinger, Joseph. See Benedict XVI, Pope

reason: and revelation, 39–40, 57n136,
64–65

Reformation, Protestant, 22, 25n26, 248

ressourcement, 22, 24, 54n130, 73, 81, 84,
135n235, 136n238

Revelation, Book of, 49

revelation, divine, 13–14, 19–20, 25–46,
47n109, 48–49, 53, 55–58, 61, 63, 65–74,
78, 89–90, 99–100, 103n135, 104–5, 110,
115–22, 124–25, 127, 131–32, 134n234,
135–39, 141–43, 146, 186, 207, 226–27,
230n154, 233, 236–40, 242, 247–48, 250,
255, 267–69, 272, 274–83, 285–89; Christ
as fullness, 35–38, 40, 42–43, 67, 132,
136–37, 191, 230n154, 237, 247, 288

Rice, Joseph, 153n37, 158n54

Rite of Christian Initiation of Adults,
283n134

Romans, 35, 38, 61n149, 83n47, 205n60,
222n126, 228

Ruddy, Christopher J., 135n235, 289n10

Ryan, Mary Perkins, 7n16, 75n14, 106,

Ryba, Thomas, 155n45

Rymarz, Richard, 129

sacrament, 29, 82, 90, 112, 140n3, 209,
245n9, 247, 257, 260, 263–65, 283–85;
sacramentality, 64–65, 191, 194, 265,
276–78, 280, 283; sacramentum, 27, 29

Sacrosanctum Concilium, 21n12, 47, 80n37

salvation history, 30, 33, 35, 56, 68, 79,
84–85, 91n85, 103n135, 104, 126, 128,
274, 276

Salzman, Todd A., 57n136

Scheler, Max, 150n27, 151, 152n32

Schenk, Richard, 50n118, 51n121

Schillebeeckx, Edward, 39n77, 130

Schindler, David L., 59, 217, 235n172

Schmitz, Kenneth, 16, 143n11, 144n13,
145n15

scholasticism, 22, 31, 37, 58, 78, 83, 104, 109,
116, 135, 144, 239

Schoonenberg, Piet, 107n149

scripture, sacred, 25, 27–31, 34–35, 40–41,
45–46, 56–57, 62n157, 67–69, 78n29,
83–84, 103n135, 104, 106, 118, 119n196,
122–27, 135–36, 138, 146, 242, 252, 266,
274–75, 280; historical-critical method,
105, 266

Scotus, John Duns, Bl., 22n14

2 Corinthians, 54n130, 210n83, 214

2 Thessalonians, 5n8, 135n236

2 Timothy, 83n47, 135n236

Second Vatican Council, 6–14, 17, 19–66,
71–74, 78–81, 95–96, 107–11, 122–45,
187–88, 190–91, 207–8, 210, 213, 217, 226,
231–39, 242–44, 252, 265–68, 274–76,
281n129, 283, 286–90

seeds of the Word, 97, 273–274, 280

Seifert, Josef, 150n28

sensus fidei, 45, 69; and sensus fidelium, 45n102

Sheed, Frank, 234n166

Sheridan, Terrence J., 98n113

Sherwin, Michael S., 161n64, 172n114,
223n127

signs of the times, 20, 46, 48–57, 60, 99,
106, 138, 267–68

Simplicianus, 5–6

Simpson, Peter, 143nn10–11

sin, 61, 66, 69, 219, 257; as disunity, 204–7,
271

Sloyan, Gerard S., 75n13, 105n141, 136n238

Socrates, 4

Stieglitz, Heinrich, 76

Study Weeks, catechetical, 85–102, 132;
Bangkok (1962), 85n61, 93–95, 102, 279;
Eichstätt (1960), 85n61, 86–93; Katigondo (1964), 85n61; Manila (1967), 85n61,
95–99, 102; Medellín (1968), 85n61,
98–106, 112, 120n199, 125, 128, 267;
Nijmegen (1959), 85n61

Synod of Bishops: 1967, 244n5; 1974, 11,

Catechesis for the New Evangelization: Vatican II, John Paul II, and the Unity of Revelation and Experience was designed in Quadraat with Quadraat Sans and Anzeigen Grotesk display type and composed by Kachergis Book Design of Pittsboro, North Carolina. It was printed on 60-pound House Natural Smooth and bound by Sheridan Books of Chelsea, Michigan.